# Postcards from a Bilingual Family
日×米家族の11年

本書は、週刊英和新聞『朝日ウイークリー（Asahi Weekly）』（朝日新聞社）にて2011年～2022年に連載された英文イラストエッセイ「Postcards from a Bilingual Family」を、書籍化にあたって再編集・再構成したものです。現在とは情勢や通念が異なる内容が含まれている場合もありますが、内容は基本的に連載時のままとしています。

# POSTCARDS FROM A BILINGUAL FAMILY

## 日×米家族の11年

田村 記久恵 著
Steve Ballati 訳

IBCパブリッシング

## まえがき

近年日本でも、国際結婚家庭や外国にルーツを持つ子どもたち（いわゆるハーフ）は珍しくなくなりました。我が家もそんな家庭の一つです。

道祖神や石碑は見過ごせない日本民俗学好きなアメリカ人のオット・スティーヴと、民藝や職人など匠の技に関するものに強く惹かれる日本人の私。そんな私たちの間に生まれ、日本で生まれ育ったのが息子ハルと娘ミドリです。

ドアよりも引き戸が多い家に暮らし、具だくさんの味噌汁を好み、夏には草履や下駄を好んで履いたりするような暮らしを送りつつ、しっかりアメリカ的な感覚も持ち合わせている子どもたち。彼らを見ると、私たちの暮らしそのものだなと感じます。

うちが国際結婚家庭だとわかるとよく、こんなふうに聞かれます。

「家では何語で話すの？」「子どもたちはやっぱり英語ペラペラ？」「旦那さんとはどうやって知り合ったの？」「子どもたちの国籍は？」「学校は？」「このままずっと日本に住むの？」などなど。

こうした疑問に答え、誤解を解けたらと始めたのが、イラストエッセイ「Postcards from a Bilingual Family」です。『Asahi Weekly』（朝日新聞社）で2011年から隔週で連載した、全275話。長く続ける中で、私自身の新たな発見や気づきを共有する場にもなりました。それを加筆修正してまとめたのがこの本です。

連載開始当初、子どもたちはまだ幼く、ハルは小学1年生になりたてほやほや。ミドリもおままごとに夢中な3歳児でした。それが11年の月日を経て、連載終了時には高校2年生と中学2年生に。世話が焼けてもなんだかんだかわいい幼児時代、自我が頭をもたげる小学校時代、生意気さもありつつオトナの会話も楽しめる思春期……と、振り返るとそれぞれにそれぞれのむずかしさとおもしろさと愛しさがありました。

そんな成長に伴って、私たちのバイリンガル育児（子どもたちに日米両方の言葉や文化を伝える）も新たなステップを踏んできました。この本はそれらの記録とも言えます。

国際結婚家庭のルポとして、またバイリンガル育児の記録として、私たちはほんの一例に過ぎません。でも、この本を通して少しでも理解が深まり、より身近に感じてくださったら、とてもとてもうれしいです。

田村記久恵

## Writing Postcards in English

Each time a Postcard arrived in my email inbox, I knew I was in for a treat and a challenge.

Kikue has an uncanny way of connecting points across cultures. It was thoroughly enjoyable to set down sentences about events I remember and often had a part in. She picked up some very specific points to write about, always with a fresh perspective.

When Kikue sent me an illustrated draft written in Japanese, my first step was to write out a fairly directly translated (直訳) English draft. I did my best to use straightforward sentence construction and clear wording while also making the English natural, easy to follow, and engaging.

When translating from Japanese to English, word-for-word translation inevitably falls flat. Words are just the tools used to convey meaning. Especially in a personal column like Postcards, it's the meaning and message behind the words that give the text life. Adjusting and filling in words to bring out the underlying meaning (意訳) often leads to a text that looks quite different from the original Japanese on the surface, but the meaning and message are faithful.

The beginnings and endings are where I often changed the most. I wanted to create openings and closings that resonate with the English reader's sensibilities of structure and flow. Most times, Kikue's openings worked fine in both languages, but sometimes the English needed to take a different tack to engage the reader. On occasion, I even proposed completely new openings, which I'm sure were a shock to Kikue. But with some persuasion, she usually went along with my proposals.

Likewise, when I recast endings, it was to create the closure that English readers expect. In English, an ending that links with something from the beginning of the column creates a feeling of coming full circle and gives a sense of completion.

The writing style of the Postcards was designed for readers to brush up their English, learn some new vocabulary, and also to introduce new perspectives. I hope you will find something fresh in each one.

Steve Ballati

# 家族紹介

え
碑

おおっ?!
Steve
スティーヴ

日本在住
30年越えの
アメリカ人。
日本民俗学好きで
石碑は
素通りできない。
我が家の企画部長。

電車の中で
人物観察中
Kikue
記久恵

イラストレーター。
メモ魔。
和モノ好き。
Steveとは
独身時代に
習っていた
津軽三味線が縁で
知り合った。
当時の英語力は3級
→現在2級程度。

Midori
ミドリ
明るく元気な社交家。情に厚く涙もろい。
最寄り駅から家まで歌いながら帰ってくる。
No Music No Life
穏やかだが芯がぶれない理数系&アート系男子。
Haru
ハル
年度始めにはノートを独自のタイポグラフィで飾る習性あり。
MUJIのノートがお気に入り

目　次

まえがき　田村記久恵……004
Writing Postcards in English　Steve Ballati……005
家族紹介……006

1st Year 2011……011

2nd Year 2012……035

3rd Year 2013……061

4th Year 2014……087

5th Year 2015……115

6th Year 2016……143

7th Year 2017 ······ 171

8th Year 2018 ······ 199

9th Year 2019 ······ 227

10th Year 2020 ······ 253

11th Year 2021 ······ 279

あとがき　田村記久恵 ······ 306

The Gift of Cultural Diversity　Steve Ballati ······ 307

テーマ別索引 ······ 308

COLUMN① *From Steve* ······ 034

COLUMN② *From Haru* ······ 060

COLUMN③ *From Midori* ······ 086

COLUMN④ *From Midori* ······ 114

COLUMN⑤ *From Steve* ······ 142

COLUMN⑥ *From Haru* ······ 170

COLUMN⑦ *From Midori* ······ 198

COLUMN⑧ *From Haru* ······ 252

STEVE
日本在住25年の
江戸好きアメリカ人
KIKUE
ワタクシ
HARU
息子。
小学1年生
MIDORI
娘。
3歳

# 1st Year

2011

アメリカ人の夫と結婚して以来、何十回となく聞いた言葉があります。それは――

since　〜して以来
dozens of times　何十回も，何度も何度も
fluent　〔人が言語に〕堪能な，流ちょうな
translator　翻訳者，通訳者
proficiency　〔能力・技能などの〕熟練，習熟（度）
depend on　〜によって決まる
complicated　複雑な，込み入った
pretty　とても，非常に

# Vol. 1 What Language Do We Speak?
## （英語と日本語、どっちで話す？）

Since I married my American husband 10 years ago, I have heard this dozens of times:

あー、じゃあ
英語ペラペラなんだ
いいなー


But there was only one person who was fluent in our house:

こっち
日本語がペラペラ
神前式でした
15 years living in Japan (当時)
Japanese-to-English translator
Interested in Japanese folklore (日本民俗学).
Born and raised in Tokyo
Eiken Grade-3-level English (英検3級止まり).


We talked to each other in Japanese.

ケンカだって日本語でできる人
母国語でケンカしても負ける人


This changed, however, six years ago when our first child was born. We now talk in English or Japanese depending on who we are talking to.

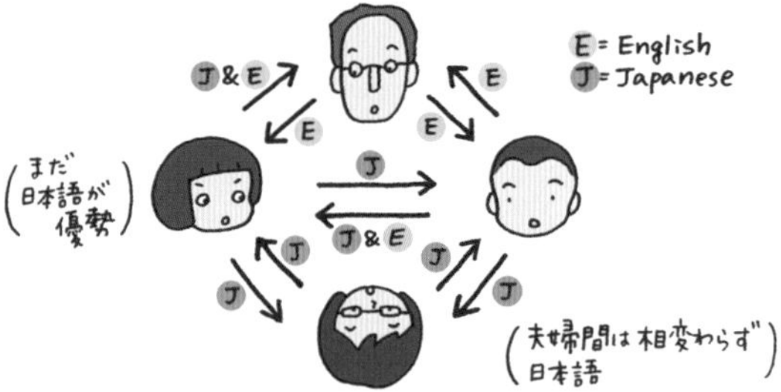

E = English
J = Japanese
J & E
E
E
E
J
J & E
J
J
J
J
（まだ日本語が優勢）
（夫婦間は相変わらず日本語）


It looks complicated, but it's really pretty simple. The kids speak English to their dad and Japanese to their mom. I'm the only one who speaks all Japanese.

# Vol. 2 Does "Half" Equal Bilingual?
(ハーフ＝バイリンガル？)

With a father from the United States and a mother from Japan, our kids are often called "half."

Isn't it more correct for a person who can speak two languages or who lives in two cultures to be called "mixed" or "double"?
"half"には半人前の意味もあるしね


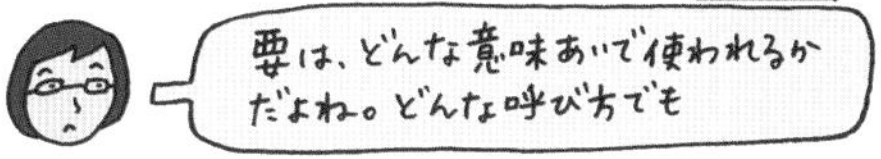

要は、どんな意味あいで使われるかだよね。どんな呼び方でも


At the same time, being "half" doesn't necessarily mean the person can speak both languages.

見ため西洋人。でも関西弁バリバリ
うちのオカンたらびっくりやで！


There are lots of people like this.

Our kids' language abilities are like this:

Haru (age 6)
I can read English too.
English 50%
Japanese 50%
Midori (age 3)
Understands English but
speaks mainly in Japanese.
English 15%
Japanese 85%


Haru grew up in a bilingual environment but spoke mostly Japanese at first, and Steve worked hard to build up his English ability.

3歳くらいで50:50になった
Pump it up!
Japanese
English
シュコ シュコ シュコ


Children easily absorb and learn to speak the language they hear around them. But it takes extra effort to support the development of a second language.

Haru in Action
ハル、Daddyにごはんよって言ってくれる?
はーい
Daddy! It's dinner time!
OK! I'll be right there!
すぐ行きまーす だって
ありがとね


Midori is still at the early learning stage. Steve is working every day to help his "half" daughter become a native speaker of two languages.

アメリカ人の父親と日本人の母親を持つ私たちの子どもたちは、しばしば「ハーフ」と呼ばれます。

**equal** 等しい，同一の
**correct** 合っている，的確な
**at the same time** それと同時に
**necessarily** 必ずしも～でない
**language ability** 言語能力
**pump it up** 〔勉強などの〕ペースを上げる
**absorb** 吸収する，自分のものにする
**take an extra effort** さらなる［特別な］努力が必要である

言語の習得は、その言語にどれだけ触れているのかが大きく関係すると言われています。我が家の子どもたちの英語環境は……

acquisition 取得，習得

exposure 〔環境に〕さらされること，〔人前や社会に〕出る［触れる］こと

spend as much time as possible with （人）と可能な限り多くの時間を過ごす

even so たとえそうであっても

range of vocabulary 語彙の幅

plenty of たくさんの

don't care 気にしない，関係ない

encounter 出合う，遭遇する

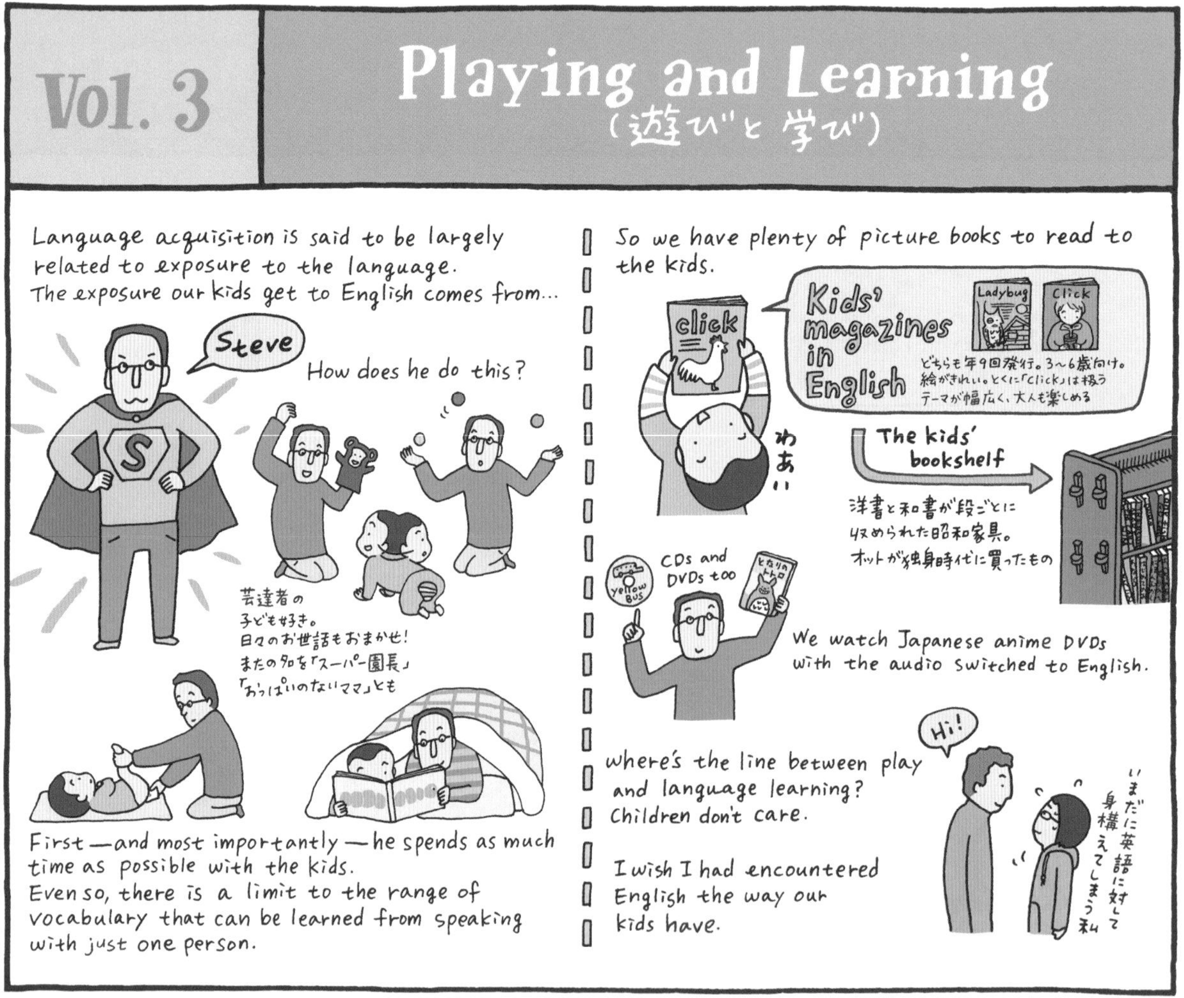

Vol. 3
Playing and Learning
（遊びと学び）
Language acquisition is said to be largely related to exposure to the language.
The exposure our kids get to English comes from...
Steve
How does he do this?
芸達者の子ども好き。日々のお世話もおまかせ！またの名を「スーパー園長」「おっぱいのないママ」とも
First — and most importantly — he spends as much time as possible with the kids.
Even so, there is a limit to the range of vocabulary that can be learned from speaking with just one person.
So we have plenty of picture books to read to the kids.
click
わあい
Kids' magazines in English
Ladybug
Click
どちらも年9回発行。3〜6歳向け。絵がきれい。とくに「click」は扱うテーマが幅広く、大人も楽しめる
The kids' bookshelf
洋書と和書が段ごとに収められた昭和家具。オットが独身時代に買ったもの
CDs and DVDs too
yellow bus
となりのトトロ
We watch Japanese anime DVDs with the audio switched to English.
Where's the line between play and language learning? Children don't care.
Hi!
I wish I had encountered English the way our kids have.
いまだに英語に対して身構えてしまう私

# Vol. 4 Choosing a School (学校選び)

When people meet international couples with kids, they nearly always ask:
やっぱり学校はインターナショナルスクールとか?
NO
Tuition at international schools is very high — at least two or three million yen each year.
And that's for one child; we have two!
うちには無理っす
On the other hand, if we had sent our kids to public school, they would undoubtedly have lost most of their English ability.
日本語ばかりになるのはよくある話
親との時間より友達との時間が増えることで
After much agonizing, we chose a private school that specializes in accommodating returnee students.
ピカピカの一年生
電車通学にもすっかり慣れました
The school staff includes native English teachers, and the class lessons are presented in a more Western style (although they are conducted in Japanese).
You might say it's halfway between an international school and a public school.
おまけ
Steve's Surprise #1
Massive shoe racks
おおー日本的
そうか、アメリカだと外履きのままだもんね
Steve's Surprise #2
Randoseru (School Backpacks)
普通のリュックで十分
Expen-sive
Heavy!

子持ちの国際結婚夫婦が、必ずと言っていいほど聞かれる質問があります。それは――

- **tuition** 授業料
- **million** 100万
- **on the other hand** その一方で，他方では
- **public school** 公立学校
- **undoubtedly** 疑いようもなく，明らかに
- **agonize** 〔難しい判断・選択などに〕苦悩する
- **specialize in** ～に長けた
- **accommodate** 〔人の〕世話をする，収容できる
- **returnee** 帰国者，帰国子女
- **conduct** 行う，実施する
- **you might say** ～と言ってもいいでしょう

アメリカの祖母（義母）がミドリの誕生日プレゼントに人形を送ってくれました。祖母が選んでくれたのは……

- **complexion** 肌の色，外観
- **Hispanic** ヒスパニック，〔スペイン語圏の〕ラテン・アメリカ
- **feature** 特徴（づけるもの），容貌
- **ethnicity** 民族性
- **Caucasian** コーカサス人，白色人種
- **roughly** おおよそ，大体
- **cuddly** 抱き締めたくなるほど愛らしい
- **aromatherapy** アロマセラピー

# Vol. 5 Ethnic Dolls

## （人形の人種）

Midori's grandmother in the United States sent her a doll for her birthday.

さあ
メリーちゃん
着替えましょよ〜
「メリーちゃん」と命名。
「さっちゃん」とかではないらしい（笑）

Her grandmother chose the doll that looked the most like Midori. It has the same hairstyle and skin complexion. We were surprised to see that it was described as having "Hispanic" features. Dolls have ethnicities too. The Amazon.com site has various models.

商品数がいちばん多い
同じくらいの商品数
Caucasian
Hispanic
African-American
All by the same maker

When I thought about it, I realized that the doll ethnicities roughly reflect the makeup of the U.S. population. But for some reason, the faces of the Asian dolls remind me of traditional Japanese dolls.

ザンギリ頭と
ハチマキに見えるリボン
まるで日本人形の顔をそのまま使ってみた、みたいな顔立ち
商品数も少ない

I love that there are now Asian dolls too, but they still don't seem cuddly to me.

As an added feature, the doll is made of a material with a mild vanilla fragrance. At night, the whole family falls asleep while enjoying vanilla aromatherapy.

川の字で寝てます

# Vol. 6 The Tooth Fairy
（歯の妖精）

Haru recently lost his first tooth.
In Japan, when we lose a tooth, we throw it under the house or up on the roof.
歯がはーえろっ
30年前の私
「ねずみの歯がはえろ」という地域も（なんでもかじる丈夫な歯）
In America, losing a tooth is a major event for a kid.
A kid who loses a tooth saves it, and then puts it under their pillow at night when they go to bed.
いそいそ
わくわく
Then, the next morning…
The Tooth Fairy came!!
The Tooth Fairy takes the tooth and leaves a coin in its place.
（もちろん親がこっそりとやる）
For Haru's first tooth, the Tooth Fairy left a special coin — a gold-colored $1 coin.
ABRAHAM LINCOLN
（歴代大統領の肖像が描かれた特別シリーズ）
フフフ
His dad had been prepared for this day for over a year.
Along with the coin, the Tooth Fairy also left the tooth!
したり顔
Maybe she left it so you can throw it on the roof.
— Haru knows the truth:
しんけん
She left it because she was afraid she might drop it in the ocean on her way back to America.


初めてハルの歯が抜けました。日本では抜けた歯を家の下か屋根の上に放り投げますが、アメリカでは違うようです。

- **Tooth Fairy**　歯の妖精
- **recently**　最近，つい先日
- **first tooth**　乳歯
- **save**　取っておく，残しておく
- **pillow**　枕
- **in its place**　その代わりに
- **prepare**　準備する
- **along with**　～と一緒に，～と共に
- **might**　～かもしれない，～の可能性がある
- **drop**　落とす
- **on one's way back to**　～へ帰る途中で

アメリカの人はバーベキュー好きで、週末によく、家の裏庭に集まって楽しみます。

relative　親類，親戚
get together　集まる，集合する
backyard　〔家の〕裏庭
at any time　いつでも
contribute　貢献する，寄与する
specific　特定の
chore　雑事，雑用，作業
role　役割，役目
father-in-law　義父
show off　〔～を〕誇示する
mosquito　蚊

# Vol. 7 Men and BBQs
## (オトコのBBQ)

ガス式のパワフルなもの
Nearly all of our relatives and friends in America have large barbecues (BBQs) at their homes.
People like to get together for BBQs in their backyards on weekends, not just in summer but at any time of year.
When we barbecue in Japan, it's common for people to each contribute by doing a specific chore.
火起こしは男性陣
調理は女性陣
In America, it is the man's role to do the actual barbecuing.
Men, who might not do any other food preparation, cooking, or cleaning up, take over the job.
義父
Once, when I asked my father-in-law if I could help, he said:
No, thank you.
It's my job.
柔和だけどキッパリと
Men like to show off their skills with BBQs.
A few years ago, we bought our own BBQ for summer BBQ parties.
But with all the mosquitoes in our yard, our BBQ mostly stays in its box.
庭でBBQやりたい
…
薪を使う日本式。コンパクト
サビも…

# Vol. 8 The Celebrate Plate
（記念のお皿）

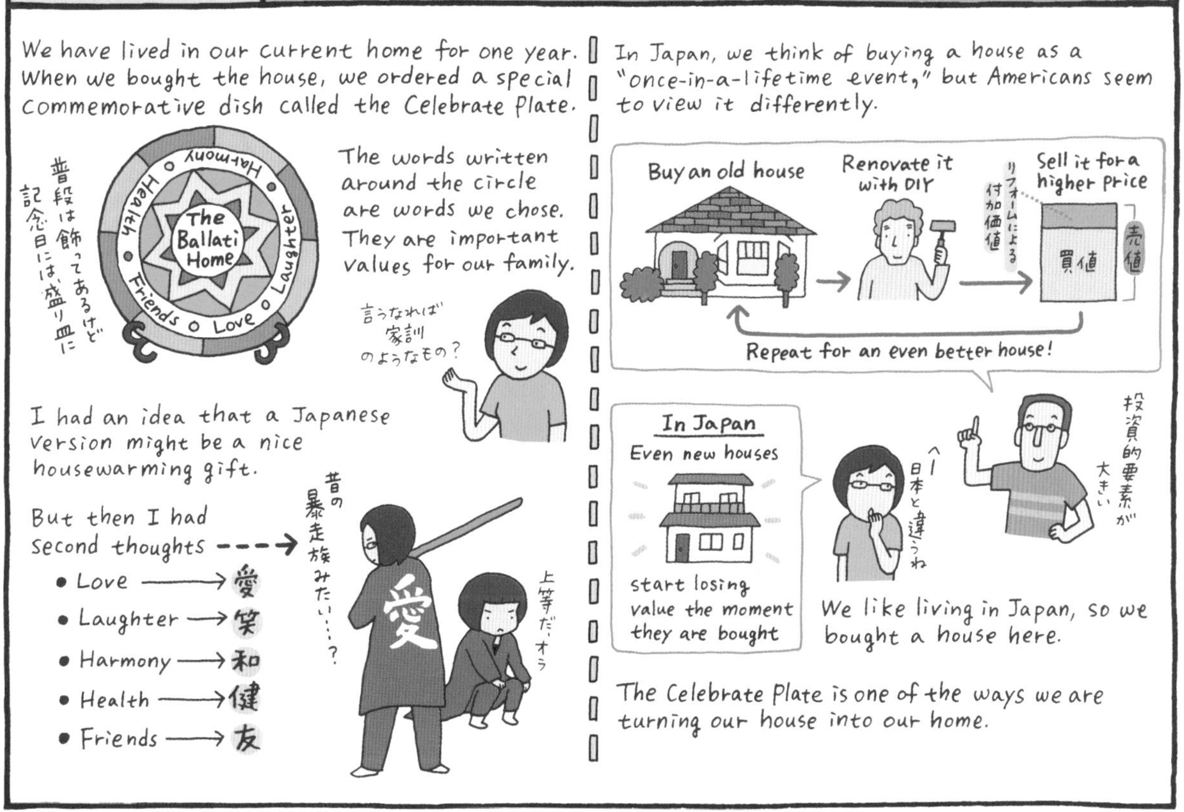

We have lived in our current home for one year. When we bought the house, we ordered a special commemorative dish called the Celebrate Plate.
The Ballati Home
Harmony
Laughter
Love
Friends
Health
普段は飾ってあるけど
記念日には盛り皿に
The words written around the circle are words we chose. They are important values for our family.
言うなれば家訓のようなもの？
I had an idea that a Japanese version might be a nice housewarming gift.
But then I had second thoughts
● Love → 愛
● Laughter → 笑
● Harmony → 和
● Health → 健
● Friends → 友
昔の暴走族みたい…？
愛
上等だ、オラ
In Japan, we think of buying a house as a "once-in-a-lifetime event," but Americans seem to view it differently.
Buy an old house
Renovate it with DIY
Sell it for a higher price
リフォームによる付加価値
買値
売値
Repeat for an even better house!
投資的要素が大きい
In Japan
Even new houses
start losing value the moment they are bought
へー日本と違うね
We like living in Japan, so we bought a house here.
The Celebrate Plate is one of the ways we are turning our house into our home.


家を購入したとき、「セレブレート・プレート」という記念のお皿を特別に注文しました。

**commemorative** 記念の，記念となる

**value** 〔望ましい〕価値観，基準

**housewarming gift** 新築［引っ越し］祝いの贈り物

**once-in-a-lifetime event** 一生に一度の出来事

**renovate** 〔古い建物・家具などを〕修理する

**even better** さらに良い

**turn ~ into ...** ～を…にする

**home** 家庭，〔安心できる心の〕ふるさと，我が家

# Vol. 9 Seal and Signature
## （ハンコと署名）

日本人にとって「ハンコ」は、子どもの頃から身近な存在です。アメリカでは、手書きのサインが日本の印鑑と同じように使われます。

**seal** 〔印影を残すための〕印鑑, ハンコ, 〔印鑑で押された〕印影

**adult** 大人, 成人

**several** 数個の

**handwritten signature** 手書きの署名

**officially registered seal** 印鑑証明

**carve** 〔文字や像などを〕刻む, 彫刻する

**find out** 発見する, 気がつく

**health insurance card** 健康保険証

For Japanese, "hanko" seals are an everyday part of our lives even from when we are children.
おかーさん今日プールあるからハンコ押して
ポン
はーい
When we become adults, many of us have more than one. I have several.
銀行印
習字用
遊び用
仕事の請求書用
久記
き
田村
In America, where Steve is from, a person's handwritten signature is used in all the ways that a seal is used in Japan.
右腕とペンさえあればOK
日本の銀行口座もサインで
Last year, Steve made his first officially registered seal.
馬楽亭ステ吉
自慢！
The shop where he had it carved said it was all right to use kanji characters to write his name.
実は
同じ当て字で千社札も持ってる
We found out later that the name registered for the official seal also appeared on his health insurance card.
馬楽亭ステ吉さーん
は…はいっ
この人が？
Worried this could be a problem at a hospital,
he quickly had a new seal made.
結局すごくシンプル
スティーヴン・バラティ
ちぇっ つまんないの

# Vol.10 Sports Meets (運動会)

With autumn in the air, people across Japan are gearing up for their annual undokai, sports meets.
What's this race called? What do you have to do?
えっ
アメリカではやらないの？
パン食い競争
Sports meets in Japan usually have lots of fun competitions. School sports meets in America are more like track and field competitions.
High Jump
Long Jump
Sprint
とかね
日本人的には物足りない…
体育の授業の延長？
Americans are more likely to play fun games at family events or group picnics in a neighborhood park.
Egg Toss
raw egg
Teams of two people line up across from each other and toss a raw egg back and forth. With each successful catch, everyone takes one step backward. If the egg breaks, your team is out.
Sack Races
Sack races are relay races where participants hop around a course in large potato sacks.
Steve is getting ready for this year's Japanese-style sports meet. It's a fun day for the whole family.
イチニ！イチニ！
ムカデ競争


秋の気配を感じると、日本各地では毎年恒例の「運動会」が開催されます。しかし、アメリカでは少し事情が異なるようで……

**sports meet** 運動会，体育祭

**in the air** 〔気配・匂いなどが〕漂って

**gear up for** ～の準備をする

**annual** 年に一度の，毎年恒例の

**competition** 競争，試合，競技会

**track and field** 陸上競技

**across from** ～の真向かいに

**raw egg** 生卵

**back and forth** 行きつ戻りつ，往復して

**potato sack** ジャガイモを入れる（麻）袋

**get ready for** ～の準備をする

# Vol.11 Happy Halloween!?

## （ハッピー？ハロウィン）

10月も終わりに近づき、ハロウィン気分を味わいたくて楽しい飾りつけにしようとするも、スティーヴには違和感があるようです。

approach 〔時間・空間的に〕近づく，近くなる

get into the spirit of 〜の雰囲気を堪能する

festive decoration お祝いの[お祭り気分の]飾り

think something is not quite right 何かがおかしい気がする

creepy-crawly 恐怖感，嫌悪感

cardboard ボール紙，段ボール

poisonous 毒のある

With the end of October approaching, I wanted to get into the spirit of Halloween.
じゃーん
I found this at the ¥100 shop!
HAPPY HALLOWEEN
I thought this would be a festive decoration. But Steve thinks something's not quite right.
Halloween is more like monsters and creepy-crawlies!
Mummy
Franken-stein
It's a day for scary things.
まあたしかに
ハロウィンって日本のお盆みたいなものだしね
うらめしやー
We designed, cut out, and colored our own decorations made of cardboard.
ジョキジョキ
ぬりぬり
Every day in the week building up to October 31, we put more decorations on the wall.
Poisonous Spider
Giant bat
Black cat
Daddy, Let's make more!
なんか落ちつかないなぁ

# Vol.12 Trick or Treat?
（おやつをくれないとイタズラするぞ）

Halloween has finally arrived. Our kids decided they wanted to be pirates for Halloween.
Avast!
練習した海賊語
A group of kids, all about the same age, from international families joined us for a Halloween party. They came as:
The Hungry Caterpillar
Little Devil
Skeletons
After a hearty meal with lots of pumpkin, we were ready to go trick-or-treating.
一応はカボチャ料理ってことで
ほうとう
We recruited neighbors by explaining how trick-or-treating works.
このお菓子を子どもに渡してください
あら楽しみ
6軒まわった
ピンポーン
Trick or Treat!!
One Neighbor
Extra candy in specially made bags!
ぬっ
Another Neighbor
Counterattack!
わあっ
こわいよー
And Another Neighbor
Gifts too!
Each kid received a hand-made temari ball.
We planned the trick-or-treating for the kids, but the parents and all the neighbors enjoyed it too.


いよいよハロウィンがやってきました。我が家の子どもたちは、海賊の仮装をすると決めていました。

**avast** やめ《stopの意味で使われる号令》

**Hungry Caterpillar** はらぺこあおむし

**hearty meal** ボリューム満点の［栄養たっぷりの］食事

**go trick-or-treating** 〔ハロウィンに〕お菓子をねだりに行く

**recruit** 〔人を〕募集する，採用する

**counterattack** 反撃，カウンター攻撃

３歳のミドリは、けんかしながらも兄を慕っています。小学１年生のハルが宿題をするとき、自分も宿題をしているつもりでマネをしています。

have a quarrel with　～とけんかする
idolize　崇拝する，心酔する
first-grader　小学１年生
pretend　～のふりをする
be proud of　～に満足する，自慢に思う
creation　創作，作品
secret code　暗号
letter　文字
compare　比べる，比較する
construction　構造

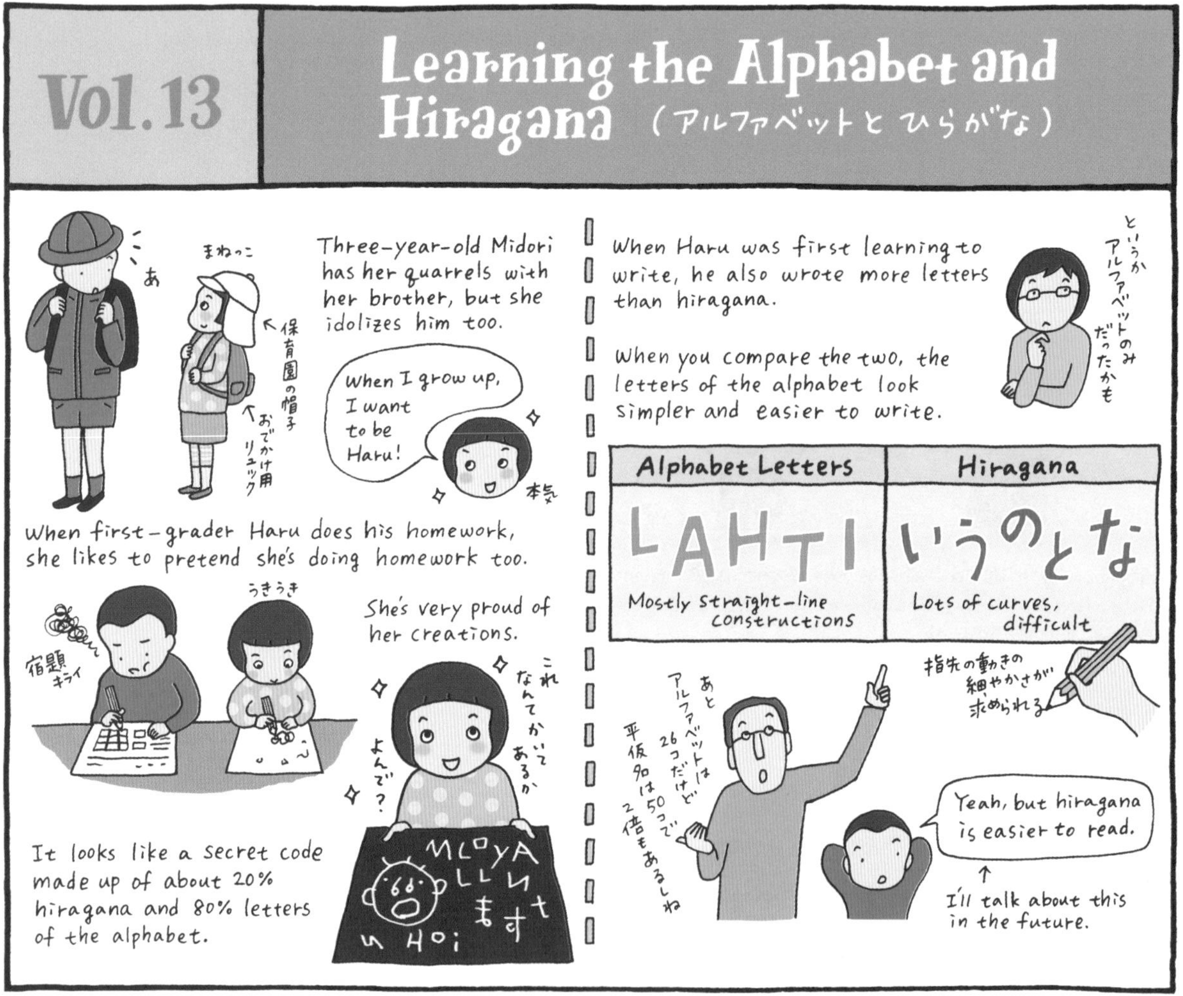

Vol.13
Learning the Alphabet and Hiragana (アルファベットと ひらがな)
あ
まねっこ
Three-year-old Midori has her quarrels with her brother, but she idolizes him too.
保育園の帽子
おでかけ用リュック
When I grow up, I want to be Haru!
本気
When first-grader Haru does his homework, she likes to pretend she's doing homework too.
宿題キライ
うきうき
She's very proud of her creations.
これなんてかいてあるか
よんで？
MLOYA
LLい
ますt
い HOi
It looks like a secret code made up of about 20% hiragana and 80% letters of the alphabet.
When Haru was first learning to write, he also wrote more letters than hiragana.
When you compare the two, the letters of the alphabet look simpler and easier to write.
というかアルファベットのみだったかも
Alphabet Letters
LAHTI
Mostly straight-line constructions
Hiragana
いうのとな
Lots of curves, difficult
指先の動きの細やかさが求められる
あとアルファベットは26コだけど平仮名は50コで2倍もあるしね
Yeah, but hiragana is easier to read.
I'll talk about this in the future.

# Vol. 14 Colors
## (色の認識)

About four years ago, Haru said to me:

パッ
あ、青になったよ。渡ろうか
ちがうよ、ママ。「あお」じゃなくて「みどり」だよ!
きっぱり
Age 3


In English, crosswalk signals are red and green. In Japanese, we say they are red and "ao," which usually means blue. This is confusing for bilingual kids.

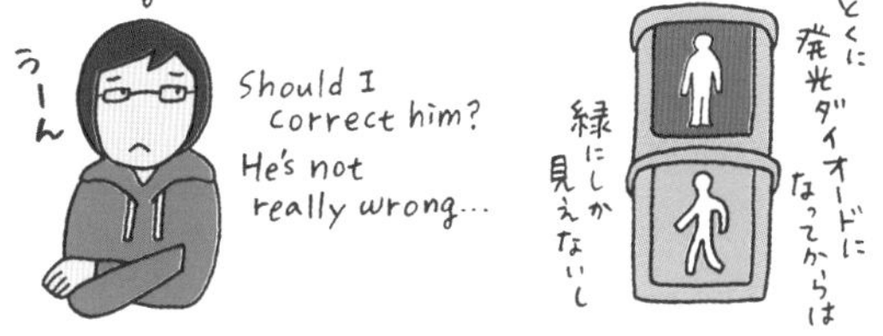

うーん
Should I correct him?
He's not really wrong...
とくに発光ダイオードになってからは
緑にしか見えないし


(Now that he's 7 years old, he sees the color of crosswalk lights as green but calls it "ao" in Japanese.)

Japanese and American kids also color the sun differently. Japanese kids color the sun red, but American kids color it yellow.

赤に近いオレンジとか


Just for fun, I asked Steve, Haru, and Midori to draw the sun. Here's what they drew:

STEVE
MIDORI
HARU(赤も入ってる)


(ちなみに日本の太陽が"赤"なのは、国旗の日の丸からきているらしい)

あれま、ほんとに黄色だ


I had never thought twice about the colors of the sun or crosswalk signals. I realized I was coloring them how I had been taught, not how I actually saw them.

まだ刷り込み以前の人


横断歩道の前でハルと信号待ちをしていたときのこと。「青になったよ」と声をかけると、ハルが否定して言いました——

crosswalk signal 横断歩道の信号
usually 通常，たいてい
confusing 紛らわしい，ややこしい
correct 訂正する，正す
now that 今や〜だから
just for fun 興味本位［面白半分］で
think twice about 〜について熟考する
realize 〔〜に〕気づく
actually 実際に，実質的に

アメリカでは、クリスマスには遠方からも家族が集まります。大切なこの日のためにいろいろな準備をします。

# Vol.15 Christmas Tree
(クリスマスツリーを手に入れる)

Christmas is approaching. In America, families gather from far and wide to be together at Christmas. In that way, Christmas for Americans is similar to New Year's for Japanese. A lot of preparations are made for the holiday.
Artificial Christmas trees have become more and more common in recent years.
Every year, our family goes to a Christmas tree farm to cut down our own tree.
いい香りがするしね
アメリカの親せき
This one looks good!
When you find one that is the right height and has the look you want, you cut it down, tie it on top of your car, and bring it home.
We bought an artificial tree this year.
(In Japan, cutting your own tree is not really an option.)
The artificial tree looks very nice and is just what we wanted. But my husband wanted a little more... a tree with lights already on it!
毎年本物の木を買うのも
高くつくしね
そして少しずつだけど葉も落ちる
こんなの
(枝先に電球がついていて、こういうのをいちいち巻きつけなくていい。すごく楽!)
義母宅のは回転もする
わー
Our tree is up! Our preparations are just getting started, but we are beginning to feel the Christmas spirit.


gather 集合する

from far and wide あちこちから

be similar to ～と同じようである

preparation 準備，支度

holiday 休日，祝祭日，クリスマス休暇

artificial 人工の，人工的な

become more and more common ますます一般的になる

in recent years 近年，ここ数年

option 選ぶこと，選択肢

just getting started まだ始まったばかりだ

Vol.16
Making Christmas Magic
(クリスマスの魔法)
We have spent most Christmases in the United States in recent years. Here are a few of the things that parents in the U.S. do to make Christmas a magical time for their children.
① Bring the kids to meet Santa Claus
この時期、アメリカのショッピングモールなどにはたいてい撮影用サンタが常駐している
Look! There's Santa!
Hi, Santa!
ちょっとこわいらしい
② Read a Christmas story
"The Night Before Christmas" is a classic story evoking the magic and spirit of the Christmas holiday.
しんけん
つい正座
トナカイのそりに乗ってサンタがおもちゃを届ける様子を描いたもの。描写が細かく鮮明
③ Leave milk and cookies for Santa on Christmas Eve
The children put out a dish of cookies and a drink for Santa to snack on when he visits.
それを…
After the kids go to sleep, the parents eat the snacks.
もぐもぐ
(わざと食べかすを残しておく)
After all the buildup, Christmas Day finally arrives when the children wake up on the morning of the 25th.
Presents!
He ate the cookies!
Santa came! Santa came!
今年も無事任務終了
ホッ
This year we'll be in Japan for Christmas. We're busy preparing to make another magical Christmas.
しーっ
娘が通う保育園のクリスマス会に参加予定

クリスマスが子どもたちにとって魔法のような時間になるよう、アメリカの親たちがしていることをこっそり紹介します。

- **here are** 〜は以下のとおりである
- **classic** 昔ながらの，よく知られた
- **evoke** 〔感情・記憶などを〕呼び起こす，想起させる
- **dish of** 一皿の〜
- **snack on** 軽食として〜をつまむ
- **buildup** 築き上げること，積み重ね

日本人の私は、お正月はアメリカよりも日本で過ごしたいという思いがあります。アメリカのお正月は私にはちょっと物足りないのです。

- **fresh start** 再出発，仕切り直し
- **have a soft spot in one's heart for** ～に弱い，～に愛着がある
- **rather than** ～よりはむしろ
- **right after** ～の直後に
- **live** 生放送の，実況中継の
- **day off work** 〔平日に取る〕休日
- **Rose Parade** ローズ・パレード《カリフォルニア州パサデナで新年祝賀行事として毎年元日に行われる》
- **atmosphere** 空気，雰囲気

# Vol. 17 A Fresh Start (お正月気分)

Being Japanese, I have a soft spot in my heart for spending New Year's in Japan rather than in America. New Year's in America seems like a minor holiday since it comes right after Christmas.

お正月になってもツリーは出したまま
1月上旬〜中旬に片付ける家がほとんど

3,2,1...
Happy New Year!
2011
TOSHIBA
HAPPY NEW YEAR
花火や街中の紙吹雪がすごい


On New Year's Eve in America, it's very popular to watch the countdown to the New Year at Times Square in New York. We usually watch it "live" on TV at my husband's family home in California.

いまいちしっくりこない。
こっちはまだ9時だしなあ


There's a three-hour difference between New York and California

In the U.S., it's common for people to have only one day off work for the New Year holiday.

大晦日もしっかり働く
学校も3日にはスタート


On New Year's Day, people like to relax and watch football games or the Rose Parade, which is held in Pasadena, California.

テレビを見てるだけじゃ
気分が出ないよ


The atmosphere of New Year's in Japan makes me feel like it's a fresh start. It's one time of year that I really feel my Japanese identity.

お年玉
寿
今年もよろしくお願いします

# Vol.18 The Terrible Twos (魔の2歳児)

When children reach about age two, they start wanting to feel more independent. They often start asserting themselves by saying, "No!" and throwing tantrums. This stage in their development is often called "the Terrible Twos."

やだ
NO
日本語でも「魔の2歳児」って言いますね
くつ履こう?
ちがうくつが…!
やだっ
NO
Let's read this book tonight.
じゃんけんで決めよう?
やーだっ

The Terrible Twos can be a trying time for parents, and I was looking forward to easier days ahead.

いつまで続くんだろう

However, the Terrible Twos are not limited to two-year-olds. Three-year-olds can also be very insistent about what they do and don't want.

A friend in America told me what stages to expect next: "The Horrible Threes" and then, finally, "the Wonderful Fours."

かーっ うまいこと言うね
たしかにハルのときもそうだったかも

Every child is different. Midori's Terrible Twos didn't start until she was nearly three.

"The Horrible Fours" だったりして…!
フフフ
まだまだ
Oh no~!

I'm feeling a mixture of anticipation and anxiety as she approaches her fourth birthday.

Look! I'm a princess!
Aren't I cute?
今まで兄のお下がりばかりだったのでピンク色やスカートというだけで幸せな人

2歳くらいになるとやってくる子どものイヤイヤ期。「魔の2歳児」とも呼ばれるこの時期の子どもは、なかなか手強いです。

**terrible twos** 魔の2歳児
**independent** 独立した
**assert oneself** 自分の主張を押し通す
**throw a tantrum** 駄々をこねる
**trying time** 試練のとき
**be looking forward to** ～を楽しみにしている
**insistent** 〔主張が〕屈しない，断固たる
**horrible** 恐ろしい
**mixture** 混じり合い，入り交じり
**anticipation** 期待，予想
**anxiety** 心配，不安

私が病気で寝込んでしまい、食事を作る気力もなかったとき、スティーヴが協力を申し出てくれました。本当にありがたかったのですが……

nourishing 体を健康にする，栄養になる

be sick in bed 病気で寝ている

steamed vegetable 温野菜

sesame dressing ごまドレッシング

brown rice 玄米

feel under the weather 具合が良くない

feel like ~ing ～したい気分である

get-well 元気になる

give it a try 試しにやってみる

# Vol.19 Get-Well Food (療養食)

One time when I was sick in bed and didn't have the energy to make a meal, Steve offered his help.
うーん
Can I make something for you?
I really appreciated his offer.
Whatever you make will be fine. Thanks a lot.
おかゆ
うどん
あっさり
さっぱり
胃にやさしい
He made this for me.
どどーん
Veggie Donburi
けっこうずっしり
Steve's original recipe of steamed vegetables with sesame dressing on a bed of brown rice.
ありがたい。ありがたいけど
なんかちがう
あっさり
さっぱり
胃にやさしい
When I'm feeling under the weather, I naturally feel like eating O-kayu (rice porridge) or udon. Steve's idea was, um, different.
American Style
Bread & Chicken Soup
ちなみに
本来ならこういうものを作ります
でも子どものときからスープ嫌いのため作らない
After I felt better, we talked about what he could make if I got sick again. We decided that this could be our family's basic get-well food.
Green Smoothie
ミキサーで作る
ギュイーン
(バナナ、りんごジュースをベースに、ほうれん草やにんじんなどの野菜をmix。見た目よりおいしい)
More, please!
子どもにも大好評
Even I like it! Give it a try!

# Vol.20 Sharing the Bath
(親子のお風呂)

One time a few years ago, we were looking at homes in America. In Japan, homes are described as 2LDK or 4LDK, but in America they are listed by the number of bedrooms, such as 2BR or 4BR.

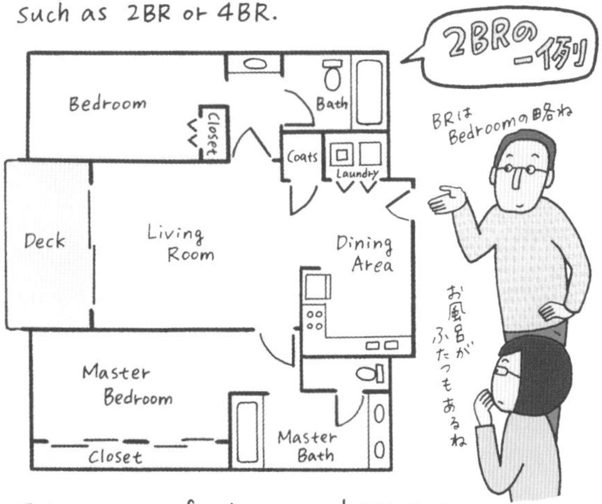

2BRの一例
Bedroom
Closet
Bath
Coats
Laundry
Deck
Living Room
Dining Area
Master Bedroom
Closet
Master Bath
BRはBedroomの略ね
お風呂がふたつもあるね


It's common for homes to have two bathrooms. One is usually connected to the master bedroom to be a private bathroom for the parents. Americans generally wash in the morning, and separate bathrooms help avoid having to wait for the shower.

寝室も赤ちゃんのときから別にするしね
We usually think of bathrooms and bedrooms as private spaces, even between parents and children.
!
そういえば
里帰りの渡米中も…

はーい流すよ
手桶代わりにペットボトルで
固定されてて出が悪いシャワー
洗い場がないので流し湯もこの中に…


In America, parents help young children to take a bath, but they don't get into the bath with them.

I like taking a bath with Haru and Midori because it naturally becomes a time when we talk. In America, they call this "quality time." For me, bathing in Japan is quality time with my kids.

さっきは怒りすぎてゴメン
いいよ


数年前、アメリカで住宅を見ていたときのこと。間取りの表記が日本とアメリカでは異なることに気がつきました。

**describe** 言い表す，描写する

**the number of** ～の数

**master** 主人，所有者

**avoid ~ing** ～することを避ける

**get into the bath** 風呂に入る

**quality time** 最も楽しくて価値のある時間

花粉症シーズン到来。スティーヴも私も花粉症なので、この時期はたいていマスクを装着。でもスティーヴは本当は嫌なのだそう。理由は——

**hay fever** 花粉症

**pleated** プリーツの，ひだのある

**stick out** 突き出る，目立つ

**descent** 〔人の〕系統，血統，祖先

**bump** 突起，隆起

**bridge of one's nose** 鼻筋

**surgical mask** 外科手術用マスク

**dust mask** 防塵マスク

**infectious disease** 感染症

# Vol. 21 Masks
（マスク）

It's the middle of hay fever season. Both my husband and I get hay fever, so at this time of year we're usually wearing masks. Steve puts them on, but he really doesn't want to. Why?

They don't fit!
大小含め
いろいろ
試したけど
どうしても
隙間が…
Pleated type
3D type
Cup type
Flat type


The problem is his nose. It sticks out more than the average Japanese nose. People of European descent have a wide variety of nose shapes.

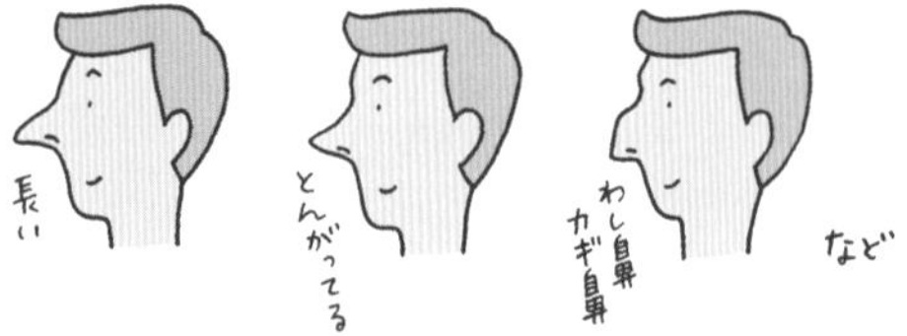

長い
とんがってる
わし鼻
カギ鼻
など


Steve is of Italian descent and has a typical Italian bump on the bridge of his nose. When he puts on a mask, there are big gaps between the bridge and his cheeks.

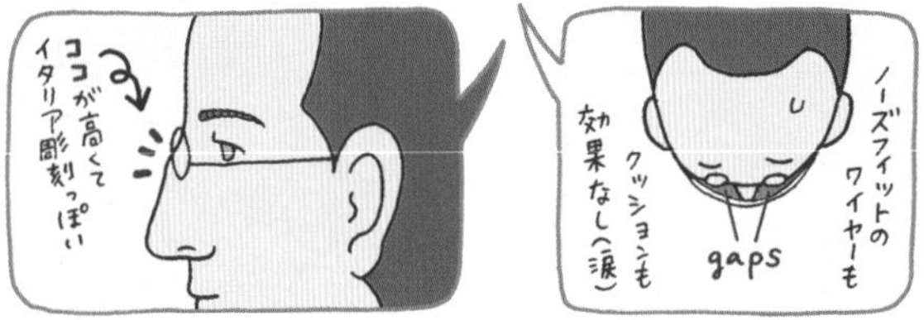

ココが高くて
イタリア彫刻っぽい
ノーズフィットの
ワイヤーも
クッションも
効果なし（涙）
gaps


In America, it's not common to see people wearing masks. The masks we see often in Japan are really only used as surgical masks or dust masks.

Do they have an infectious disease!?
At this time of year, I wonder what visitors think when they see so many people wearing masks.

# Vol.22

# St. Patrick's Day
## (聖パトリックデー)

March 17 is St. Patrick's Day. Saint Patrick is the patron saint of Ireland. People of Irish descent celebrate their heritage on St. Patrick's Day. Every year, we receive a St. Patrick's Day card from Steve's Irish-American mother.

HAPPY ST. PATRICK'S DAY!
Symbol①
SHAMROCK
アイルランドの国花。四つ葉ではなくて三つ葉
Symbol②
LEPRECHAUN
いたずら好きの小人


On St. Patrick's Day, it's a custom to wear something green.

緑のものをつけてないと小人につねられるんだって
SHAMROCKのシールをつけたり
緑の服を着たり
アクセサリーを緑色にしてみたり


America has a large number of Irish immigrants, and they and their descendants celebrate their roots with parades and shenanigans.

At school
Ouch!
PINCH
If you don't wear something green on St. Patrick's Day, you might get pinched.

Adults
緑のシャツ率高い
Irish pubs burst with beer and laughter.


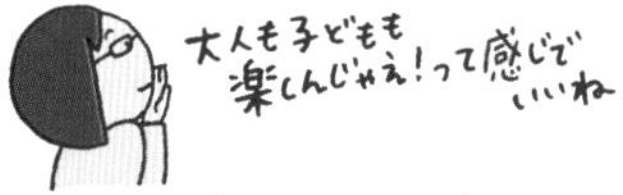

大人も子どもも楽しんじゃえ！って感じでいいね

島根の松江等でもパレードが
バグパイプの演奏などがあることも


The fun of St. Patrick's Day can also be experienced in Japan in the Irish pubs and at the parades in Omotesando and Yokohama. You don't have to be Irish to join in the fun. Be sure to wear green and watch out for leprechauns!

3月17日は聖パトリックデー。聖パトリックはアイルランドの守護聖人です。この日はアイルランド系の人々にとって伝統を祝う大切な日です。

**patron saint** 守護聖人
**heritage** 遺産，伝統
**shamrock** シャムロック
**leprechaun** レプラコーン《アイルランドの伝説の妖精》
**immigrant** 〔外国からの〕移民
**descendant** 子孫，末裔
**shenanigan** いたずら，悪ふざけ
**get pinched** つねられる
**burst with** ～であふれそうである
**be sure to** 必ず～しなさい
**watch out for** ～に気をつける

馬楽奈郵便
COLUMN 1

## Making Our House a Home: The Celebrate Plate

When we bought our house, we reformed the interior, moved in all of our stuff, purchased some new furniture, and did everything we could think of to make it a nice place to live. The house came out very comfortable for us. But it wasn't complete, it needed a soul.

We knew that, as the years went by, the rooms would fill with personal and shared remembrances that would transform the house into our home. But we wanted to set a spiritual cornerstone on the day we moved in.

I found a woman online who made hand-painted dishes called "Celebrate Plates" for commemorating special occasions, and we asked her to make one for family events. When one of us had a birthday, achieved something, or had some sort of special experience, we would serve them dinner on the plate and ask them to talk about the event.

With the plate came a Celebrate Plate Journal in which we wrote short descriptions of what we were commemorating.

***Midori's 3rd birthday.*** Today we hiked up a steep mountain and Midori insisted on walking all by herself. She likes to watch Dora the Explorer and still loves bananas.

***Haru won the 2nd grade running race.*** He said he felt like crying at one point but told himself he could cry after the race if he wanted to.

***Midori's 8th birthday.*** She wants to be a pilot when she grows up so she can fly people to where they want to go. No, that was yesterday. She wants to draw picture books. Maybe a story with a log cabin and a dog.

***Kikue's 37th birthday.*** Haru and Midori sang Twinkle, Twinkle Little Star. Kikue's family visited our new home for the first time and liked it!

***Dad's 58th birthday*** *(written by Haru)*. Midori and I gave Dad tons of chocolate, enough to keep him from stealing the chocolate we got from Jiiji and Baaba.

The journal is precious to us. We love to read it aloud and laugh and laugh together.

■ **remembrance** 思い出，記念 ■ **cornerstone** 土台，基礎 ■ **commemorate** 祝う，記念する ■ **Dora the Explorer** 『ドーラといっしょに大冒険』《アメリカのテレビアニメ作品》 ■ **log cabin** 丸太小屋 ■ **read ~ aloud** ～を声に出して読む

STEVE
日本在住25年の
江戸好きアメリカ人
KIKUE
ワタクシ
HARU
息子。
小学2年生
MIDORI
娘。
4歳

# 2nd Year

2012

ミドリの自己主張が強くなってきました。それが時には、わがままに感じられることもあります。

sound　～に聞こえる，思われる

demanding　注文の多い，手のかかる

tried-and-true　実証済みの，確実に信頼できる

polite　丁寧な，礼儀正しい

ask for something　何か依頼する

May I have ~?　～を頂戴したいです

respond　応じる，取り入れる

have the same ring to it　同じ響き［感じ］がする

Vol.23
The Magic Word
（魔法の言葉）
Midori is beginning to assert herself by telling us what she wants. Sometimes, she sounds very demanding.
Carry me!
Read it!
Do it!
穏やかなスティーヴもさすがに…
ムッ
いったい何様のつもりだ
Steve uses an American tried-and-true tool for teaching how to be polite when asking for something.
Soy milk!
What's the magic word?
ハッ
Soy milk, please!
"Please" is the "magic" word because it helps you get something you want, like a magic wish.
After the kids learn to say please, then we'll teach them other polite ways to ask for things.
×
I want some soy milk!
○
May I have some soy milk, please?
ちゃんと言うまで言い直させます
I thought this was a great teaching method, so I quickly started responding the same way in Japanese.
「please」に代わる日本語は…
えーっと
「～ください」かなあ
豆乳ください
手伝ってください
I've been trying the same with "kudasai" but it doesn't have the same ring to it.
Still, English is helping us learn to speak politely in Japanese too.
あれ？
なんかカタイなあ

Vol.24

# Riding the Train
## (電車に乗るとき)

Sunny spring has arrived. A ride on a warm train is a nice opportunity to refresh yourself.

あふ
zzz
老若男女でうたたねの図

Steve sometimes naps on the train too. But he says he was in Japan for five years before he allowed himself to take a nap on a train. Part of the reason was that he grew up where cars are the main mode of transportation, and he wasn't used to riding trains every day.

ドキドキ
(日本語学校の生徒時代)

He couldn't read much Japanese yet.

The main reason was Americans are careful in public places. All kinds of people mix in public, so it's important to protect your belongings. A nap is out of the question.

Don't be an easy target for a thief.

In San Francisco, I noticed that the ambience on the BART trains was different from trains in Japan.

つり革がない。あまり混んでない
No one napping.
Few announcements.
何度も繰り返したりしないので、うっかりすると乗り過ごしそう…

There certainly are a lot of announcements on Japanese trains. Maybe it creates a sense of protection and safety. Perfect for napping.

本日、傘のお忘れものが増えております。
ご注意ください
間もなく発車します

春眠暁を覚えず。日本では、電車に乗るとうたた寝する人たちを見かけるのは珍しいことではありませんが——

**opportunity** 良い機会，好機

**(take a) nap** うたた寝する

**allow oneself to** 思い切って～する

**transportation** 移動手段

**be used to ~ing** ～することに慣れている

**belongings** 持ち物，所有物

**out of the question** 問題外である

**be an easy target for** ～の格好の餌食になる

**ambience** 〔ある場所が醸し出す独特の〕雰囲気

**BART** バート《サンフランシスコ市の通勤用高速鉄道》

初夏の気配を感じるやいなや、スティーヴは夏の装いに早変わり。でもこれは彼に限った話ではないようです。

**warm up** 暖まる，温かくなる
**be quick to** すぐに～する
**bring out** 持ち出す，取り出す
**climate** 気候
**tolerance level** 許容範囲
**feel right** しっくりくる，納得できる
**it doesn't matter** ～は構わない，問題ない
**chilly** ひんやりする，肌寒い
**bring oneself to** ～する気になる

# Vol.25 Dressing for the Season
## （体感温度の壁）

As summer approaches and the weather warms up, Steve is quick to bring out his warm-weather clothes.
T-shirt and shorts
It's California weather!
口グセ
（スキをみては日焼けしたがる人）
ちょっと早すぎない？
Long-sleeved shirt and long pants
It's not just us. We've met many international couples that seem to be dressed for different seasons.
GWのピクニックで
イギリス人
アイルランド人
日本人
日本人
There could be many reasons why people dress so differently.
People originally from different climates must have different tolerance levels for the cold.
寒いねえ
（と言いつつも、コーデュロイのジャケットで十分らしい人）
冬だってこんなに違う
I just wear what feels right for me.
It doesn't matter what the calendar says.
衣替えとか海開きとか
That may be true.
But my body is telling me that it's still too chilly. I can't bring myself to wear shorts in early May.
言われてみればたしかに。
でもそんな節目も四季の一環という気も…
うーん
制服とか

# Vol.26 Rock-paper-scissors (じゃんけん)

Rock
Scissors
Paper
Steve is not good at rock-paper-scissors. He knows the rules and how to do it, but he's not used to playing it. He has a hard time keeping up with the speed of the game.
Rock, paper, scissors! (じゃーんけーん, ぽいっ!)
また後出し!
ちゃんと「ぽいー」で出してよー
あんまりやったことないからうまくできないんだよ
Steve says they play rock-paper-scissors in America, but not nearly as much as the Japanese do.
えー
Then how do you decide who goes first?
We work out a deal or some other way.
flip a coin とか
Brothers deciding who gets a piece of cake:
日本では…
First, cut the cake.
じゃんけんぽいっ!
The winner gets first choice.
よっしゃ!
あー、負けた
"Janken" clearly decides the winner.
アメリカでは…
One person cuts it, the other person chooses which half they want.
OK!
等分にしないと自分が損をする
切る人も真剣
Half
選ぶ人も真剣
They negotiate a fair way to do it.
ほーなるほど
面倒だけどとってもフェアな感じ
Our young kids do "janken" almost every day and are already experts. Steve is doing his best to keep up. He's getting lots of practice.
さいしょはグー
じゃんけんぽい!

スティーヴはじゃんけんが苦手です。ルールややり方は知っているものの、やり慣れていないのです。なぜなら——

**be not used to ~ing** ～することに慣れていない
**have a hard time ~ing** ～することに苦労する
**keep up with** ～に遅れずについていく
**go first** 最初にやる，先に行く
**work out a deal** 何とか折り合いをつける
**flip a coin** 硬貨を指ではじく《表か裏かで物事を決める》
**expert** 専門家，エキスパート
**do one's best** 最善を尽くす
**get lots of practice** たくさん練習する

私たち家族はみんな同じ部屋で寝ていますが、アメリカでは、子どもは赤ちゃんのときから自分の部屋で寝る習慣があります。

**go to bed** ベッドに入る，就寝する

**retire to** 〜に引っ込む

**recently** 最近，近頃

**bond with** 〜と親密な絆を結ぶ

**have no plans to** 〜する考えはない

**by oneself** 自分ひとりで

**downstairs** 階下［１階］で

**anymore** もはや〜ない

Vol.27
Sleeping Alone
(ひとり寝)
When we go to bed at night, we all retire to the same room.
Queen-Size futon
Single futon
6畳にいっぱいいっぱい
In America, the custom is for children to sleep in their own room from the time they are babies. Recently, however, sleeping together has become more common in the United States and Europe.
①夫婦のプライバシーを守るため
②子どもの自立を促すため
独り寝させる理由
It's a great way to bond with your children.
うちも「川の字」でいこう!
We had no plans to change, until one day when Haru announced:
I'm going to sleep by myself downstairs!
キッパリ
おおっ
大丈夫?
1F
Good night
Good night
So that night…
2F
なんか落ち着かないね
きっと途中でこっちに来るんじゃない?
And the next morning…
おはよう!
誇らしげ
Children grow up before we know it. As parents, we are proud of our child's independence. At the same time, we feel a little sad that our little boy is not so little anymore.

# Vol.28 Rain Gear (雨具)

The rainy season will soon be here.

Four-year-old Midori, who loves to wear her rain boots even on sunny days, can't wait to splash in some puddles.

Steve's rain gear is simple.

どしゃぶりでなければこれで十分
野球帽は眼鏡を水滴から守るために

When I think about it, I haven't ever seen an umbrella stand when we visit his parents' home in Northern California.

?
Don't they use umbrellas?
It certainly rains enough.

I asked my mother-in-law where she keeps her umbrella.

Um. I think it's in the car.
CA.....
Yep, it was there. It looked like it hadn't been used in a long time.

Umbrellas don't seem to be needed as much in America as in Japan. Maybe it's because Americans rely mostly on cars to get around.

In Japan, many people have umbrella collections.

私の実家では傘立てひとつに入りきらない状態
ほとんどはビニール傘

How many umbrellas do you have at your house?

もうすぐ梅雨の季節。晴れた日でも長靴を履くのが大好きな4歳のミドリは、早く水たまりで水しぶきを上げたいようです。

rain gear　雨具

can't wait to　〜するのが待ち遠しい

splash　〔しぶきを〕跳ね上げる

puddle　水たまり

umbrella stand　傘立て

certainly　確実に、必ず

rely mostly on　ほとんど〜に頼る

get around　動き回る

我が家のDVDプレーヤーは、子どもたちが英語に触れる大切な情報源。ビデオを観るときはいつも、英語音声に日本語字幕をつけて楽しんでいます。

**come in contact with** ～と接触する

**subtitle** 〔映画などの〕字幕

**expose ~ to** ～を…にさらす

**all sorts of** あらゆる種類の～

**follow the story** 話についていく

**ignore** 無視する

Vol.29
Watching DVDs
(DVD鑑賞)
Our DVD player is a source of entertainment and also an important source for our kids to come in contact with English. We always watch videos with English audio and Japanese subtitles.
(テレビなしの生活ゆえ、PCモニターで)
Viewers who listen to the English audio
Viewer who reads the Japanese subtitles
Steve is the main source of everyday English for the kids, but English videos are a great help.
会話は英語。絵本の読み聞かせも。
子どもたちの英語の源のほとんど
責任重大
Movies and TV shows expose the kids to English used in all sorts of situations.
内容のすべてを吸収して糧にしている
I need the subtitles to follow the stories. The kids are still quite young and ignore the subtitles. But we've heard stories that this could change.
ニュージーランド人の父と日本人の母を持つ12歳
字幕、ウザイから消していい？
なんか悔しい～！
国際結婚の先輩ママさん

Vol.30
Reading and Writing
(英語の読み書き)
Four-year-old Midori is excited about learning to read and write hiragana.
そぉーこぉーにぃー あぁーひぃー るぅーがぁー…(すべて平たんに発音)
お経っぽい
単なる文字の羅列&鏡文字率が高い
あひるのおやこ
She started trying to read hiragana before trying to read English. This may be because she hears mostly Japanese, or it could be because, at the start, English is more difficult to read.
English letters, especially vowels, can have more than one pronunciation.
ひらがなは一文字につき一音のみ。(例外は「～へ」の「へ」は「え」と読むとか)
cup [ʌ]
use [juː]
[uː] blue
など。
大変だなあ
混乱しないの?
How do English speakers teach kids how to read and pronounce the words?
I watched Steve teaching Midori how to read.
Reading
BUS
B says buh[b]. U says uh[ʌ]. S says sss[s]. So…?
buh-uh-sss b-u-s… bus…
BUS!
He reads each letter's sound one by one and then strings them together into a word. They practice this over and over until kids can do it themselves.
Writing
[bʌs]
[b][ʌ][s]
B U S
かな?
Midori is slowly starting to read English words. Right now, Japanese is easier, but she still has to learn katakana and kanji.
As they say, "There's no shortcut to learning a language."

ひらがなの読み書きができるようになってきた4歳のミドリ。英語の読み書きはどうやって習得するのでしょうか。

**be excited about** ～にワクワクする

**at the start** 初めは

**vowel** 母音

**pronunciation** 発音

**pronounce** 発音する，話す

**one by one** 一つずつ

**string ~ together into** ～をつなぎ合わせて…にする

**over and over** 何度もくり返して

**right now** 現時点では

**shortcut** 近道，手っ取り早い方法

誰かの話を聞くとき、私はよくうなずいたり相づちを打ったりします。でも、スティーヴは、たいてい黙って聞いています。

interjection 間投詞

how often どのくらいの頻度で

show respect 敬意を表する

quiet 静かな，〔人が〕寡黙な

one-third 3分の1

sentence 文

bother 困らせる，落ち着かない気分にさせる

excitable 興奮しやすい

generally speaking 一般的に言えば

flexible 自由自在な，融通の利く

Vol.31
Interjections
（相づち）
When you are listening to someone speak。how often do you nod or say "hai" or "so desu ne" or "naruhodo"? I do it a lot。
例えば この文章だったら 3回ぐらいかな
（句読点ごとに）
To me, interjections are a way of showing respect and support to the speaker.
Steve, however, is usually quiet when listening to someone talk. He seems to use interjections about one-third as often as I do. Sometimes I get the feeling that he isn't listening.
ねえねえ
Are you listening to me?
疑いのまなざし
Yes, of course!
ぬれぎぬだよー
Steve might make one interjection for each sentence or wait until the sentence is finished to say something.
We're taught that it's polite to listen quietly when someone is talking.
Conversation
浮き彫りになる感覚の違い
Too many interjections can bother the speaker.
そうかなあ？
Of course, everyone's personality is different.
A quiet Japanese
えっと それで
じっ
言葉数少ない
An excitable American
No kidding!
Oh really?
You did?
Oh boy!
Generally speaking, Japanese people interject quite often during conversations.
So, what does Haru do?
Ya gotta be flexible!
日本語のときは多めに
英語のときは少なめに
ほー
そんなところまでバイリンガルなのね

Vol.32
American Breakfast
(洋風?な朝食)
I had always thought a Western breakfast was this:
Orange juice
Toast
Sausage
Greens
Egg
ホテルの洋食朝ごはんもこんな感じだよね
But when I started living with Steve, I learned this is not what he eats on a daily basis. He eats something more like this:
Cereal
The breakfast I had imagined is eaten mainly on special days.
On weekends or holidays, we might have something different, like pancakes.
The word "cereal" can mean many different types of grains.
Corn-flakes
Made from corn. Possibly the most common breakfast in the U.S.
Oatmeal
Made from oats. A very nutritious whole grain. Very filling.
Muesli
A mix of oats and cornflakes mixed with dried fruit, nuts, and seeds. Often eaten with yogurt.
Granola
Oatmeal baked with vegetable oil and sweetener, like maple syrup, and mixed with dried fruits, nuts, and seeds.
At our house, we mix oatmeal and muesli and eat it with soy milk. I usually have a Japanese-style breakfast. The kids can choose which they want that day.
具だくさんみそ汁とおしんこがあれば幸せ
そして納豆
おはよう
Which do you want, oatmeal or natto?
オハヨー
Our days always start with this breakfast question.


私が「これぞ洋風な朝食」と思っていたものと、スティーヴの日常的な朝食とはだいぶ異なっていました——

**on a daily basis** 毎日のように，日常的に

**cereal** シリアル，穀物

**grain** 穀物，穀類

**oat** オート麦

**nutritious** 栄養価が高い

**filling** 食べ応えのある

**muesli** ミューズリー《オート麦とコーンフレークをドライフルーツやナッツ、種子などと混ぜた朝食用シリアル》

**seed** 種子，種

**sweetener** 甘味料

もうすぐ新学期。またお弁当作りが始まります。前の晩ごはんの残り物もフル活用する「詰め弁」が多い我が家のお弁当ですが――

Vol.33
Bento Lunches
(お弁当)
いってきまーす!
The new school term is about to begin. That means I will be making school lunches again.
給食のない学校に通っています
I say "making," but what I usually do is gather leftovers from the previous night's meal.
厚揚げのしょうゆ焼
梅干し
サツマイモのみそ煮
キュウリとワカメの酢のもの
ニンジンとマイタケ煮
キャラ弁
には程遠い地味弁
The bento lunches I make are very basic. But our relatives in America surprise me by saying things like:
WOW
Your lunches are so creative and look so beautiful!
アハハ
Oh, I'm sure you're exaggerating...
The other day, I saw pictures of American school lunches that were praised on a website.
ジャムサンドイッチ
カットフルーツ
キュウリの輪切り
チーズスティック
So few veggies. It's more like raw food.
スカスカ&パサパサだし
The comments were praising the mere presence of vegetables.
ワックスペーパーに包んで持っていく
When I brought bag lunches to school, a peanut butter and jelly sandwich and an apple were the basic ingredients.
There seems to be a really high standard for school lunches in Japan. I would say this is something about our culture that we can be proud of.
実はもっと手抜きしてもいいくらいかも?


**new school term** 新学期

**be about to** まさに~するところだ

**leftover** 料理の残り物, 余り

**previous** 前の

**exaggerate** 誇張する

**the other day** 先日, この間

**be praised** 称賛される

**mere** ほんの, たったの

**peanut butter and jelly sandwich** ピーナッツバターとジャムを2枚のパンで挟んだサンドウィッチ

**ingredient** 〔特に料理の〕材料

# Vol.34 More than Leaves Fall in Autumn（費用がかさむ里帰り）

季節は夏から秋へ。でも、私たちの思いはすでに年末へと向かっています。なぜなら――

The weather is gradually shifting from summer to autumn. Our thoughts, however, are already jumping ahead to the end of the year.

Air Ticket/
Air Ticket/
We have to reserve air tickets now so we can go home for Christmas!
子連れには日系が親切で人気


Christmas is an important family event in the U.S. and Europe, very much like the New Year's holidays in Japan. Schools and companies also have vacations around that time. Demand is so high the airlines even sell out.

なにしろ4人分だし
We have to go. But it's so expensive...
燃料費もばかにならないし
格安航空券でもひとり10万くらい。
もちろんエコノミークラスで


We used to save several hundred dollars by avoiding the high-demand periods. Now that our son is in grade school, however, we're stuck with flying when the prices are high.

ピポパ
なにしろ4人分なので真剣


I often hear comments like this:

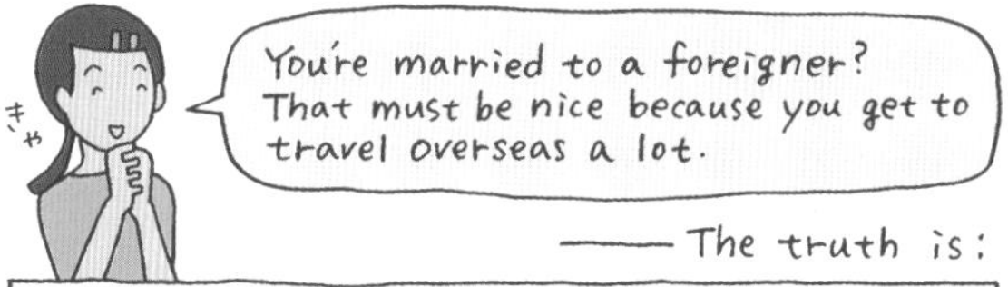

きゃ
You're married to a foreigner? That must be nice because you get to travel overseas a lot.


—— The truth is:

Family visits eat a large chunk of our savings.
里帰り以外の旅行なんてしばらくしてない
周りの国際結婚ファミリーの人たちも…
We haven't been back in five years.
Just my husband and kids went this year.


Autumn is the season of good appetites and curling up with good books. For us, it's also a time when our savings fall like autumn leaves.

**gradually** だんだん，徐々に

**jump ahead** 先んじる，先を行く

**very much like** ～のようなものである

**demand** 要求，必要，需要

**sell out** 完売する，〔在庫を〕切らす

**grade school** 小学校

**be stuck with** ～に行き詰まっている

**eat a large chunk of** かなり多くの～を食いつぶす

**good appetite** 旺盛な食欲

**curl up with a good book** 体を丸めて良い本に夢中になる

スティーヴの国籍はアメリカ、私の国籍は日本です。子どもたちはアメリカと日本の２つの国籍、そしてそれぞれの国のパスポートも持っています。

multinational　多国籍の

nationality　国籍

have to be careful　注意しなければならない

recognize　認める，受け入れる

dual nationality　二重国籍

get to　～できる機会を得る

have to　～する必要がある

be forced to　～せざるを得ない

# Vol.35 Our Multinational Family
## (家族の国籍)

My husband's nationality is American and mine is Japanese. Our children have two nationalities — American and Japanese — and they have passports for each country.

日本のと
アメリカのと
日本国旅券
JAPAN PASSPORT
PASSPORT
United States of America


We have to be careful how we use them.

日本の出入国時は…
In Japan, the kids use their Japanese passports.
こんにちは
アメリカの出入国時は…
In America, they use their American passports.
Hi


Before they are 22 years old, they will have to choose which nationality they want to keep.

The United States recognizes dual nationalities, but Japan doesn't.
それにしても二十歳そこそこで決めるなんてむずかしいよね


People sometimes comment:

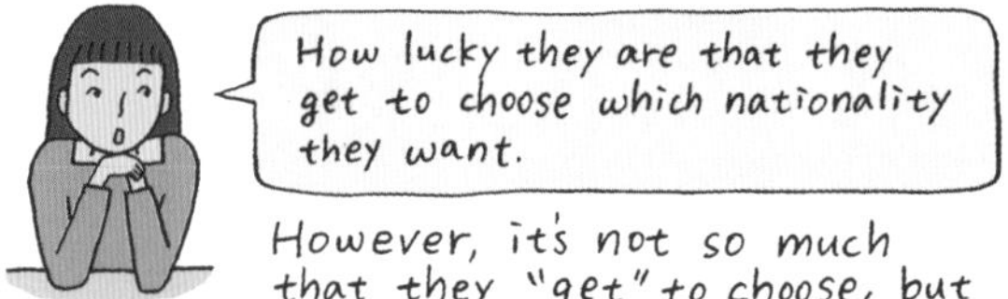

How lucky they are that they get to choose which nationality they want.


However, it's not so much that they "get" to choose, but that they "have" to choose. I also feel like our kids will be forced to lose one of their nationalities.

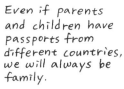

ママの国か、Daddyの国か…


Even if parents and children have passports from different countries, we will always be family.

Vol.36
Bobbing for Apples
(ハロウィンのりんごゲーム)
The kids are looking forward to Halloween. They are already excited about their costumes.
I'm gonna be Spiderman!
I want to be a princess!
We could buy costumes, of course, but they are expensive when you consider that they will probably only be worn once. So we parents get creative.
高っ!
1万円とか
その結果…
ざっとこんなもんよ
Mask from an old stretchy T-shirt.
Red garden gloves.
Drawn with fabric paint.
Rain boots.
Fairy dress she received last Christmas.
Every year, we invite friends and their kids to a Halloween party at our house. The kids love to play in their costumes. We also have another Halloween tradition.
Bobbing for Apples
← アメリカではハロウィンによく楽しまれているゲーム
小さめのリンゴ 紅玉などでやるのがおすすめ
Apples are put into a tub filled with water. Without using their hands, each person must dip their whole head in the cold water to bite an apple and lift it out.
The kids have a blast, and the parents do too.
Apples always taste better on Halloween.
Apples can also be hung up by strings.
パン食い競走のリンゴ版?

我が家の子どもたちはハロウィンをとても楽しみにしています。どんな仮装にするか盛り上がっているようで……

**bob for** 〜を口にくわえようとする

**probably** 高い確実性で，十中八九

**get creative** 創造力を発揮する

**stretchy** 伸縮性のある

**tub** たらい，おけ

**filled with** 〜で満たされている

**dip ~ in the cold water** 〜を冷水に浸す

**bite** かむ，かみつく

**lift ~ out** 〜を取り出す

**have a blast** とても楽しい時間を過ごす

スティーヴの両親が３年ぶりに来日することになりました。彼らの来訪が楽しみでならない私たちです。

**in-laws** 義理の両親
**come to visit** 訪ねてくる
**because of** ～のために
**nuclear** 核の, 原子力の
**first ~ in ... years** …年ぶりの～
**have a special affection for** ～に対して特別な愛情を持っている
**section** 部分, 区画
**every time** 毎回（～するたびに）
**intricate** 〔構造・模様などが〕複雑な
**knot** 結びかた, 飾り結び
**enthusiasm** 熱中, 熱烈な興味
**unfamiliar** 慣れていない

Vol.37
Fun with the In-Laws
（義・両親の視点）
My in-laws (Steve's parents) are coming to visit us soon. They didn't come last year because of the Fukushima nuclear disaster. This will be their first visit in three years, and we are really looking forward to seeing them in Japan again.
Not all of our international friends are happy when relatives come to visit.
あーストレス
I never know what to cook for them when they're here. They won't even touch Japanese food.
My in-laws have a different opinion.
Japanese food is very healthy. I love it!
日本酒もいけるクチ
It's yummy.
My mother-in-law has a special affection for Japanese things. She even has a Japanese section in her garden in California.
庭を彩る紅葉
ちょうずばち
手水鉢とひしゃくもある。
池には鯉も
Every time she comes, she finds something new to get excited about.
Bamboo Fences
写真に撮ってた
One time when she was taking pictures of fences, I noticed for the first time the intricate rope-work and the varieties of knots.
梅結び
玉結び
総角結び
I really enjoy the enthusiasm my in-laws have for unfamiliar things. I wonder what my mother-in-law will discover this time.

Vol.38
Japanese Appliances
(日本の家電)
Japanese appliances are one of the things about Japan that our foreign friends often comment about. They are amazed at the over-the-top level of service from the products themselves.
Hot water heater
低めの女性の声で
The bath is ready.
電子音で十分じゃない!?
Car navigation system
ドライブして2時間を過ぎた頃から
You've been driving for some time and may be tired. Please be careful to drive safely.
親切だけど余計なお世話?
It always tells us the day and date, but on Dec. 25 it says "Merry Christmas" too.
There are many more examples too. Trucks say "moving back" when reversing, and home security systems say "The system will secure your home while you're out."
However, there's one product that never fails to generate comments.
Washlet toilet
There're too many buttons!
I'm always surprised when I hear music in public toilets.
The bidet scares me!
不評が多い
ミドリも!
よく分からないままビデのボタンを押してしまう人が多いらしい
One time, my inquisitive mother-in-law was so impressed by an automated toilet she saw at a hotel that she had one installed in her own home.
フフフ
The toilet was completely automated, opening and closing the lid and even flushing by itself.
However, the one she bought in America is not completely Japanese.
あれっ
足が届かない…

日本を知る外国人たちがよく話題にするもののひとつに、サービス過剰ともいえる家電の機能があります。例えば――

**appliance** 〔家庭用〕電化製品, 電気器具

**over-the-top** 度を超えた, やり過ぎの

**reverse** 〔エンジンやギアを〕バックにする

**never fail to** 必ず～する

**generate comments** コメントが寄せられる

**bidet** ビデ

**inquisitive** 探求心のある, 好奇心旺盛な

**install** 取り付ける

**lid** ふた

**flush** 水を流す

両親に対して使う呼び名は、家庭によってさまざまです。我が家では、アメリカ的な呼び名と日本的な呼び名が入り交じっています。

**vary from family to family** 家族によって異なる

**a bunch of** たくさんの

**from then on** それ以降

**tend to** ～する傾向がある

**abruptly** 突然

**address** 〔人を～と〕呼ぶ

**reach adolescence** 青年期［思春期］になる

**homonym** 同音異義語

**fairly common** かなり一般的な

**feel awkward** 気まずい

**become hesitant in** ～への意欲がそがれる

Vol.39

# Mom and Dad

（父と母の呼び方）

お父さん
お母さん
パパ
ママ
父ちゃん
母ちゃん


The names people use for their parents vary from family to family. We have a bunch of names.

Daddy, do you know where my hat is?
I don't know, ask your mom.
ママー、ぼくの帽子、どこか知ってる？
知らない
ダディーに聞いてみた？

Daddy
ママ
って呼んでるよ


In English, the names you call your parents change as you grow older.

うちは今、ココ

| Names | Ages |
|---|---|
| Dada, Mama | until about age 4 |
| Daddy, Mommy | until about middle school |
| Dad, Mom | from then on (even as an adult) |

In Japanese, we tend to abruptly change how we address our parents when we reach adolescence. English has more of a feeling of a transition.

日本の場合
ハハハ
パパー
これが…
おいヒロシ
何、オヤジ
本人も切り替えるタイミングがむずかしかったりね


In both languages, after getting married, you can call your parents-in-law mom and dad. Japanese uses homonyms with different kanji. In English, at least in the United States, it's fairly common for a person to call their in-laws by their first names.

日本語だとお義父さんお義母さんだけど
For me personally, I feel awkward calling my in-laws o-tōsan and o-kāsan.


Steve has a very good relationship with my parents, but he still becomes hesitant in situations when he could call them mom and dad.

なんとか呼ばずに済ませて11年
あの～

Vol.40
The Christmas Spirit
（クリスマス・スピリット）
Soon after marrying Steve, I got my first taste of a real American Christmas. The biggest surprise was how many presents people gave to each other, not just to kids but to the adults too. As Christmas approached, we were spending most of our weekends shopping for gifts.
えーっとあとはおばさんと義妹と…
これ、どう？
うーん前に似たのをあげたかも
結婚当時在日15年。すでにいろいろ贈り済み
List（大人だけで12名分）
Walking around shopping all day was exhausting.
The o-seibo gift system is so much easier for choosing presents for so many people.
買いものが楽しくない
In fact, it was a lot of work for everyone. And now, the adults exchange presents by drawing lots.
今ではアミダくじであげる人を決めることに
Christmas is not about getting gifts, it's about giving.
どういうこと？
?
Showing love and gratitude and helping others. That's the Christmas spirit!
ぐっ
Let's teach this to the kids!
Steve's first plan
In this shop, choose one thing to give to each person in our family.
100円ショップにて
ウーン
what would be good to give to mom?
ヨシヨシ
This is for Daddy!
え
Midori is still learning the nuances of the Christmas spirit.

スティーヴと結婚してすぐ、初めてアメリカのクリスマスを体験しました。一番驚いたのはお互いに贈り合うプレゼントの量で……

**Christmas spirit** クリスマス気分

**soon after** ～から間もなく

**get one's first taste of** 初めて～を体験する

**spend ~ doing** 〔時間を〕～して過ごす

**drawing lots** くじ引き

**gratitude** 感謝の気持ち

**nuance** 微妙な差異，あや

日本の冬にミカンは必需品。その感覚はアメリカでも一般的になりつつあるようです。

**a big sack of** ～が詰まった大きな袋

**mandarin orange** ミカン，マンダリンオレンジ

**notice something odd** 何かおかしいことに気づく

**peel** 〔皮や膜を〕むく，〔果物などの〕皮

**exclaim** 叫ぶ，大声で言う

**be very impressed** 大いに感銘を受ける

**fold** 折る，折りたたむ

**on the lookout for** ～に目を光らせて

# Vol.41 Mikan (みかん)

こたつでみかん。最高ね
In Japan, winter wouldn't be winter without mikan. It seems they are becoming more common in America as well.
Every year my in-laws living in California go to a nearby mikan farm to buy a big sack of mikan.
The farm grows several varieties of mikan, which are called mandarin oranges. On my last visit, I noticed something odd.
1袋に20〜30個入っている
箱買いならぬ袋買い
SATSUMA?
えっ
「薩摩」ってこと？
SATSUMA
CLEMENTINE
Satsuma mandarins are the same as Unshu mikan but are called Satsuma because they originated in Kagoshima.
もちろん味も温州みかんそのもの
手でむけて種がなくて食べやすいと人気。
I once had a funny experience with mikan. After I peeled it and put the peel on the table, my mother-in-law exclaimed:
Wow! How did you do that?
え？
いつも通りにむいただけだけど…
She was very impressed, just like the first time I folded a paper crane for her.
I'm always on the lookout for new ways to surprise her.
フフフ
みかん1個を動物などの形にむく方法が載っている本

Vol.42

# Nice Casual
## （ドレスコードはナイスカジュアル）

The company I worked at before I was married had a very relaxed atmosphere, and I dressed pretty much the same as I did when I was a student.
This presented a problem when I was preparing to travel to America to visit Steve's family for the first time.

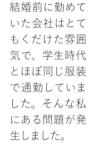

オハヨウゴザイマース
コンタクトだった
エスニックシャツ&アクセサリー
ベルボトムのジーンズ
トランク
(小さい出版社の編集者でした)

This is all I have that might be appropricate for the occasion.
The suit I wore when interviewing for jobs


Steve went with me to shop for clothes.

Something like this?
いいお嬢さん風
It's too formal. Nice casual is fine.
Nice Casual? What's that?


Steve says that Japanese formal wear often comes across as being overdressed in America.

女性向けファッション誌にありそうな装い
Nice Casual
Cotton shirts are OK if they have a touch of style.
Jeans are even OK if they are nice looking.
日本だとこういう感じが多いけど
カタイ感じ


So, "nice casual" is nice-looking, slightly stylish casual clothing.
That's simple. Or is it?

I still have a hard time picking clothes that fall between too casual and too formal.

どうも華やかさが出ないなぁ
アクセサリー足すかな


結婚前に勤めていた会社はとてもくだけた雰囲気で、学生時代とほぼ同じ服装で通勤していました。そんな私にある問題が発生しました。

---

**pretty much the same as** ～とほとんど同じだ
**present a problem** 問題を起こす
**appropriate for the occasion** その場にふさわしい
**interview for a job** 就職の面接を受ける
**come across as** ～のような印象を与える
**overdressed** 過度に着飾って
**touch of style** 雰囲気，感じ
**slightly** わずかに，少し
**fall between** ～の中間に位置する

下の子であるミドリは、いつも兄に勝とうと躍起になっています。でも、英語に関してはなかなかうまくいきません。

language environment 言語環境

sibling きょうだい，兄弟姉妹

competitive 競争心の強い

eager to ～したくて仕方がない

show up ～に打ち勝つ，勝る

appear to ～するように思われる

extended vacation 長期休暇

by leaps and bounds 飛躍的に

review 復習，おさらい

# Vol.43 The Power of the Language Environment（言語環境のチカラ）

Younger siblings are often very competitive, and Midori is always eager to try to show up her brother. With English, however, she doesn't seem to speak as well as Haru did when he was her age.

ずいっ
あ
あのね ミドリね
ドン


They both would appear to have the same English-language environment. But, in fact, the family situation has been different.

3歳くらいまでこうだった
English 50
Japanese 50
English 30
Japanese 70
ずっとこんな感じ


Before Midori was born

The kids speak mostly Japanese to each other.

We decided Midori should spend some extra time in an all-English environment. This winter, Steve and Midori went to America for an extended vacation so Midori could speak English for a full month.

ENG-LISH 100%
後から行くからねー


（2週間後に合流した）

She improved by leaps and bounds.

It's my turn!!
NO
おー
They even argue in English!!


Children have an amazing ability to absorb languages. The other side of the coin is they also have the ability to forget.

9×3は16だっけ?
漢字も思い出せないよ
たった2週間で…


Don't worry, with a little review the kanji came back quickly.

Vol.44

# If the Shoe Fits
## （大きい靴天国）

I'm 1.65 meters tall. In Japan, I'm pretty tall for a woman, but when I go to America, I shrink.

How nice to feel small for a change!
180cmのスティーヴでも小柄に見える
足首は締まってる


I really feel small when I try to find my size in clothing.

XXXL
こんな大きいのも！
自分にちょうどいいのはSサイズかMサイズ


There's one kind of store that I love to visit when I'm overseas. A shoe store.

I've got huge feet in Japan. Many shoe stores don't even stock shoes in my size.

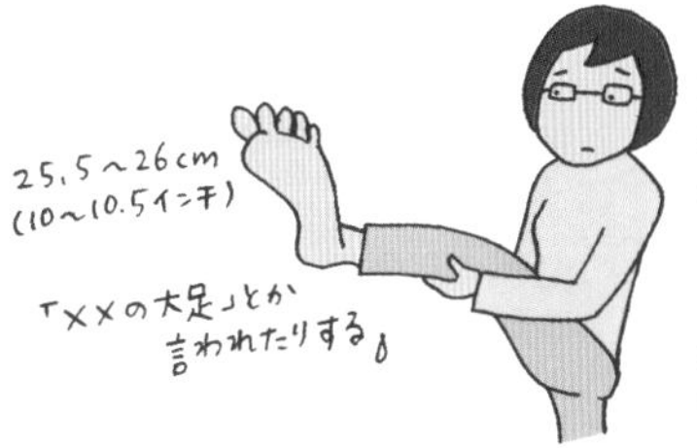

25.5〜26cm
(10〜10.5インチ)
「××の大足」とか言われたりする。


I usually have to choose from:
a) men's shoes
b) imported shoes
c) order-made shoes
Choices b and c are expensive.

In America, lots of women have feet my size. It's normal! There's a full selection of shoe types, styles, and colors.

9
9 1/2
10
10 1/2
11
わあ！
よりどりみどり
たいてい12インチ(28cmくらい)まである
感激


It may be out of the ordinary, but going to a shoe store is one of the big highlights of my trips. They say "If the shoe fits, wear it." I do.

身長165cmの私は日本の女性としては背が高い方ですが、アメリカに行くと小さくなったように感じます。そんな私が海外で必ず訪れるお店は──

**shrink** 小さくなる，縮まる
**How nice to** 〜してうれしい
**for a change** いつもと違って
**overseas** 海外に，外国に
**huge** 巨大な
**stock** 〔店に商品を〕仕入れる，置く
**imported** 輸入された
**out of the ordinary** 並外れた，普通ではない
**highlight of the trip** 旅の中で最も印象深いこと［場所］

アメリカの絵本や子ども向けの雑誌、さらには大人向けの洋服のカタログにいたるまで、登場する人物の多様性には、いつも驚かされます。

melting pot 〔人種・文化などの〕るつぼ
variety of 多様性，さまざまな〜
amazing 驚くほどの
purposely わざと，意図的に
motto 座右の銘，モットー
seal 標章，紋章
exemplify 典型的な例となる
give a glimpse of 〜をそれとなく示す
aspect 側面，見方

# Vol.45 From Melting Pot to Salad Bowl
（るつぼからサラダへ）

The variety of people in American picture books and magazines for kids, and even clothing catalogs for adults, is always amazing to me.

白人の主人公に黒人の親友とかその逆とか
アジア人の登場人物も
こっちの本もだ
It seems like they are purposely trying to show many different types of people.


America's motto is "e pluribus unum," which is Latin for "one from many," and it appears on American coins and the Seal of the United States.

UNITED STATES OF AMERICA
E·PLURIBUS UNUM
ONE CENT
ね


America has been called a "melting pot," and I had always thought the image really exemplified the country. But Steve recently told me —

Instead of a melting pot, people are now saying it's more like a salad bowl.
昔 Melting Pot → 今 Salad Bowl
Different ingredients mixing together to make one flavor.
とかして混ぜてひとつにする
Different ingredients mixing together but keeping their own flavors.
ありのままでおいしい


The picture books and catalogs that give a glimpse of this aspect of America are like menus of the different flavors America has to offer.

Although we live in Japan, our kids are also part of the American salad bowl. I wonder what flavor they will see today?

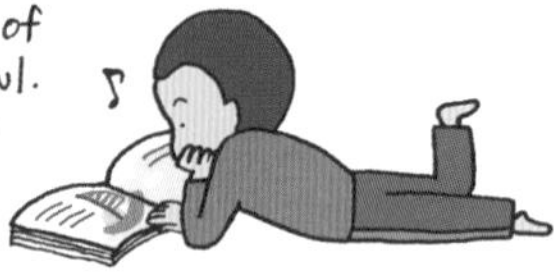

# Vol.46 Taboos and Manners

## （タブーとテーブルマナー）

スティーヴは日本の習慣やマナーにかなり通じていますが、時々、不作法をしてしまうこともあります。

Steve is very familiar and comfortable with Japanese customs and manners. But sometimes, he commits a faux pas.

わーダメナー
それは拾い箸!!
拾い箸（合わせ箸、箸渡しともいう）
マナー違反とされる嫌い箸のひとつ。お骨拾いを想起させるため


I've told him many times that it's taboo for two people to hold something with chopsticks at the same time.

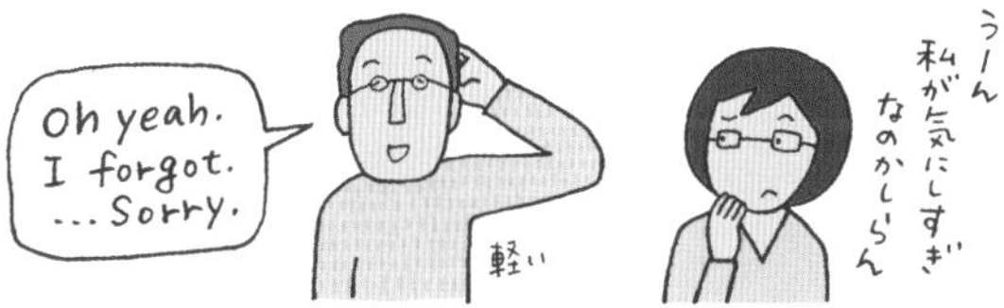

Oh yeah. I forgot. ...Sorry.
軽い
うーん 私が気にしすぎなのかしらん


Things like this make me realize again just how deep and different our cultural backgrounds are.

America has its taboos and faux pas too.

あ〜お腹いっぱい
Burp
あ
Slurp
ズズーッ


We once took Steve's family to a Soba restaurant in Japan.

You're supposed to slurp to bring out the full flavor.
We're not in America, so let's all give it a try!


They gamely tried to slurp, but it was pretty obvious they weren't really enjoying it.
No matter where you're from, it takes a strong will to try something you've always considered taboo.

ズズーッ
...
義父
ズ...
いいとわかってても やっぱり静かにすすってしまう人


**be comfortable with** 〜に対して心配がない

**commit a faux pas** 失礼なことをしてしまう

**make someone realize** （人）に気づかせる

**cultural background** 文化的背景

**burp** げっぷ

**slurp** 〔飲食するときに〕ズルズル音を立てる

**bring out the full flavor** 本格的な風味を出す

**gamely try to** 果敢に〜しようとする

**no matter where someone is from** （人）がどこの出身でも

**take a strong will** 強い意志が必要である

馬楽奈郵便
COLUMN 2

## 「ハーフ」であること

半分とか半人前という意味につながる「ハーフ」という言葉は良くないという意見もありますが、「ハーフ」と呼ばれることに僕は抵抗がありません。僕は日本とアメリカ双方の文化や価値観を知った上で、部分部分で好きな方を選び、アメリカ人らしいところや日本人らしいところを混ぜて自己を形成しています。それが僕のアイデンティティです。

他の人に片方だけ注目されて都合のいいようにされても、自分も都合よく日本人とアメリカ人を使い分けているのでお互い様だと思っています。僕はアメリカ人でも日本人でもあります。二つのナショナリティが共存しているのです。

とはいえ、「ハーフ」であることが元でモヤモヤした気持ちにさせられてしまうこともあります。

ある日曜日、父が前々から行きたいと思っていたところに僕と父の二人で出かけることにしました。木造船に乗って川下りをしたり、和風なアンティークショップで買い物をしたりと楽しい時間を過ごしていました。昼頃になってお腹が空いたのでじゃがいもの味噌焼きを買ったのですが、支払いのときに店の人に「それ味噌入ってるけど大丈夫？」と聞かれました。その場では「大丈夫です」と答えましたが、後から嫌な気持ちが込み上げてきました。見た目が外国人っぽいからという理由で間違った思い込みをされたことが心に引っかかりました。父もそう感じていたのですが、父は心配をして一言かけてくれた優しさに目を向けるべきだと言い、そのままその場を去りました。

こういった優しさは様々な形をとります。納豆や枝豆が食べられるか聞いたり、箸で食べる食事をフォークと共に出したり、片言でも英語で話してくれたり。相手のことを知らないわけですから、最悪の場合を考えて動くのはとても良いことです。きっとその優しさが、勝負で手加減をされているかのような、居心地の悪さと軽い侮辱を感じてしまうのでしょう。しかし、これもしょうがないことです。自然な考え方や関わり方が浸透していくのは時間がかかるのかもしれません。それまでは、自分でどう考えてどう関わるのが良いのかを考えてみるしかないでしょう。その一歩一歩によって、個人がより尊重される世の中につながっていくと思います。

STEVE
来日27年目の
江戸好きアメリカ人
KIKUE
ワタクシ
HARU
息子。
小学3年生
MIDORI
娘。
5歳

# 3rd Year

2013

典型的な日本の家庭で育った私。結婚後、「スキンシップ」に関して日本とアメリカの家族がいかに違うかに気づかされました。

typical　典型的な
when it comes to　～に関して言えば
physical contact　身体的接触，スキンシップ
awkward moment　気まずい瞬間
instigator　扇動者
wordless　無言の，言葉にできない
cheerful　陽気な，元気のいい
celebration　お祝い，称賛
bonding　絆

# Vol.47 Hugs

## （ハグ）

I was raised in what I believe is a typical Japanese family. After I married my American husband, I realized how different our families were when it comes to physical contact, or "skinship" as we say in Japanese.

もー何言ってるんだか
物心ついてからのボディタッチはツッコミのときくらい
弟

This led to some awkward moments for me when I would meet his family.

強さはこれくらいでいいのかな
HUG
義妹
KISS
く、口と口?! 初めて同性とキスしちゃった
義母

After 11 years of marriage, I've gotten used to expressing my feelings with physical contact. I've even become an instigator of hugs when greeting or saying goodbye.

Thank you for everything! I love you!
ぎゅっ
義母

遠い親せき→
儀礼的なハグはあっさりめ

Once I got used to it, I understood how a hug can communicate something that words can't.

Living in Japan, we don't hug as often as we would if we lived elsewhere. But hugs are certainly a part of our family life.

照れつつもうれしそう→
だいすきー
…
…
不安に押しつぶされそうなときにも

A wordless hug helps heal the heart when you're sad, and a cheerful hug shares a celebration.

Hugs are one of the bonding points of our family.

# Vol.48 The Joy of Reading
## （読書の楽しみ）

My husband and I are avid readers. Before our kids were born, we often spent our free time browsing in bookstores and reading in cafe's.

ぜったい和書
ほとんど洋書
都心の大型書店には洋書も結構ある
当時は都心暮らしで書店も喫茶店もよりどりみどりだった


I read books in Japanese, and he reads books in English. Sometimes we talk about a great book we are reading, but if it hasn't been translated then we can't recommend that each other read it.

After our kids were born, I started using the library as my main source for new books to read.

子連れで本屋とかムリ…
本
あそんで〜
書店より山が近い環境に


Libraries in Japan stock very few, if any, books in English. My husband now searches for new books on the Internet.

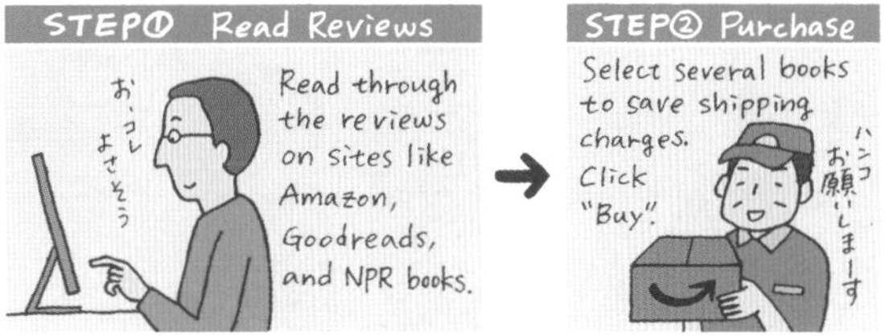

STEP① Read Reviews
お、コレよさそう
Read through the reviews on sites like Amazon, Goodreads, and NPR books.
STEP② Purchase
Select several books to save shipping charges. Click "Buy".
ハンコお願いしまーす


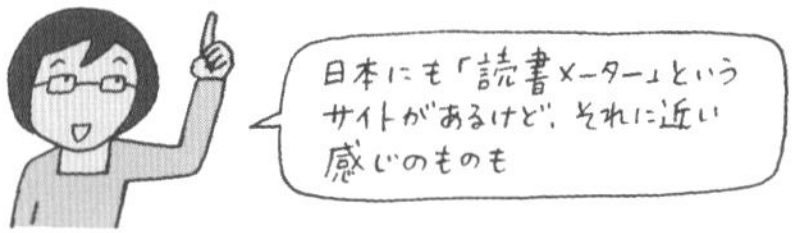

日本にも「読書メーター」というサイトがあるけど、それに近い感じのものも


We still love to read, but how we buy books and where we read them has changed drastically.

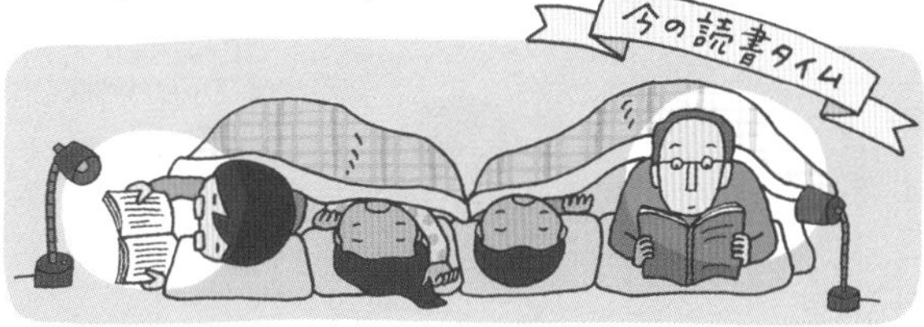

今の読書タイム


私たち夫婦は読書好きです。子どもたちが生まれる前は、暇さえあれば本屋をぶらぶらしたり、カフェで本を読んだりしていましたが――

**avid** 熱烈な，熱心な

**browse** ざっと見る，閲覧する

**recommend** 推薦する，おすすめする

**main source** 主な情報源

**if any** たとえあったとしても

**read through** 読み通す，最後まで読む

**shipping charge** 送料，配送費

**drastically** 〔変化などが〕大幅に

「出身はどこ?」としょっちゅう聞かれるスティーヴ。彼の答えは決まって「カリフォルニアです」。

hundreds of times　何百回も
it stands to reason that　～というのも当然である
the rest of　～のその他の部分
bountiful　豊かな，豊富な
tolerance　寛容，容認
insist　主張する
divide　区分，相違
in terms of　～の面から言うと［見ると］

# Vol.49 California
## (カリフォルニア)

Steve's been asked, "Where are you from?" hundreds of times.

I'm from California.
Wouldn't you normally say, "America?"
?
お、どうも
自治会の飲み会などで


We all know America is a large country. But California is also big. Very big. In fact, it's about 10 percent bigger than Japan. It stands to reason that there are some differences from the rest of America.
California is known for its bountiful nature and free-thinking people.

Central Valley Produce
ぶどうやオレンジなどの果物、ナッツ、野菜など
Californians
様々な人種
Liberal Tolerance
同性愛カップルなど


On the map, California's two major cities, San Francisco and Los Angeles, may seem close, but they're actually 610 kilometers apart. Californians insist there is a cultural divide between North and South, or as locals say: NoCal and SoCal.

大阪
東京
約550km
これより離れてるのか!

So Cal
映画やビーチ、日差しなど
やや軽薄なイメージ
SF (NoCal)
LA (SoCal)
No Cal
コンピューターや食べもの、霧など
やや気取っているイメージ

日本でも東京と大阪じゃいろいろ違うもんね


Steve is an American, but in terms of culture, he thinks of himself as a Northern Californian.

# Vol.50 The Pleasures of Bicycling
## （サイクリングを楽しむ）

When the sun comes out and the weather warms up, a new group of people dressed in colorful clothes begins to appear on the roadways. Steve is one of them.

He takes 1- to 2-hour rides most mornings and weekends.
He has toured Tohoku, Kyushu, and other areas of Japan by bicycle.


Bicycling in Japan is great, Steve says, but transporting your bike is a challenge.
Trains are a good example. To bring a bike on a train, you have to disassemble it and cover it up.

めんどくさい
輪行袋という専用の袋に入れる


Getting around with a bike is a lot simpler in the San Francisco Bay Area.

You simply wheel your bike on the train. During rush hour, designated cars are provided.
◀電車の場合
▼バスの場合
Look! That bus has bike racks on the front.


With Japan's fantastic public transportation system, just think of the possibilities if moving bicycles around were that easy here too.

いつか親子で自転車旅行するのが夢


暖かくなってくると、カラフルなウェアに身を包んだグループが車道に現れ始めます。スティーヴもその一人ですが……

**come out** 出てくる，姿を現す
**dressed in** ～を着ている
**roadway** 車道
**transport** 運ぶ，輸送する
**challenge** 挑戦，課題
**disassemble** 分解する，ばらばらにする
**wheel** 動かす，押す
**designated** 指定された，特定の
**provide** 提供する
**fantastic** 非常に優れた，素晴らしい
**public transportation system** 公共交通機関

ひらがなの読み書きに興味を持ち始めて、1年後にはスムースになったミドリ。でも、英語の読み書きになると……

---

**show an interest in** ～に興味を示す

**a series of** 一連の

**carefully** 注意深く，入念に

**add** 加える，つけ足す

**simplicity** 簡単，平易

**word choice** 言葉の選択

**give someone a new appreciation for** 〔主語のおかげで〕(人)は～の価値を改めて実感する

**humor** 面白さ，ユーモア

**perennial favorites** 根強い人気

**fixture** 定番，欠かせない存在

Vol.51
Bob Helps Midori Read
(英語のおすすめ絵本)
When Midori was 4, she started showing an interest in reading and writing hiragana. One year later, she reads and writes pretty smoothly.
Her progress reading and writing English, however, has been a series of stops and starts.
手紙を書くのがマイブーム
← 鏡文字もだいぶ減ってきた
日本語はひとつの平仮名にひとつの音が基本だけど
Cup
Ocean
Century
One letter can have several pronunciations.
There are special books written to help young children get started reading English. This is the set we are using.
Bob Books published by Scholastic, Inc.
(現在、日本のAmazonでも取り扱い中)
アメリカの教材の店で見つけた
BOB BOOKS®
SET 1. BEGINNING READERS
SCHOLASTIC
$16.99 US
Sam sat.
Mat sat. Sam sat.
(大人の手のひらサイズの薄い冊子が12冊で1セット)
Bob Books use simple words and sounds in very short sentences. Then they carefully add new words and sounds one by one.
Jig is a big pig.
Jig
big
Pig!
できた!
1冊が短いので達成感も得やすい
The simplicity of the word choice gave me new appreciation for Dr. Seuss, whose genius using simple words with rhythm and humor makes his books perennial favorites. His "Hop on Pop" is a fixture at our house.
鉄板です
Hop on Pop
By Dr. Seuss

Vol.52
Learning by Listening
(リスニングで言語習得)
The other day on the radio, I heard a song by Chris Hart, an American who sings in Japanese.
♬涙そうそう♪
夏川りみの曲と徳永英明の「レイニーブルー」をアカペラで
PCで聞くラジオ radiko
えっ、これ外国人なの?!
うまいっ! 歌も日本語も
I know many people who speak Japanese very well as a second language.
浄土宗の宗紋がついてるね このお寺には
ハゲるなら いっそ月代(さかやき)にするとかね
月代 チョンマゲにするために剃り落とす部分
なにそのコアな知識…
But Chris Hart's fluency was at another level. I think it was the naturalness of his pronunciation that made me think so.
They say that people who are good singers are also good at learning languages.
I think it is their ability to hear that sets them apart.
あの美空ひばりも英語はほとんどしゃべれなかったけど英語の歌は抜群にうまかったそう
I remember what a friend once told me in high school.
What do I have to do to get better at English?
英語が不得意なワタシ
英語が得意な友人
I sing my favorite song over and over until it sounds perfect.
Studying the structure of a language is the most common way to acquire a foreign language, but learning the sounds and rhythms of the language seems to be another path to fluency.
いやいや それ違うし
イヤイヤ ソレチガウシ
意味がわからなくてもとにかく真似してみる
20年くらい前、日本語勉強中のスティーヴ

ラジオでクリス・ハートというアメリカ人が日本語で歌っている歌を聴きました。日本語が上手な外国人の中でも彼の流暢さは別格です。

**second language** 第二言語
**fluency** 流暢さ
**at another level** 別の次元で
**naturalness** 自然さ
**set ~ apart** 〔他の人よりも〕~を際立たせる
**get better at** ~するのが上手になる
**structure of a language** 言語の構造
**most common way to** ~する最も一般的な方法
**acquire** 習得する, 自分のものにする
**path to** ~への道

Vol.53

# Letting Go
## (開き直りの英語力)

スティーヴと結婚した当初、私の英語力は本当に頼りないものでした。アメリカの彼の家族に会いに行くと、英語の悪夢にうなされて……

pathetic　哀れな，情けない

shortcoming　短所，弱点

haunt　つきまとう，悩ませる

in the form of　～の形をして

anxiety dream　不安な夢

fret　思い悩む，くよくよする

unicycle　一輪車

perhaps　もしかすると

improvement　改善，向上

get it　理解する

let it go　〔他者の言動に対して〕そのままにしておく

When Steve and I got married 12 years ago, my English was truly pathetic.

!
高1のときの英語のノート
過去の自分が書いた英文が理解できない
Wow, your English was really good when you were a student.
NOTE


My English ability is not a problem at home because Steve and I usually speak Japanese. It's when we go to visit his family in America that my shortcomings haunt me in the form of anxiety dreams.

Daytime
しどろもどろ
心の命綱
Night-time
I am… I mean… I'm sorry…
うーん


It took six years for these dreams to stop, and 10 years until I finally stopped fretting about my English skills. Hearing Steve and the kids talk to each other in our home must have been a big help.

聞くともなしに聞いている
What did you do at school today?
I rode a unicycle!
(父子間は英語)


But perhaps the most important improvement came when I learned how to not worry about not understanding something.

① If you don't get it, just let it go.
(とくにグループのとき)
② It's OK if I don't say it right, just say it anyway.


I became a better English speaker when I stopped worrying if my English was perfect.

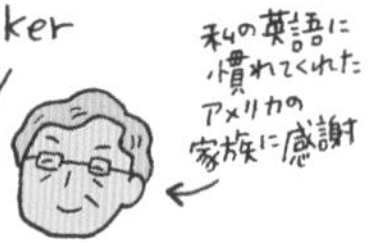

私の英語に慣れてくれたアメリカの家族に感謝

# Vol.54 R and L
## (RとLの発音)

Every once in a while, a scene like this happens in our house.
たまには英語を使ってみる
Is there any YOUGULT in the fridge?
ないなら買ってくるけど
Um, what did you say?
ええーだから一
ヨーグルトだよ、YOUGULT!
豆乳ヨーグルト
なーんだ
あはははは
何かと思ったよー。「yogurt」ね（Lじゃなくて R）
There's no denying it: Japanese have a hard time differentiating between R and L. I'm no exception.
軽くショック
R seems easier for Japanese to say, so concentrating on good L pronunciation might help clarify the difference.
えっそうなの？
R
舌を丸め気味にノドの方へ向ける
舌を上あごに押しつける
L
日本語のラ行よりも力が要る
To make sure the kids could hear the difference, Steve made up some silly songs to train their ears when they were babies.
Lovely ladies like to live in little little homes,
Lovely ladies like to listen to lovely lullabies...
It worked. Now I have three teachers.
Right
Light
どっちも同じに聞こえる!


多くの日本人がRとLの区別に苦労していますが、私も例外ではありません。

**every once in a while**　たまに，時々

**fridge**　冷蔵庫

**There's no denying...**　…は否定できない，紛れもない事実だ

**differentiate between A and B**　AとBを区別する

**no exception**　例外ではない

**concentrate on**　～に意識を置く

**clarify**　〔～を〕明確にする

**make sure**　確実に～する

**make up a silly song**　ばかばかしい歌を作る

**lullaby**　子守歌

日本語にも外来語がたくさんあり、その多くは英語に由来したものです。しかし、外来語の中には英語では通用しないものもあります。

loanword　外来語，借用語

describe what ~ is　～がどのようなものか説明する

make the mistake of　～という間違いをする

assume〔～と〕推測する，思い込む

confuse〔人を〕混乱させる

I'll bet　～だと確信している（賭けてもいい）

deal with〔問題などに〕取り組む，対応する

at one time or another　一度は，いつか

faithful to　～に忠実である

# Vol.55 Loanwords Don't Always Have the Same Meaning（外来語とのつき合い方）

Like any language, Japanese has many loanwords. Lots of our words come from English. But many of these don't work in English.
ミキサー
長年使っていたのが壊れてしまった
ミキサー、買い替えなきゃだね
えっ？ミキサー、持ってたっけ？
うちで一番ミキサーを使う人
When I described what it was, he finally got it.
Oh, you mean "blender".
えっ?! 英語でもミキサーっていうんじゃないの?!
（mixerは泡立て器のことらしい）
Steve has had to learn many new "English" words.
㊐ ホチキス
Ⓔ Stapler
㊐ ベビーカー
Ⓔ Stroller
㊐ ミシン
Ⓔ Sewing machine
ちなみに「アルバイト」はドイツ語から来てるんだよね 実は
㊐ アルバイト
お待たせしました〜
Ⓔ part-time job
I made the mistake of assuming all loanwords were from English.
油断ならない
Loanwords are also confusing for our kids. I'll bet all bilingual families have to deal with this at one time or another.
Midori
アルモンド食べるね
アルモンド？
【解説】
ALMOND → アルモンド
Faithful to the English pronunciation
Haru
Hey! This isn't right.
こくご
キャンデーだって おかしいよ
昔の文章だとそう書くんだよ
でもおかしいも〜ん

# Vol.56 Home after Birth
## (産後の里帰り)

Haru turned 9 last month. I can remember all the uncertainty I had about giving birth and raising our first child.
What!? You and the baby are going to stay at your parents' house? What about me?
長いと数か月も?! そんな大事なときに家族がバラバラなんて
No way!
In Japan, it's quite common for a mother and a newborn to go stay at the new mother's parents' house. In America, it seems to be unthinkable.
Even the time the new mother stays in the hospital after birth is very short by comparison.
The baby's coming…
Admission
Discharge
One or two nights
(日本だと約1週間)
自宅に戻る
※U.S. hospital fees are also pretty high.
不安～
I've never given birth before.
10年前の私
They say good postnatal care is critical.
産後1か月間はなるべく横になって過ごすこと
お世話になった助産師さん
But I can do it! I can take care of all your needs and do the house work too.
うーん…
We worked out a compromise. Steve would come and stay with us at my parents' house for two weeks.
Find a compromise and don't be bound by convention. That's pretty much become our family motto.
よろしくお願いします
はいはい こちらこそよろしく
私の実母

日本では、出産に伴い実家に里帰りする人も珍しくありませんが、それを聞いたスティーヴは驚いて……

- **uncertainty** 不確実なこと
- **give birth** 出産する
- **No way** ありえない，とんでもない
- **newborn** 新生児
- **by comparison** 比較して
- **admission** 入ること，入院
- **discharge** 退院
- **postnatal care** 〔母子の〕産後ケア
- **critical** 非常に重要な
- **work out a compromise** 妥協案を考え出す
- **bound by convention** 因習にとらわれている

ハルが生まれた後、結核予防のBCG接種案内の手紙が届きました。でも、アメリカでは一般的に推奨されていないようで……

vaccination　ワクチン接種
remind　〔人に〕気づかせる
tuberculosis　結核
germ　細菌
weakened　弱体化した
toxicity　毒性
antibody　抗体，免疫体
prevent　防ぐ，阻む
opt to　～することを選ぶ
scrutinize　精査する，注意深く調べる
dose　〔薬の〕一服，1回分
thigh　もも，大腿部

# Vol.57 Vaccinations

## （どうする？ 予防接種）

Nine years ago, after Haru was born, I received a letter reminding me that our son needed to get his BCG vaccination shots for tuberculosis.

BCG shots?
They aren't generally recommended in America.
結核の予防接種だよね
えっ？
予防接種ってどこも同じじゃないんだ！
接種のスケジュール

The vaccine works by introducing germs with weakened or no toxicity into the body so the body will make antibodies to fight off the germs. The person then has antibodies for preventing the disease.

However, whenever they are tested for tuberculosis in the future, the results will come out "positive." This can be a problem for kids entering school in America.

日本では陽性だと「免疫アリ」でOKなツベルクリン反応だけど…
⊕ positive
You should take the medicine.
結核だと診断されてしまうことも

We thought a lot about which country's recommendations we should follow. In the end, we opted to have our kids vaccinated.

副作用のことも含めて検討
結果的に任意のもの以外は全て日本の制度に合わせて受けています。
（BCG、日本脳炎、はしか、風疹など）

I had never thought twice about vaccine shots, but after this experience, we are careful to scrutinize each one.

Vaccine shots are also given in different places and different doses.

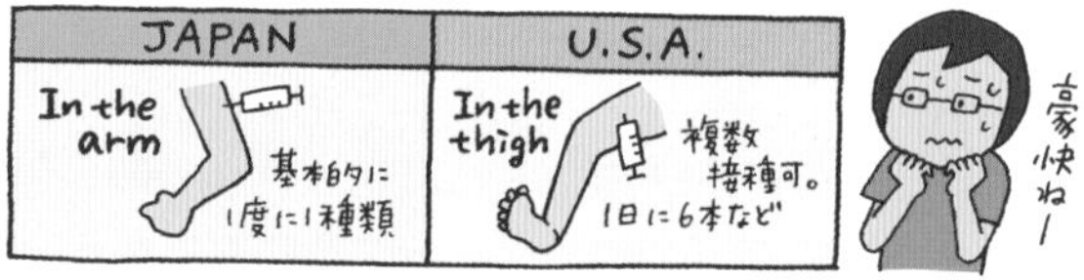
JAPAN
In the arm
基本的に1度に1種類
U.S.A.
In the thigh
複数接種可。1日に6本など
豪快ね！

One thing's the same in both countries. Children hate getting shots!

ヤーだー！
でも凝視しちゃう
ポリオの不活化ワクチン

# Vol.58 Gummy and Sakura
## （ぬいぐるみの交換留学）

One day last spring, Haru came home from school with a koala bear named Gummy. Haru's school and a school in Australia had each sent dolls for "homestay" visits.

SAKURA
GUMMY
※名前はそれぞれの生徒たちが考えた


Each student brought Gummy home for one week to take pictures of it experiencing different things and write about what the doll did.
When everybody's turn was finished, they would send the doll and the reports back to Australia.

Gummyのレポート。それによると…
the night before. We woke up early in the morning when it was still dark outside.
なんと！富士山にも登ったらしい


Haru showed Gummy lots of sites in our area.

Udon restaurant
Buddhist temple
Tama River
ぬいぐるみを持ち歩いて撮影するのはちょっと恥ずかしかったけどおもしろかった！
撮るよー
英語でレポートをまとめる
? ?


It was a good opportunity to look objectively at the things we do and where we live.

We're all looking forward to reading about Sakura's adventures when she's sent back from Australia. In the meantime, it's also been a lot of fun taking Gummy on various adventures in Japan.

ハルが学校からコアラのぬいぐるみを連れて帰ってきました。ハルの学校とオーストラリアの学校では、ぬいぐるみを「交換留学」させているのです。

- koala bear　コアラ
- bring ~ home　家に連れて帰る
- someone's turn　（人）が～する番
- site　場所
- Buddhist temple　仏教寺院
- good opportunity to　～するいい機会
- look objectively at　～を客観的に見る
- in the meantime　それまでの間
- various　さまざまな

この夏、スティーヴの家族を訪ねました。義父のサプライズ誕生日パーティーに参加するためです。

family event　家族の一大イベント
midyear　1年の中頃，年半ば
attend　出席する，参加する
stepfather　義父，継父
in secret　秘密に，こっそり
up to　～に至るまで
big day　重要な日
big success　大成功
memorable day　思い出に残る日

# Vol.59 Surprise Party
## (義父のサプライズ祝い)

We visited Steve's family this summer. We usually go in winter for Christmas because it's such an important family event. This year, however, we went in midyear to attend a surprise birthday party for Steve's stepfather, Don.

日本式に言えば傘寿のお祝い
旅行や野球観戦、アンティークボートが好きな義父
80

Steve's mother set up the whole event in secret. Up to the big day, we had to be very careful about what we said when we talked with them.

チケット取れたよ
義兄
義母 →
義父に隠れてこっそり連絡したりする
よし航空券ゲット！
行く前に夏休みの宿題終わらせなくちゃ
私も仕事、終わらせないと…

On the big day, we all met early at a San Francisco Giants baseball game and waited for Don to arrive.

Surprise!
ジャイアンツのカラーオレンジと黒を身につけて応援
Giants
GIANTS
SF
45

They showed his name on the scoreboard.

Happy 80th Birthday
DON SMITH!
You can have your message shown for about $150.

The surprise party was a big success. It was a fun and memorable day for everyone.

# Vol.60 The Retirement Community
## (義両親のリタイア生活)

Steve's mother and stepfather live in a retirement community. Their home is one of some 7,000 that a construction company designed and built in the California countryside.

何度来ても迷ってしまう
町全体に手入れが行き届いていて整然としている。
でも家の趣がすべて似ていて、映画「トゥルーマン・ショー」の町並みを彷彿(ほうふつ)とさせる


To live in the community, at least one member of the family must be age 55 or older and no one can be under the age of 45. In other words, no kids allowed.
The services available are quite different than those offered by retirement homes in Japan.

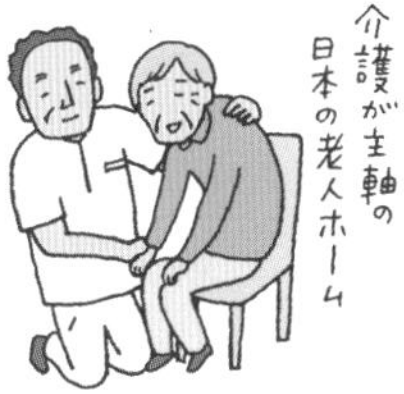

介護が主軸の日本の老人ホーム


The community provides an active culture center, puts on various events, and contains golf courses, tennis courts, a swimming pool, and other sports and exercise facilities that only residents and their guests can use.

Beautiful shot!
「ナイスショット」は和製英語
近所の人と誘い合ってゴルフを楽しむ人多し
コミュニティ内の道路はゴルフカートで走ってもOK


The concept of the community is to cater to retirees and senior citizens desiring active and independent lifestyles.
America has more than 2,000 communities catering to different desires from independence to assisted living or being cared for by their children.
America seems to offer more options than Japan for people who want to live independently in their senior years.

スティーヴの両親は高齢者居住地区に住んでいます。郊外に作られた大規模な高齢者居住地区とはどんなところなのでしょうか。

**retirement community** 〔退職後の〕高齢者居住地区
**countryside** 田舎，地方
**at least** 少なくとも
**in other words** 言い換えれば
**available** 利用できる
**provide** 提供する
**facility** 施設，設備
**resident** 居住者，入居者
**cater to** ～向けの，～に応じる
**retiree** 退職者
**independent** 独立した，自主性がある

# Vol.61 Making Meals in America
（アメリカでの食事作り）

私たちがアメリカに行くときは、たいてい義母の家に数週間滞在します。その間、食事は義母と私が交代で用意します。

- take turns　交代でする
- rice cooker　炊飯器
- pot　〔調理用の〕深鍋
- camping pot　飯ごう
- swallow one's pride　恥を忍ぶ
- embarrassing　恥ずかしい気持ちにさせる
- in the end　最後には，結局
- learn a good lesson　いい勉強［教訓］になる
- confident　自信に満ちた
- blackout　停電
- emergency　緊急事態

When we go to America to visit Steve's parents, we usually stay a few weeks at his mother's house. His mother and I take turns preparing the meals. The meals I make usually follow this pattern.
BREAKFAST
Oatmeal or Cereal
デザートに果物とか
子どもたちにはCheeriosというリング状のシリアルが人気
LUNCH
Sandwich or Udon
Tuna Sandwich
Udon
乾麺は地元スーパーで買える
DINNER
Japanese-style food
豆腐ステーキと温野菜サラダ
ひよこ豆のハンバーグ＋煮物＋サラダなど
Everyone loves noodles.
義父
白米より玄米の方が好き。味があるから
義母
これらにプラス
炊き込みごはんやチャーハン。
白飯で出すとしょうゆをかけて食べているので
I remember the first time I started to make meals there.
Where's the rice cooker?
I make it in a pot.
え゛
水加減や火加減はどうしたらいいの？
I had never made rice in anything but a rice cooker or camping pot.
しかもずっと昔、子どもの頃
I had to swallow my pride and ask her to show me how to cook rice in a pot.
How embarrassing…
お米の国の人なのに…
In the end, I learned a good lesson. Now I'm confident that I can cook rice even during a blackout or an emergency.
鍋で炊いたごはんっておいしいね

# Vol.62 At the Supermarket

（アメリカのスーパーで）

私がアメリカで日本食を作るとき、必要な食材はたいてい近所のスーパーマーケットで手に入れることができますが――

When I make Japanese-style meals in the United States, I can usually find most of the ingredients I need at the local supermarket.

カリフォルニアは移民の多い州だからかもしれないけど
日本食の他、中国や韓国、タイの食材もあるセクション
Asian food
わぁーこんなにいっぱい!!
しょうゆやみりん、みそ、ゴマ油などの調味料の他、こんなものも…
SUSHI NORI 寿司
Seaweed $5くらい
Soba
$4くらい
$2くらい
POCKY
CUP NOODLES
$1くらい
$3くらい
日本のより固め
TOFU
SILKEN 絹ごし
FIRM もめん
$4くらい
GOLDEN CURRY
せんべい
Rice Crackers $2くらい
$3.5くらい
ふりかけ


California grows nearly half of all of the produce in the United States, and the abundance is eyepopping. Nevertheless, it's still hard to find the right vegetables to make Japanese food. For example, there are several types of eggplants and bell peppers, but they're all huge! And, oddly, the variety of root vegetables is very limited.

Lotus root (レンコン)
Taro (里芋)
Daikon (大根)
Burdock root (ゴボウ)
根菜、あんまりないなぁ
葉物は豊富なんだけどなぁ。
ま、あるものでどうにかするか
Kale 1束$2くらい
Arti-choke 1コ $2くらい


Such abundance also means that many items that are prohibitively expensive in Japan are super cheap. Steve always looks forward to eating lots of his favorite fruits and veggies.

1コ $1くらい
Melon (品種はいろいろアリ)
1lb(ポンド) $3くらい
1lb≒500g
Asparagus
1lb $2くらい
Seedless grapes
感激!!
日本だと高くてあんまり食べられないんだもん


**Japanese-style meal** 日本食，和食

**produce** 生産する，〔野菜や果物の〕農産物

**nearly half of** 〜のほぼ半数

**abundance** 豊富さ

**eyepopping** 目玉が飛び出るほどの，驚くべき

**nevertheless** それにもかかわらず

**eggplant** ナス（の実）

**bell pepper** パプリカ，ピーマン

**root vegetable** 根菜

**prohibitively expensive** 法外に高価な

**seedless grape** 種なしブドウ

クリスマスの準備といえば、なんといっても飾りつけです。ツリーの飾りには、自然にその家庭らしさが表れます。

**ornament** 装飾品，飾り

**sight** 見えるもの，近い将来

**turn to** ～に変わる

**prepare for** ～に備えて準備する

**put up the decorations** 飾りつけをする

**in one's own way** 自分なりのやり方で

**lavish** 豪華な

**resplendent** キラキラ輝く，まばゆい

**fragile** 壊れやすい，もろい

**trinket** ちょっとしたアクセサリー

**in a way** ある意味では

# Vol.63 Christmas Ornaments

## （クリスマスオーナメント）

After Halloween in October and Thanksgiving in November, our sights quickly turn to Christmas in December. Preparing for Christmas means gift shopping, but it also means putting up decorations, including ornaments on the Christmas tree. Each family decorates a tree in its own way.
スティーヴの両親は離婚して、それぞれ再婚しています
Steve's father's house : Lavish
His stepmother trades ornaments each year with friends from her school days.
うっとり
The tree is resplendent with fragile ornaments.
Steve's mother's house : Nostalgic
Holland
浅草
日本のもある！
His mother turns trinkets from her travels into ornaments.
キーホルダーやストラップとおぼしきものもオーナメントに
Russia
Texas
Hawaii
In a way, the tree decorations reflect the personality of each side of his family.
I wonder how our tree will look in 10 years' time.
まだシンプルな我が家のツリー

# Vol.64 Gift Wrapping and Unwrapping（ギフト包装とその開け方）

Christmas is a time of gift giving. Americans give gifts to family and children, friends, and lovers.
Just like in Japan, Americans customarily wrap the gifts they give.
Unlike in Japan, they usually wrap the gifts themselves.
Supermarkets and other stores often have a section dedicated to low-priced wrapping paper and other goods to help prepare and decorate the gift packages.

うちも毎年、家族以外のために12コくらい用意してます


**Wrapping paper** シートじゃなくてロールで売ってる（80cm×4mが$4くらい）

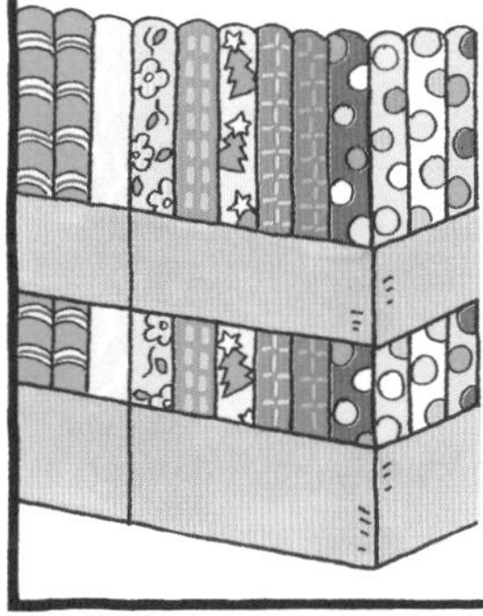

その他にも…

**Ribbons**

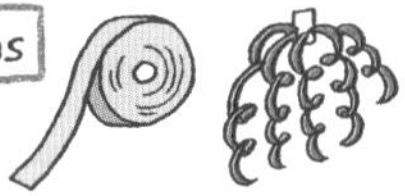

**Stickers** 誰から誰へのプレゼントかを記入して包みに貼るもの

GIFT TAGS


In Japan, "department wrapping" is probably the most common way to wrap. Americans prefer the more frugal "caramel wrapping" method.

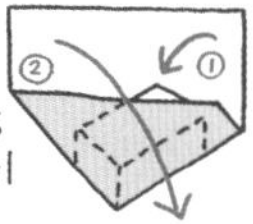

日本で主流のデパート包み


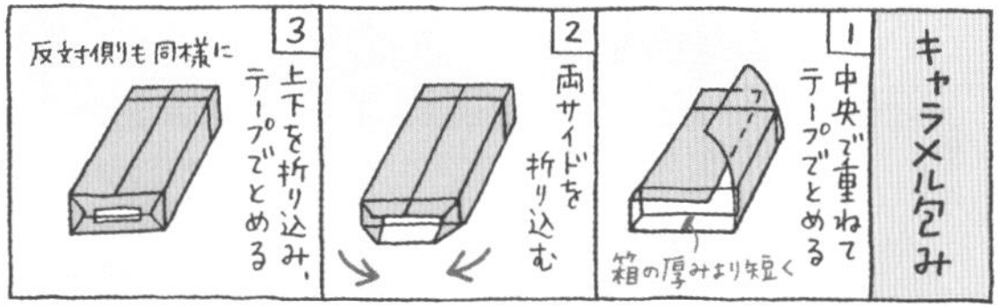

キャラメル包み
1 中央で重ねてテープでとめる
箱の厚みより短く
2 両サイドを折り込む
3 上下を折り込み、テープでとめる
反対側も同様に


Americans also have a different way of opening presents. Some people carefully peel off the tape and try to preserve the pretty paper. Others like to rip off the paper to show how excited they are about the gift.

ビリビリ
ビリッ
勢いよく開ける = 待ちきれないほどうれしい
ということになるらしい。


Although we may have different ways of wrapping and unwrapping gifts, the sense of appreciation in the giver and recipient is the same in both cultures.

クリスマスといえばプレゼント。日本と同じように、アメリカにもプレゼントを包む習慣がありますが、自分で包むのが一般的なようで……

- **unwrap** 〔～の〕包装を解く
- **customarily** 通例，習慣的に
- **dedicated to** ～に充てられている
- **prefer** ～する方を好む
- **frugal** 質素な
- **peel off** はがす
- **preserve** 〔～を〕保存する
- **rip off** はぎ取る
- **although** ～だけれども
- **sense of appreciation** 感謝の気持ち
- **recipient** 受領者，受け取る人

アメリカのクリスマスは家族で過ごす休日で、日本のお正月と似ています。毎年行くようにしていますが、今年は日本で年末を過ごすことに……

**plan to** 〜を計画する，〜するつもりである

**element** 要素

**somehow** どうしたものか

**though** 〜だけれども

**get in touch with** 〜と連絡を取る

**take advantage of** 〜をうまく活用する

**There's no comparison.** 比べ物にならない

**at once** すぐに，同時に

**cousin** いとこ

**make a face** 面白い顔をする

**giggle** クスクス笑う

# Vol.65 Skype

## (家族をつなぐスカイプ)

Christmas is a major family holiday in the United States and in many ways is similar to the New Year holidays in Japan. Although we try to go every year, this year we plan to spend the year-end in Japan.

思いっきり満喫するぞー!

The elements that make a Japanese New Year
年越しそば
初詣
おせち料理
謹賀新年
正月飾り
お雑煮
あけましておめでとう
年賀状
田村家のお雑煮は具だくさんの関東風。けんちん汁っぽい


Somehow, though, we will need to get in touch with family in America. This is when we can really take advantage of the Internet. We use software called Skype, which lets us make video contact anywhere in the world.

The best thing about it? It's totally free!

International phone calls cost about ¥180 per three minutes. There's no comparison.
※日本↔カリフォルニアの場合。電話会社によって料金も様々
ちなみにボクが初来日した1986年頃は3分1530円とかだった


Skype lets us see their faces and talk to many people at once.

国際電話だと密室の中のマンツーマン状態で、英語力に自信のない私にはかなりのプレッシャーだった
?


It's a great way for the kids to see and talk to their cousins. The truth is, they mostly just make faces and giggle.

Maybe it's the smiles of family members that make the Christmas and New Year holiday so special.

Vol.66
Passport Renewal
(パスポートの更新)
Haru and Midori have dual citizenship. They are both Japanese and American. They each have two passports.
日本国旅券
JAPAN PASSPORT
PASSPORT
United States of America
22歳になるまでにどちらかに絞ればよい
Japan and America both put limits of five years for children's passports. This seems short compared to the 10 years for regular passports. But it also seems too long considering how fast kids grow and change.
First ID Photo
5 Years Old
※ Taking the first ID photo requires a little bit of creativity.
注意を引きつける係
(まだ首が据わっていないので、無地の布団に寝かせて、上から撮る)
The usefulness of a baby's photo ID really doesn't last very long. At the same time, renewing a passport can be a hassle, so 5 years comes too soon.
理由① Must go to the embassy
理由② The passport office is only open on weekdays
理由③ Ideally, both parents must be present
家から片道約2時間
これが遠いんだ
しかも予約制
片親による勝手な国外への連れ出しを防ぐため
結果的に…
Passport renewal =
① Choose a school holiday
② Take a day off work
③ Make it a family outing
よしっ
Let's make the most of it and do something fun!
Renewing the kids' passports has become another type of family outing.
We can always use more of those!
水族館とか博物館とか


日本もアメリカも、子どものパスポートの期限は5年です。子どもの5年は成長も、それによる変化も大きくて……

**renewal** 更新

**dual citizenship** 二重国籍

**put a limit of** ～の期限を設ける

**consider** 考慮する，〔～と〕考える

**require** 必要とする，要求する

**last** 持続する

**hassle** 困ったこと，苦労

**embassy** 大使館

**ideally** 理想的に

**present** 出席して，居合わせて

**outing** お出かけ

**make the most of** ～を最大限に活用する

**use more of** ～さらに利用する

日本はハーグ条約に加盟しました。片親が子どもを連れて旅行する場合、もう一方の親の同意を証明する必要があります。

**comply with** 従う，応じる
**child abduction** 子どもの誘拐，拉致
**divorced** 離婚した
**give permission** 許可する
**family registry** 戸籍
**split with** （人）と決別する
**custody** 子どもの養育権，親権
**be granted** ～が認められる
**joint custody** 共同親権
**consent letter** 同意書
**don't mind** 差し支えない，気にしない

# Vol.67 The Hague Convention（ハーグ条約）

Last year, Japan agreed to comply with the Hague Convention, an international law for dealing with child abduction. Under the law, a divorced parent traveling with their child must show proof that the other parent has given permission.

勝手に連れ出しちゃダメ！
ハーグ条約
裁判所
子どもを戻して下さーい
故郷に帰ります！
誘拐だ！返せ！

ただし、DVなどの危険性がある場合は、その限りではないという規定もあるそう


When a couple divorces in Japan, the family registry is split, with one parent maintaining custody of the child or children.

In America and many other countries, parents are often granted joint custody, so both parents have rights over the child.

The Hague Convention affects international couples like us, even though we are not divorced.
When one of us travels abroad with the kids, we have to be sure to bring a consent letter from the other parent.

Yes, I have it right here.
両親ともにこの子どもの渡航を承知しています ということを示すもの
昨年二手に分かれて渡米したときも用意した
Letter of Consent
出入国の際、提示を求められることも


The Hague Convention is important to prevent illegal abductions.
We don't mind that we now have one more thing to be sure not to forget.

パスポートにお土産に渡航同意書に……
えっと

# Vol.68 Divorce and Child Custody Rights

（離婚と親権）

Have you seen the movie "Kramer vs. Kramer" about a divorce and the court battle for child custody?

Kramer vs. Kramer
(1979年、アメリカ)
ダスティン・ホフマンが夫役、メリル・ストリープが妻役を演じた、離婚と親権の問題を真正面から取り上げた映画。
法廷で
Billy's only 7 years old. He needs me. I'm not saying he doesn't need his father. But I really believe he needs me more.


When this movie came out in 1979, single-parent custody was still the norm in America. Like Japan now, when parents with children divorce, one parent was chosen to have sole custody of the children.

Now joint-custody is common in America. Steve's brother, for example, has joint custody of his daughter.

家がふたつになりました
日・水はマミィの家、木・土はダディの家
こういうのは珍しくない


Joint custody usually means the divorced parents must live fairly close to each other. For the children's sake, divorced parents often try to remain on friendly terms. At school and other events, all parents often show up to support the children.

父
母
母の再婚相手
授業参観、試合の応援、誕生日会など


Even if a husband-and-wife relationship ends, the relationship between the parents and children continues. Thinking of it this way, joint custody makes total sense.

いろいろ大変だけど子どものためには良さそう

別れてもマメに連絡
日曜、朝10時に迎えに行く
次は…


離婚と親権を巡る法廷闘争を描いた映画『クレイマー、クレイマー』が公開された1979年当時、アメリカではまだ片親の親権が主流でした。

**court battle** 法廷闘争

**norm** 規範，基準

**sole custody** 単独親権

**fairly close to** 〜からかなり近い

**for one's sake** 〜のために

**remain on friendly terms** 友好的な関係を保つ

**make sense** 道理にかなう，うなずける結婚すると親戚が増えるのは誰でも知っていますが、スティーヴと結婚して、私は家族という概念を考え直すことになりました。

gain　増える
reconsider　再考する，考え直す
concept　概念，考え
strictly　厳密に，正確に
blood relation　血縁関係
in ways other than　～以外のさまざまな点で
twists and turns　込み入っていること
third-generation American　移民三世のアメリカ人
it'll be fun to　～するのは楽しいだろう

# Vol.69 Family and the Family Tree
## （家族のくくりと家系図）

Everyone knows that when you get married, you also gain a lot of relatives. When I married Steve, though, I had to reconsider my concept of family.
Oh! Good to see you!
そういえばこの人、いつもクリスマスを一緒に過ごしてるけど、血縁ではないんだよね。これって、どういう関係になるんだろう？
スティーヴの母の再婚相手とその先妻の子。スティーヴは同居したこともない
In Japan, we think of family as strictly blood relations.
この人は、この③にあたる
Family① 父，母，子 祖父母など
Family② おじ，おば いとこなど
Family③ 血縁ではないけど，何かつながりのある人
Sometimes it feels a little awkward to me. But when I think about it, you can be related to someone in ways other than by blood.
そういう意味では「Family」という言葉は広義にも使えて便利
マフィアのFamilyとか（ちょっと違う？）
ちなみに家系図のことを英語で"Family Tree"といいます。
My family tree is pretty simple, since it's all Japanese. Steve's tree has a few twists and turns.
Italian American
Italian American
Irish American
German American
再婚
離婚
再婚
All four are third-generation Americans.
Brazilian
Irish Italian American
Japanese
It'll be fun to teach our children about their family tree.

Vol.70

# DUI
## (飲酒運転)

「飲んだら乗るな」が日本では常識ですが、アメリカではちょっと事情が異なるようで……

Drinking and driving don't mix. If someone is driving under the influence (DUI), both the person who drinks and the person who serves the drink are responsible. That's become common sense in Japan.

春はお酒の席も多い季節。
でも「飲んだら乗るな」ってね


Recently, lots of non-alcoholic drinks have come out.

カンパーイ♪
FREE
ALC 0.00%
ゼロ
ZERO
Beer
Cocktail
Sake
Wine


America's DUI laws are not as strict as Japan's. Most people believe it's still safe to drive after having a couple of beers.

| BAC (Blood Alcohol Content) Limits 違法な血中アルコール濃度 | |
|---|---|
| Japan | California |
| 0.03% or higher | 0.08% or higher |

↑呼気中アルコール濃度0.15mg/Lに相当　↑州によって異なる。これは厳しい方

!
The legal limit is higher than in Japan.


California's Department of Motor Vehicles (DMV) provides estimates for how many drinks a person can have and still legally drive based on their sex and weight.

| 酒量(杯) \ 体重(lb) | | 100 (約45kg) | 120 (約54) | 140 (約64) | 160 (約73) | 180 (約82) | 200 (約91) | 220 (約100) | 240 (約109) | Driving Condition |
|---|---|---|---|---|---|---|---|---|---|---|
| 0 | 男 | 0% | 0 | 0 | 0 | 0 | 0 | 0 | 0 | Safe |
| | 女 | 0 | 0 | 0 | 0 | 0 | 0 | 0 | 0 | |
| 1 | 男 | 0.06 | 0.05 | 0.04 | 0.04 | 0.03 | 0.03 | 0.03 | 0.02 | Impaired オススメはしないけど違法ではないレベル |
| | 女 | 0.07 | 0.06 | 0.05 | 0.04 | 0.04 | 0.03 | 0.03 | 0.03 | |
| 2 | 男 | 0.12 | 0.10 | 0.09 | 0.07 | 0.07 | 0.06 | 0.05 | 0.05 | |
| | 女 | 0.13 | 0.11 | 0.09 | 0.08 | 0.07 | 0.07 | 0.06 | 0.06 | |
| 3 | 男 | 0.18 | 0.15 | 0.13 | 0.11 | 0.10 | 0.09 | 0.08 | 0.07 | |
| | 女 | 0.20 | 0.17 | 0.14 | 0.12 | 0.11 | 0.10 | 0.09 | 0.08 | Intoxicated 違法なレベル |
| 4 | 男 | 0.24 | 0.20 | 0.17 | 0.15 | 0.13 | 0.12 | 0.11 | 0.10 | |
| | 女 | 0.26 | 0.22 | 0.19 | 0.17 | 0.15 | 0.13 | 0.12 | 0.11 | |
| 5 | 男 | 0.30 | 0.25 | 0.21 | 0.19 | 0.17 | 0.15 | 0.14 | 0.12 | |
| | 女 | 0.33 | 0.28 | 0.24 | 0.21 | 0.18 | 0.17 | 0.15 | 0.14 | |

↑※1杯はおよそビール1缶くらい(約340ml)で考えられている

If you get caught driving drunk, you go to jail and can be fined up to $22,500, which is a lot higher than in Japan. Next time I drink alcohol, I'll be reminded of a basic American tenet — with freedom comes responsibility.

飲むべきか飲まざるべきか…


**DUI (driving under the influence)** 飲酒および麻薬の影響下の運転
**responsible** 責任を負うべき
**Department of Motor Vehicles** 車両管理局
**estimate for** ～の見積もり，概算
**impaired** ほろ酔いの
**intoxicated** 酔って，酩酊して
**get caught** 逮捕される
**go to jail** 刑務所に行く
**be fined up to $...** …ドル以下の罰金に処せられる
**tenet** 教義，信条

COLUMN 3

# ハグ

ハグというと欧米をイメージする人が多いかもしれない。何しろ日本ではあまりない習慣だから。

私の家庭はご存知の通り、日本の文化も大切にしながらアメリカの文化も大切にしている。その一つがハグだ。アメリカの親戚に会ったときは必ずするのだけれど、それまで離れている時間が長くても、ハグをすることで心の距離がぐっと縮まる気がする。

思うに、日本でも幼児のときはハグをする、と言っていいのではないだろうか。安心・落ち着きを求めてハグをする――実際、私はハグをすることによってこのどちらも得られていると実感している。

うちでは、兄が中２になるくらいまでは家族みんなが日常的にハグをしていたけれど、今も頻繁にハグをするのは母と私くらいだ（お祝いのときやクリスマスなどのイベントのときは別）。私と母は寝る前の、おやすみを言うときに必ずハグをする。

他にも、疲れやストレスがかなり溜まってしまったとき、悲しい出来事があったときなどにもハグをする。私から母に求めに行くこともあるし、母が私に求めてくることもある。そういうときは大抵、黙って目を合わせ、腕を広げ、ギュッとする。長い時間そうしていることもある。

アメリカで生まれ育った学校の友達の家も同じらしい。その友達ともたまに、学校でハグをする。癒しが必要なとき、信用できて、安心できる人のところへ行き、ハグをするのだ。

その人を丸ごと受け入れるハグは、家族や友達との絆を深めることができるし、困っている人に安心できる環境を作ることもできる、本当に素晴らしいものだと思う。癒しをもたらすことのできるハグは私の人生にとてもいい影響を与えていて、そのおかげで自分を見失わないようにもできていると思う。

これからもハグの文化、ハグによる癒しを身の回りの大切な人たちと分かち合えたらいいな。

STEVE
来日27年目の
江戸好きアメリカ人
KIKUE
ワタクシ
HARU
息子。
小学4年生
MIDORI
娘。
小学1年生

# 4th Year

2014

結婚後、洗濯物の干し方でもめました。外干し派の私と乾燥機派のスティーヴ。その違いは根深くて……

compromise　妥協，和解
figure out　〔答えを〕見つけ出す
ruin　台無しにする，損なう
perspective　見方，視点
come out of　～から生まれる
household　家庭，世帯
clothes dryer　衣類乾燥機
ban　禁じる
clothesline　物干し用ロープ
nag　〔しつこく〕文句を言う
discontentment　不満，不平
It's a deal.　よし、決まりだ。これで手を打とう。

Vol.71
Our Compromises
（私たちの妥協線：衣類乾燥編）
After we got married, one of the things we had to figure out was how to dry clothes.
外干し派 VS 乾燥機派
It's a perfect day to dry the clothes outside.
日光には殺菌作用もあるし
But it ruins the material.
タオルも固くなっちゃう
These different perspectives come out of our family experiences. In America, they say about 80 percent of households use clothes dryers. Some managed communities ban drying clothes in front your home.
条例で禁止されている地域も
No clotheslines. They ruin the scenery.
地域の不動産価値が下がるので近所迷惑
日本では晴れると「洗濯日和」って言うけどね
外干し = 貧しい というイメージが根強い
When we got married I was happy to have our own dryer. After the 2011 earthquake, however, we both agreed line drying would conserve energy.
ホカホカ
なんだかんだラク
省エネ! 外干ししよう!
OK!
But about one month later...
I think we should switch back to using the dryer.
がんばったけど もう限界
ゴワゴワ
Saving electricity is important, but it's not good to live with nagging discontentment.
All right. We'll use the dryer for Steve's clothes and nice clothes.
It's a deal!
Not everyone may agree with this compromise. But it works for us. We make cultural compromises for sure, but like everyone, we also make compromises in our everyday lifestyle.

Vol.72
Commuting to School
(通学)
Midori started first grade this spring. She joins her brother at a school that caters to returnee students. One of the school's advantages is that it provides special classes for native English speakers. One disadvantage is that the kids have to commute to school by train.
Pi
Aren't you worried about the kids taking the train by themselves? 乗りすごしとか迷子とか
はじめのうちは親が同伴。徐々に一人で行き来できるようにします。
送るとき、今日は学校まで、明日は学校の最寄り駅まで、という具合に。
We heard this a lot from friends in Japan, but our American family was even more worried.
アメリカでは考えられないわ
Isn't it dangerous?
Pick-pockets?
What about strangers?
Conventional wisdom in America is that kids under 12 should be accompanied by a parent. That applies to commuting to school too. So schools provide school buses or parents drive their children to school. If the kids walk to school, then a parent goes with them.
現地の日本人母の声
お迎えが来ないと下校させないよね、学校が。
親が行けないならシッターに頼むとか
サンフランシスコ在住
放課後のプレイデート(遊びの約束)も親がかり。
大変よー
NY在住
私が子どもの頃はこんなに厳しくなかったんですけどね
幼少期もアメリカ在住
ボストン在住
Looking back, Steve and I appreciate that we grew up in times when it was normal for kids to walk to school by themselves. I wonder what our kids will tell their children when they grow up.
早く早く
行ってきまーす!


ミドリはこの春から小学1年生。兄と同じ学校に一緒に通うことになり、電車通学を始めました。

**commute** 通勤する，通学する

**first grade** 小学1年生

**advantage** 有益な点，強み

**even more** さらにいっそう

**pickpockets** スリを働く

**stranger** 見知らぬ人

**conventional wisdom** 社会通念

**accompanied by** ～が同伴する

**looking back** 思い返せば，今考えると

**appreciate** 〔～を〕ありがたく思う

スティーヴは、ミドリの保育園で子どもたちに英語を教えていたことがあります。「スティーヴ先生」に子どもたちがした質問は……

**day care** 託児所，保育園
**Itsy Bitsy Spider** ちっちゃなクモさん
**innocent** 率直な，純真な
**in simple terms** 簡単な言葉で
**assumption** 想定，思い込み
**problematic** 問題のある，解決の難しい
**accurate** 正確な，間違いのない
**less than whole** 完全でない
**multiracial** 複数民族の
**mixed race** 人種が入り交じった
**distressing** 悩ませる，苦しめる

# Vol.73 Dual Ethnicity and "Half"
## （「ハーフ」の概念）

Steve used to teach English to the kids at Midori's day care.
英語の手遊び歌をみんなで歌ったり踊ったり。替え歌にすることも
"Itsy Bitsy Spider"や"Walking Walking" "The Pinocchio"など
The kids called him "Steve-sensei" and often described Midori as "Steve-sensei's daughter."
ねえねえ
ミドリちゃんってスティーヴ先生から生まれたの？
えっ？
Their innocent questions were cute, and we did our best to answer in simple terms.
In Japan, we often describe people with dual ethnicity as "Half." But the assumptions it generates can be problematic. Some think "double" or "mixed" are more accurate and sound more positive.
ハーフ＝半分
パカッ
一人なのに半分？
日本人
米国人
Some international parents think "half" sounds less than whole.
In America, "multiracial" or "mixed race" are common.
In addition, all "halves" are not alike. "Half" suggests that one parent is Japanese, but it says nothing about the other parent.
The assumptions that people have with the word "half" can lead to some distressing situations.
ハーフはみんなバイリンガルってことはないよね
伝統工法の大工職人（日米ハーフ）
よく「英語で話してみて」って言われるけどお父さんフランス人だし
日仏ハーフ（９才）
人種のるつぼ、カリフォルニアでは「ハーフ」なんて珍しくもなんともないんだけどね

ハルが少年野球チームに入りました。私たちは週末になると、いろいろなグラウンドに出かけて行っては、彼の試合を観戦しています。

# Vol.74 The Green Green Grass of Home（芝生を求めて）

Haru joined a baseball team last year. On weekends, we travel to various playgrounds to watch him play his games. Steve's not impressed with the all-dirt fields at many playgrounds.

It's so much better to play on grass.

Back home in California, he says, most of the playing fields are covered in grass.
Last year, we watched our 9-year-old cousin play soccer on a big field covered in thick grass.

土ぼこりがたたない
転んでもケガをしにくい
水はけがよくなる
などのメリットの他にも——
Go Girls!
観客席もピクニックムードでいい感じ♪


Many schools in Japan have been replacing their dirt playgrounds with grass. But the schools face significant upkeep costs, mainly owing to the country's climate.
Once Steve started thinking about grass, he started yearning for it. Then he had an idea.

Hey! I can plant some grass in our backyard.
芝生の庭でBBQとかいいよね〜


So, last year, he dug up our backyard and planted several packets of seed.

It's not picture-perfect, but it really is nice to relax on green grass.

時々庭でごはんを食べることも
裸足サイコー
週1の芝刈りは子どもに人気
電動じゃないので扱いやすい
次、ボクの番だよ


grass　草，芝生
impressed with　〜に感心する
dirt　土，泥
thick　厚い，密集した
replace ~ with　〜を…と交換する
significant　多大な，かなりの
upkeep costs　維持費
owing to　〜のために，〜のせいで
yearn for　〜に憧れる，〜を切望する
dig up　〔土を〕掘り起こす
picture-perfect　〔見た目が〕完璧な

日本国内でもゴミの分別方法は地域によって異なりますが、それ以上に日本とアメリカでは異なるようで……

sort　分類する
trash bin　ゴミ箱
curb　縁，歩道の縁石
rumble down　ガタガタと音を立てながら走る
empty　中身を出す，空にする
collection facility　収集施設
separate out　取り出す
put in so much effort　相当な努力を注ぐ
I did a little digging.　ちょっと調べてみた。
The Council for PET Bottle Recycling　PETボトルリサイクル推進協議会
fiscal　年度の

# Vol.75 Trash Sorting and Recycling

## （ゴミの分別とリサイクル）

How do you sort the trash where you live? In our community, we separate it into 12 different categories.
ゴミ収集カレンダー 6
えーと今日出せるのは…
12種
可燃ゴミ
不燃ゴミ
有害ゴミの他…
ビン,カン
ペットボトル
プラスチック
新聞紙
雑誌&雑紙
紙パック
ダンボール
繊維
などの資源ゴミ
At Steve's family home in California, there're just three categories. Each is put into a large trash bin and rolled out to the curb on designated days.
ゴロゴロゴロ…
大人2人は入れそうな大きさのコンテナ
RECYCLABLE
YARD WASTE
GARBAGE
RECYCLABLES
ビン,カン,ペットボトルなどの資源ゴミ
YARD WASTE
切った枝や落ち葉,刈った芝生など
GARBAGE
左の2種以外何でも
A garbage truck rumbles down the street and empties the bins.
① 車についているアームでコンテナをつかむ
ガシッ
車から降りないでOK
② コンテナを丸ごとひっくり返して回収
ザザザーッ
ひょーダイナミック!!
Machinery at the collection facility separates out the recyclable materials.
えー
It makes me wonder why we put in so much effort in Japan.
I did a little digging. The Council for PET Bottle Recycling here in Japan reports that in fiscal 2012 the U.S. recycled 21.1% of plastic bottles, while Japan recycled 85%.
That's pretty impressive.
The little effort we put in at home seems to have a big effect.
ホッ
よし これからも 分別 がんばろっと

Vol.76
All the Colors of the Rainbow
(虹の色はいくつ?)
About a month ago, we saw something pretty fantastic.
The arc is upside down?!
Look, a rainbow!
Oh yeah!
あれっ
It really must be rare because that evening it was reported on the news. It's called a circumzenithal arc.* It's like a rainbow, but the light refracts through ice crystals in clouds rather than through raindrops.
(* Circumzenithal arc →環天頂アーク。逆さ虹とも)
I asked Haru how many colors he thought there were.
7!
Yep, he's Japanese.
即答
I thought this because...
赤橙黄緑青藍紫
Ask any Japanese and they will say there are seven colors in a rainbow. Ask an American and they will usually say six. Once, when we asked our cousin Emily, she answered:
6!
やっぱり即答
Emily (当時9歳)
日本の7色から藍を引いた6色が一般的
国や地域によっては5色や2色としているところも
The number of colors one sees depends on where the color spectrum is divided. People decide for themselves how many colors they choose to identify.
実際、見極めるのも難しいし
People from different countries and cultures can look at the same thing and still see something different. One thing that seems true about rainbows around the world, though, is that everyone thinks they are special.

日本では「七色の虹」と言いますが、実は国や地域によってその表現は異なるようです。

**rainbow** 虹
**arc** 弧状のもの
**upside down** 逆さまで
**refract** 〔光などを〕屈折させる
**ice crystal** 氷の結晶
**raindrop** 雨粒
**color spectrum** 色のスペクトル
**divided** 分かれた，分断された
**identify** 識別する，確認する

ハルが招待されたクラスメートのアメリカ式誕生日パーティー。最近のアメリカでは子どもの誕生日パーティーは大イベントなのだそうです。

Vol.77
American-Style Birthday Parties
(アメリカ式誕生日パーティー)
Haru was recently invited to an American-style birthday party for one of his classmates. In America, birthday parties for kids have become big events in recent years.
Lots of kids
Sometimes even a whole class is invited to make sure no one is left out.
ホスト。日米ハーフ
Party theme
plates, napkins, tablecloths, decorations... all follow the theme.
Invitation
BIRTHDAY PARTY
今回はバスケットボールだった
HAPPY BIRTHDAY RIN
Big birthday cake
Amazing designs and colors!
でかっ
ケーキもバスケがテーマ。A3サイズくらい
HAPPY BIRTH
Games and attractions
お皿の絵付けもやりました
Piñata
Piñatas are popular. Kids whack them with a pole until candy pours out.
Take-home goody bag
THANK YOU
Some candy or a small toy
It looks like a lot of fun to participate, but a lot of work to organize.
参加するだけでも大変よ。今月なんか毎週末だし
米国在住のママ友
There's even a growing industry in America of event sites designed mainly for birthday parties. One party can cost several hundred dollars or more.
Haru will turn 10 this summer. We'll certainly do something special, but the party is going to be just family.
Haru
Make a wish!


invited to　～に招待される

whole class　クラス全員

no one　誰も～ない

left out　仲間外れになる

piñata　ピニャータ，福人形

whack　強く打つ，叩く

pour out　あふれ出る

growing industry　成長産業

event site　イベント会場

cost　〔お金・費用などが〕かかる

make a wish　願い事をする

## Vol.78

# Hand Gestures

（ハンドジェスチャー）

Hand gestures are a natural way to communicate, and people rarely give them much thought. Well, our family has two types.
JAPAN The Peace Sign
It feels odd to make the peace sign.
ピース♥
パシャ
I like it as a hippy sign of peace from the '60s, but it seems odd to use it to look cute.
LOVE PEACE
イエーイ
Beware: The backhanded peace sign that's become popular lately is really rude in England.
ほぼ
手の甲を見せるピースサイン
AMERICA Beckoning Someone
おいで おいで
JAPAN
Does she want us to go over there?
Dad's calling us.
Come here
AMERICA
Both kids recognized the American gesture.
People learn those signs very naturally. Imagine how stunned I was to find my kids didn't use the same gestures that I do.
やっぱり
AMERICA Stop!
?
ダメ
Stop! No!
AMERICA
JAPAN
Some American gestures are quite useful.
評価
Good
Bad
So-so
幸運を祈る
Good Luck!
(Crossing the index and middle fingers)
引用
He said It's "free."
文中のダブルクオーテーションのところで
お金
Rubbing the thumb against the index and middle fingers
他の人に気付かれないようにこっそり支払いを済ませたい時など
In Japan where these are not so well known, they come in handy for communicating on the sly.

同じハンドジェスチャー（手ぶり）でも国によって意味が違ったり、同じことを表すのに動作が違ったりします。我が家の場合は……

rarely　めったに～しない
give much thought　熟慮する
beware　注意する，気をつける
lately　最近，この頃
rude　不作法な
beckon　手招きする
stunned　がく然として
index finger　人さし指
rub　こする
thumb　親指
come in handy for ~ing　～するのに役立つ
on the sly　ひそかに，こっそりとハルを妊娠するまで考えたこともありませんでしたが、赤ちゃんの誕生を祝う風習は国によっていろいろ。アメリカでは……

pregnant with （人）を身ごもっている

celebrate 〔誕生日・特別な出来事などを〕祝う，記念する

due date 出産予定日

feature 特色となる，特徴づける

expectant mother 妊婦

work out nicely うまくいく，良い結果をもたらす

word of encouragement 励ましの言葉

congratulations お祝いの言葉

afterward その後，後に

# Vol.79 Baby Showers

## （ベビーシャワー）

I had never thought about it until I was pregnant with Haru 10 years ago, but every country must have its own way of celebrating the birth of a baby.
In Japan, we usually send gifts after the birth. In America, gifts are given before birth, usually at a party called a "baby shower."

BABY♥SHOWER
BABY GIRL
It's a girl!!
It's a girl!
おなか周りのサイズ当てゲームなども
BABY

Baby showers are usually held a couple of weeks before the due date and are usually for women only.

The event features light snacks, talk, funny games and opening presents.

It's common for guests to choose presents from a "baby registry" set up by the expectant mother.

Babies"Я"Usのものが人気
The Baby Registry System
贈られる人
店のサイトで欲しいものリストを作成
I'll get this one.
リストの中から贈りたいものを選ぶ。他の人とプレゼントが重複しないので便利
贈る人

We didn't have a baby shower, but before Haru arrived our American relatives sent us things we put on our registries.

無駄がなくて
合理的なシステムは
いかにも米国的!?

It worked out really nicely for me because I received lots of words of encouragement before the birth from my American relatives and then congratulations from my Japanese family and friends afterward.

# Vol.80 Parent-Child Resemblance
## （親子で似ているところ）

Haru used to have straight hair like mine. He's been letting it grow out, though, and the longer it gets, the wavier it gets. He doesn't get that from me, because my hair is emphatically straight.

半年ほど前から伸ばし中
Before
After
That DNA has to come from Steve.
あれま
伸びるとウェーブヘアの人
ストレートヘアの人たち


Since they were literally once a part of me, finding something in them that is different from me always fills me with a sense of wonder. I had that feeling when my kids were born without a Mongolian blue spot.

友だちの赤ちゃんナツくん
もうこはん
蒙古斑
（ハルとミドリにはなかった）
The spots are common among East Asians and can be anywhere on the body.
ほー これがあの
本を読んで知ってはいたけど初めて見た人


When I hear other parents say they feel like their kids are part of them, I often become more aware of how my kids are different from me.

高い高い〜
You're my baby, but you're your own person too.


I also find lots of ways that our kids' personalities resemble ours.

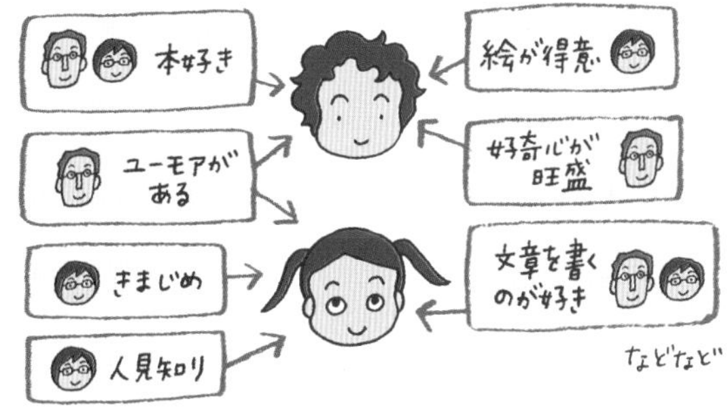

本好き
ユーモアがある
きまじめ
人見知り
絵が得意
好奇心が旺盛
文章を書くのが好き
などなど


The resemblances are more than skin deep.

以前は私と同じ直毛だったハルの髪の毛ですが、伸びたらウェーブが出てきました。スティーヴからの遺伝のようです。

**resemblance** 似ているところ
**grow out** 伸びる
**emphatically** 断固として
**literally** 文字通り
**fill someone with** （人）を〜でいっぱいにする
**sense of wonder** 不思議さに驚嘆する感性
**anywhere on the body** 身体のどこにでもある
**become more aware of** 〜をより意識するようになる
**one's own person** 本来の自分
**personality** 個性，人となり
**more than skin deep** 表面上だけではない

長い夏休みをどう過ごすか――アメリカの子どもたちは、日本の子どもたちと同じように過ごしているのでしょうか？

finally come to an end　ようやく終わる

alternate between A and B　AとBの間を行ったり来たりする

boredom　退屈

struggle　取り組む，悪戦苦闘する

I wish I were ～　～だったらよかったのに

extend over ～　～に広がる，及ぶ

overnight　泊まりがけの

niece　めい，姪

unforgettable　忘れられない，いつまでも記憶に残る

# Vol.81 Summer Vacation（夏休み）

The long summer vacation from school is finally coming to an end. The kids have been passing their days alternating between summer activities, fighting boredom, and struggling to sit down and do their homework.

I wish I were going to school in America. They don't have summer homework.
ずるーーい！
ヤル気出ない…
えっ そうなの?!

In America, summer vacation often extends over two months from mid-June to late August. While that's pretty long compared with Japan, most schools don't give homework over the summer.

The academic year begins in September in the U.S. So summer is between grades.
日本の春休みに宿題がないのと同じ
FREE

What do kids in America do over the long summer break?

## 1 Go to Summer Camp

Day camps, commuter camps, and overnight and weeklong camps offer various activities. Summer camps are a great help to working parents.

アウトドア系
アート系
科学系
健康サポート系
などなど
料金もいろいろ

ボクは参加したことないけど

## 2 Go Traveling

Extended vacations for the whole family: Some of our friends return to Japan to visit relatives and attend local schools.

1カ月間よろしくお願いします
あー レオくんだ！
毎年のことで友達もいたりする

Japanese and American parents both seem to view summer vacation as a chance to introduce kids to new experiences.

Steve's niece will visit us during her summer vacation. We're all looking forward to creating unforgettable experiences for her... and us.

# Vol.82 Typhoon Season
## (台風到来)

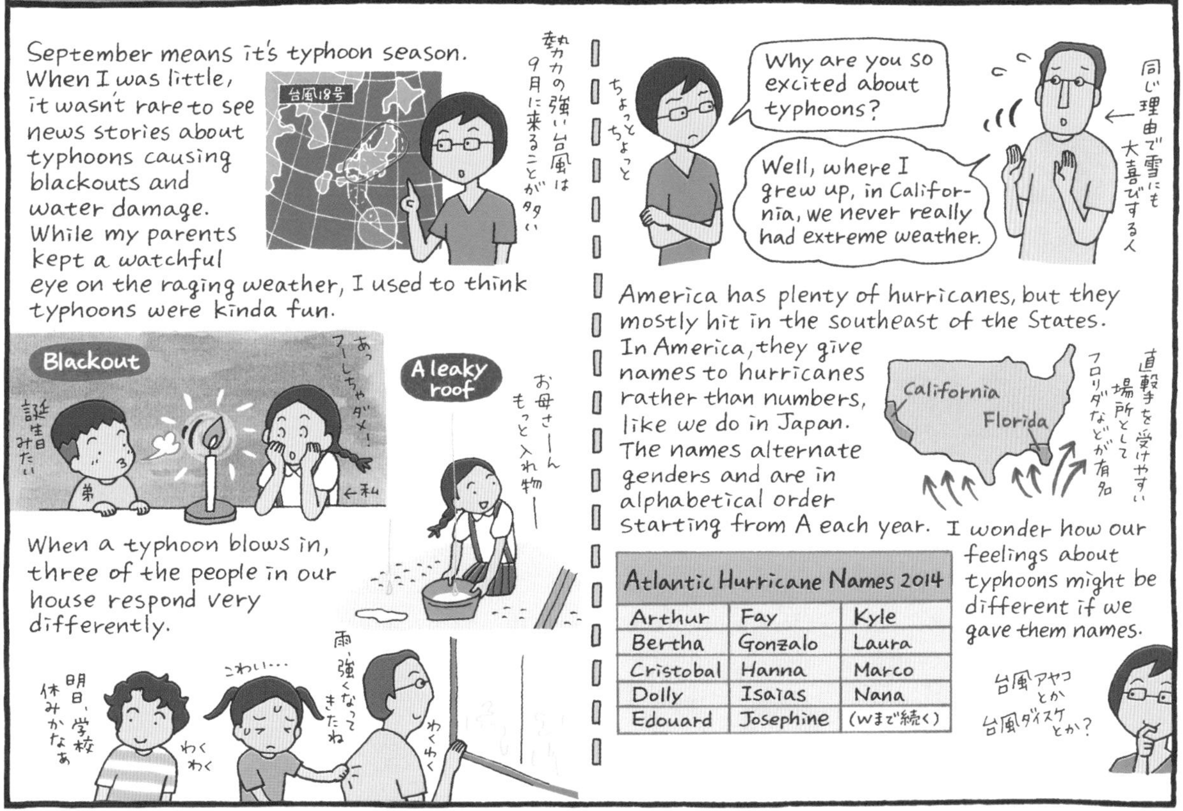

September means it's typhoon season.
When I was little, it wasn't rare to see news stories about typhoons causing blackouts and water damage.
While my parents kept a watchful eye on the raging weather, I used to think typhoons were kinda fun.
台風18号
勢力の強い台風は9月に来ることが多い
Blackout
あっフーしちゃダメー!
誕生日みたい
弟
←私
A leaky roof
お母さーんもっと入れ物ー
When a typhoon blows in, three of the people in our house respond very differently.
明日、学校休みかなあ
わくわく
こわい…
雨、強くなってきたね
わくわく
Why are you so excited about typhoons?
ちょっとちょっと
Well, where I grew up, in California, we never really had extreme weather.
同じ理由で雪にも大喜びする人
America has plenty of hurricanes, but they mostly hit in the southeast of the States.
In America, they give names to hurricanes rather than numbers, like we do in Japan.
The names alternate genders and are in alphabetical order starting from A each year.
California
Florida
直撃を受けやすい場所としてフロリダなどが有名
I wonder how our feelings about typhoons might be different if we gave them names.
台風アヤコとか台風ダイスケとか?


| Atlantic Hurricane Names 2014 | | |
|---|---|---|
| Arthur | Fay | Kyle |
| Bertha | Gonzalo | Laura |
| Cristobal | Hanna | Marco |
| Dolly | Isaias | Nana |
| Edouard | Josephine | (Wまで続く) |

9月といえば、台風の季節です。カリフォルニア育ちのスティーヴには物珍しいようで……

**typhoon** 台風, 暴風
**news story** 〔解説やコメントのない〕ニュース記事
**water damage** 水害
**keep a watchful eye on** ～から目を離さない
**raging** 荒れ狂う
**kinda** ～のようなもの（= kind of）
**leaky roof** 雨漏りする屋根
**extreme weather** 異常気象
**hurricane** ハリケーン
**give a name to** ～に名前をつける
**in alphabetical order** アルファベット順に

ハルは先日、英検３級を受験しました。バイリンガルの子どもたちが英検を受験する意味とは……

**in ninth grade** 9年生で，(日本の)中学3年生で

**confirm** 確認する，確かにする

**motivator** きっかけ，動機づけ

**keep working at** 〜をし続ける

**get used to ~ing** 〜することに慣れる

**fill in** 記入する

**have a contest to** 〜する競争をする

**much less ~ than** …よりずっと〜でない

**stressful** ストレスの多い

**aim for** 〜を目指す

# Vol.83 The Eiken Test (英検3級にチャレンジ)

Haru recently took the Eiken Grade 3 test. It seemed about the right level for him, but when I told my friend, she was shocked:

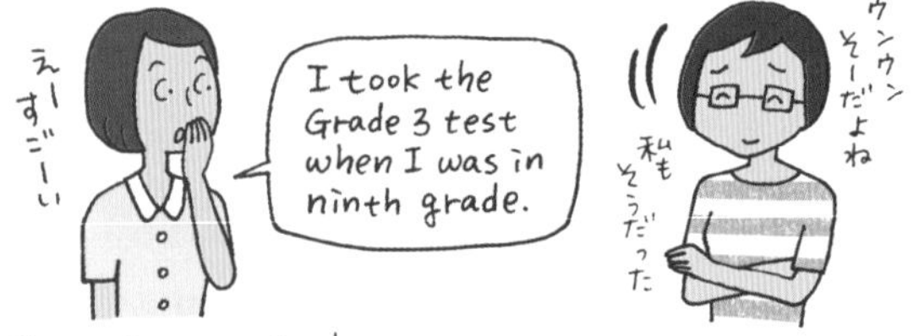

えーすごーい
I took the Grade 3 test when I was in ninth grade.
ウンウン そーだよね
私もそうだった


Some have asked:

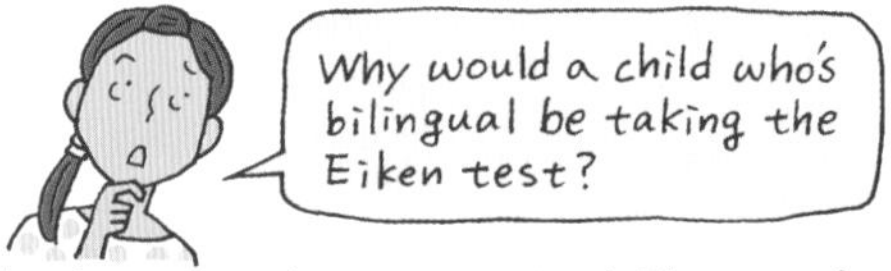

Why would a child who's bilingual be taking the Eiken test?


Haru's situation is certainly different from most of the kids who take the test. Most kids are testing their proficiency, while it's more like Haru is confirming his.
Nevertheless, he's learning English too. We thought the tests could be good motivators for him to keep working at it.

ハルの学校の同級生も一緒に受けました
父親の仕事で6歳まで中国に住んでいたRちゃん
日米ハーフのハル
両親がともに日米ハーフのLくん


We downloaded a practice test so Haru could get used to filling in the answer sheets. We had a contest to see who would get the better score, him or me.

親の意地
実は英検3級止まりの母
問題を読むのも解くのも母より速い息子
パサッ


Haru finished well before I did, but our scores were pretty close.

The test was much less stressful than I remember it.
中3の時の私
よく分かんないから適当に答え書いとこ
おー！バツはひとつだけ！感激〜♪


Haru and his bilingual classmates all passed the test. We're aiming for the next level next year. When I say "we," I mean me too!

ママのこと抜いてやる〜
そう簡単に抜かれないもんねーだ

# Vol.84 Autumn Is for Reading

（読書の秋）

Is everyone hunkered down with a good book? I'm a bookworm.

就寝前はもちろん
読みながら
食事することも
（※独りのとき）
4日で1冊のペース。
幸田文や有吉佐和子の
作品が大好き


I borrow books from the library. If I really like a book, I'll buy my own copy to read over and over.

Steve's a bibliophile too, but he buys the books he wants to read.

But there are no English libraries nearby…
…and I like to write in the margins.
それは確かに
買うしかないね
壁一面の本棚。
1/3が和書で
残りは洋書


The kids' school has two libraries, one for Japanese and one for English books. The kids can conveniently borrow books in both languages.

Haru gets completely wrapped up in the books he reads.

ごはんだよー
…
おーい
ごはんだよ！
生返事
んーー
ごはん！
って言ってるでしょ
はーい
チラ
（まだ見てる）


His most recent favorite book is a boy's coming-of-age story set in medieval Japan and written in English.

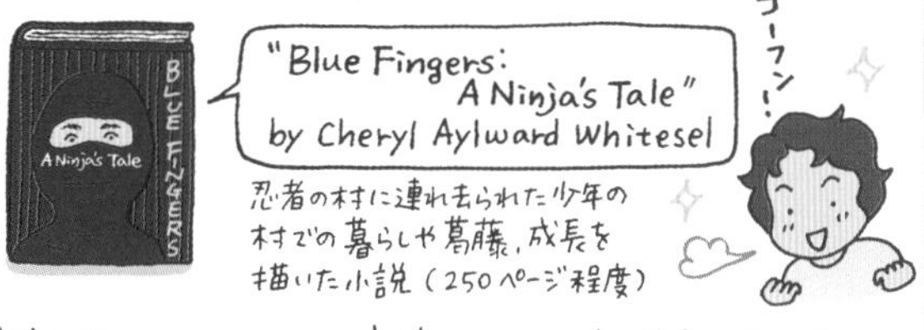

BLUE FINGERS
A Ninja's Tale
"Blue Fingers: A Ninja's Tale"
by Cheryl Aylward Whitesel
忍者の村に連れ去られた少年の
村での暮らしや葛藤，成長を
描いた小説（250ページ程度）
コーフン！


We encourage our kids to read all kinds of books for language acquisition and intellectual growth.

As the nights grow cooler, I hope you find a real page-turner to fire your imagination.

読書の秋がやってきました。最近のハルはまさに本の虫です。

**hunker down** 本腰を入れる，熱中する

**bookworm** 本の虫，大の本好き

**copy** 〔本などの〕部，冊

**bibliophile** 愛書家

**write in the margin** 余白に書き込みをする

**get wrapped up in** ～に没頭する，夢中になる

**coming-of-age story** 成長物語

**medieval** 中世の

**intellectual growth** 知的成長

**page-turner** 読み出したらやめられない本

**fire someone's imagination** （人）の想像力をかき立てる

毎年、我が家でハロウィンパーティーをします。作った料理を持ち寄ってシェアするポットラック・パーティーです。

potluck　持ち寄り料理の食事会
gathering　集まり，集会
baking soda　ベーキングソーダ，重曹
yeast　酵母，イースト
lentil beans　レンズ豆
witch　魔女，魔法使い
criminal　犯罪者，犯人
zombie　ゾンビ

# Vol.85 Potluck Party
## (一品持ち寄り)

Every year, we host a Halloween gathering at our house for over 20 monsters, superheroes, and princesses. We invite over some families for a potluck party where each brings a dish they made for all to share.

持ち寄り品の例
Irish Soda Bread
Made with baking soda instead of yeast.
Vegetarian Meatloaf
Made from lentil beans
Spanish Omelet
Egg omelet with lots of ingredients
かぼちゃサラダ
おにぎり
けんちん汁
うちでも3品くらい用意します
BEER
作るのが苦手な人は飲みもの担当とか


At a potluck party, each guest brings a part of the meal, such as the main dish, salad, or dessert.
We ask everyone to bring a dish their kids like to eat.

これ、おいしい！どうやって作るの？


Everyone always brings such interesting dishes. Learning about them is nearly as fun as tasting them.

The witches, criminals, and zombies are coming back this year. What dish would you make for them?

囚人と刑事の仮装をする日英カップル
毎年魔女の友人M
ヒッピーになったスティーヴ

# Vol.86 Kids and Movies
## （子どもに見せる映画）

Every once in a while, we rent a movie for the whole family to watch on the weekend. Pretty much every time, though, we end up renting a kids' movie.

食傷気味
It'd be nice to see a story that is more interesting for adults.
いや、Disneyとかのアニメもよくできてるけどさー
「アナと雪の女王」がいいー！
いや、ぜったい「プレーンズ」


On those occasions, we pick movies that we think will be wholesome and interesting for the kids, but we're often surprised by some of the things we see or hear.

げげっ
Shit!
Dammit!
ギョッ
子どもに使わせたくない言葉が出てきたり、きわどい性描写があったり。
Shitなどのfour-letter wordは独りきりのときにしか使わない人


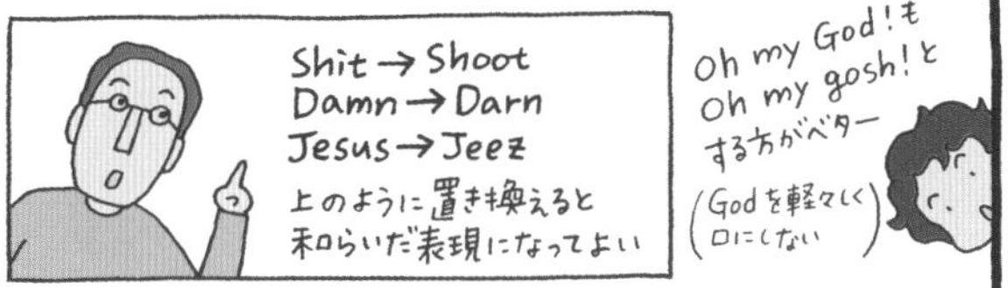

Shit → Shoot
Damn → Darn
Jesus → Jeez
上のように置き換えると和らいだ表現になってよい
Oh my God!もOh my gosh!とする方がベター
（Godを軽々しく口にしない）


Steve looks at the Common Sense Media website to find movies that are appropriate for our children's ages. The site provides movie reviews and recommendations from a parent's perspective.

ふむ
Common sense media
Ages 2–17
Violence
Sex
#! Language
作品に添えられた項目の例
詳しく見ると…
細かいなー！
Scene with a man threateningly waving a knife
A long kiss, some nudity
#! A few uses of s--t, d--n, hell


While we don't want to be overprotective of our kids, we also don't want to traumatize them. So we'll continue doing our best to choose family-friendly movies we can all enjoy.

時々週末にビデオを借りてきて、家族みんなで映画を見ます。たいていは子ども向けの映画を借りることになりますが……

**end up ~ing** 結局～することになる

**on those occasions** そのときは

**wholesome** 健全な，有益な

**dammit** ちくしょう

**four-letter word** 4文字語，禁句，汚い言葉

**appropriate for** ～にふさわしい

**from someone's perspective** （人）の観点から

**threateningly** 脅迫的に

**nudity** 裸（の状態）

**overprotective** 過保護な

**traumatize** 傷つける，精神的ショックを与える

我が家の子どもたちは、夫とは英語で、私とは日本語で話しています。2つの言語が入り混じることなく共存している感じです。

**switch** 切り替える

**mishmash** ごちゃ混ぜ，寄せ集め

**blend** 混ぜること，混合

**weaving** 織ること

**get one's wires crossed** 混線する，行き違う

**block out** 遮断する

**process** 処理する

**go in one ear and out the other** 右から左へと聞き流す

# Vol.87 Language Switching（言語スイッチ）

Our kids speak English with their dad and Japanese with their mom.

English
日本語
日本語
兄妹間は英語だったり日本語だったり

A lot of our conversations are a mishmash of the two languages. However, it's not a blend. It's more like a weaving of the languages.

交差する家族の会話
アンケートの締め切り明日だって
I finished my English homework!
That's good!
あ、そう

It's still surprising to me that we don't get our wires crossed. But each of us seems to be able to switch on whichever language we want to listen to.

That also means, however, one language can be blocked out.

日本語スイッチONの状態
日本語
K
P
J
N
R T S Y
H C
Q U F

There's no way of telling which language the brain is processing. At those times, words in the other language can go in one ear and out the other.

この間も言ったのにー
えー覚えがないなあ

E
英語スイッチON

Sometimes I wish we had a sign or a switch to make sure the right language is on.

# Vol.88 Thanksgiving（感謝祭の料理）

日本で暮らしているとつい忘れがちなアメリカの祝祭日ですが、11月の第4木曜日の感謝祭はいつも覚えているスティーヴです。

Steve admits he forgets many of the U.S. holidays each year. One he has always remembers is Thanksgiving.★ Thanksgiving is celebrated on the fourth Thursday of November, and the next day is also a holiday in some states. Thanksgiving and Christmas are the two major holidays when family members gather for big feasts.

Thanksgivingといえば七面鳥
ローストターキー
中に詰め込んだ野菜や米などに肉汁がしみ込む
パンプキンパイ
など
マッシュポテト
グレービーソースつき

クリスマスもだいたいこんな感じ


★Thanksgiving…感謝祭。開拓者が最初の収穫を神に感謝したことに由来する

Turkey is a Thanksgiving tradition. Because we don't eat much meat, Steve made a special dish.

バジル
マイタケ
トマト
ナス
えっへん
Yay, pizza!
It's a turkey!


The day after Thanksgiving is called Black Friday. It's the biggest shopping day of the year. Shoppers vie to take advantage of special sale prices and buy popular items before they sell out. The checkout lines can get crazy with hour-long waits not uncommon.

店が黒字になるから「ブラック」フライデー
SHOPPING

クリスマスに向かってGO!
大掃除と餅つきも。師走だ〜!


After a relaxing Thanksgiving Day, Black Friday is the starting line to buy presents, put up decorations, plan dinner, and get ready for the next family holiday—Christmas.

---

**Thanksgiving** 感謝祭
**admit** 〔〜を〕認める
**feast** ごちそう，祝宴
**turkey** 七面鳥
**tradition** 伝統，慣習
**the day after** 〜の翌日
**vie** 競う，先を争う
**checkout line** レジ待ちの行列
**get crazy** 熱狂する，正気を失う
**not uncommon** 珍しいことではない

結婚してから12月が急に忙しくなりました。クリスマスの準備はやることが多くて大変ですが、子どもたちもいろいろと大忙しのようです。

**endless** 終わりのない，永遠の

**meanwhile** その間に，その一方で

**mail** 郵送する

**North Pole** 北極

**have mixed feelings** 複雑な心境である

**chimney** 煙突

**go all the way** はるばる行く

**brilliant** 素晴らしい，見事な

**reaffirm** ～を再確認する

# Vol.89 The Secret Truth about Santa Clause（サンタの秘密）

After I married, December suddenly became a busy month. Preparing for Christmas is a lot of work. We have to decorate the tree, shop for presents, plan the day… the "to do" list seems endless. Meanwhile, the kids are busy deciding what they want for presents and writing to Santa Claus.

Dear Santa,
My name is Midori. I have been quite good this year. I want a unicycle for Christmas.
Love, Midori
HOHOHO
しんけん


When they finish writing their letters, we mail them to Santa Claus at the North Pole.

Santa Claus
Santa Claus' Main Post Office, Tähtikuja 1
FI-96930 Arctic Circle
ネットで調べると
送り先候補は
他にも
いろいろあります


Ten-year-old Haru wrote a letter to Santa, but he's having mixed feelings. He's beginning to wonder, "Is there really a Santa Claus?"

Our house doesn't have a chimney, so how does he get in?
?
How does he go all the way around the world in just one day?
お


How would you, dear reader, respond to these questions?

Luckily, there's a brilliant picture book to help answer these questions.

Yes Virginia There's a Santa Claus


"Yes, Virginia, There Is a Santa Claus"
by Francis P. Church

1897年に米国の新聞The New York Sunに掲載された社説を元にした絵本。
8歳の女の子から寄せられた投書に答えたもの。
日本語版は「サンタクロースっているんでしょうか？」（偕成社）

The book reaffirms the magic of Santa for kids—and parents too!

# Vol.90 Spreading the Christmas Spirit
（広がるクリスマス・スピリット）

In the buildup to the Christmas holiday, television in America is saturated with special holiday programs. Many of the shows are aired every year and have practically become tradition in the U.S.

Thanks to modern technology, we have DVDs of several of the classic shows.

Some of our favorites, which have been around since I was little, are:
① "A Charlie Brown Christmas"
② "How the Grinch Stole Christmas"
③ "A Christmas Carol"
まだまだ米国流クリスマス初心者
毎年ワクワクして見てる人たち

When we think of Christmas, the first thing most people probably think of is receiving presents. For children, this surely is the highlight of the holiday. But there's a greater "Christmas spirit." The spirit of Christmas is the sense of gratitude and giving.

The Christmas spirit is in the giving.
This is for you.

In the past few years, we've been following the example of Steve's parents and giving small gifts to people we see on or around Christmas, such as the postman and delivery people. It's quite similar to what we do during the New Year holidays in Japan.

いつもありがとう。メリークリスマス!
ありがとう
ちょっとしたお菓子など

These little actions bring joy to both the giver and receiver. Merry Christmas to all!

クリスマスが近づくと、アメリカのテレビはクリスマス特別番組でいっぱいになります。毎年放送される番組も多く、伝統のようになっています。

**buildup** 準備期間

**be saturated with** ～でいっぱい［飽和状態］である

**air** 放送する，放映する

**practically** ほとんど，実質的に

**sense of gratitude** 感謝の気持ち

**postman** 郵便配達員

**delivery people** 配達員の人たち

**bring joy to** 喜びをもたらす

新年が訪れても、まだクリスマスの名残りがあるのが我が家のお正月です。

transition　移行，移り変わり
best wishes for　～を祈る
bask in the afterglow of　～の余韻に浸る
come knocking　やって来る
even though　～にもかかわらず
overshadow　〔～を〕暗くする，見劣りさせる
calligraphy　カリグラフィー，書道
bonfire　大かがり火，たき火
unique　唯一無二の，ユニークな

# Vol.91 The Transition from Christmas to New Year's（クリスマスからお正月へ）

Happy New Year! Best wishes for a happy and healthy year.
Christmas and New Year's are important family holidays in our family. We're usually still basking in the afterglow of Christmas when the new year comes knocking.
米国では1月に入ってからツリーを片付けるのが一般的
いつもの手まりのオーナメントも
お年玉♥
お年玉
年賀状来たよー
After the New Year's greeting cards are sent, the kids write "Thank you letters" for the Christmas presents they received.
The kids must send thank you letters to everyone who gave them a present.
Dear Uncle Randy Thank you for the game. I enjoy it a lot. It's fun! Love, Midori
夏休みの終わりに宿題に取り組むときみたいになっている
このときのために、プレゼント開封時に贈り主ともらった物のリストを作成します
Even though we live in Japan, Christmas could easily start to overshadow the New Year's holidays. So we try to give New Year's a real Japanese flavor by visiting a shrine, doing kakizome calligraphy, and joining community events like a dondo-yaki bonfire.
できた！
RAINBOW MIDORI
あれま
We're rarely completely American or completely Japanese. But I guess that's what makes our family unique.

# Vol.92 Open Doors
## (ドアの役割)

When no one is in the bathroom, we leave the door open. This may sound strange, but that's what they do in America.

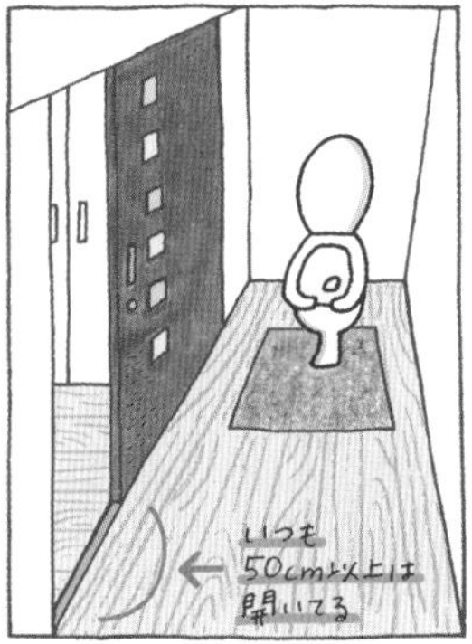
いつも
50cm以上は
開いてる

Odors waft away.
おすすめ！
ある意味、合理的
It's easy to tell if someone is inside or not.

My family usually leaves most doors open. Doors are really only closed for privacy, such as when someone is dressing or sleeping.

There are two good reasons for leaving doors open.

### 1 Air Circulation

Central heating is common in America, so there's no need to contain heat or cold in a room. In fact, doors need to be open for the air conditioning to work effectively.

高断熱・高気密の
建物向き
うっとり
真冬でも廊下もトイレも寒くないんだよねー

### 2 Maintains Open Relationships

A closed door can be taken as a strong sign of wanting to shut people out.

NO
米国でも思春期の子どもは自室のドアを閉める傾向が強い

ドアは心の鎧？

Our home in Japan is about 40 years old and we rely on space heaters in the winter. Even so, we keep as many doors open as possible for fresh air and warm relations.

我が家ではトイレに誰もいないときは、ドアを開けっ放しにします。不思議に思うかもしれませんが、アメリカでは当たり前のようです。

**odor** におい
**waft** 漂わせる
**dress** 服を着る
**air circulation** 空気循環
**central heating** 集中暖房，セントラルヒーティング
**contain** 含む，封じ込める
**air conditioning** 空調（設備）
**effectively** 効果的に
**taken as a strong sign of** ～の強いメッセージだと見なされる
**shut someone out** （人）を中へ入れない
**rely on** ～を頼りにする

昨年のバレンタインデーにチョコをもらったハル。相手のお母さんにお礼のメールを送ったら、彼女もプレゼントに大喜びだったそうです。

**eat ~ for a snack** おやつに～を食べる

**homemade** 自家製の，手作りの

**excited about someone's gift** もらったプレゼントに（喜びで）興奮する

**over the moon** 大喜びしている，有頂天になっている

**not unexpected** 予想外というわけではない

**common practice in** ～では一般的なこと

**busy with** ～で忙しい

# Vol.93 Valentine's Day

## （我が家のバレンタインデー）

Haru received chocolate from "S-chan" on Valentine's Day last year.
I'm going to eat some of S-chan's for a snack, OK?
~♪
Wow! It's homemade.
あとで Sちゃんママに お礼のメールを しなくちゃ
ハル
Sちゃん
両思いで何をするわけでもないけど
同級生
公認の仲
I sent a thank-you e-mail to S-chan's mom, and she said S-chan was very excited about her gifts too.
Haru-kun gave S-chan a gift and a love letter. She was over the moon.
キャー
Sちゃんママ
自分の宝箱の中から オモチャの宝石や ブレスレットなどを
いつの間にっ
S-chan and her mother's surprise were not unexpected. It's common practice in the United States for men to give women Valentine's gifts.
In our mixed-culture house, the gift giving goes both ways.
ミドリと記久恵に
Happy Valentine's Day!
I love you!
ママとミドリに
スティーヴとハルに
※ホワイトデーは省略
ダディーとハルくんに
手紙書いたよ
So with Valentine's Day approaching, we're all busy with our private preparations.
I want to make cookies this year!
ミドリもー
ひー

Vol.94
Table Manners
(テーブルマナー)
Dinnertime is an important time for family bonding. As parents, it's also important to teach table manners. This leads to a lot of demands from us parents.
モゴモガ
Don't speak with your mouth full!
Elbows off the table!
コラッ
ちょっとトイレ
Stay at your seat during the meal!
トイレは先に行っとこうね
Many of the table manners are the same in Japan and the U.S. Some, however, are specific to our different cultures.
Lift your rice bowl when you eat!
左手出して
I wouldn't notice that because it's Japanese etiquette.
そもそも米国じゃ茶わんを使わないし
器は持ち上げない
Of course, it goes the other way too.
ちょっとゴメン
Rather than reaching across the table, it's better to say "Would you please pass the salt."
SALT
なんでダメ?
答え
食卓にも各人のスペースがあり、それを尊重するため
While teaching the kids table manners, we adults are learning too.

夕食は、家族の絆を深める大切な時間ですが、親としてテーブルマナーを教えることも大切。そのため、あれこれ注意することになります。

**demand** 要求，要望，求めるもの

**elbow** ひじ

**off the table** テーブルから下ろす

**specific to** ～に特有である

**rice bowl** ごはん茶わん

**etiquette** 礼儀作法，エチケット

**go the other way** 反対の方に行く，逆を行く

**reach across the table** テーブル越しに手を伸ばす

子どもたちと私は毎晩お風呂に入りますが、スティーヴは朝にシャワーを浴びます。その理由は……

**bed hair** 寝ぐせ（のついた髪）
*bad hair day ヘアスタイルがうまくいかない日
**bathe** 入浴する
**grooming** 身づくろい，身だしなみ
**chronic** 頻発する，習慣的な
**couldn't care less** 少しも気にしない
**au naturel** 自然のままの
**hygiene standards** 衛生基準
**despite** ～にもかかわらず
**morning ritual** 毎朝の日課
**put up with** ～に耐える，我慢する

# Vol.95 Bed Hair Day（寝ぐせ）

The kids and I bathe every night. Steve usually showers in the morning. I like to feel clean and refreshed at the end of the day. Steve showers to wake up and get ready for the day.
Start your day with a shower and a smile!
水道代を考えると夜にまとめて済ませてほしいけどねえ
The morning shower is also part of grooming for the day. Without it, you could have a "bed hair day."
You don't see bed hair so often in America.
なんと！寝グセの土壌が、日本のお風呂文化にあったとは！
Haru and I have chronic bed hair.
ママ、鬼みたい〜
ほんとだ〜
さらさらロングヘアで寝グセ知らず
そういうハルも鳥の巣みたいよ
Haru couldn't care less and goes to school with his hair au naturel.
My hat'll fix it.
行ってきまーす
Oh No〜!
せめてブラッシングだけでも〜
無造作ヘアってことでいいんじゃない？
Notices immediately
VS
Doesn't care
Japan's bath culture and America's hygiene standards both value cleanliness. Despite his morning ritual, Steve still has to put up with everyone else's bed hair.

# Vol.96 Same Meaning, Different Language
## （同じことをそれぞれの言語で）

Wake up! It's time to get up.
ほら起きて。朝だよ——
In our house, the kids often have to hear the same thing twice in different languages.
Sometimes they even have to listen twice to things they don't want to hear.
One time, for example, Haru brought home a low score on a kanji test.
I was higher than the class average.
へらへら
That's good enough, right?
平均は52点、ボクは58点だった
As parents, we both wanted to share our thoughts about that attitude.
みんなもそうだからって…。自分は自分で100点取るつもりでがんばらないと
You shouldn't measure yourself by others. Always do your best to get 100 points.
事前に出題範囲もわかってたんだし
Sometimes we catch ourselves repeating what the other just said.
They both say the same thing!
いつものことだけど
でも
It makes the lecture twice as long…
It only feels like the important points have been said when we hear it in our own language.
んね
For Haru's sake, though, we're trying to be short and to the point.


我が家の子どもたちはよく同じことを二度、違う言語で聞くはめになります。時には小言も。なぜなら——

twice　二度

class average　クラスの平均点

good enough　十分である

attitude　態度, 考え方

measure oneself by others　他人の尺度で自分を評価する

catch oneself ~ing　気がつくと～をしている

to the point　要領を得た

COLUMN 4

## 夢と独り言

「夢は何語で見るの？」「独り言とか考え事は何語なの？」

こうした質問は、二カ国語以上を喋る人の多くが一度は聞かれたことのある質問だと思う。私はたいてい「そのときによるなー」と答えることが多い。独り言も夢もそのときの雰囲気、気持ち、そして状況に合わせて言語が変わる。

私の周りにいるバイリンガルの友達に聞いても同じらしい。ただ、英語に慣れていて、持っている語彙も英語の方が多い人は英語の夢を見ることが多いようだ。最近は私も、英語の方が多いなと思う。

中学生になって、帰国子女などの英語の得意な友達(以下、国際生の友達)が増えた。休み時間になるとその子たちと過ごすことが多く、そんなときは会話の9割が英語になる。

私が小さかった頃は友達とも日本語を喋ることの方が圧倒的に多かったし、本を読むのが苦手だったこともあって、英語の語彙は同年代のネイティブに比べるとかなり少なかった。

でも今は、友達との日々の会話で新しい英語の語彙に触れる機会が増え、使えるようになってきている。見ている動画も英語のものが圧倒的に多い。だから最近は、夢も独り言も基本、英語が多いのだと思う。

そんなわけで、最近の夢に登場する人はたいてい英語を喋っている。普段日本語でやりとりしている友達でも、だ。

逆に、最近数少ない日本語の夢には国際生の友達は登場しない。たとえば、国際生がいない一般の授業の夢であったり、学校の外で習っているバレエの夢だったりするときだ。

自分でも不思議だ。

ただ一つはっきりしているのは、独り言も夢も場面によって言語が変わる、ということだ。言葉は場に呼応する“反応”みたいなものなんだと思う。

STEVE
来日30年目の
江戸好きアメリカ人
KIKUE
ワタクシ
HARU
息子。
小学5年生
MIDORI
娘。
小学2年生

# 5th Year

2015

日本に住む外国人なら一度は「なぜ日本に来たの？」と聞かれたことがあるのではないでしょうか。スティーヴは今でも年に数回聞かれます。

**at one time or another** 一度は，いつか

**virtually every** ほとんどすべての

**Why don't you ~ ?** ～したらどう？

**know little of** ～についてほとんど知らない

**have no expectations** 何も期待していない

**step off the plane** 飛行機から降りる

**curiosity** （知的）好奇心

# Vol.97 Why Did You Come to Japan?

## （どうして日本へ？）

At one time or another, I would bet that virtually every foreigner living in Japan has been asked, "Why did you come to Japan?" Steve still gets asked several times a year.

Why did you come to Japan?

Steve first came to Japan in 1985 after spending half a year traveling, mostly around Europe.

フランスの牧場で働いたり、イタリアの教会に滞在させてもらったり、インドでお腹をこわしたり…
チーズ作り
Are you OK?

When he was finally thinking of returning home to California, a friend invited him to visit Japan.

Why don't you come to Japan?
当時日本在住のスティーヴの友人

Could you～?
英会話スクールで先生をしたりも
（バブル初期の頃だった）

Steve knew little of Japan and had no expectations when he stepped off the plane. He says that allowed his curiosity to drive his learning of our country's culture and customs.

Wow, this is all so amazing!
漢字の成り立ち
文化
習わし
風景
歴史
道具
などなど

米国に比べると人も暮らしも穏やかで安心なのもいいなと思いました

When he finally returned to California, his interest in Japan only grew. He decided to come back to become a translator. That was 30 years ago!

Steve's deep roots in Japan grew from a seed planted by a friend. Steve may be the most surprised of all about how that seed has grown.

かれこれ人生の半分以上、日本にいるんだもんね

# Vol.98 Youth Baseball, Part I
## (少年野球①)

ハルは少年野球チームで練習や試合に励んでいます。スティーヴは、コーチの指導方法に少し疑問を抱いているようです。

Haru is on the local youth baseball team. The team practices or has games every Saturday, Sunday, and on holidays. Steve respects the dedication of the coaches but feels a bit at odds with their coaching methods.

Baseba
正面で捕れって言ってんだろ!!
オラもう一回いくぞ!!

弁当持参で朝から夕方まで

これぞザ・スポ根ってやつ?
The practices last all day long.
There's so much yelling and berating. It can't be fun for the kids.
米国じゃ考えられないよ


In the U.S., even highly competitive youth teams usually practice only half a day and not at all during the off-season, when many kids play other sports.

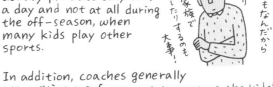

まだ子どもなんだから
いろいろ体験したり
家族で過ごしたりするのも大事!


In addition, coaches generally use positive reinforcement to nurture the kids' development by praising rather than criticizing their abilities. For example, a coach might say:

Good Swing!
三振しても…
Nice try!
など
日本ならドンマイ!かな
ほめて伸ばす!
打とうとしたその積極性をほめる


They say Japanese kids are losing interest in baseball. I wonder if this would change if the practices weren't year-round and coaches created a positive and constructive atmosphere for the kids. That's something to ponder.

**dedication** 献身，熱心さ

**feel a bit at odds with** ～に少し違和感を覚える

**berate** 〔人を〕ひどく叱りつける

**highly competitive** 非常に競争力のある

**positive reinforcement** 正の強化，積極的に促すこと

**nurture** 育てる，助長する

**criticize** 批判する，批評する

**year-round** 年間を通した

**constructive atmosphere** 前向きな雰囲気

**ponder** じっくり考える，熟考する

最近、日米の少年野球の違いをテーマに書かれた本に出合いました。とても興味深い内容でした。

come across ～に出くわす
insight 洞察, 見識
eye-opening 目を見張るような, 目からうろこの
emphasize 強調する, 力説する
objective 目的, 方針
recreational 〔活動が〕楽しみを得るための
compete in ～で競う
tryout 入団［適性］テスト
it's hard to say ～とは言い難い, わからない
dilemma 〔二者択一の〕ジレンマ, 板挟み

# Vol.99 Youth Baseball, Part II

(少年野球②)

I recently came across a book with many interesting insights about the differences between youth baseball in Japan and the United States.

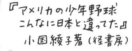

野球に詳しくない私でもすいすい読めました！
アメリカの少年野球こんなに日本と違ってた


『アメリカの少年野球 こんなに日本と違ってた』小国綾子著（径書房）

米国で4年間を過ごした一家が、少年野球を通して、日米文化の差異を学んでいく様子を描いたノンフィクション

The book was really eye-opening. Here are a couple of the points that left a strong impression on me.

## 1 Japanese baseball emphasizes good form

Japanese coaches teach players to have picture-perfect form, while American coaches prefer to let each player develop their own form.

Wow! Beautiful Swing!


## 2 American youth baseball teams have different objectives

Youth baseball in the United States generally divides into two categories.

| Recreational Team | Travel Team |
| --- | --- |
| Teams for kids who want to have fun playing without the pressure. | Kids compete in tryouts for the team, which plays teams from other cities, or even other states. |

日本の少年野球は
どちらかというとトラベルチームっぽいよね


It's hard to say which has more advantages, Japanese or American style.

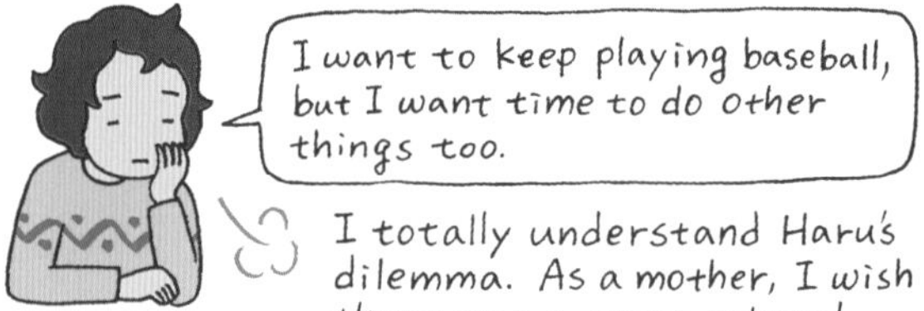

I want to keep playing baseball, but I want time to do other things too.


I totally understand Haru's dilemma. As a mother, I wish there was a more relaxed recreational team for him to join in our area.

Vol.100
Losing Teeth
(前歯が抜けたら)
Midori has lost her two front teeth. When each one fell out, she carefully put them under her pillow at night. As is the custom, she was hoping the Tooth Fairy would take the teeth and leave some money for her.
イーッ
She had a dilemma, though. She wanted the money, but she also wanted to keep the teeth. So she put a message under her pillow with each of her teeth.
Dear Tooth Fairy,
Here is my tooth. Could you please leave a coin? But I want to keep my tooth. Can you leave my tooth too, please?
Love, Midori
Next Morning
珍しい1ドルコインゲット!
歯も残ってた♪
Happily, the Tooth Fairy left a coin and the tooth. However, Midori now has a new dilemma.
…
モゴ
Without my front teeth, it sounds funny when I try to say the "th" and "f" sounds.
TH
舌を前歯の後ろに軽くつける
F
下唇を前歯につける
ちなみに日本語では困ることはないらしい
Teeth
Fluff
あれー?変になっちゃう
Front teeth may be small, but they play a big part in creating clear pronunciation.

前歯が抜けて歯の妖精から硬貨を手に入れたミドリ。しかし前歯がないせいで、ちょっと困ったことが起きたようです。

**front teeth** 前歯
**fall out** 抜け落ちる
**pillow** 枕
**as is the custom** いつものように，恒例により
**though** 〜だけれども，でも
**leave** 〜を残す，置いておく
**fluff** 綿毛，へま，言い間違い
**play a big part in** 〜において大きな役割を果たす

子どもと一緒にお風呂に入ることは、父親の育児参加でまず思い浮かぶもののひとつでしょう。しかしアメリカでは……

time-honored tradition　昔ながらの伝統
come to mind when someone thinks of　（人）が～のことを考えるとき思い浮かぶ
Ministry of Foreign Affairs　外務省
warn　警告する
indeed　確かに
golden opportunity　絶好の［またとない］機会
strengthen　強固にする
definitely　最終的に

# Vol.101 Bath Time
## （お風呂の時間）

Sharing the bath is a time-honored tradition in Japan and may be one of the first things that comes to mind when we think of ways fathers participate in raising their children.
In the United States, however, sharing the bath with children is practically taboo. The Ministry of Foreign Affairs even warns on its website to be careful about it when traveling in the U.S. and Europe.
MOFA 外務省
海外安全ホームページ
ヨーロッパやアメリカでは（中略）たとえ親子であっても一緒に入浴することは非常識な行為で、特に父親と娘の場合は性的虐待が強く疑われることになります。
ええっ?!
Indeed, I have noticed that my American relatives treat bath time a little differently.
Small kids
Bathe with help from a fully clothed parent
Kids aged about 6 or older
Shower alone
子どもは親の裸を見たことないのが一般的
ええっ
私、毎日目の前で裸になってるよ
In our home in Japan, we want to have an open understanding of our bodies and how bodies change. We see bath time as a golden opportunity to strengthen parent-child relationships. We definitely take a Japanese approach to bath time.
心も体もほぐれてリラックス～♪
Bath time is great quality time with the family.
一緒にお風呂入るの大好き！

Vol.102
Quality Time
(子どもとの大切な時間)
In the last Postcard, I talked about how bath time is quality time with the kids. There are other ways to spend quality time too.
就寝前の読み聞かせ
など
Ex. ② Gold Panning with Midori
Swish it back and forth carefully.
ok!
※砂金採りはスティーヴの趣味のひとつ
Every once in a while, Steve takes one of the kids for an outing for just the two of them.
Ex. ① Batting Center with Haru
Keep your eye on the ball!
One-on-one time really strengthens the parent-child bond.
ポイント!
※野球は2人の共通の趣味
When I get the feeling that my interaction with the kids is sounding like nagging — Elbows off the table! Brush your teeth! — that's when I know we need some quality time together.
Steve is pretty good at making time to bond with the kids. I think I need to set aside some special time too.
Besides, it's always fun for me too.
気負わずに、自分がやりたいことを子どもと一緒に
Making desserts
Eraser Stamps
Dyeing
T-shirt art
やってみようかな


たまにスティーヴが子どもたちのどちらかだけを連れて、２人きりで外出することがあります。これもまた、子どもとの大切な時間です。

---

**one-on-one** 1対1の

**keep one's eye on** ～から目を離さない

**gold panning** 砂金採り

**swish** 〔物を〕サッと動かす

**interaction** 交流，意思の疎通

**nagging** 口やかましい，しつこい

**good at ~ing** ～するのが上手である

**set aside** 〔時間・金などを〕残しておく，確保する

**besides** その上，さらに

漢字テストで思うような点が取れなくなってきた小学２年生のミドリ。どうやら語彙の問題が関係しているようで……

Vol.103
Missing Vocabulary
(語彙の欠落)
Midori is learning more-difficult kanji now that she's in second grade. Her test scores have dipped from the perfect 100 points she used to earn in first grade.
二年生 かん字テスト
やっちゃった…
She obviously needs to practice writing more. However, her teacher also said we should help her increase her vocabulary.
担任のY先生
It's not unusual for bilingual children to be missing some common vocabulary.
目からウロコ
When I heard this, it was immediately obvious to me how this could happen.
Even though our kids are learning two sets of vocabulary, our focus at home has been mainly on helping the kids develop their English abilities.
就寝前の読み聞かせは洋書が中心
日本在住の我が家の場合、どうしても英語が不足するしね
Increasing time using one language (English) necessarily means less time for the other language (Japanese).
寝る
学校(ほぼ日本語)
は家にいる時間。日本語も英語もアリ
ぎゅうぎゅう
日本語
英語
押しくらまんじゅう状態
Haru confirms what the teacher said:
Sometimes I don't know some words that other kids know.
「非難」とか「あんぽんたん」とか
Now I understand that, along with helping our kids maintain and develop their English, we also need to provide a little extra support for learning Japanese.
それ取って?
「それ」じゃなくてちゃんと名前で言って
おまけ
名誉挽回
今度は100点だったよ!


---

**vocabulary**　語彙

**dip from**　～を下回る

**earn**　得る，獲得する

**not unusual for**　～にとっては珍しいことではない

**obviously**　明らかに，どう見ても

**immediately obvious**　一見してわかる

**provide extra support**　特別な援助を与える

# Vol.104 Units of Measurement
## (単位の違い)

No matter how proficient a person becomes in English, there's one thing that may always seem awkward — units of measurement.

Measurements don't come up a lot, but they do cause communication gaps every now and then when we are talking with relatives in the U.S.

他にも…
キロ(km)とマイル(mi)
グラム(g)とオンス(oz)
めんどくさい!
そろえてほしい!
リットル(ℓ)とガロン(gal)
など

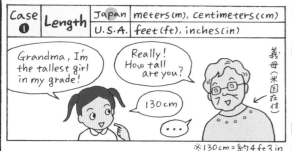

| Case ❶ | Length | Japan | meters(m), centimeters(cm) |
| --- | --- | --- | --- |
| | | U.S.A. | feet(ft), inches(in) |

Grandma, I'm the tallest girl in my grade!
Really! How tall are you?
130cm
...
義母(米国在住)


※130cm=約4ft3in

The U.S. tried to introduce the metric system, but the cultural attachment to its customary units is too strong. By law, however, food packages must show both the customary and metric units.

例えば…
Potato Chips
9½oz.(269.3g)
移民が多く、メートル法に慣れてる人も多いので

| Case ❷ | Temperature | Japan | Celsius(℃) セ氏 |
| --- | --- | --- | --- |
| | | U.S.A. | Fahrenheit(°F) カ氏 |

It's going to be 90 degrees today.
えっ90度?!
義母のオーブンを借りても設定できない…
?
180℃ってカ氏だと何度?


※90°F=約32℃　※180℃=356°F

Experience has helped Steve adjust to the metric system. He says units of length are pretty easy to grasp, but metric weight is best left to the scales.

If you're trying to lose weight, it's easier to lose pounds than kilograms.
増減の幅が大きく実感できる
kg
キログラム
lb
ポンド
kgだと
56
lbだと
123


※1lb=約0.454kg

どんなに英語が堪能な人でもつまずくのが、単位です。アメリカの親戚と話していると、時々混乱することがあります。

- units of measurement 単位
- no matter how どんなに～であろうとも
- proficient 熟達した，堪能な
- awkward 扱いにくい
- come up 話題に出る
- every now and then 時々，時折
- metric system メートル法
- attachment to ～への愛着
- customary unit 慣用単位
- grasp 把握する
- best left to ～に任せるのが一番
- lose weight 減量する，痩せる

もうすぐ夏休みがやってきます。国際結婚の家庭では、親戚に会うために遠方まで飛行機で行くことも多いのですが……

distant land　遠方，遠い国
upcoming　今度の，もうすぐやって来る
get a discount on　〜の割引を受ける
fare　運賃
get around　〔問題などを〕うまく避ける
take special care of　とりわけ〜に配慮する
in transit　移動中で
bienvenue　〈フランス語〉歓迎（= welcome）
economically　経済的に
practical　実際上の，現実的な
on one's own　自力で，単独で

# Vol.105 Flying Home
## （里帰りの渡航）

The kids' summer vacation will soon begin. Have you made your summer plans yet? International families often fly to distant lands to see their relatives. We're excited about our upcoming trip. But with the joy, there's a little pain too.

わーい
Yay! We can see Grandma!
2年ぶり!!
楽しみ〜
喜
Air ticket
I got a discount on the air ticket by making the reservations early.
Children's ticket prices end up being about the same as discount regular fares.
（※ちなみに12歳からは大人料金）
悲


Even with discounts, it takes quite a lot of money to pay for a whole family to fly. Some families get around this by sending just their kids to relatives overseas.

One family we know sends their 10-year-old daughter to stay with relatives in France.

心配だわ…
楽しんでおいで。
仏語の勉強にもなるよ


The airline companies understand the situation and take special care of kids in transit.

### Special services for kids aged 5 to 11

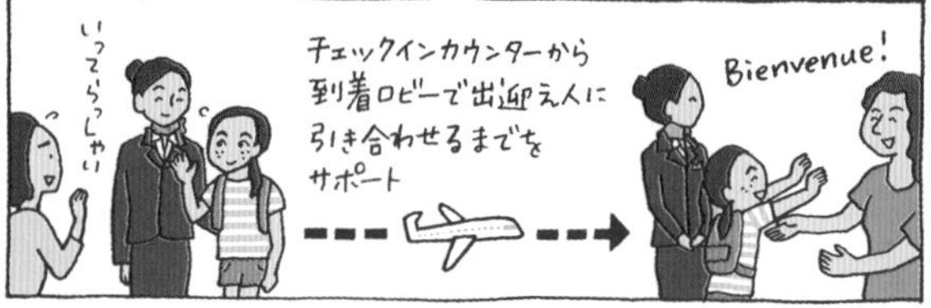

いってらっしゃい
チェックインカウンターから到着ロビーで出迎え人に引き合わせるまでをサポート
Bienvenue!


We all enjoy flying home, but the day may come when it is not economically practical. Haru and Midori may be flying on their own (or together) someday. That may be part of growing up for international kids.

でも、たまには純粋な「旅行」もしたいなー
「里帰り」は親戚まわりだしね

Vol.106
Kids & Money, Part I
(子どもとお金①)
おこづかい
Steve and I agree that the kids can learn financial responsibility if they have their own spending money to manage.
The kids have reached the age when they can start appreciating the value of money. So we're considering giving them some cash on a regular basis.
In my experience Japanese parents give their children cash monthly. However in the U.S. most kids are required to earn a weekly "allowance" by doing small chores around the house.
日本式
毎月定額を渡す
Here's your pocket money for the month.
ありがとう
米国式
手伝いの報酬として払う
Nice work doing your chores this week.
Thank you
ボクも子どもの頃お皿洗いをして週に25セントもらってました
Naturally, we have different views.
家族なんだから手伝うのは当たり前と思ってほしい
If it's based on work, the kids might say,
I won't do it if you don't pay me.
カネクレカネ
It doesn't make sense just to give them money if they haven't earned it.
お金は「もらうもの」じゃなくて「稼ぐもの」
Should we just give them money or make them earn an allowance? We need to decide what we want to teach the kids. And, how we want to teach it. In our next Postcard, we'll show you what we've decided to do.


どんなふうにお小遣いをあげるのが子どもたちのためになるのか――スティーヴと私は、定額制か報酬制かで悩んでいます。

---

**financial** 金銭上の
**responsibility** 責任, 義務
**spending money** お小遣い
**appreciate the value of** ～のありがたみを正しく理解する
**cash** 現金
**on a regular basis** 定期的に
**required to** ～するように求められている
**earn** 〔労働の対価として〕金を得る
**weekly allowance** 週給, 1週間分のお小遣い
**chores** 家事
**pocket money** お小遣い

アメリカの子どもたちは、家事をした報酬としてお小遣いをもらうのが一般的です。中には家事以外で小遣い稼ぎをする子どもたちも――

**do household chores** 家事をする

**get the hang of** ～のコツをつかむ

**entrepreneur** 起業家，請負人

**snow shoveling** 雪かき

**go out ~ing** ～しに出かける

**look for** ～を探す

**put ~ to good use** ～を大いに利用する

**hire** （人）を雇う

**tutoring** 個別指導，家庭教師

**lawn mowing** 芝刈り

**encourage** 勧める

Vol.107
Kids & Money, Part II
（子どもとお金②）
In Japan, parents often give kids pocket money. In America, kids can earn an allowance by doing household chores, like washing dishes or cleaning the yard.
When they get the hang of how to earn money, some kids even become entrepreneurs.
LEMONADE STAND
（自宅前などで販売。親が一緒だったり家の中から見守っていたり）
LEMONADE 50¢
チャリティーのためにしている子も多い
SNOW SHOVELING
近所へ御用聞きに回ることも
Hi, Mrs.Goodneighbor. Do you need any snow shoveled today?
かわいくてつい頼んじゃいそう♡
When they become teenagers and go out looking for their first job, the work experience and negotiation skills are put to good use.
チラシを作って配ったり
Hire me for small jobs
I have experience with all of the jobs listed below.
Babysitting
Pet Sitting
Tutoring
Car Washing
Lawn Mowing
Junior / 16 years old
3.4 GPA / 3 Siblings
AMANDA
セールスポイントも。GPAはGrade Point Averageの略で、米国式の成績評価方法。4が最高
They learn more than how to handle money, they also learn responsibility.
これはいいかも
雇う側もプロに頼むより安く抑えられるし
We've decided to try the American system. We will give the kids special chores to complete.
If they want more spending money, we will encourage them to think of ways they can earn it.

# Vol.108 Blue Jeans
## (伝統のブルージーンズ)

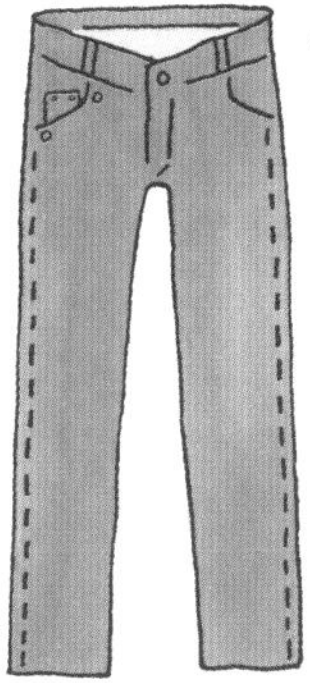

California helped bring the world hippies, computers, blockbuster movies, and mountain bikes. Steve is proud of one more California invention — Levi's blue jeans.

The Levi Strauss headquarters in San Francisco is fun to visit.


Jeans were invented during the California Gold Rush.

Gold Rush
1848年にカリフォルニアで金鉱が発見され、一攫千金を狙う人々が世界中から押し寄せた


Gold miners often returned from the gold fields with their pants in tatters. Levi Strauss and his partner, Jacob Davis, decided to make pants that were sturdier by using denim reinforced with metal rivets. The blue dye coats the fibers and helps the material get softer with each washing.

ふっ…
カウボーイハットやブーツと
合わせれば完璧
So blue jeans are traditional clothing of the United States. Right?
Isn't that a bit of an exaggeration?


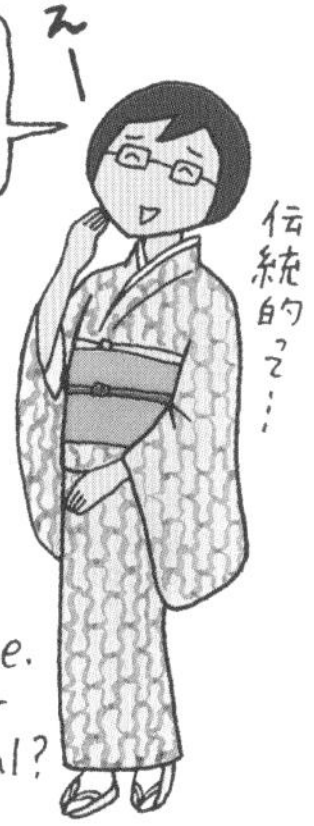

えー
伝統的って…


Well, the cultural importance of a type of clothing that has been around for about 150 years in a country that has existed for about 250 years is unquestionable. So how much time is needed for something to be called traditional? Jeans are very versatile, but on some occasions wouldn't be appropriate dress. Steve, however, would wear them every day if he could.

伝統的なのに
あくまでも
格下なんて…
お正月の
親戚まわりだって
ジーンズでもいいと
思うんだけどなー


カリフォルニア出身のスティーヴにとって、お国自慢はいろいろあるけれど、絶対に外せないのはジーンズです。

**bring the world** 世界に～をもたらす

**blockbuster movie** 大ヒット映画

**invention** 考案

**headquarters** 本社，本部

**miner** 鉱夫

**in tatters** ボロボロにちぎれて

**sturdy** 頑丈な

**reinforce** 補強する

**rivet** 鋲，リベット

**exaggeration** 誇張すること，〔話の〕尾ひれ

**unquestionable** 疑う余地のない，確かな

**versatile** 用途の広い，万能の

夏の大半を、北カリフォルニアに住むスティーヴの両親と一緒に過ごしました。記録的な暑さと干ばつに見舞われた現地では……

drought　干ばつ
spend a good part of　〜の大部分の時間を過ごす
sweltering hot　うだるように暑い
humidity　湿度
sticky　蒸し暑い，べたべたする
muggy　蒸し暑い，暑苦しい
step out into the sun　日なたに出る
desert　砂漠
record　記録的な
wildfire　山火事
hazy　もやのかかった，かすんだ
oppressive　〔天候が〕あまりに蒸し暑い

Vol.109
Summer Adventures－Drought
（夏の思い出：干ばつ）
We spent a good part of this past summer with Steve's parents in Northern California. It was our first visit in two years.
だいぶラクになりました
子どもたちが自分で荷物を運べるようになって
数年前までは子どもたちもベビーカーもで大変だった
While Japan was sweltering hot, California was also burning under the sun.
!!
TVで言ってる
It's going to be 108 degrees F again today!
°Fで聞くとなお暑く感じるよね
米国では力氏（Fahrenheit）が使われており，日本の七氏（Celsius）にすると，約42°c
However, the humidity in California is low, so you don't feel sticky like in Japan's muggy climate. But the moment you step out into the sun...
あ…暑っっ
Moisture
Heat
It feels like my whole body is drying out.
This is what a desert must be like.
Although the temperatures were normal for summer, the state is also experiencing record drought this year. The hot and dry conditions are combining to produce wildfires all over the state. California, which is just about 10% larger than Japan, was battling over 20 separate wildfires while we were there.
（風向きによっては義両親宅周辺にも煙が流れてきた）
It's hazy today
At the same time, the weather was not oppressive, and we were out and about having all sorts of adventures. More next time...

# Vol.110 Summer Adventures－RV Trip
## （夏の思い出：RVでの旅行）

On our summer trips to California, we spend most of our time visiting with family and relatives. This year Steve's parents had special plans for us — an extended trip in their RV.

Let's go to Yosemite!
80代
70代
年に1度はRVで米国国内を旅している義父母


RVとは RV stands for recreational vehicle, a large vehicle equipped with beds, a kitchen, and a lounge area.

電気コードや水道&排水ホースを接続すると、電気も水も自由に使える


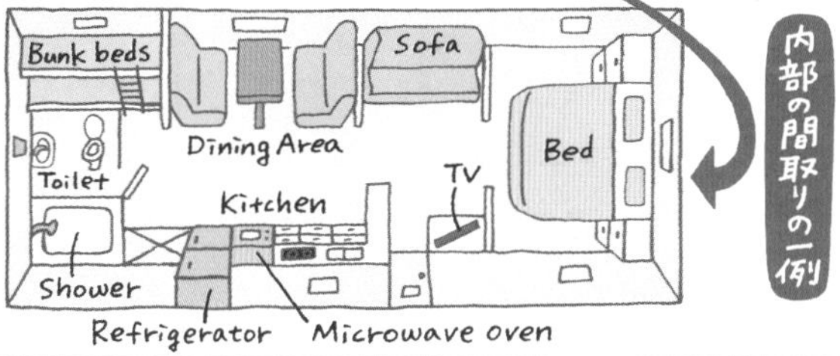

Bunk beds
Sofa
Dining Area
Bed
Toilet
Kitchen
TV
Shower
Refrigerator
Microwave oven
内部の間取りの一例


All across America, in or near virtually every major city, tourist area, and national park, there are RV parks with facilities to hook up RVs to electricity and sewage systems.

After spending the day sightseeing, people return to their RV sites for a barbecue dinner and to relax inside the vehicle.

スイッチON
Air conditio-ning
今日は寒いな
Watching TV
Go! Giants!
サンフランシスコジャイアンツのファン
A warm shower
An RV has all the basics of home, but it's very compact.
RVs are so cool!!


As Steve's parents get older, they are using the RV more and more to travel and see the beauty and history of their country. We were lucky to get to enjoy part of it with them.

家として住む人がいるのもナットク!
実は日本にもあるらしいですよ、RVパーク♪


いつもアメリカ滞在中は親戚を訪ねて過ごすことが多いのですが、今年はスティーヴの両親が特別にキャンピングカーでの旅行を計画してくれました。

**extended trip** 長期旅行
**stand for** 〔略語などが〕～を表す
**recreational vehicle** RV車，キャンピングカー
**equipped with** ～を備えている
**bunk bed** 2段ベッド
**all across America** 全米で
**park** 駐車場
**hook up** つなぐ，留める
**sewage system** 下水設備
**compact** コンパクトな

毎年我が家で開くハロウィンパーティーも今年で5年目。最初は手づくり感いっぱいだった飾りつけも、徐々にグレードアップしています。

# Vol.111 Halloween Decorations
## (ハロウィンの飾りつけ)

Come October, we start preparing our house for our annual Halloween party. We used to make our own party decorations but have gradually accumulated more decorations over the past five years.
5年前
On the walls and windows, we hung homemade cardboard and origami decorations.
工作好き↓
切り紙楽しい
Now, we put up several store-bought knickknacks and even prepare some ghoulish appetizers.
現在
未だ現役
義母にもらったものがいろいろ
スーパーボールやカリフラワー with ドライアイス
EYEBALL JUICE
BRAIN SOUP
だいぶ充実してきたなぁ
But our Halloween decorations can't hold a candle to the front yard of one of Steve's friends in the United States.
RIP
フフフ…
イベント好きな知人のレさん
Yard Decorations
ウズウズ
Maybe it's time for us to have something scarier.
Steve as 1960s hippy
Well, it can't be too scary because some of the kids are still small. And it might surprise the neighbors too.
ギャーこわい〜
し…心臓がっ
うちの周りは70〜90代の人が多いので とくに心配…
We're thinking up something new for this year's party. Do you have any ideas?


come 〔時が〕来ると

annual 年に1度の，毎年恒例の

used to 以前は〜（したもの）だった

accumulate 積み重ねる，（少しずつ）ためる，積もる

cardboard ボール紙，段ボール

knickknack 小間物，雑貨

ghoulish 残忍な，おぞましい

appetizer アペタイザー，前菜，期待を持たせるもの

can't hold a candle to 〜の足元にも及ばない

neighbor 近所の人

# Vol.112 Homestay, Part I
（ホームステイ①）

When I was 11 years old my family participated in a homestay program. My mother did all she could to make our visitor, Kimberly, comfortable.
私→（11歳）
弟（7歳）キンバリーとケンカばかりしていた
キンバリー（11歳）沖縄の米軍基地から来た
30年前の母→
Would you like orange juice?
わー豪華！
いつもはごはんとみそ汁なのに
Western-style breakfast
Thinking back, I probably did too much to fit her lifestyle rather than helping her experience ours.
現在の母
My mother's comments made a deep impression on me. Treating a homestay visitor as a guest may not provide the best homestay experience. The most memorable experience may come from the opportunity to participate in our everyday lifestyle.
Two years ago:
Here's an ad seeking host families. Shall we contact them?
いつ？
おっいいね
シアトルの高校生だって
それなあに？
市報
でも…
Wait a minute! We speak two languages and have a blend of cultures. Would we be a good host family?
Well, most families communicate with their guests in English anyway.
大丈夫！
In fact, that would be an advantage.
←STAFF
With those words of encouragement, we decided to give being a host family a try. In our next Postcard, we'll show you how that worked out.


私が子どもの頃、ホストファミリーになったことがあります。心を尽くしたものの、母には反省も多いようで……

**participate in**
～に参加する，加わる

**do all one can**
全力を尽くす

**think back**　～を振り返って考える

**make a deep impression on**
（人）に強い印象を与える

**memorable experience**
心に残る経験

**ad**　広告，宣伝

**seek**　探し求める

**Wait a minute.**
ちょっと待って。

**give ~ a try**　～を試してみる

**work out**　やり遂げる，実現するホストファミリーとしてシアトルで日本語を勉強している高校生を受け入れました。できるだけ普段通り、を心がけて過ごしました。

**host** 主人役として接待する，客を泊める
**adopt** 選ぶ，採用する
**easygoing** のんびりした，おおらかな
**regular** 習慣的な，いつもの
**fellow** 同期生，仲間
**take part in** ～に参加する
**have a blast** とても楽しい時間を過ごす
**would love to** ぜひとも～したい

Vol.113
Homestay, Part II
（ホームステイ②）
Two years ago, we hosted a student studying Japanese at a high school in Seattle. All of the students had adopted Japanese names for the class. "Yasuo" was the name of the boy who stayed with us.
コンニチハ
ヤスオデス
Yasuo was a shy and easygoing 16-year-old.
He had been studying Japanese for half a year and had just learned hiragana.
Fumiko
Izumi
Takumi
Hiroshi
同級生たち（マンガ好きが多い）
不思議とみんな合ってるんだよね
Remembering my mom's thoughts, we decided to let Yasuo experience our regular lifestyle. We had our usual breakfast of natto or oatmeal, and dinners that were mainly Japanese.
納豆は薦めたものの拒否されました（笑）
Ah—...
No thank you.
Yasuo and his fellow visitors were busy nearly every day climbing Mount Fuji, watching a taiko drum performance, and taking part in cultural activities. We usually only saw him when he returned in the evening.
少し前まで習ってた
津軽三味線を手ほどき
かるた遊び
平仮名は読める
互角の勝負
平仮名勉強中の5歳
折り紙や簡単な漢字も教えた人（小3）
紙風船が意外に大ヒット
He was one of our family when he was with us, and he and the kids had a blast together. Of course, we can see some things we could have done better, but the homestay was a memorable experience for all of us. We'd love to do it again.

# Vol.114 Grandparents' Visit
## （義両親の来日）

Since they became grandparents, Steve's parents have been coming nearly every other year to visit us in Japan. They're coming for two weeks again this year.

We're looking forward to spending time with them but are not sure how to keep them entertained. They've seen and experienced much of Japan already. Also, the kids will be going to school most days, so any travel would have to be on the weekends.

今までに行った場所、したことのリスト
浅草
京都
鎌倉
吹きガラス
日光
かれこれ来日10回を超える強者
ミドリが行ったことないところもいっぱい！
どうしよう


Nevertheless, being grandparents, they've told us that they are most looking forward to just spending time doing ordinary things.

This means doing stuff like going for walks and shopping. After the kids come home from school, we can have dinner and play cards together.

Hmmm...
ZIP
31やゴルフというトランプゲームをすることが多い


Since we usually only get together once every year or two, the time we spend together is precious no matter what we do.

おまけ
ホッ
結局今回は
富士山
周辺へ行くことに
ヨカッタヨカッタ


孫が誕生してから、ほぼ1年おきに来日してくれている義両親。今回はどんなふうに楽しませようかと悩みましたが……

**every other year** 1年おきに，隔年で

**keep someone entertained** （人）を楽しませ続ける

**ordinary thing** ありふれたこと

**do stuff like** ～のようなことをする

**play cards** トランプをして遊ぶ

**once every year or two** 1年か2年に1回

**precious** 貴重な，大切な

**no matter what someone does** （人）がどんなことをしようと

学生時代にホームステイ先で作ったときも、結婚後スティーヴの家族に作ったときも不評だったそうめん。その理由は──

taste preference　味の好み
extended family　〔近親者を含む〕拡大家族
soupy　スープのような
rich flavor　豊かな風味
fried　炒めた
broth　だし汁，スープ
appealing　魅力的な，好ましい
full-flavored　風味が濃厚な
strong-tasting　濃い味のする
make someone smile　（人）をほほ笑ませる

# Vol.115 Different Cultures, Different Taste Preferences（外国人受けする和食）

The first time I made Japanese food for a foreigner was when I was a high school student. I made somen noodles for my homestay family in England. Unfortunately, they didn't like it very much.

Thank you. But I can't eat any more.
（1杯目で）
ホストファーザー
作り過ぎて余ったそうめんを犬にあげるも…
拒否！
No
ガーン
高校生の私


I never understood why they didn't like the somen until I started making Japanese food for Steve's parents. I found that there are two things about the taste preferences of foreigners ── well, at least Steve's extended family.

## 1 Many people don't like soupy dishes

ズズッ
食事中に音を立てるのは欧米でタブー
食べにくい


## 2 Most people prefer rich flavors

白ごはんにしょうゆをかける義母
あ…ちょっと
なんか敗北感
ショウガじょうゆや練りゴマを使った料理は好評


Udon and other noodles are preferred fried rather than in a broth. White rice is not appealing unless it is mixed with other foods. Full-flavored, strong-tasting items make better snacks than simple, plain flavors.

一般的に人気とされるものは…
お好み焼き
焼きギョーザ
とんかつ
天ぷら
カレーライス
焼き鳥など


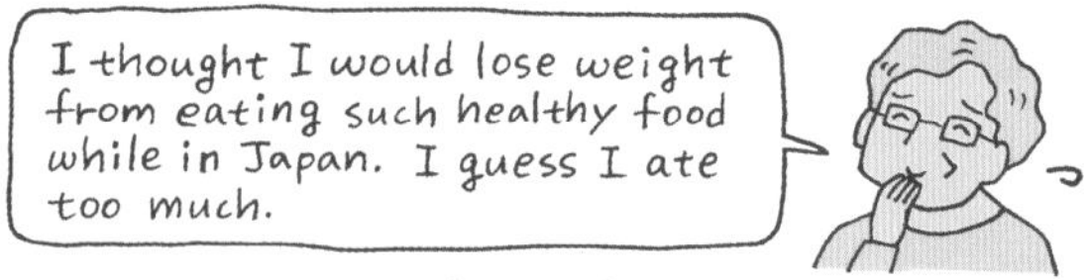

I thought I would lose weight from eating such healthy food while in Japan. I guess I ate too much.


My mother-in-law's words made me smile to myself.

Vol.116
The Peanuts Museum
（スヌーピーミュージアム）
Every year as Christmas approaches, we all look forward to watching "A Charlie Brown Christmas" on DVD.
The show is a hugely popular TV special for the message it has about Christmas Spirit.
「A Christmas Carol」とかももちろんいいけど"
音楽もすごくいいよね
↑ Charlie Brown's Christmas Tree
「I won't let all this commercialism ruin my Christmas」というチャーリーのセリフの象徴
This summer in California, we visited the Charles M. Schulz Museum, a museum dedicated to the Peanuts comic strip and its creator.
わー
あっちにチャーリー・ブラウンのツリーもあるよ！
「Peanuts」の原画がいっぱい！
The museum exhibits were fun, interesting, and educational, but we were most impressed by the volunteer who guided groups through the museum. He was very engaging and knowledgeable. His enthusiasm for Peanuts really showed.
Charles modeled this character on one of his childhood playmates…
Ask me!
へぇ～
作者がいかに身の周りのものを作品に盛り込み、愛情深く描き続けたかがよくわかるなあ
We stopped for lunch at the adjacent skating rink and café. The kids couldn't resist ordering the meal that came in a reusable dog dish —just like Snoopy's.
犬食い♪なんちゃって
There's good news for all fans of Charlie Brown and all the Peanuts characters. A Snoopy Museum Tokyo is scheduled to open in Roppongi in the spring of next year. Merry Christmas to all!

老いも若きも大好きなスヌーピー。その美術館にみんなで行ってきました。

**hugely popular** 絶大な人気がある
**commercialism** 商業主義，もうけ本位
**ruin** 台無しにする
**Charles M. Schulz** チャールズ・M・シュルツ《『ピーナッツ』でよく知られるアメリカの漫画家。1922–2000》
**comic strip** 〔新聞などに掲載される〕連載漫画
**exhibit** 展示品
**engaging** 魅力のある，〔人が〕愛嬌のある
**knowledgeable** 〔人が〕博識な
**enthusiasm for** ～に対する思い入れ
**adjacent** 隣接した
**can't resist** 〔ひどく魅力的で〕たまらない

あけましておめでとうございます！　クリスマスの飾りつけがまだ残る我が家ですが、お正月飾りにも力を入れています。

changeover　切り替え
laden with　～でいっぱいの
will most likely be ~ing　たぶん～すると思う
surrounded by　～に取り囲まれる
hang on　～にぶら下がる
take down　下げる，降ろす
store　保管する，格納する

# Vol.117 Not-So-Quick Holiday Changeover
（季節の飾りの後片づけ）

Happy New Year!
日本酒も結構いけるクチ
今年もよろしくお願いします

Like many families in America, we have a house that is still laden with Christmas decorations when we welcome the New Year.

Last year a friend of mine showed me how to make a shimekazari. So this year I'll most likely be making a Japanese New Year's decoration while surrounded by a Christmas tree, Christmas stockings, and newly opened presents.

稲わらをなうのが結構むずかしい
こんなのを作った
基本の「ごぼうじめ」

I've come to enjoy the walk to the shrine at New Year's because it gives me a chance to see the different kinds of shimekazari that people hang on their front doors.

会社などに多いごぼう型
旧家の柱につけられていた縦型のもの
気をつけてみるといろんなのがあっておもしろい
わりとよく見る輪っか型
珍しい鳥型など

The tradition is to take down the shimekazari on Jan. 7. That's about the same time we take down our Christmas tree to store it for next year.

| 飾る期間 | | |
|---|---|---|
| | Christmas Tree | 12/1頃から 1/上旬まで |
| | しめ飾り | 12/28から 1/7まで |

I wish the New Year's holiday season were longer. I'm sure the kids would like Christmas to last longer too.

ツリーは1カ月間も楽しめるのに、しめ飾りは10日間だけ
せっかく作ったのに～

# Vol.118 Cultivating Languages
## （言語が育つきっかけは）

Some years ago, I published a book of illustrated essays about our international family and raising bilingual children.

悦楽バイリンガル子育て
田村記久恵


The book contained anecdotes from our family as well as stories and questionnaire results from families of various mixed nationalities.

We learned so much from their experiences, and one particular comment has really stayed with me.

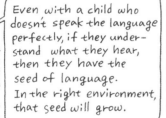

Even with a child who doesn't speak the language perfectly, if they understand what they hear, then they have the seed of language.
In the right environment, that seed will grow.

大丈夫！どうにかなるって
長女のたまきちゃん。日本語優勢だった
ニュージーランド人のSimonさん
Seed of language


Now, Tamaki is perfectly bilingual.

Of course, that seed needs constant watering and care.

毎朝出勤前の20分間、子どもたちに英語を教えていたサイモンさん
もうやだ。やりたくない
フーん
ラクじゃないよね


Tamaki always seemed to resist learning English all through her younger years. However, the seed suddenly germinated and blossomed when she reached middle-school age and discovered Western music and a TV show she liked.

Western music
Western TV show
English
日本語


Ten years ago, Simon's insight made me think that a language will develop if given the right environment.

Now I realize that the person's internal motivation is also a key element, and that needs to be cultivated, too.

他の家庭の話が参考になることは多々あります。バイリンガル育児についても同様で——

**cultivate** 育てる，耕す

**anecdote** エピソード，逸話

**questionnaire result** アンケート結果

**right environment** ふさわしい環境

**constant** 絶えず続く，くり返される

**resist** 抵抗する

**all through** ～を通してずっと

**germinate** 発芽する，成長する

**blossom** 咲く，開花する

**internal** 〔人の〕意識内の，内面の

**key element** 重要な要素

スティーヴが来日して30年。日本に住む外国人への扱いは確実に良くなってきているそうですが……

**relatively rare** 比較的まれな

**experience highs and lows** 浮き沈みを経験する

**extremely** 非常に，とても

**frustrating** 〔思いどおりにならず〕じれったい，もどかしい

**handful of** ほんの一握りの，わずかの

**annoy** 困らせる，悩ませる

**virtually** ～も同然で

**fluent** 流ちょうな，堪能な

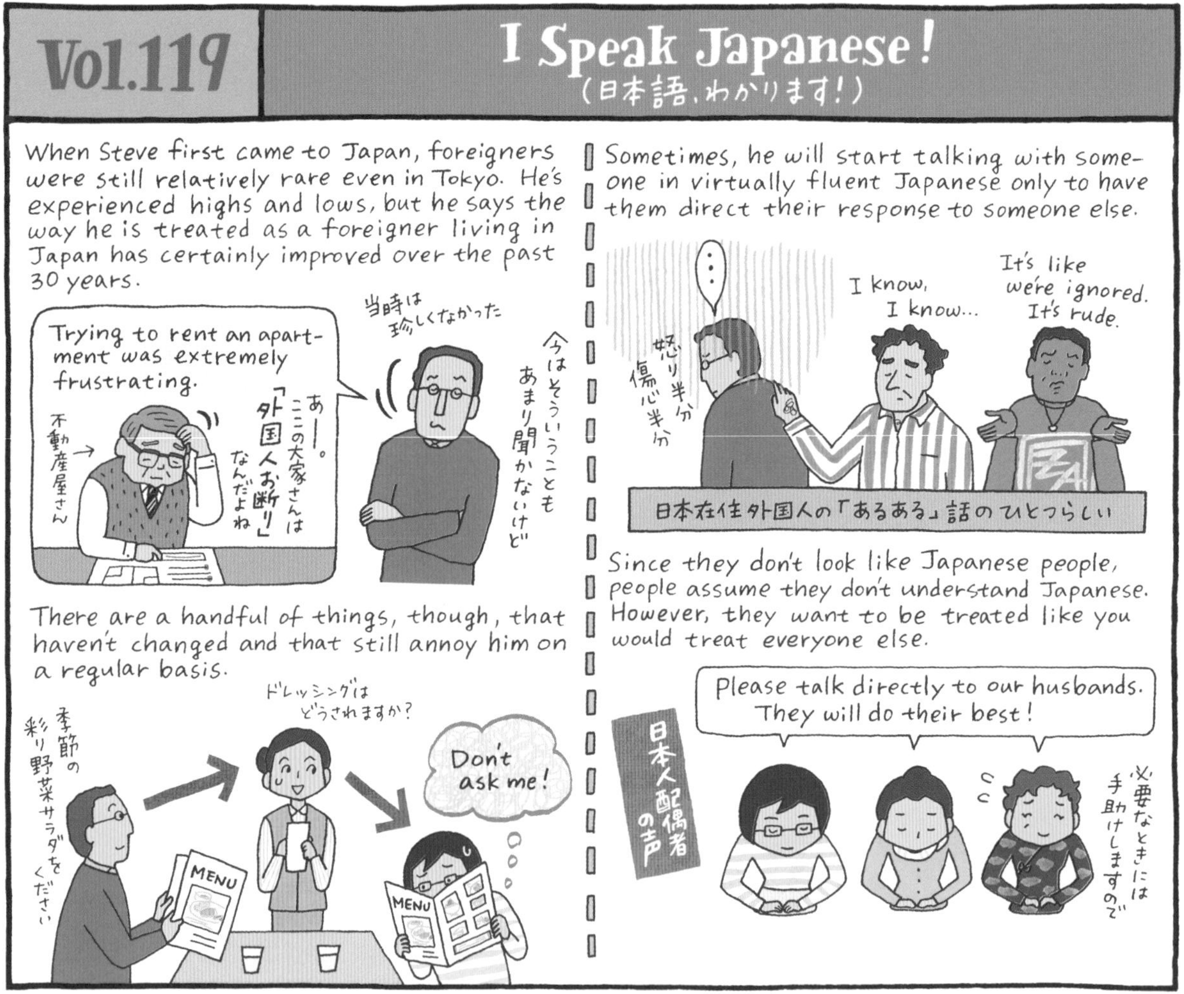

Vol.119
I Speak Japanese!
(日本語、わかります!)
When Steve first came to Japan, foreigners were still relatively rare even in Tokyo. He's experienced highs and lows, but he says the way he is treated as a foreigner living in Japan has certainly improved over the past 30 years.
Trying to rent an apartment was extremely frustrating.
不動産屋さん
あー。ここの大家さんは「外国人お断り」なんだよね
当時は珍しくなかった
今はそういうこともあまり聞かないけど
There are a handful of things, though, that haven't changed and that still annoy him on a regular basis.
季節の彩り野菜サラダをください
ドレッシングはどうされますか?
Don't ask me!
Sometimes, he will start talking with someone in virtually fluent Japanese only to have them direct their response to someone else.
怒り半分傷心半分
I know. I know...
It's like we're ignored. It's rude.
日本在住外国人の「あるある」話のひとつらしい
Since they don't look like Japanese people, people assume they don't understand Japanese. However, they want to be treated like you would treat everyone else.
日本人配偶者の声
Please talk directly to our husbands. They will do their best!
必要なときには手助けしますので

Vol.120
Is Common Sense Always Reasonable? (常識? 理不尽?)
Midori started ballet lessons two years ago when she was 5 years old. She has since improved quite a bit and is really starting to look like a ballerina.
かわいい うれしい
ピンク〜 ひらひら♡
5 years old
Now
人前で踊るのは緊張するけど楽しい♡
For Steve and me, our first foray into the ballet world was full of surprises, especially when it came to the recitals.
わ—…
うっかりすごいものに手を出しちゃったな!
例1 They're expensive.
にわか黒子に
例2 Parents must help put them on.
The biggest surprise was that we could not take Midori's picture when she performed. We were supposed to buy pictures from a hired photographer. No less surprising was the fact that most of the other parents thought this was perfectly normal.
Shouldn't professional photographers make us want to buy their photos with the strength of their skills? It doesn't seem right to tell us we can't take pictures of our own child.
プロの公演じゃないんだし
I once saw some photos of a friend's recital in the U.S.
客席にカメラやスマホがいっぱい!
What!? It's OK for parents to take pictures?
Americans have little tolerance for things they think are unreasonable. I think parents would complain strongly if they couldn't take pictures at a recital.
友人C
プロのカメラマンも入ってたけど購入は希望者のみだったよ
Sometimes, common sense is not common. What do you think?

ミドリがバレエを習い始めて2年。子どもも親も慣れてきましたが、スティーヴにはどうしても納得できないことがあります。

**common sense** 常識，共通感覚

**reasonable** 合理的な，筋の通った

**ballet** バレエ

**quite a bit** 相当に，かなり

**foray into** 〔新しい分野など〕への進出

**recital** 〔ピアノ・バレエ・ダンスなどの〕発表会

**no less** それでもなお，やはり

**have little tolerance for** 〜はとうてい我慢できない

**unreasonable** 理不尽な，不合理な

**complain** 不満を言う，訴え出る

きちんと自分の意見を述べられるように教育されているアメリカの子どもたち。どんなふうに鍛えられているかというと――

presentation skills　プレゼンテーション技能
encouraged to　～することが推奨される
debate　討論会，ディベート
pro and con　賛成と反対の
issue　論点
foster　発展させる，育成する
biography　伝記，経歴
Henry Ford　ヘンリー・フォード《自動車王として知られるアメリカの企業家。1863–1947》
presentation material　プレゼン資料
drive　傾向，動き

# Vol.121 Presentation Skills
## (鍛えられるプレゼンの力)

It's well known that American school kids are encouraged to express their opinions. Did you know they are also given plenty of opportunities to practice how they express themselves? One way is class debates. Students take pro and con sides on an issue.

**Issue** Should art and music be part of the school curriculum?

They foster imagination and expression.
Emotional development is also important.
They're not practical like the other subjects.
必要ない！
必要！
中学・高校生くらい
That means less time for more important subjects.
Pro VS Con


(個人の意見に関係なくどちらかに振り分けられ，そのグループに適した意見を出さなくてはいけない場合も)

Students begin developing their debating skills by building their speaking abilities in lower grades. Haru's native-English class recently did presentations for their classmates and then for parents and visitors. The students read biographies and organized their own presentations. Haru's presentation was about Henry Ford, the first person to mass-produce automobiles.

**STEP**
1. Research
2. Prepare report
3. Decide how to present the information
4. Present report

point 1 Make it interesting
point 2 Make your own presentation materials

Hi, I'm Benjamin Frank-lin.
米国に住むおいがプレゼンしたときは仮装したそう
↑ よくあること

うわあ
こんな小さいうちからプレゼン力を培わされてるのか。こりゃ差がつくわ


Japan's drive to be more international includes learning English from a young age.
I think that's a great idea.
But it might also be important to practice presentation skills in English or Japanese.

# Vol.122 Languages on Clothes
## （英字プリントにご用心）

Kids grow out of clothes so fast. Or they wear them out.
My shirt's too short.
I got a hole in the knee.
気に入ってたのに…
えー
この間買ったばっかりなのに
Because the clothes don't last long, we look for low-cost options. This leads to a problem for bilingual families —— the English words on kids' clothing.
BABY 西●屋 KIDS
ファッションセンター
し●むら
ENCHANTED REALM OF FAIRIES
HAPPY KISS
Happy Tomorrow For You
KIDS' CATALOGUE
ひらひらやキラキラ大好き
Before we buy shirts with words printed on them, Steve checks each one.
No way.
It's just a bunch of words.
It doesn't mean anything.
FINE SHAPER
GOODMAKE STAY UP
どっ？コレ
I see the words as simply part of the design, but Steve and the kids spontaneously read them. And they react immediately if the meaning is odd.
以前、海外で間違った漢字のタトゥーを見たときの違和感と同じなのかも
ブッ
あれきっと「永遠」のつもりだよね…。気の毒
氷遠
Despite wanting to save money, we ultimately end up buying a fair amount of clothes at multi-national chain stores.
JUST DO IT!
英字プリントがちゃんとしていて安心です


子どもたちはすぐに大きくなったり着古したりしてしまうので、服は低価格のものを探します。そこで問題になるのが、服の英字表記です。

**grow out of** ～を着ることができなくなる

**wear out** 〔衣類・靴などを〕着古す

**bunch of words** 言葉の寄せ集め

**spontaneously** 無意識のうちに，自然と

**immediately** すぐに，すかさず

**ultimately** 最終的に

**despite** ～にもかかわらず

**fair amount of** 〔量・金額・程度などが〕かなりの

**multinational** 多国籍（企業）の

COLUMN
5

## Color Me In

Kikue and the kids always give me thoughtful gifts on Father's Day. However, my favorite gift is for them to indulge me by listening to a story from my past. This is a family favorite.

I was a typical self-conscious teenager who was constantly insecure about my place in my group of school friends. I felt I had to be similar to them to be accepted.

My stepfather was a women's stocking salesman. He occasionally would bring home a boxful of brightly colored samples for my brother and I to wear if we wanted to. But no two socks were alike. We matched them as best we could so people wouldn't easily notice that they were different. To cover my secret, I only wore them with long pants, never short pants.

But I was hiding an even bigger secret. My friends didn't know that every day before school I had the chore of feeding our barnyard animals.

I had to be quick so I wouldn't get dirty. I'd slip into the chicken pen and scatter feed, dash to the goats and set out hay and grain and then, carefully not to splash, plop slop in the pig trough. On rainy days, I would tuck my jeans into rubber boots and try to stealthily deliver the food before the muddy pigs could rub against me.

Then one day at school, a friend pointed at my leg and said, "What's that?"

On my jeans was a mud-encrusted, perfectly round circle with two nostril holes. Undeniably, it was the shape of a pig's nose. This was my moment of truth.

I said, "One of the pigs must've got me."

"What!? You have pigs!"

"I feed them in the mornings," I said, "with the chickens and goats."

"Goats!! When can we come see them?"

I realized that being open and honest about yourself takes courage, but delivers peace. My friends were still my friends, and maybe even wanted to know me more. From that day onward, when I wore short pants, I was especially sure to wear my mismatched, colorful socks.

■ **color someone in**　(人)を仲間に入れる　■ **thoughtful**　心のこもった　■ **indulge**　甘やかす, 気ままにさせる　■ **self-conscious**　人目を気にする　■ **barnyard animal**　家畜　■ **pen**　囲い　■ **plop**　ポチャンと　■ **slop**　〔ブタなどのエサにする〕残飯　■ **trough**　エサ入れ　■ **mud-encrusted**　泥で覆われた　■ **nostril**　鼻孔　■ **undeniably**　まぎれもなく

STEVE
来日31年目の
江戸好きアメリカ人
KIKUE
ワタクシ
HARU
息子。
小学6年生
MIDORI
娘。
小学3年生

# 6th Year

2016

本好きが多い我が家の本棚は、ジャンルも言語もいろいろ入り混じっています。本好き同士、本談議を楽しみたいものの……

**majority** 大半，大部分
**clearly** 明らかに
**translation** 〔他の言語による〕訳文，訳本
**neither of** どちらも～でない
**trade** 〔人や物を〕交換する
**unfortunately** 残念ながら
**sophisticated** 洗練された，高尚な

# Vol.123 Book Talk (憧れの、本談義)

We're all bookworms in our family. But we each read different types of books. Even the languages are different.

KIKUE
ほとんど和書のみ
KIDS
和書 7
洋書 3
STEVE
洋書 9
和書 1
小説好き
洋書なら小説かエッセー
最近のヒットは宮下奈都さんの「羊と鋼の森」
宿題の途中で読書していて叱られることも
和書なら江戸や民俗学についての本が好き
Homework


Steve and I sometimes read books in other languages, but the majority are clearly in our native language. The kids, however, easily switch between Japanese and English.

同感
他言語本だと勉強モードになっちゃって楽しめない…


Reading translations is one way we could read the same books. But for different reasons, neither of us likes to.

翻訳ものって文章がちょっとカタイ感じがしたりしてのめり込みにくい
This could've been translated better.
職業病


Trading and talking about books you like is one of the pleasures of reading and also leads to discoveries of new books. Unfortunately, it's rare when Steve and I can do this. However, Haru is starting to read more-sophisticated books. We're looking forward to adding more book talk to our dinner conversations.

Haru's Choice
江戸川乱歩や星新一を愛読
和書
星新一
WARRIORS
洋書
"Warriors" by Erin Hunter
全米で100万部突破を誇るファンタジー小説シリーズ

# Vol.124 How to Make a Speech

## (英語のロジック)

Our kids' school recently held an English-language speech contest. As I listened to fifth to eleventh graders give their presentations, I began to wonder:
5年生だったハルはヘンリー・フォードの生涯についてプレゼンしました
What makes a good presentation?
Content?
Pronunciation?
Language skill?
それもあるけど…
Sure, all of those. But the logical progression is key.
In English, a good speech or presentation basically leads the listeners through a logical progression to a new idea. To help the listeners, start by telling them the conclusion, so they know exactly where you are taking them. Then guide them step-by-step through examples and ideas that progress toward the conclusion.
English logical progression
Conclusion
STEP ①
こっち こっち
A
B
Point of View
STEP ②
Conclusion
うまく組み立てないと納得させられない
具体例など
導入
B
A
The basic technique is to create a logical progression from A to point B, then C to D and onward until you reach the conclusion.
ね？
日本語は「同調」を促すために外堀を埋める感じ
結論
A
The TED Talks website has some great presentations.
優良講演動画が無料でたくさん見られます。(日本語字幕つきのものも)
TED
www.ted.com
Ken Robinson's "Do schools kill creativity?" is very popular.


先日、子どもたちの学校で英語スピーチコンテストが行われました。生徒たちの発表を聞きながら私は疑問を持ち始めました。それは――

**begin to wonder** 疑問に思い始める

**content** 内容, 項目

**logical progression** 論理的進行

**basically** 基本的に, 大筋で

**conclusion** 結論, 結果

**exactly** 正確に, ちょうど

**step-by-step** 1段ずつ, 着実に

**progress toward** ～の方向で進む, ～へ向けた進展

**onward** 前方へ, 前進する

外で過ごすとき、スティーヴはいつも帽子とサングラスを持参します。本当に必要なのか少々疑わしく思っていましたが……

**sun's glare** まぶしい太陽光
**bright** 〔強い光で〕輝く, まぶしい
**suspicious** 不審な, 怪しい
**it's pretty common to** ～するのが割と一般的だ
**protection** 保護するもの, 防護物
**to be honest** 正直[率直]に言うと
**sensitive** 敏感な, よく反応する
**pupil** 瞳, 瞳孔
**apply** 塗る, つける
**meant to** ～するように意図されている
**cut down on** ～を減らす

# Vol.125 Battling the Sun's Glare
## (日差し対策)

When we're going to spend some time outside, Steve always brings a cap and sunglasses.

① Cap
It's just too bright without these.
SF
② Sunglasses


A baseball cap and dark glasses can make him look a bit suspicious sometimes. It's pretty common to see people wearing so much protection from the sun in the United States. But, to be honest, I wonder how necessary it really is.

こんな小さな子も
Do you really need it?
Isn't it just a fashion thing?


One thing I have noticed, though, is that our kids seem to be a little more sensitive to bright sunlight than other kids in Japan.

まぶしくて目が開いていないハルとミドリ


I did a web search and found out that lighter-colored pupils let in more light. Blue and green eyes are more sensitive to glare than brown eyes.

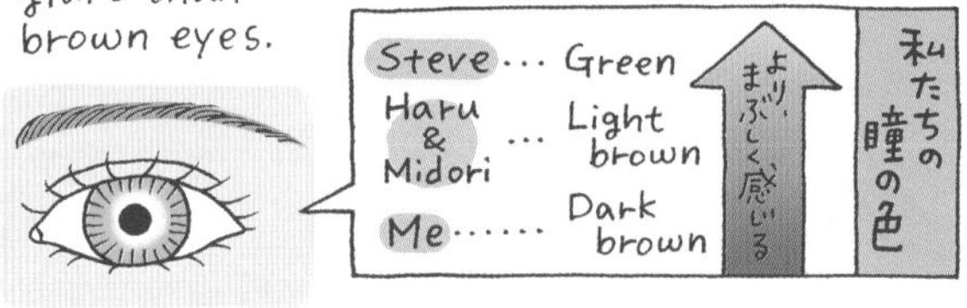

私たちの瞳の色
Steve … Green
Haru & Midori … Light brown
Me …… Dark brown
より、まぶしく感じる


I also recently learned that the eye black that Major League baseball players apply under their eyes is meant to cut down on glare.

威嚇用メイクかと思ってた人
コレ
WIL 55


I see the world differently now.

# Vol.126 Mailboxes
## (郵便配達)

In the United States, mailboxes are used not just to receive mail, but to send it too.
It's so nice not to have to bring it all the way to a collection box.
いつも最寄り駅のポストまで使いっ走りさせられてる人
How to mail a letter from a home mailbox
1 Put letter in mailbox
2 Put up the flag to show there's a letter to pick up
3 Mail carrier picks up the mail
The United States has strict laws about home mailboxes. It's against the law for anyone other than the homeowner and the mail carrier to open a mailbox.
POST
こういうのはダメ！
昔は給料の支払小切手なども郵送だったため、ポストに触る他人は盗人を疑われた
You might be wondering, "How are newspapers delivered?"
こんなふうに
I would throw it from the sidewalk and try to make it land on the doorstep.
雨の日はビニール袋に入れてある
乗ったままどんどん投げ込んでいく
この辺りを目指して投げ込む
（ドアの近くであればOK）
Sometimes I would miss and hit the door with a BAM. That was bad because I might not get a tip when I collected subscription payments.
小6のときと高校生のときに少しやっていた
Newspapers delivered near the front door and mailing from your own mailbox — the system certainly offers some conveniences.


アメリカでは、郵便受けは郵便物を受け取るだけでなく送るのにも使われます。そして、郵便受けについての厳しい法律があります。

- **all the way to** はるばる～まで
- **collection box** 回収箱
- **put up a flag** 旗を掲げる
- **mail carrier** 郵便配達員
- **anyone other than** ～以外の人
- **sidewalk** 〔舗装された〕歩道
- **land on** ～に着地する
- **doorstep** 玄関前の階段
- **bam** バン，ガン，ドスン（という音）
- **subscription payment** 予約購読料
- **offer convenience** 利便性を提供する

日本の国際結婚家族の比率は以前より上がりましたが、互いに知り合うにはちょっとした工夫が必要です。

marriage　結婚
congregate　集まる，集合する
take some effort to　～するにはある程度の努力が必要になる
seek out　～を捜し出す
as is often the case　よくあることだが
hail from　～の出身である
all corners of the globe　地球［世界］の至るところ
hit it off　仲よくなる，意気投合する
in touch with　～と連絡を取って
reach out to　～と接触する
treasure someone's friendship　（人）の友情を大切にする

# Vol.127 Relationships with Other International Families I（国際結婚家族のつながり①）

They say that 1 in 30 marriages in Japan are international couples. On the school level, that would mean one student in every classroom also has non-Japanese roots.

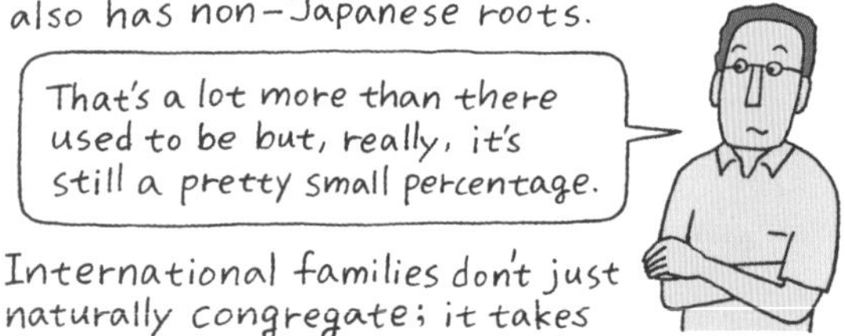
That's a lot more than there used to be but, really, it's still a pretty small percentage.

International families don't just naturally congregate; it takes some effort to seek each other out. Seven years ago, we joined a picnic organized by people connected via social media.

Hi!
Hi! I'm Steve.
はじめまして〜
3か月と3歳だったミドリとハル

As is often the case, most of the non-Japanese people were the husbands. They hailed from all corners of the globe.

イギリス人
スペイン人
アイルランド人
オーストラリア人
会話は英語か日本語

We met about 20 families that day. Of course, we didn't automatically hit it off with everyone. Now, we're in regular touch with just three of the families. We all get together about four times a year.

| | | | |
|---|---|---|---|
| Picnic | 春 | 夏 | BBQ |
| Christmas Party | 冬 | 秋 | Halloween Party |

うちはコレ
持ち回りで担当。

One of the reasons we reached out to other international families was for the kids to have a chance to use English outside our family. The kids have grown closer over the years and they're kind of like our local relatives now.

また背が伸びたじゃーん
いてーよ
Hey! Let's play baseball!
Yeah!
会話は英語になったり、日本語になったり

We adults have formed strong bonds too. So much so that the relationships are actually really important to us now, and we treasure our friendship. More on that next time.

# Vol.128 Relationships with Other International Families II（国際結婚家族のつながり②）

The number of kids in our group of international families has doubled from 5 to 10, and they are participating in various outside activities and developing their own social lives. In fact, there are so many activities that it has become a challenge to find times for the families to get together.

今どきの小学生って忙しいよね
野球やサッカーをやってると、土・日・祝は試合や練習
他にも習いごとがあったり


So we parents have taken a new course of action. We've started getting together separately for dinner and drinks on Mom's Night Out and Dad's Night Out. Can you guess what we talk about the most on Mom's Night Out? Yep, the kids.

最近また子どもたちが日本語ばかりで心配
航空券、高い！里帰り、大変！
3人で35万！
だよね
12歳になったら大人料金だしね


But there is another topic that has risen to prominence. And that is peer pressure. Not on the kids, but on us mothers.

**Peer Pressure** ※日本語では「同調圧力」

「こうあるべき」という無言の圧力。
空気を読んで同調することが全体のため、という風潮

空気読むの苦手～
わかるー
私も苦手
子どもでも関係のグループとかであるよね


For international families, highlighting the advantages of being different and of being proud of who you are are fundamental to fostering a positive self-image. Dealing with peer pressure can create a lot of stress. Mom's Night Out is a great opportunity to share our experiences and insights—and relieve stress.

I wonder what the fathers talk about on their night out.

子どもの習いごとなどで、全員揃うのが難しくなってきた国際結婚家族の集い。ならば、と「ママ会」をすることに──

**double** 倍にする，倍増させる

**outside activities** 外部での活動，課外［社外］活動

**social life** 社会生活

**night out** 外出して楽しく遊ぶ夜

**guess** 推測する，言い当てる

**rise to prominence** 有名になる，注目されるようになる

**highlight** 強調する，目立たせる

**fundamental to** ～にとって重要である

**deal with** 対応する，対処する

他の国際結婚家族とのつながりから生まれた「パパ会」。彼らはどんなことを話しているのでしょうか。

**occasionally** ときどき，たまに
**have in common** 共通点がある
**nothing in particular** 特にない
**filter** フィルターをかける，選別する
**liberating** 解放感のある
**likely to** ～しそうである
**wordplay** しゃれ，言葉の軽妙なやりとり
**initial** 初めの，当初の
**circumstance** 事情，状況，境遇
**turn out** 結局～になる
**lasting** 長続きする，持続的な

# Vol.129 Relationships with Other International Families III （国際結婚家族のつながり③）

We've started meeting occasionally with the other international families without the main thing that brought us together — the kids. We now have Mom's Night Out and Dad's Night Out.

Cheers!
Dave (30代) 剣道と歴史マンガ、そしてスターウォーズにハマっているアメリカ人
David (30代) 車とサッカーに夢中なイギリス人
Steve (50代) 日本民俗学、野球、健康好きのアメリカ人
Frankie (40代) 本好き＆創作好きアイルランド人


The fathers are different ages and nationalities, and have various interests. The one thing they have in common is that English is their native language. With such different backgrounds, what do they talk about? That's a good question.

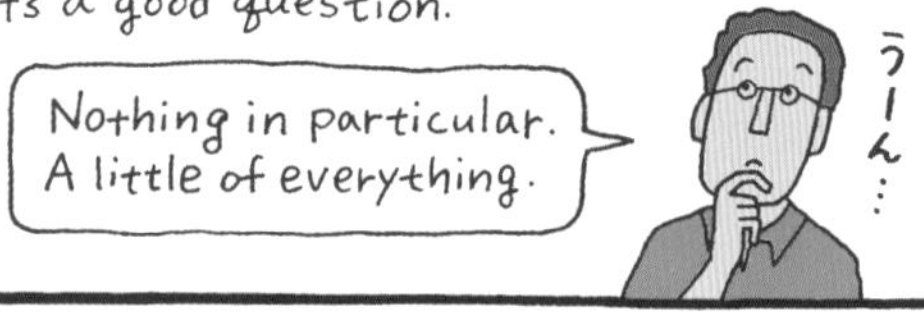

Nothing in particular. A little of everything.
うーん…


They don't have a particular topic they want to discuss.

The best part of getting together with the guys is that we can talk freely. We can say what we think without filtering our words. It's liberating.
ものすごい解放感!!


When they speak English to their wives or other non-native speakers, they have a helpful habit of using words the listener would be likely to understand. When they talk to each other, however, they can let fly with jokes, slang, and wordplay.

スラングもOK!
シニカルなジョークも通じる!
地方出身者が郷里の方言に触れて、心が開いたり言葉がするする出てくるのと似てるかも?


Our initial motivation for contacting other international families was so our kids could meet other kids in similar circumstances. It turns out that we parents are forming lasting relationships too.

# Vol.130 The Vegetarian Lifestyle I
## (ベジタリアン生活①)

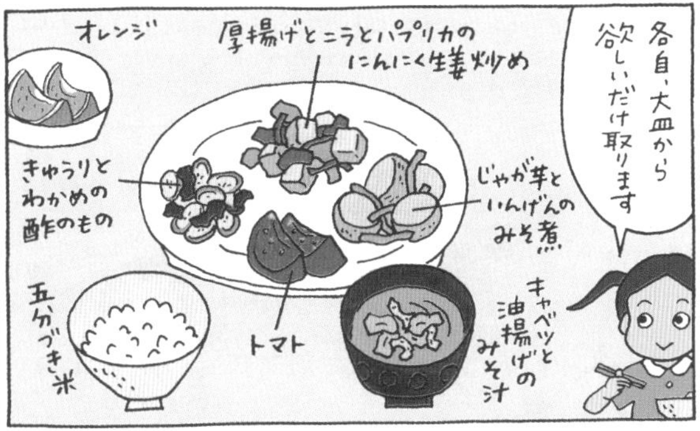

オレンジ
厚揚げとニラとパプリカのにんにく生姜炒め
各自、大皿から欲しいだけ取ります
きゅうりとわかめの酢のもの
じゃが芋といんげんのみそ煮
五分づき米
トマト
キャベツと油揚げのみそ汁


This is an example of what we might have for dinner. It's about 90% Japanese-style food. But it's still a little different than usual. Can you guess what's different?

実は…
Our meals do not have any meat or fish.
We follow a mostly vegetarian diet.


Nowadays, there are different levels of vegetarians.

| | meat | fish | eggs | dairy products (milk, cheese, etc.) |
|---|---|---|---|---|
| Semi-vegetarian | △ | ○ | ○ | ○ |
| Pescatarian | × | ○ | × | × |
| Lacto-ovo vegetarian | × | × | ○ | ○ |
| Lacto vegetarian | × | × | × | ○ |
| Vegan | × | × | × | × |

(※and many more categories)

In our case we aim to be vegan inside our home but have some fish products. When we eat out, we take a semi-vegetarian approach.

家ごはんは極力ヴィーガンで
毎日のお弁当には魚が入ることも
外食時は何でもOK!
うなぎ


Next time, we'll talk about the reasons for being vegetarian and how it affects our lifestyle.

我が家の食事は和食が約9割です。でも、肉や魚がほぼない、ベジタリアンな食生活を送っています。

- **follow** 従う, 守る
- **vegetarian diet** 菜食
- **nowadays** 最近は, 今日では
- **dairy product** 乳製品
- **semi-vegetarian** セミ・ベジタリアン, 半菜食主義者
- **pescatarian** ペスクタリアン, 魚菜食主義者
- **lacto-ovo vegetarian** ラクト・オボ・ベジタリアン, 乳卵菜食主義者
- **lacto vegetarian** ラクト・ベジタリアン, 乳菜食主義者
- **vegan** ヴィーガン, 完全菜食主義者
- **aim to** ～を目指す, 心がける
- **affect** 作用する

ベジタリアンになる動機も目指すレベルも人それぞれ。我が家の場合は――

animal product 動物性食品，畜産物

plant-based diet 野菜中心の食事

eat out 外食する

numerous 数多くの

compassion for ～への思いやり，深い同情

vary 変わる，多様にする

settle on 〔～という考え〕に落ち着く

current 現在の

good decision 英断

constipation 便秘

stay on the ~ path ～の道を歩み続ける

let someone in on 〔秘密などを〕（人）に打ち明ける

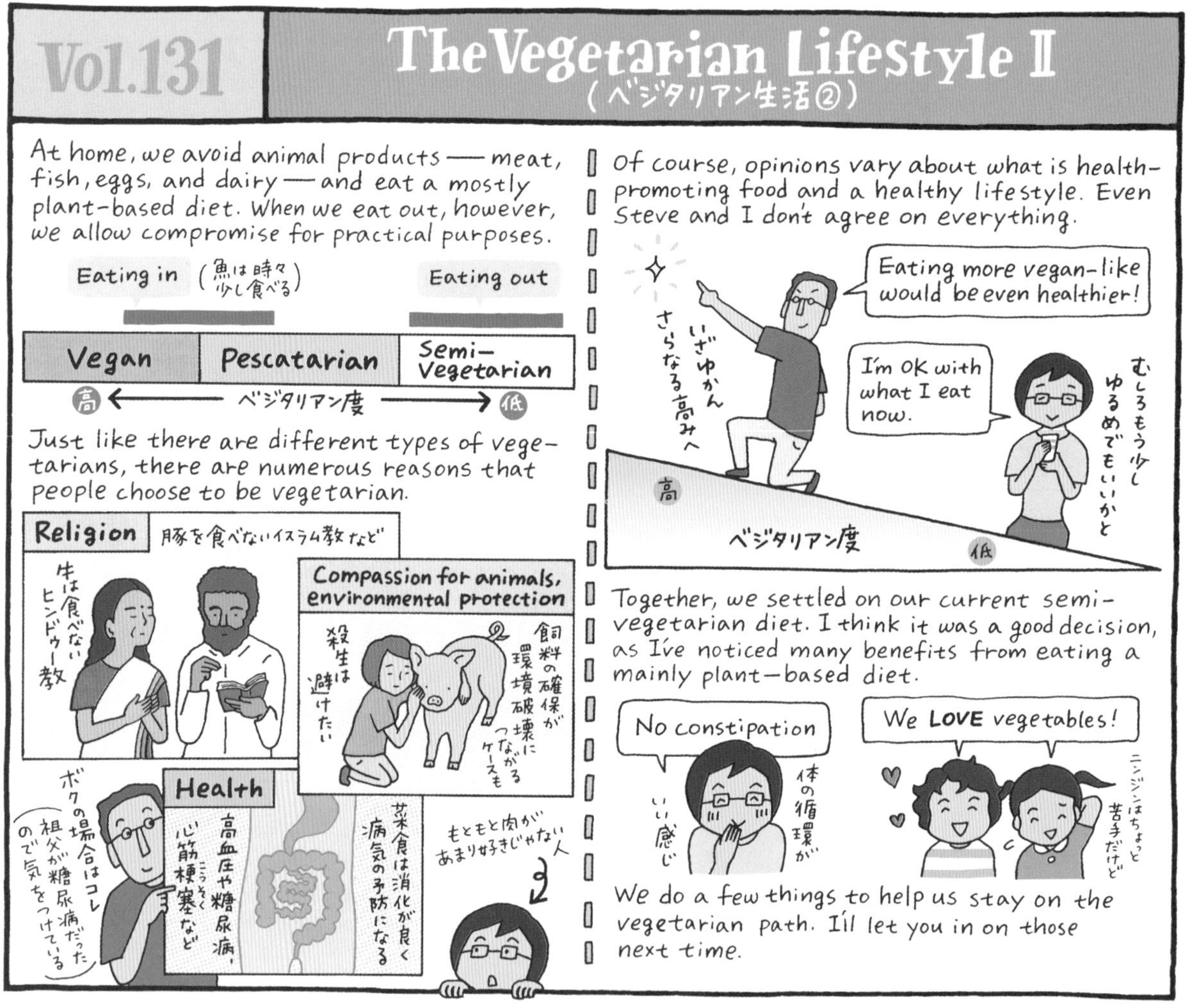

Vol.131
The Vegetarian Lifestyle II
（ベジタリアン生活②）
At home, we avoid animal products — meat, fish, eggs, and dairy — and eat a mostly plant-based diet. When we eat out, however, we allow compromise for practical purposes.
Eating in
（魚は時々少し食べる）
Eating out
Vegan
Pescatarian
Semi-Vegetarian
高 ← ベジタリアン度 → 低
Just like there are different types of vegetarians, there are numerous reasons that people choose to be vegetarian.
Religion
豚を食べないイスラム教など
牛は食べないヒンドゥー教
Compassion for animals, environmental protection
殺生は避けたい
飼料の確保が環境破壊につながるケースも
Health
ボクの場合はコレ
祖父が糖尿病だったので気をつけている
高血圧や糖尿病，心筋梗塞（こうそく）など
菜食は消化が良く病気の予防になる
もともと肉があまり好きじゃない人
Of course, opinions vary about what is health-promoting food and a healthy lifestyle. Even Steve and I don't agree on everything.
Eating more vegan-like would be even healthier!
いざゆかんさらなる高みへ
I'm OK with what I eat now.
むしろもう少しゆるめでもいいかと
高
ベジタリアン度
低
Together, we settled on our current semi-vegetarian diet. I think it was a good decision, as I've noticed many benefits from eating a mainly plant-based diet.
No constipation
いい感じ
体の循環が
We LOVE vegetables!
ニンジンはちょっと苦手だけど
We do a few things to help us stay on the vegetarian path. I'll let you in on those next time.

# Vol.132 The Vegetarian Lifestyle Ⅲ
## （ベジタリアン生活③）

長らくベジタリアン生活を続けている私たち。具体的にどんなふうにしているかというと──

The main reason that we continue following the vegetarian lifestyle is nutrition. Instead of meat and fish, we get a balance of protein and vitamins from plants. We choose plants that provide plentiful plant protein and vitamins, with a special focus on vitamin B12 (which is not widely found in the plant world).

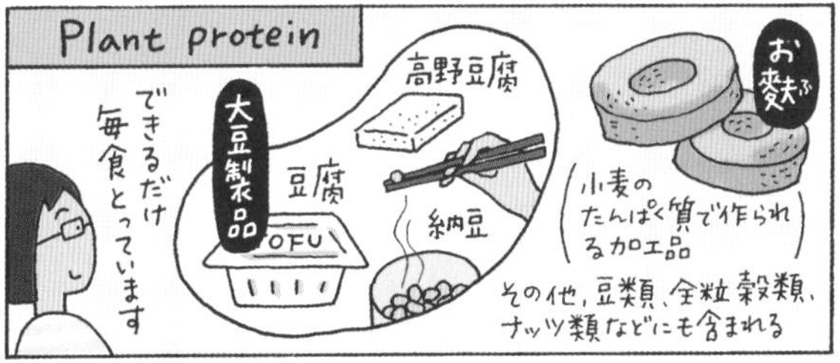

Plant protein
できるだけ毎食とっています
大豆製品
高野豆腐
豆腐
TOFU
納豆
お麩
小麦のたんぱく質で作られる加工品
その他、豆類、全粒穀類、ナッツ類などにも含まれる

Vitamin B12
海苔
茶葉
限られた食品にしか入っていないのでサプリメントを使うことも


When people learn we are vegetarians, they often will take pains to try to accommodate our food preferences. So we don't burden anyone, we take an approach of being grateful for any meal.

わー
「食は楽しくが大事だしね
meat


When we bring food or dishes to a barbecue or potluck, we always bring a vegetarian dish. Most people enjoy trying a new type of food. Although I really only make pretty simple dishes, people often think I'm a good cook.

Hit food #1
Tofu-based shortcake
うちの誕生日ケーキはコレ!
見た目は普通のショートケーキだけど、豆腐、ピーナッツバター、メイプルシロップ、レモン汁で作ったクリーム
つい食べすぎちゃう
あっさりしてて、胃もたれなし。


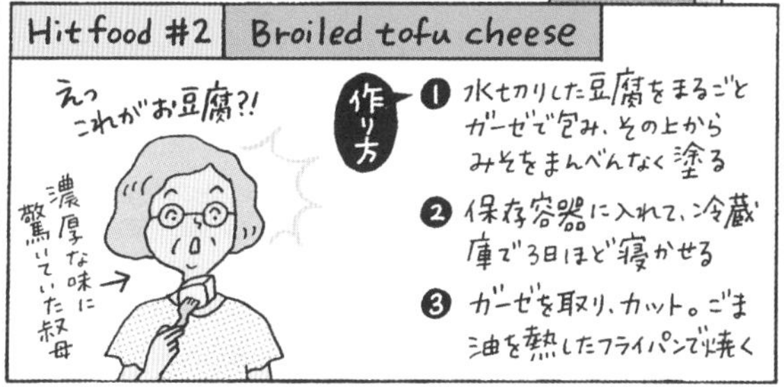

Hit food #2
Broiled tofu cheese
えっ これがお豆腐?!
濃厚な味に驚いていた叔母
作り方
❶ 水切りした豆腐をまるごとガーゼで包み、その上からみそをまんべんなく塗る
❷ 保存容器に入れて、冷蔵庫で3日ほど寝かせる
❸ ガーゼを取り、カット。ごま油を熱したフライパンで焼く


For us, being vegetarian is not a hard-and-fast rule, it's a preference. We enjoy knowing that what we eat is promoting our health.

---

**nutrition** 栄養摂取，栄養素
**protein** たんぱく質
**plentiful** ありあまるほどの，豊富な
**plant protein** 植物性たんぱく質
**take pains to** ～するのに苦労する
**accommodate** 適応させる，受け入れる
**food preference** 食べ物の嗜好
**burden** 〔人に〕面倒なことを押しつける
**broil** 〔直火で〕焼く
**hard-and-fast rule** 厳格な決まり，鉄則
**promote** 促進させる

ベジタリアンは何からたんぱく質を摂るのか──大豆にはたんぱく質がたっぷり含まれていて、見渡せばたくさんの大豆製品があります。

- **soybean** 大豆
- **packed with** ～でいっぱいである
- **staple** 必需品，特産品
- **seek and ye shall find** 尋ねよ、さらば見出さん
- **substitute** 代用品，代替
- **accommodating** 融通の利く，寛容な
- **leave off** ～を除く
- **catch on** 人気を博する，受ける
- **abundant** たくさんある，富んだ
- **another option** 〔主語〕という選択肢もある

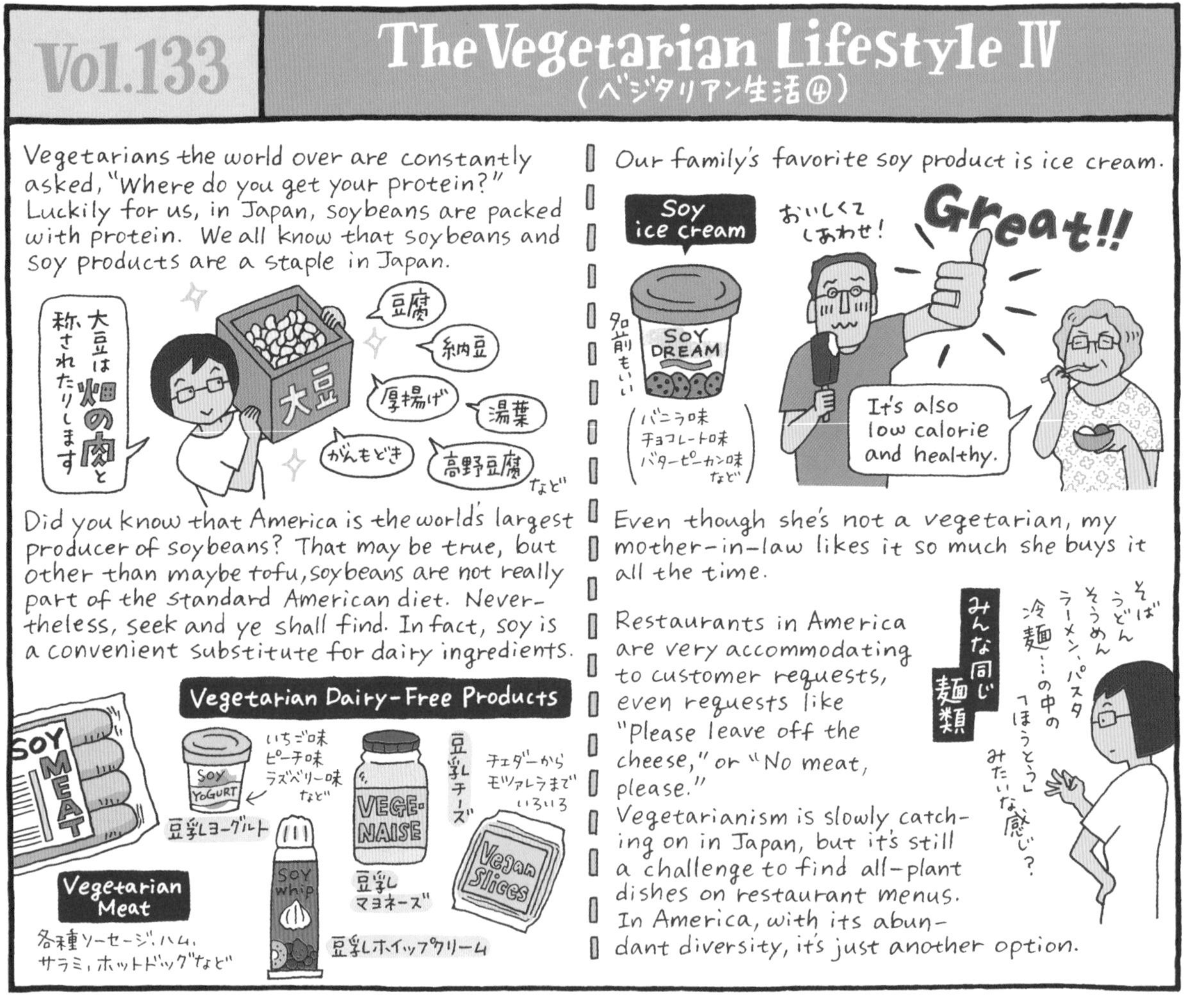

Vol.133
The Vegetarian Lifestyle IV
(ベジタリアン生活④)
Vegetarians the world over are constantly asked, "Where do you get your protein?" Luckily for us, in Japan, soybeans are packed with protein. We all know that soybeans and soy products are a staple in Japan.
大豆は畑の肉と称されたりします
大豆
豆腐
納豆
厚揚げ
湯葉
がんもどき
高野豆腐
など
Did you know that America is the world's largest producer of soybeans? That may be true, but other than maybe tofu, soybeans are not really part of the standard American diet. Nevertheless, seek and ye shall find. In fact, soy is a convenient substitute for dairy ingredients.
Vegetarian Dairy-Free Products
SOY MEAT
Vegetarian Meat
各種ソーセージ，ハム，サラミ，ホットドッグなど
SOY YOGURT
いちご味
ピーチ味
ラズベリー味
など
豆乳ヨーグルト
SOY whip
豆乳ホイップクリーム
VEGE-NAISE
豆乳マヨネーズ
豆乳チーズ
チェダーからモツァレラまでいろいろ
Vegan Slices
Our family's favorite soy product is ice cream.
Soy ice cream
SOY DREAM
名前もいい
バニラ味
チョコレート味
バターピーカン味
など
おいしくてしあわせ！
Great!!
It's also low calorie and healthy.
Even though she's not a vegetarian, my mother-in-law likes it so much she buys it all the time.
Restaurants in America are very accommodating to customer requests, even requests like "Please leave off the cheese," or "No meat, please."
Vegetarianism is slowly catching on in Japan, but it's still a challenge to find all-plant dishes on restaurant menus.
In America, with its abundant diversity, it's just another option.
みんな同じ麺類
そば
うどん
そうめん
ラーメン、パスタ
冷麺…の中の「ほうとう」みたいな感じ？

# Vol.134 How Good Are You at Swiming?
## （「泳げる」という認識）

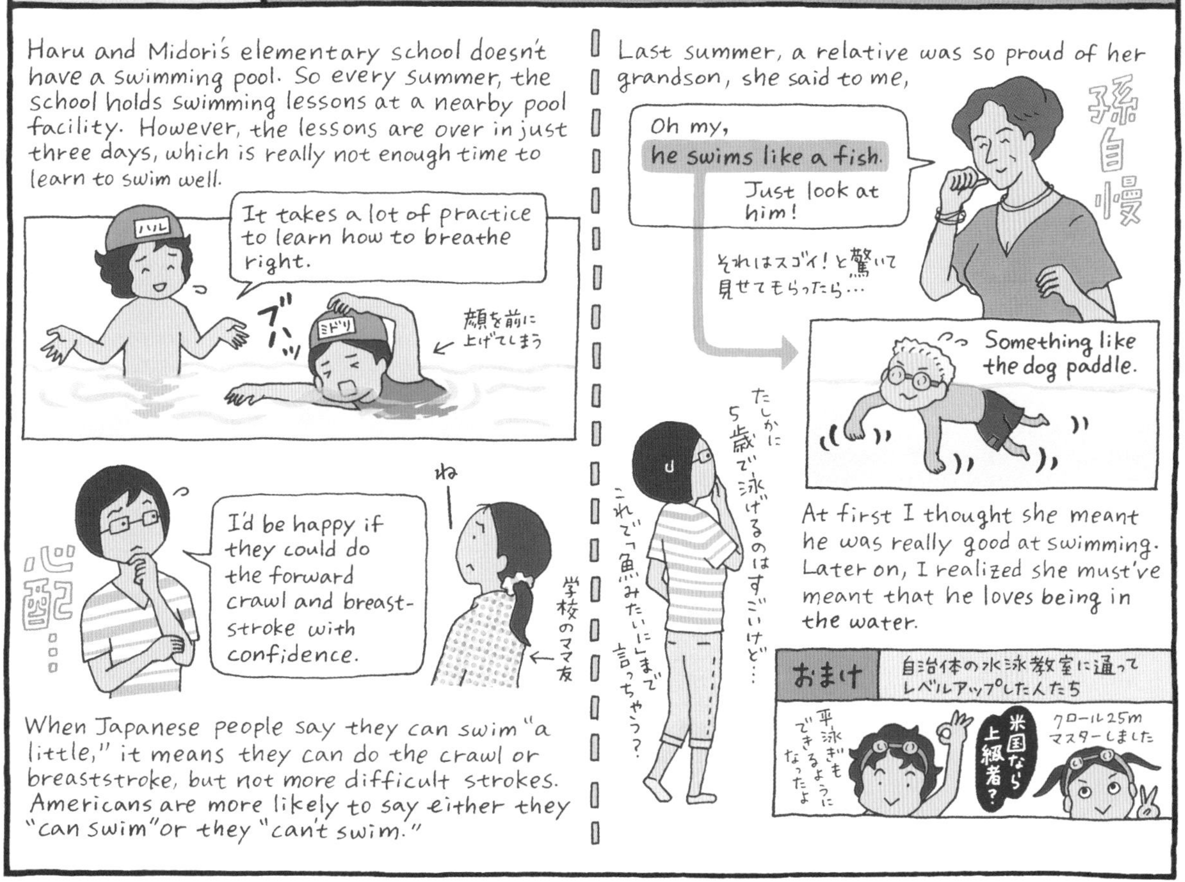

Haru and Midori's elementary school doesn't have a swimming pool. So every summer, the school holds swimming lessons at a nearby pool facility. However, the lessons are over in just three days, which is really not enough time to learn to swim well.
ハル
It takes a lot of practice to learn how to breathe right.
ミドリ
ブハッ
顔を前に上げてしまう
I'd be happy if they could do the forward crawl and breast-stroke with confidence.
心配…
ね
学校のママ友
When Japanese people say they can swim "a little," it means they can do the crawl or breaststroke, but not more difficult strokes. Americans are more likely to say either they "can swim" or they "can't swim."
Last summer, a relative was so proud of her grandson, she said to me,
Oh my, he swims like a fish. Just look at him!
孫自慢
それはスゴイ！と驚いて見せてもらったら…
Something like the dog paddle.
たしかに5歳で泳げるのはすごいけど…これで「魚みたいに」まで言っちゃう？
At first I thought she meant he was really good at swimming. Later on, I realized she must've meant that he loves being in the water.
おまけ
自治体の水泳教室に通ってレベルアップした人たち
平泳ぎもできるようになったよ
米国なら上級者？
クロール25mマスターしました


日本で「ちょっと泳げる」と言ったら、クロールや平泳ぎがまあまあできるという意味になりますが、アメリカでは――

**facility** 施設，設備

**breathe** 呼吸する，息をする

**forward crawl** クロール

**breast stroke** 平泳ぎ

**with confidence** 自信をもって

**a little** 少し，ちょっと

**either A or B** AかそれともB

**dog paddle** 犬かき

**later on** あとで

**must've** ～に違いない（＝must have）

人種によっても異なる髪質。それぞれに合った理髪店や美容院を利用する必要があるようです。

fine hair　繊細な毛

compared with　～と比べると

hair follicle　毛包

as you can imagine　あなたのご想像通り

angst　不安，懸念

uneven　平らでない，でこぼこの

charged extra　別料金を請求される

overdo　やり過ぎる，度を超す

cater to　～に対応する

for a decade　10年間（にわたって）

American military base　米軍基地

Vol.135
Hair and Hairstyling
（髪と美容院）
Haru and Midori have different types of hair.
Wavy
Brown
くりくり
まっすぐ
Straight
Brown
Wavy
Brown
Brown
Straight
Wavy
Brown
Straight
Black
They both have fine hair like their father.
Most people of European descent have hair that is fine and soft compared with Japanese hair. The hair follicles can even be half as thick as Japanese hair. As you can imagine, the barbershops and hair salons in the United States and Japan use different techniques. This has caused some angst among our Japanese friends living in America.
The cut is uneven!
ガタガタ!
I was charged extra for having "more hair than usual."
ふつうだもん
They way overdid it!
ゆるめにって言ったのに～
Naturally, the hair salons in America are designed for their most common customers. My friends said they have had to find salons that cater to Japanese hair.
日本人の髪を扱うときの注意点
① まっすぐなのでカットラインが際立つ
② ハリがあるのでパーマが強くかかりやすい
A friend of mine who has been in America for a decade told me:
I go to a salon in Chinatown.
Some of my friends go to salons catering to Latin Americans (who also usually have thick hair).
In Japan, we found a similar solution. We take Haru with his wavy hair to a salon near an American military base.
切ると、コイルのように丸まる
満足♡

# Vol.136 Handwriting（手書き文字）

I chose to handwrite this series rather than type it because some of my Japanese friends have told me my writing is clear and easy to read. Steve and other non-native readers, however, think my handwriting looks like it was written by a child.

Beautiful?
クセを抑えて読みやすく
活字っぽいとぎこちない感じがしちゃうんだよ
Saturday

Americans have a different concept for what makes good handwriting.
Japanese generally prefer clean lettering for everyday writing.

書店でもペン字コーナーは人気
（とくに年賀状シーズン）
きれいな字が書けるペン字
今年こそきれいな字に！

In America, the standard for everyday writing seems simply that it be "readable."

Special handwriting, like calligraphy, is reserved for occasions when nice handwriting would be appropriate.

カリグラフィー
筆記体
Happy Birthday
Enjoy your Special Day!
今の日本の草書に値する感じ？
（草書）
※昔は「筆記体＝品格を表すもの」という意識が強かったため、きれいな筆記体を書くのは年配の人が多い

These aesthetics for handwriting can be seen on chalkboards in schools.

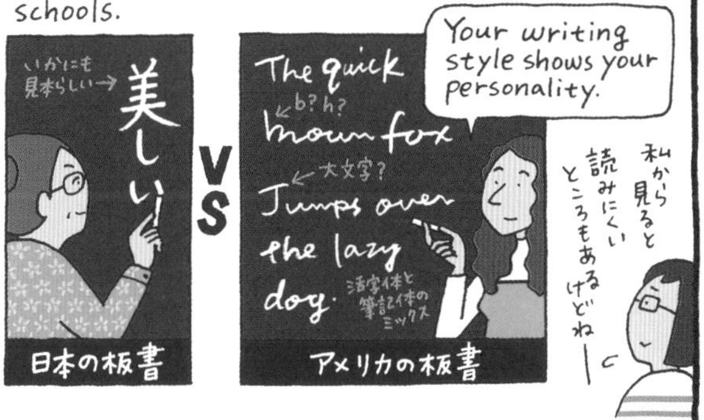
いかにも見本らしい→
美しい
VS
The quick brown fox jumps over the lazy dog.
b? h?
大文字？
活字体と筆記体のミックス
Your writing style shows your personality.
日本の板書
アメリカの板書
私から見ると読みにくいところもあるけどねー

「きれいな手書き文字」は誰もが憧れるものですが、日本とアメリカではその定義がちょっと異なるようです。

- **handwriting** 手書き，筆跡
- **type** 〔キーボードで語句などを〕タイプする
- **lettering** レタリング，文字のデザイン
- **standard** 尺度，基準
- **readable** 読める，判読できる
- **reserved for** ～向けである，～用の
- **appropriate** 適した，適切な
- **aesthetics** 美意識，美的感覚
- **chalkboard** 黒板
- **personality** 人となり，個性

日本でもハロウィンの仮装を見かけることが増えてきました。アメリカではどれくらいの人が仮装をしているのか統計を見てみました。

costume　服装，衣装
dress up for Halloween　ハロウィンの仮装をする
wonder　～を知りたいと思う
statistic　統計
witch　魔女，魔法使い
zombie　生き返った死体，ゾンビ
it's natural to　～するのは当然だ
worth every penny　価格に見合った価値がある
pirate　海賊

# Vol.137 Halloween Costumes
## （ハロウィンの仮装）

I've been seeing more and more people in Japan dressing up for Halloween and started wondering how many people actually dress up for Halloween in America. One statistic I found said that about 44% of American adults and kids dress up on Halloween.

Hmm, that's almost half of all Americans.
Kids
Adults

Popular costumes in 2015

| Kids | | Adults |
|---|---|---|
| Princess | 1 | Witch |
| Batman character | 2 | Animal (Cat, bear, gorilla, etc.) |
| Other Action Hero/Superhero | 3 | Batman character |
| Animal (Cat, dog, lion, tiger, etc.) | 4 | Zombie |
| Frozen character (Anna, Elsa, Olaf) | 5 | Star Wars character |

The statistics I saw also said Americans would spend about $28 on their costume. Some people enjoy making their costumes themselves. A friend of ours makes costumes for her son every year.

どれもこれも思い出深いわー
4歳（カボチャ）
7歳（ハチ）
8歳（孫悟空）
9歳（タコ）

It's natural to think buying a costume to wear just once is a waste of money. The first year, we thought so too, but they are worth every penny. Even after Halloween, our kids love to dress up and play as ninjas, fairies, superheros, or pirates.

友達とも

# Vol.138 Halloween Food
## （ハロウィンを盛り上げる料理）

Halloween is one of the occasions when we get together with our international family friends. Everyone dresses up and we go trick-or-treating at our neighbors' houses. Of course, everyone brings a dish for a potluck party.

British Cuisine

**Shepherd's Pie**

Meat and mashed potato pie

Irish Cuisine

**Soda Bread**

Bread made with baking soda rather than yeast

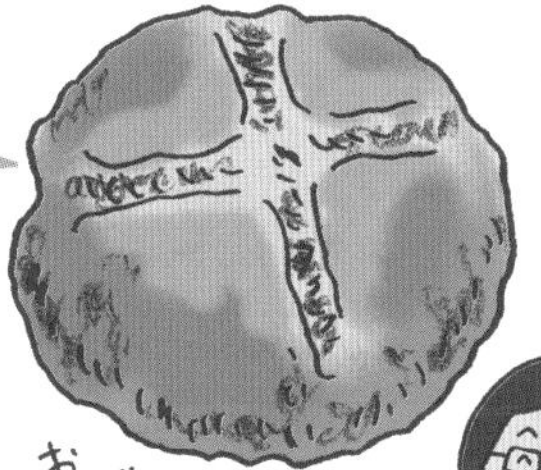

いろんな国のものがあってうれしい
普通におにぎりやサラダも用意しますが

With a little imagination, even simple dishes can be given a Halloween touch. Over the years, our friends have created some amazing dishes.

**Mashed Potato Skull**

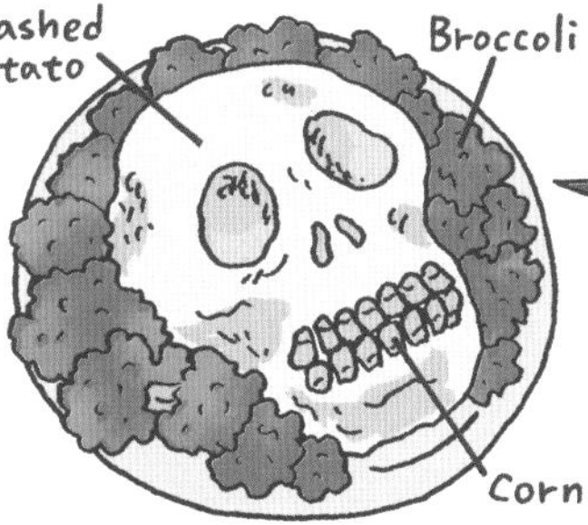
Mashed potato
Broccoli
Corn

他にも…

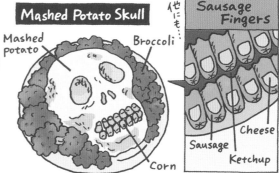

**Sausage Fingers**

Cheese
Sausage
Ketchup

**Mikan jack-o'-lantern**

油性ペンで描いただけ

ジュースパックに包帯を巻き、目玉シールを貼りつけたもの

**Zombie Juice**

We're looking forward to setting a scary table again this year.

国際結婚家族の友人たちと集まるハロウィンでの持ち寄り料理は楽しみのひとつです。様々な工夫が見られます。

- **dish** 〔皿に盛られた〕料理
- **cuisine** 〔特定の地域や店などの〕料理，食事
- **shepherd** 羊飼い
- **with a little imagination** ちょっと想像力を働かせてみれば
- **give a ~ touch** ～っぽさを与える
- **skull** 頭がい骨
- **jack-o'-lantern** ハロウィンのカボチャのちょうちん
- **scary** 恐ろしい，ゾッとするような

アメリカの義両親の家には、たくさんの収納スペースがあって羨ましくなります。でも、義父はいつも日本の床下収納に感心しきりです。

- **storage space** 収納スペース
- **storeroom** 保管室，物置
- **attic space** 屋根裏空間
- **workspace** 作業場
- **plenty** たくさんの，十分な
- **constant** 〔量・性質・温度などが〕一定な
- **cellar** 地下貯蔵室
- **basement** 〔住宅の〕地階
- **decidedly** 明らかに
- **handy** 便利な，すぐ手が届く
- **universal need** 普遍的なニーズ

# Vol.139 Storage Space
（収納スペース）

In Japan, it seems like everyone wants more storage and closet space in their homes. My in-laws' house has a closet in every room plus space in the big garage and in a storeroom under the roof.

Attic space
大人でも立てる。20畳くらいの広さ

Garage
DIYスペース
絵や写真も飾られてたり…
憧れ

A garage is not just a place to park a car; it can also provide a private workspace.

秘密基地的魅力

You would think all that storage space would be plenty. But every time my father-in-law visits us, he tells me how much he likes the storage box we have under the floor of our kitchen.

What a great idea!
I wish we had one in our house.
It's easy to get things in and out, and it stays at a constant temperature.
お酒やみそなど

While many old homes in the United States and Europe have whole cellars or basements for cool storage, the Japanese version is decidedly smaller. But its compactness and location make it very handy. It's a Japanese approach to a universal need for storage space.

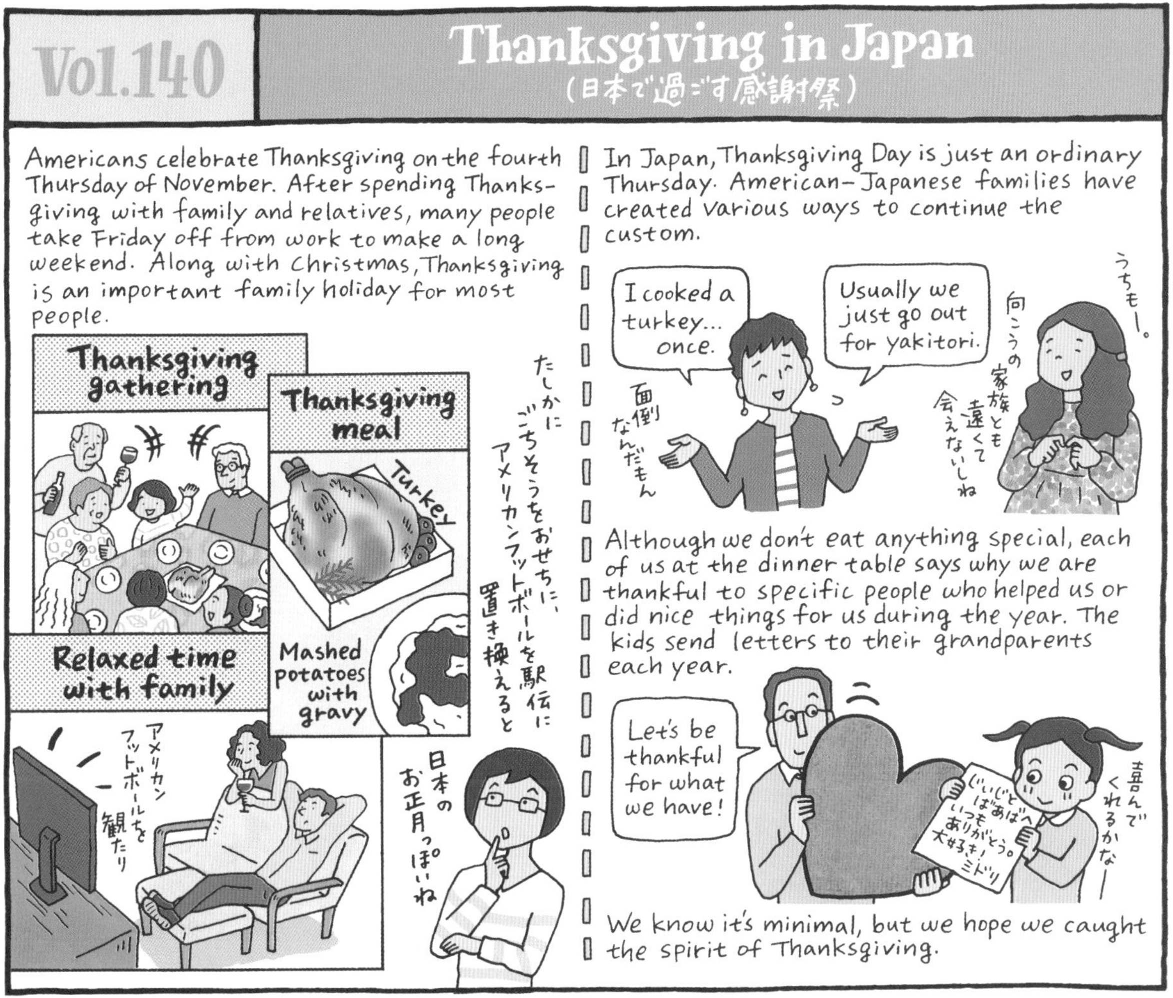
Vol.140
Thanksgiving in Japan
（日本で過ごす感謝祭）
Americans celebrate Thanksgiving on the fourth Thursday of November. After spending Thanksgiving with family and relatives, many people take Friday off from work to make a long weekend. Along with Christmas, Thanksgiving is an important family holiday for most people.
Thanksgiving gathering
Thanksgiving meal
Turkey
Mashed potatoes with gravy
Relaxed time with family
アメリカンフットボールを観たり
たしかにごちそうをおせちに、アメリカンフットボールを駅伝に置き換えると
日本のお正月っぽいね
In Japan, Thanksgiving Day is just an ordinary Thursday. American-Japanese families have created various ways to continue the custom.
I cooked a turkey... once.
面倒なんだもん
Usually we just go out for yakitori.
うちもー。
向こうの家族とも遠くて会えないしね
Although we don't eat anything special, each of us at the dinner table says why we are thankful to specific people who helped us or did nice things for us during the year. The kids send letters to their grandparents each year.
Let's be thankful for what we have!
じぃじとばぁばへ いつもありがとう。大好き！ ミドリ
喜んでくれるかなー
We know it's minimal, but we hope we caught the spirit of Thanksgiving.

アメリカでは、クリスマスに負けず劣らず大切な家族行事である感謝祭。日本にいるとごく普通の木曜日ですが――

**take a day off from work** 仕事を１日休む

**along with** ～と共に

**family holiday** 家族と一緒に過ごす休日

**gravy** グレイビー《肉汁で作ったソース》

**at the dinner table** 夕食の席で

**thankful** 感謝している，ありがたく思う

**specific** 特定の

**do nice things for** ～に親切にする

**minimal** 最小限の

**catch the spirit of** ～の気分を感じ取る

感謝祭が終わると、関心は一気にクリスマスの準備へ。まずはクリスマスまでの日を数えるアドベントカレンダーが登場します。

Advent　降臨節，待降節《クリスマスの準備をする期間》
attention　注目，関心
store-bought　店で買った，市販の
argument　口論，口げんか
craft　手作業で作ること
music box　オルゴール
tiny　とても小さい
fill up　〔穴・空席などを〕埋める
anxious　心配して，気がかりで
get going　動き出す，前進する
pretty soon　近いうちに，早急に

# Vol.141 Advent Calender
## (アドベントカレンダー)

After Thanksgiving Day, our attention quickly turns to preparing for Christmas. The first decoration that goes up is the Advent calendar. Advent calendars count down the days to Christmas. Kids love them.

**Store-bought**

ちょっとしたお菓子が入っている
MILK
12月1日から24日まで毎日ひとつずつ開ける
24
6 13
1 19 10
15 23 5 14
12 9 2 16 21
17 3 20 11 7 18
8 22 4
わくわく

Unfortunately, they can also lead to fights.

今日は私の番だよ
やだー ボクが開けるー

Some friends make a calendar for each of their children to avoid arguments. Making an Advent calendar is a fun craft project.

**Homemade**

小窓の中に小さなオモチャが
1 2 3 4
5 6 7 8
9 10 11 12
13 14 15 16
17 18 19 20
21 22 23 24
ダンボールで中を仕切って

Relatives gave us our Advent calendar. It has a music box and is shaped like a Christmas tree and has hooks for tiny ornaments. The kids put one ornament on the tree each day.

今日はコレ

As it slowly fills up, the kids get a little more excited, and I get a little more anxious.

We have to get going and put up the big tree pretty soon!!

Vol.142

# Christmas Stocking
（クリスマスの靴下）

Hanging stockings on the hearth is another Christmas tradition. On Christmas Eve, Santa fills them with small gifts when he comes down the chimney.

These are usually separate from the gifts left under the tree.

The stockings are mainly for the kids, but some families have stockings for the adults too.

HARU
MIDORI
EMILY
義母宅。孫の名前入り
Holy Night

じーん
ROSE
STEVE
KIKUE
ほー。おばあちゃんのもあるんだ
あ、私のも！


On my first Christmas at my father-in-law's after we got married, I felt I had really been accepted into the family when I saw a stocking with my name stitched on it.

Stocking Stuffers
小さいオモチャやコスメ用品、アクセサリーや実用品など、なんでもOK
UNO
Hand Care
Nail
NOTE
Pens
クリスマスのお菓子 CANDY CANE


In Steve's family, Santa and various people stuff the stockings with small gifts. On Christmas morning, we open them with our other presents.

ニヤリ
アイデア勝負！腕が鳴るね〜


Steve gets the Christmas spirit trying to think up funky and funny gifts to put in the stockings.

暖炉前に靴下を吊るすのもクリスマスの慣習のひとつです。靴下の中には小さなプレゼントが詰まっています。

**stocking** ストッキング，靴下
**hearth** 暖炉前
**accept** 認める，受け入れる
**stitch** 縫いつける，刺しゅうする
**stuff** 詰め込む，詰める
**stuffer** 入れるもの
**candy cane** 杖の形をしたキャンディ
**think up** 考え出す，思いつく
**funky** 独創的な

アメリカのスーパーには食品や日用品が数多く並んでいますが、私が最も驚かされるのは、グリーティングカード専用の通路です。

dazzling variety of　非常に種々さまざまの
aisle　〔スーパーや倉庫などの〕通路
dedicated to　～に特化した
organized in　～にしたがって整理されている
get well　〔健康状態が〕よくなる
sympathy　お悔やみ，弔慰
for a specific occasion　特定の場面用に
specialized　特化した
one-size-fits-all　汎用的な
choice　選択の範囲，品ぞろえ
clever　器用な，気の利いた

# Vol.143 Greeting Cards
## (グリーティングカード)

Supermarkets in America have a dazzling variety of food and daily goods, but nothing is so amazing to me as the aisles dedicated to greeting cards.

Greeting
BIRTHDAY
THANK YOU
GET WELL
F
G
(しかもみんな違う)
こんなにいっぱい!

Example
Card for a daughter-in-law
(全て活字)
The day that my son took a wonderful wife, she was lovable right from the start...
And today when I think of my daughter-in-law, my heart drops the "in-law" part.
Happy Birthday
(書き文字スペースはちょっとだけ)
これって限られた相手にしか使えない文章だけど…?


The cards are organized in standard categories like birthday, thank you, get well, sympathy, graduation, and anniversary. But there are also cards for very specific occasions, like changing jobs, and for specific recipients, like a niece or grandchild.

ご結婚おめでとう!
いつまでもお幸せに
(書き文字スペースたっぷり)
当たり障りのない活字メッセージ
便利だけど、選ぶのが大変かも
The purpose of each card seems highly specialized compared with the one-size-fits-all approach of Japanese card makers.
There are so many choices, it can take some time to find one with the type of message you want to send.
Many are funny and clever and fun to read.


While the Japanese approach is to write a personal message, it seems very American to have many choices to find just the right message to send.

Can you see advantages to both styles?

Vol.144

# Read-a-thons
## (読書マラソン)

We all know what a marathon is, but have you heard of a "read-a-thon"? A read-a-thon is a type of fundraising event. Participants obtain sponsors who pledge to give a certain amount of money for each book read.

"a-thon"は接尾辞で、Walk-a-thonとかJog-a-thonとかSkype-a-thonなんていうのもあるようです

Here's how a read-a-thon works.

↓

STEP 1 A student gathers sponsors (parents, friends, neighbors).

STEP 2 The student reads as many books as they can within a set period.

STEP 3 The school gives the student a certificate with the number of books they read.

賞品が出ることも♪
GIFT CARD

STEP 4 The student collects the pledged money which is given to the school or a charity.

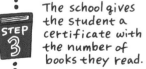

My niece's school holds an annual, school-wide read-a-thon. Students curl up in their favorite corners and read throughout the school day.

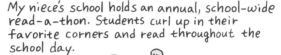

Stuffed toy
Pillow
Sleeping bag
Blanket
Drink
Pajamas

Read-a-thons are popular fund-raisers in Europe and the U.S. because they simultaneously promote reading, education, and a sense of accomplishment. They also give kids a chance to turn off their TVs and video games and rediscover the joys of reading.

日本でも広まったらいいのでは
いいね!
やりたーい♡
本好き
うえー
よくないね

姪の学校で毎年行われている「読書マラソン」は、チャリティーイベントの一種ですが、他にもすばらしい効用があるようで……

fundraising event　寄付金集めのイベント

obtain　手に入れる，獲得する

sponsor　賛助者，スポンサー

pledge to　～することを約束する

within a set period　一定期間内に

certificate　証明書，修了証書

charity　慈善団体

throughout　～の間中ずっと

simultaneously　〔複数の事柄が〕同時に

sense of accomplishment　達成感

rediscover　再発見する

アメリカで新大統領が誕生しました。ドナルド・トランプ氏の勝利は、私たちにとってかなりの衝撃でした。

**swear in** （人）を宣誓就任させる
**president** 大統領
**win an election** 選挙に勝つ，当選する
**forecast** 予想，見通し
**outcome** 結果，結末
**incredible** 信じられない
**prudent to** 慎重を期して軽々しく～しない
**contentious** 議論を引き起こす
**campaign slogan** 選挙戦で掲げるスローガン
**have a familiar ring to it** 聞き覚えのある響きがする

# Vol.145 Talking about Politics
## （政治のハナシ）

The United States recently swore in a new president. It's still hard to believe that Donald Trump won the election.
選挙前
Shut down Muslims entering the United States
女性蔑視発言も など。
ムッ
なんか問題発言ばっかり。大丈夫か？
Election Forecast
約30%
Hillary has a big lead.
大丈夫だよね きっと
約70%
We all know the outcome. Trump won the election.
約57%
WIN
It was quite a big shock to us all.
在米の日本人の友人たち →
Incredible!
What!?
How?!
I learned one more thing that surprised me. In America, people consider it prudent to avoid talking openly about politics.
意外！
I thought Americans were open about everything.
We're not so different from Japanese. It can be contentious to talk about politics or religion. Sometimes even within a family.
By the way, Trump's campaign slogan had a familiar ring to it.
Make America Great Again!
America First!
日本を、取り戻す。
自民党
都民ファースト

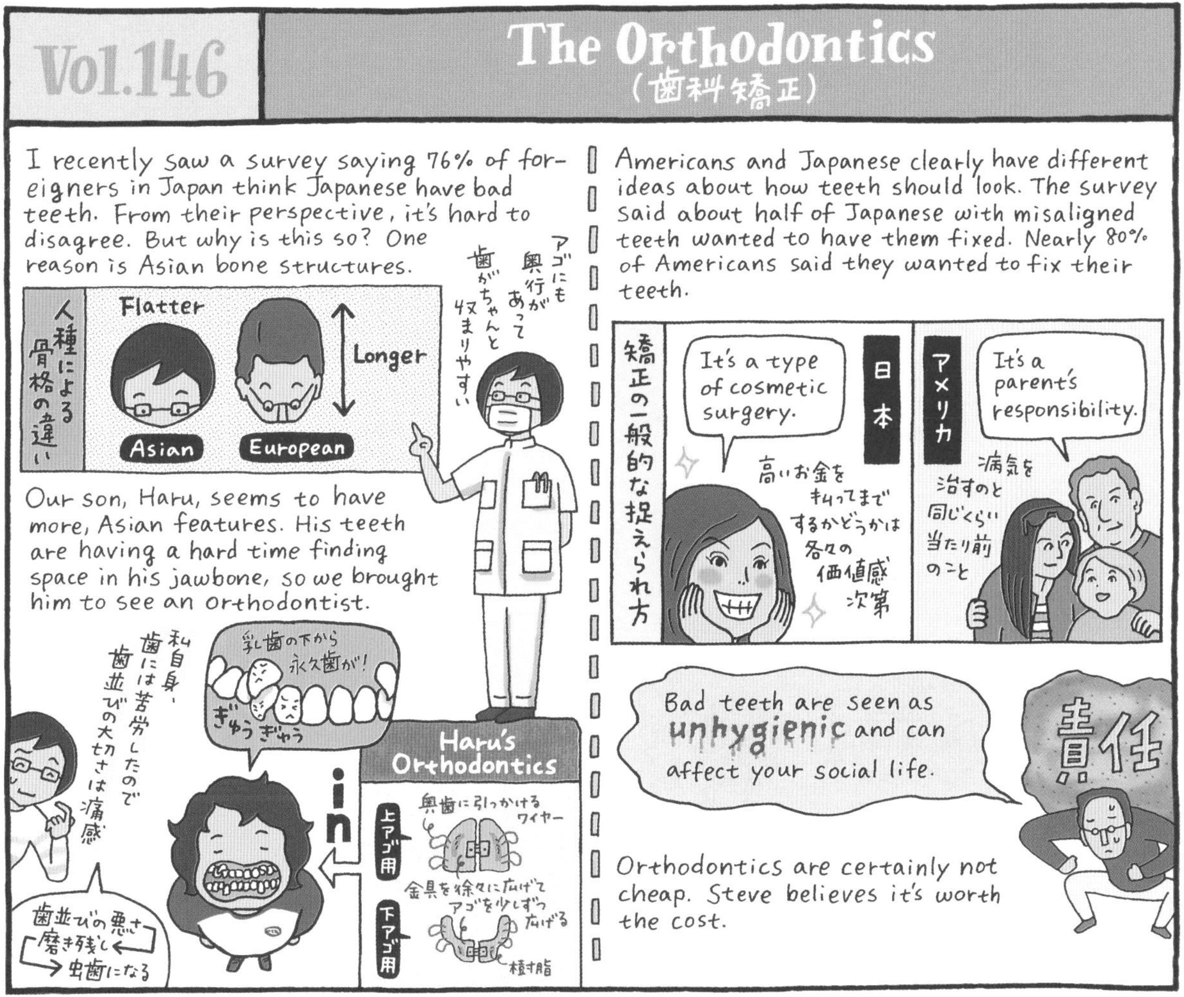
Vol.146
The Orthodontics
(歯科矯正)
I recently saw a survey saying 76% of for-eigners in Japan think Japanese have bad teeth. From their perspective, it's hard to disagree. But why is this so? One reason is Asian bone structures.
人種による骨格の違い
Flatter
Longer
Asian
European
アゴにも奥行があって歯がちゃんと収まりやすい
Our son, Haru, seems to have more, Asian features. His teeth are having a hard time finding space in his jawbone, so we brought him to see an orthodontist.
私自身、歯には苦労したので歯並びの大切さは痛感
乳歯の下から永久歯が!
ぎゅうぎゅう
歯並びの悪さ
磨き残し
虫歯になる
in
Haru's Orthodontics
上アゴ用
奥歯に引っかけるワイヤー
金具を徐々に広げてアゴを少しずつ広げる
下アゴ用
樹脂
Americans and Japanese clearly have different ideas about how teeth should look. The survey said about half of Japanese with misaligned teeth wanted to have them fixed. Nearly 80% of Americans said they wanted to fix their teeth.
矯正の一般的な捉えられ方
日本
It's a type of cosmetic surgery.
高いお金を払ってまでするかどうかは各々の価値感次第
アメリカ
It's a parent's responsibility.
病気を治すのと同じくらい当たり前のこと
Bad teeth are seen as unhygienic and can affect your social life.
責任
Orthodontics are certainly not cheap. Steve believes it's worth the cost.

ハルが歯科矯正を始めることになりました。歯並びや歯科矯正に対する意識には、日本とアメリカでは差があるようです。

---

**orthodontics** 歯科矯正

**survey** 調査，アンケート

**from someone's perspective** (人)の視点からすれば

**bone structure** 骨の構造，骨格

**feature** 特徴

**jawbone** 顎骨

**misaligned tooth** 歯並びの悪い歯

**cosmetic surgery** 美容外科

**unhygienic** 非衛生的な

**worth** ～の価値がある，～に値する

アメリカでは矯正を含む歯科治療は、ほぼ保険で賄われて安く済むと思っていましたが、それは間違いのようで――

cavity　虫歯
prevention　防止，予防
niggling　なかなか頭から離れない
presupposition　前提
eligible for　～に対して資格がある
public health insurance　公的健康保険
employer-sponsored　雇用主が提供する
attentive to　～に気を配る
fluoride　フッ化物
tooth enamel　歯のエナメル質

Vol.147
Cavity Prevention
（虫歯予防）
When we decided to bring Haru to the orthodontist, I had one niggling thought.
In America, insurance would cover the payments.
I was surprised to find out that my presupposition was wrong.
Unlike in Japan, only people that meet certain conditions, such as people with low income or disabilities, are eligible for public health insurance in the U.S. Most people join employer-sponsored health plans, but many have to take out private insurance policies—which are usually complicated and expensive.
毎月10万近い保険料を払っている在米の友人（3人家族）
It costs too much!
安いプランもあるけど それだと適用の範囲が狭まる
オバマケアでがんばりましたがうまくいかず…
Dental work isn't covered, so I have to buy a separate insurance policy.
That may be one reason why the U.S. seems to be so attentive to cavity prevention. One way they do this is by putting fluoride in the drinking water. Fluoride is believed to strengthen tooth enamel and help prevent cavities. There are lots of products to help keep your teeth white and healthy.
虫歯になったことのない人の割合は 日本では20人に1人だけど、アメリカでは4人に1人！
Electric toothbrush
Mouth wash
fresh
TOOTHPASTE
Dental floss
Of course, there's plenty of debate about whether so much fluoride is healthy or not. But everyone agrees that fluoride prevents cavities.
ヴィーン
人生、歯と目は大事
Nowadays, there are lots of things to help prevent cavities. We should do all we can so we don't have to rely on the dentist.
←電動歯ブラシとフロスを使うようになって、歯医者で歯磨きをほめられるように♪

Vol.148
Music and English
(音楽と英語)
Oddly enough, Steve and I met because we both love Tsugaru jamisen music. Other than that, however, our tastes in music are very different.
Steve listens to everything from jazz to pop and classical to country music. Asked to name just one favorite singer, he says Van Morrison.
He focuses on the lyrics.
Banjo
歌詞重視
vs
音重視
I like what they call "ethnic music." I view the singing as part of the sound. I like pop music with a sort of dark mood. Lorde is a recent favorite.
※基本的に女性ボーカルにひかれやすい
ブルガリアの女声合唱、ブルガリアンボイスなど。
雅楽なども好き
Nine-year-old Midori has also recently started developing a taste for popular music. She's a big fan of Taylor Swift.
強めの女性ボーカル
カントリーミュージック出身
自身の体験を元にした歌詞
テイラー・スウィフト
I'm going to write her a letter.
I love your songs a lot, especially "The Best Day"...
世界が近いなー
Her first fan letter. And it's in English!
I'm amazed she is so enthusiastic about Western music at such an early age. I didn't become interested until I was in middle school.

スティーヴと私とは、ある1点を除いて音楽の好みはバラバラです。最近ミドリも音楽の好みが出てきたようですが——

oddly enough 不思議な話だが

other than ～以外の

taste in music 音楽の好み

lyric 歌詞

what they call いわゆる

sort of ある種の，少し

develop a taste for ～が好きになる

big fan of ～の大ファン

enthusiastic about ～に熱心である

at an early age 幼い頃に

middle school 中学校

馬楽奈郵便
COLUMN 6

## 僕の髪の毛の話

ポストカードには反映されていませんが、僕の髪型の変化はかなり激しいです。一番短いときは数ミリ、長いときは40センチ以上の長さだったと思います。それでは僕の髪の変化を辿っていきましょう。

小学三年生頃までは僕は坊主でした。富士額に沿った逆毛や二つのつむじが僕の頭に複雑な模様を作っていたことでしょう。月に一度くらい父にバリカンで刈ってもらっていました。この頃は見た目は気にせず、とにかく楽な髪型が僕は好きでした。

小学三年生頃になって僕は外観を多少気にするようになり、周りの子達と同じように耳にかかるような長めの髪型にしたいと思い、髪の毛を伸ばしました。始めはみんなと同じ直毛になるかと思いましたが、数か月後には緩やかなウェーブが現れてきました。僕が自分の髪の毛が好きになったのはこのときです。周りのみんなと一風違う見た目であることがなんだか誇らしく感じました。

そこから僕は髪の毛を伸ばしました。寝癖などで日々変わっていくウェーブが面白く、もっと沢山欲しいと思って伸ばしていました。初めて美容院で髪の毛を切ってもらったのもこのときです。六年生になった頃には僕の髪は肩にかかり、女の子と間違われる事が増えました。美術の授業で描いた自画像は同級生にキリストの人物画と間違われました。しかし、僕が髪を切ろうと思ったのは別の理由でした。妹の七五三のときにスーツで映った写真を見て、自分の見た目が思っていたのと全く違い、ショックを受けて髪を切ることを決断しました。「ハリー・ポッター」に出てくるハグリッドとお揃いの髪型でした。

キリストの人物画と化した自画像

中学の間は耳にかかるくらいの髪型を維持しました。七三分けにしてみたり、ツーブロックを試したりしました。ツーブロックは耳が痒くないのを気に入って今でも耳周りは必ず刈り上げるようにしています。一時期結べるほどに髪が伸びた時期もありましたが、部活のときに結んでいたら先生に怒られ、これが校則改革を目指すきっかけともなりました。

高校二年生の春休み、僕は毎朝寝癖と戦うのが鬱陶しくなって思い切って坊主にしました。始業式の日、マスクをつけていたこともあって友達が僕だと気づいてくれず、駅で手を振ったら無視されてしまいました。

※強調していません

その後はそのまま伸ばし、今の刈り上げに至ります。最近は髪のボリュームが凄く、手櫛を通すと膨れ上がって顔の輪郭がまるできのこになってしまいます。

これからはまた伸ばして結ぼうかな。

STEVE
来日32年目の
江戸好きアメリカ人
KIKUE
ワタクシ
HARU
息子。
中学1年生
MIDORI
娘。
小学4年生

# 7th Year

2017

時が経つのは早いもので、ハルはもうすぐ中学生になります。ただ、日本とアメリカとでは教育制度が異なっていて――

school entrance ceremony 入学式
my 〔驚きなどを表して〕あらまあ
how time flies 時が経つのは早い, 光陰矢の如し
adulthood 大人であること, 成人期
assigned 割り当てられた
give emphasis to ～を重要視する
freshman 〔大学・4年制高校などの〕1年生, 新入生
sophomore 〔大学・4年制高校などの〕2年生
junior 〔大学・4年制高校などの〕3年生
senior 〔大学・4年制高校などの〕4年生

Vol.149
School Entrance Ceremonies
(入学式と進級)
My, how time flies! Our son, Haru, who was in first grade when this column debuted, will soon be starting middle school.
ピカピカの1年生
120cm くらいだったのが 160cmに
中学1年生
2011年
2017年
祝
入学
めでたい
School entrance ceremonies are one of the milestones on the path to adulthood. It seems that school entrance ceremonies are not so common in the U.S. Steve remembers being excited about starting a new grade, but that he simply went to his assigned classes.
We give more emphasis to graduation ceremonies.
Japan and the U.S. have different grade systems.
州によって異なります。これはカリフォルニアの場合
※別称もよく使います
This leads to some brain exercises.
例えば…
I played baseball until I was a junior in high school.
Junior = 11th grade
11th gradeは…
えーっと…
わかった
高2か!


| JAPAN | | U.S. | |
|---|---|---|---|
| 小学校 | 1年生 | 1st grade | Elementary school (5年) |
| | 2 〃 | 2nd 〃 | |
| | 3 〃 | 3rd 〃 | |
| | 4 〃 | 4th 〃 | |
| | 5 〃 | 5th 〃 | |
| | 6 〃 | 6th 〃 | Middle school (3年) |
| 中学校 | 1年生 | 7th 〃 | |
| | 2 〃 | 8th 〃 | |
| | 3 〃 | 9th (Freshman) | High school (4年) |
| 高校 | 1年生 | 10th (Sophomore) | |
| | 2 〃 | 11th (Junior) | |
| | 3 〃 | 12th (Senior) | |

# Vol.150 Getting through the Week
(1週間を乗り切る)

長年フリーランスとして働いてきたスティーヴがフルタイムの仕事に就きました。彼の1週間を乗り切るためのアイデアとは？

After many years working as a freelance translator, Steve took a full-time job in a company about a year ago. Now, after commuting five days a week, he looks forward to relaxing on the weekend. Naturally, his spirit rises on the last day of the workweek.

プレミアムフライデーの日は「TGIF」？なーんて
P…Premium

アルファベット読みして ティージーアイエフ！
Yeaaah!
T.G.I.F.!
(Thank God It's Fridayの略)


TGIF celebrates that the workweek is almost over and the weekend is about to start.

CHEERS
日本でも昔はよく花金(花の金曜日)とか言ったよね


There's another milestone during the week.

It's Hump Day!
※「Happy Hump Day」という言い方をすることも
さーて今日もがんばりますか！

Hump

Hump Day is Wednesday, the middle of the week. The thinking behind the image is: It's the halfway point and it's all downhill from today to the weekend.

Since returning to a full-time job, Steve made another special event for Wednesday. He and the kids call it ETB Day—Early to Bed Day.
We go to bed early to catch up on sleep so we have energy for the remainder of the week.

YAWN


Have a good week!

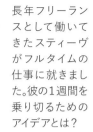

**get through** 通り抜ける，～を終える
**freelance** フリーランスの
**workweek** 1週間の労働時間
**celebrate** 称賛する，祝杯を挙げる
**milestone** 道しるべ，節目
**hump** 〔ラクダなどの背の〕こぶ，丘
**halfway point** 中間点
**downhill** 下り坂
**catch up on one's sleep** 不足した睡眠時間を取り戻す
**remainder** 残り，余り
**yawn** あくびをする

スティーヴが通勤するようになって父子の時間が減ってしまいましたが、それを補うべく、いろいろな工夫をしています。

join a company 入社する
half an hour 30分
connect with ～に連絡を取る
grandma おばあちゃん，祖母
converse 会話をする，打ち解けて話す
thanks to ～のおかげで，～の結果
chat with （人）とおしゃべりをする
across the sea 海を越えて
sneaky way コソコソしたやり方
spelling つづり，スペリング

# Vol.151 Time with the Kids
## （親子の時間）

Steve doesn't have as much time to spend with the kids now that he has joined a company.

**Before** We played cards and board games after dinner.

**Now** He helps the kids with their English homework while he eats dinner.

BLOCKERS
就寝前の読み聞かせは、今も変わらず

They found some time to spend together in the morning on the train to school and work. This gives them about half an hour to talk.

While riding the train, they also use LINE to connect with Steve's family in America.

Steveのスマホで Grandmaとチャット中

**LINE**
スマホでチャットや通話ができる無料アプリ。日本では大人気だけどアメリカではほぼ無名。（WhatsAppというアプリがよく使われる）

7:06
SUE
Hi, it's Midori. What are you doing today?
Read 6:50
Hi Midori! I'm just reading a book.
Read 6:55
Oh, really?
What subjects will you be studying today?

The Line messaging app lets them converse more quickly and easily than e-mail. Thanks to the app, they spend many of their mornings chatting with each other across the sea.

It's also a sneaky way to help the kids practice their spelling.
苦肉の策でしたが，
結果的には一石二鳥♪

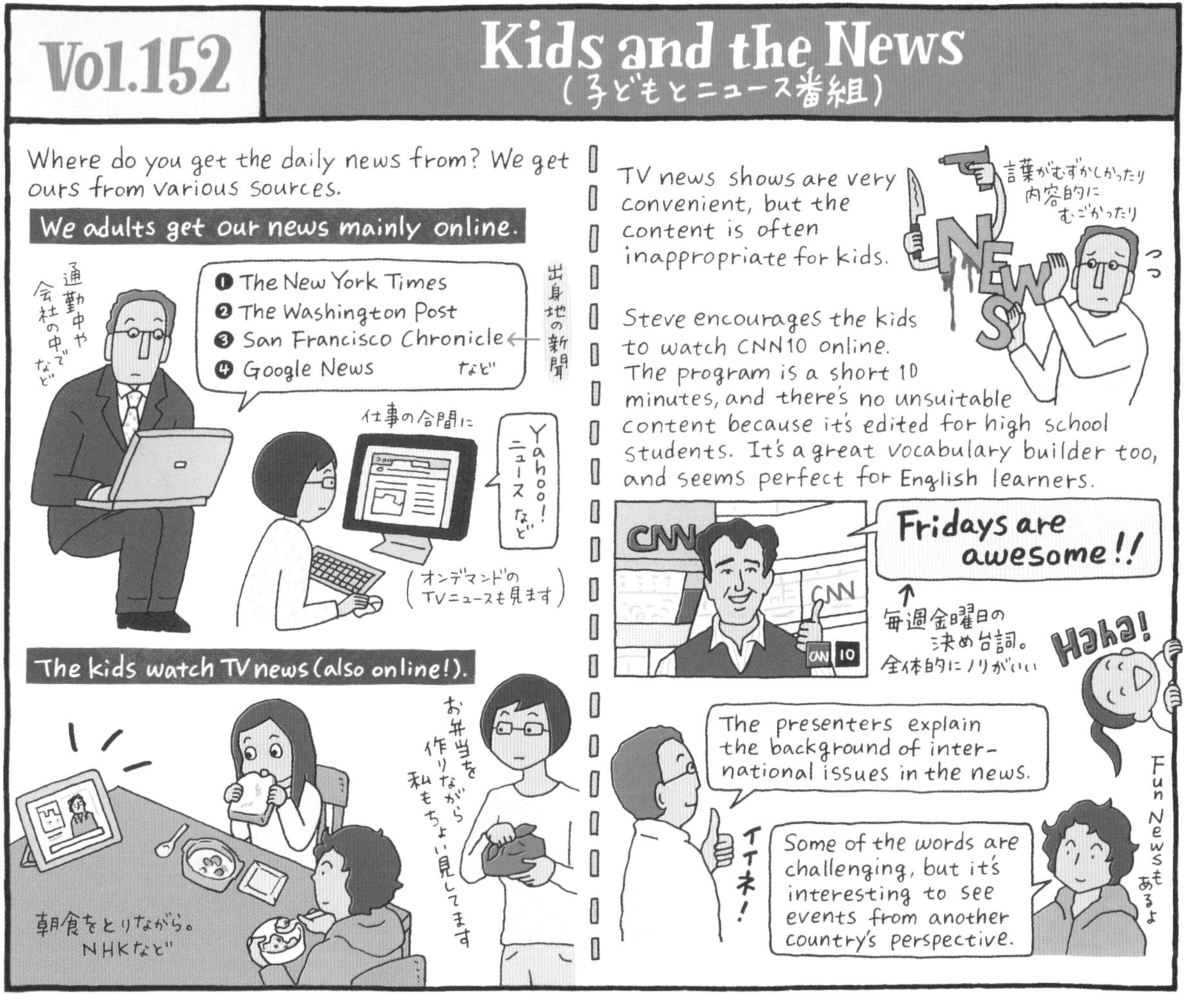
Vol.152
Kids and the News
(子どもとニュース番組)
Where do you get the daily news from? We get ours from various sources.
We adults get our news mainly online.
通勤中や会社の中でなど
❶ The New York Times
❷ The Washington Post
❸ San Francisco Chronicle
❹ Google News など
出身地の新聞
仕事の合間に
Yahoo!ニュースなど
(オンデマンドのTVニュースも見ます)
The kids watch TV news (also online!).
お弁当を作りながら私もちょい見してます
朝食をとりながら。NHKなど
TV news shows are very convenient, but the content is often inappropriate for kids.
言葉がむずかしかったり内容的にむごかったり
NEWS
Steve encourages the kids to watch CNN10 online. The program is a short 10 minutes, and there's no unsuitable content because it's edited for high school students. It's a great vocabulary builder too, and seems perfect for English learners.
CNN
Fridays are awesome!!
毎週金曜日の決め台詞。全体的にノリがいい
Haha!
The presenters explain the background of international issues in the news.
イイネ!
Some of the words are challenging, but it's interesting to see events from another country's perspective.
Fun Newsもあるよ

私たちは毎日のニュースをさまざまな発信元から得ています。テレビのニュース番組は便利ですが、子ども向けとは言えない内容もあり——

**source** 発信元，情報源
**inappropriate** 不適当な，不適切な
**encourage** 勧める，推奨する
**unsuitable** 不適切な，不相応な
**awesome** 素晴らしい，最高の
**presenter** 司会者
**background** 背景，遠因
**challenging** 困難だがやりがいのある

幼い子どもとの長時間にわたる飛行機旅には、その年齢の応じてさまざまな工夫が必要です。例えば……

progress　前進する，進歩する
toddler　よちよち歩きの小児
whine　すすり泣く，駄々をこねる
right up until　〜直前まで
relieve ear pressure　耳圧を軽減する
keep someone occupied　（人）を忙しくさせる
light-up　光を発する，点灯する
sit back　座って動かない，くつろぐ

# Vol.153 Plane Travel with Small Kids
（小さい子ども連れの飛行機旅）

We have progressed through various stages of family plane travel. Haru and Midori took their first plane trips before their first birthdays.
Look this way!!
目線集め係
撮影係
Taking the first passport photo
Taking kids on the long 10-hour-plus flights to the U.S. required a lot of planning just for the plane flight alone. Until the kids were toddlers, most of our efforts were to keep them from crying and whining during the flight.
例1 Lots of physical play right up until departure
疲れろ〜
機内で寝てくれ〜
例2 Relieving ear pressure during take off
授乳したり
飲みものやお菓子を食べさせたり
耳抜きしないと不快でグズることに
Surprising them with new toys to keep them quietly occupied.
例3
仕掛け絵本やシールブックなど
Light-up toys
わー♥
今ならタブレットとかもありますね
Once the kids became grade school age, we could sit back while they watched the in-flight movies.
ラクになったなー
寝てても大丈夫♪
This summer will bring yet another stage in our family plane travel.
Kids traveling by themselves!

Vol.154
Seasonal Wardrobe Change
（衣替え）
June in Japan is when we change our wardrobe for the season.
Summer clothes
Winter clothes
Changing the wardrobe for the coming season seems like something everyone would do, but Steve doesn't have that custom.
Where he grew up in the mild climate of Northern California, everyone usually has just one set of clothing that they use throughout the year.
We just pick out different clothes from our closet.
夏でも朝晩冷えるのでフリースや薄手のダウンを着ることも
Steve, who never had to wear a school uniform, always finds it interesting to watch the kids suddenly switch to different school clothes for the season.
June 1
学校衣替えあるある
暑くてもまだ冬服ということも
あっ
忘れてた！
Summer uniform
Winter uniform
October 1
It seems a little rigid to make them all change on a predetermined day each year.
Wouldn't it be more reasonable to just let them dress for the weather?
昨今、気候の変動も激しいしね


日本では6月や10月といえば衣替えの時期です。でも、カリフォルニア育ちのスティーヴにはその習慣がありません。

**wardrobe** 衣装だんす
**June** 6月
**mild climate** 穏やかな気候
**throughout the year** 一年を通して
**pick out** 選び出す
**school uniform** 学生服，学校の制服
**switch to** 〜に切り替える
**for the season** その季節［時期］に合わせて
**rigid** 柔軟性に欠ける，硬直した
**predetermined** 既定の，所定の

英検が近づいてきました。受験する読者も多いのではないでしょうか。我が家の9歳と12歳の子どもたちも申し込みました。

**sign up** 契約する，申し込む

**find oneself seated near** （人）と席が近くになる

**most likely** 十中八九

**side by side** 並んで，一緒に

**feel odd** 違和感を抱く

**aim at** ～にねらいを定める

**go beyond** ～の範囲を超える

**Pleistocene** 更新世《地質時代の区分の一つ》

**federation** 連邦，連合

**give someone confidence** （人）に自信をつけさせる

# Vol.155 Kids at the Eiken

## （兄妹で英検ダブル受験）

It's Eiken English-testing season. I'm sure many readers are trying to move up a level. Our kids, ages 9 and 12, are both signed up this year.

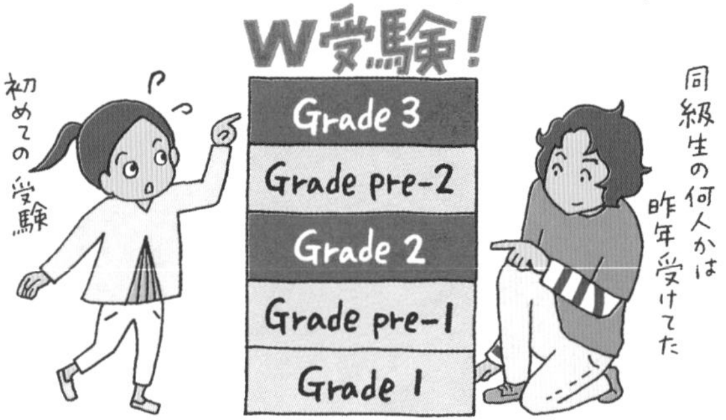

W受験!
初めての受験
Grade 3
Grade pre-2
Grade 2
Grade pre-1
Grade 1
同級生の何人かは昨年受けてた


When you take the test, don't be surprised if you find yourself seated near a very young elementary school student. In the higher test grades, the younger test-takers have most likely lived abroad or come from bilingual families.

Grade 2
会場
例


Taking a test side by side with people less than half your age may feel odd. It certainly did for me. However, the Eiken website even says Grade 2 is "aimed at Japanese high school graduates." For a native speaker, the level is about the same as a sixth-grade elementary school student's.

時事ネタとか
科学ネタとか
結構ありますよね
The Grade 2 test goes beyond language to discussion of various topics, which is probably over the heads of younger speakers.
Pleisto-cene?
federa-tions?


We hope taking the test will be a good experience for our kids and give them confidence as well as motivation to keep working at their English.

おまけ
キッズの最大の難関はマークシート!?
ナニコレ
過去問で
慣らさなきゃ

Good luck to every-one!!

Vol.156
Airlines and Traveling Children
(航空会社のジュニアサポート)
We're planning to visit Steve's family in the U.S. this summer. We have arranged to send the kids a week ahead of us so they can have a long holiday.
We'll be fine. We'd love to have them!
Thank you!
アメリカの義父母
やったー
よしっ
We only learned recently that the airlines provide support for children traveling solo. Airline staff escort unaccompanied minors to the gate and ensure they are handed over to predesignated people at their destination.
ANAの場合
(今回、ハルとミドリが利用できるサービス)
サポート内容
預り
引き渡し
出発空港
到着空港
機内でのサポートは6~11歳用の「ジュニアパイロット」のみ
Have a safe trip!
At the check-in counter
Grandma!
At the arrival lobby
これなら大丈夫だね
ホッ
友達も毎年これだって!
Knowing the children are in the hands of the airline staff is reassuring. But parents can always find something to worry about.
I just know they're going to forget something in the plane.
Will they keep up with their summer homework?
I hope they behave themselves at Grandma's house.
だいじょーぶだいじょーぶ

| 対象年齢 | 名称 |
|---|---|
| 満6~11歳 | ANAジュニアパイロット |
| 満12~16歳 | ANAエアポートサポート |

子どもたちだけ一足先にアメリカへ渡航することになり、航空会社のジュニアサポートを利用することにしました。

only ~ recently　最近になってやっと～する
travel solo　ひとり旅をする
escort　付き添う，送り届ける
unaccompanied minor　付添人のいない未成年者
ensure　保証する，確かにする
hand over　引き渡す
predesignate　あらかじめ指定する
destination　目的地，行き先
in the hands of　～の管理下に
reassuring　心強く感じさせる
behave oneself　行儀よくする

２年前に英検準２級に合格した私。次に目指すは２級ですが、そこに立ちはだかる壁を実感しています。

**pick up** 〔言葉・技術などを〕習得する，覚える

**feel good about oneself** 自分に自信を持つ，いい気分になる

**encouraged by one's success** 成功に力を得る

**have never even done** ～したこともない

**describe** 説明する，記述する

**general aspect** 一般的な側面

**real-life situation** 実際の生活の場面

**to a T** 完全に，まさに，ぴったり

**while** ～する間に，～と同時に

**build up** 高める，増大させる

# Vol.157 Where We Pick Up Words (語彙の源)

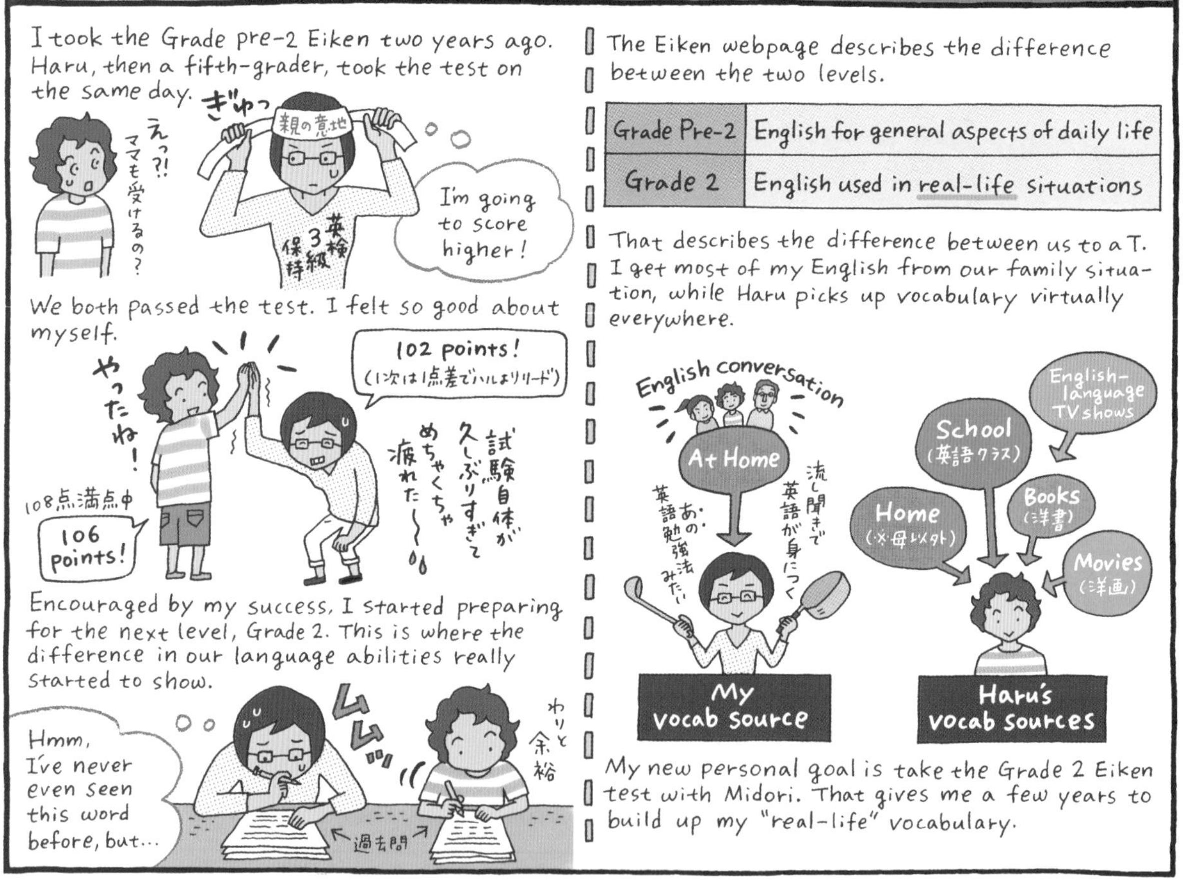
I took the Grade pre-2 Eiken two years ago. Haru, then a fifth-grader, took the test on the same day.
えっ?! ママも受けるの?
ぎゅっ
親の意地
英検3級保持
I'm going to score higher!
We both passed the test. I felt so good about myself.
やったね!
108点満点中
106 points!
102 points!
(1次は1点差でハルよりリード)
試験自体が久しぶりすぎてめちゃくちゃ疲れた～
Encouraged by my success, I started preparing for the next level, Grade 2. This is where the difference in our language abilities really started to show.
Hmm, I've never even seen this word before, but...
ムムッ
わりと余裕
過去問
The Eiken webpage describes the difference between the two levels.
Grade Pre-2 | English for general aspects of daily life
Grade 2 | English used in real-life situations
That describes the difference between us to a T. I get most of my English from our family situation, while Haru picks up vocabulary virtually everywhere.
English conversation
At Home
英語あの勉強法みたい
流し聞きで英語が身につく
My vocab source
School (英語クラス)
English-language TV shows
Home (父母以外)
Books (洋書)
Movies (洋画)
Haru's vocab sources
My new personal goal is take the Grade 2 Eiken test with Midori. That gives me a few years to build up my "real-life" vocabulary.

# Vol.158 To the Mountains!
（登山に行こう）

The mountains have been calling us this year. We've been going on more day hikes than usual.
Climbing Mt. Fuji is like beginner-level mountaineering, but the trail and guest huts make it more like hiking.
えー
日本一高い山なのに…
The different words for different types of hikes seem to influence how people think about hiking. One thing I've noticed is that my husband and his friends dress differently when we go to the mountains.
English has different words for different levels of hiking.
Japanese
Type of hike
English
どれもこれも
登山
Adven-tures
ザイルやピッケルも使用
Moun-taineer-ing
Long hikes
トレイルをたどって頂上へ
TOP
Trekking
Day hikes on trails
街歩きの延長で
高尾山とか
Hiking
場合によっては「ハイキング」と言ったり。
線引きがあいまい
They seem overdressed.
They look like they're just out for exer-cise.
いやいや
The 登山!
※夏でも極力素足は出さない
Japanese
Rugged outdoor clothes + Backpack full of supplies
Europeans and Americans
Stretch fabric and T-shirts + Carrying as little as possible
Which outfits do you think are right for a day hike? We'll explore this issue again next time.


日本語では、初心者向けでも上級者向けでもすべて「登山」の一言で言い表せますが、英語では山登りのレベルに応じて単語が異なります。

**hiking** 徒歩旅行，ハイキング

**mountaineering** 登山

**trekking** トレッキング

**hut** 掘っ立て小屋，山小屋

**overdressed** 着込んで

**rugged** 丈夫な，しっかりした

**outfit** 衣服，装備

**explore** 探索する，調査する

装備に身を固めた私と軽装のスティーヴ。一緒にハイキングしても、こんなに服装に差があるのはどうしてでしょうか？

decked-out　着込んでいる，着飾っている

preparation prevents regret　備えあれば患いなし

respect　配慮する

the more..., the more　…すればするほど～だ

injury　けが，負傷

first aid　応急処置

prepare for the worst　最悪の事態に備える

just in case　万が一～する場合に

argue in a circle　堂々巡りの議論をする

try to find a happy medium　妥協を図る

# Vol.159 To the Mountains Again!（登山の準備）

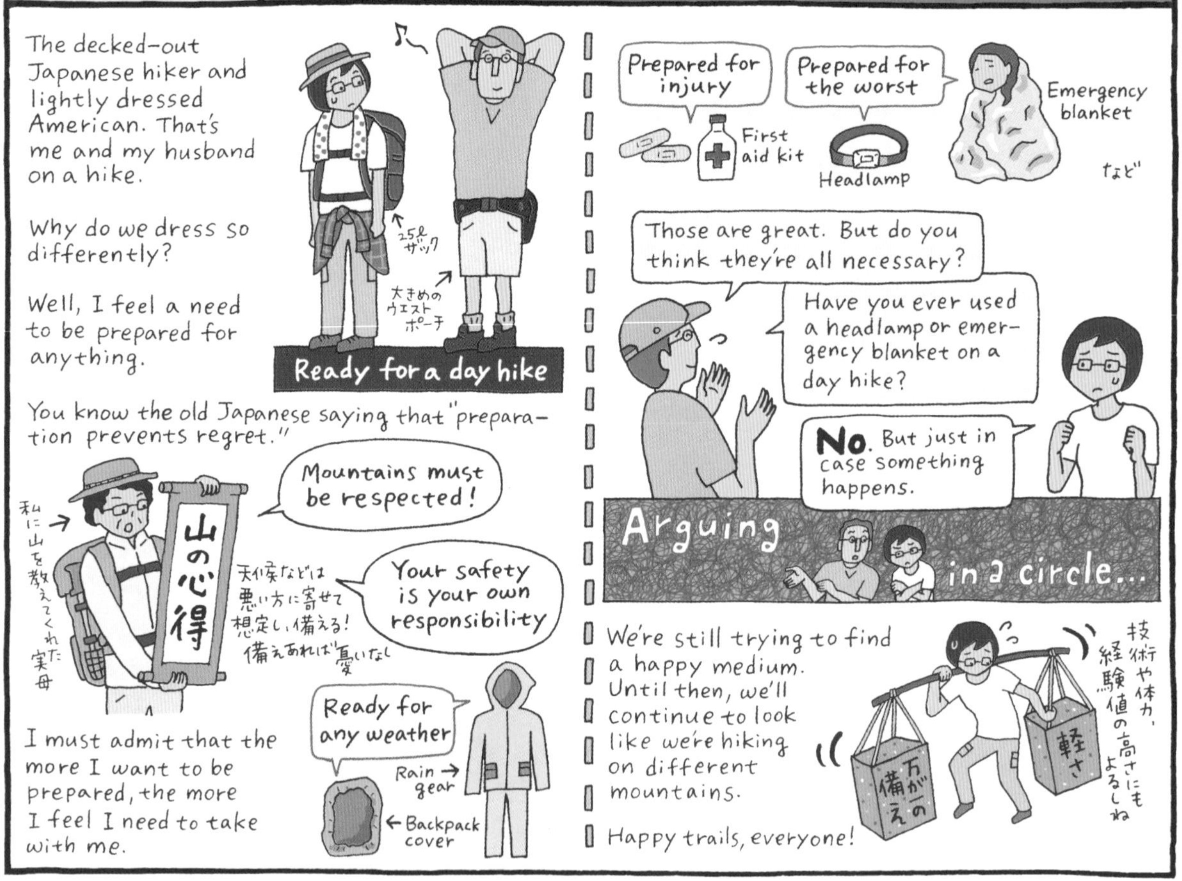

The decked-out Japanese hiker and lightly dressed American. That's me and my husband on a hike.
Why do we dress so differently?
Well, I feel a need to be prepared for anything.
25ℓ ザック
大きめのウエストポーチ
Ready for a day hike
You know the old Japanese saying that "preparation prevents regret."
私に山を教えてくれた実母
山の心得
Mountains must be respected!
天候などは悪い方に寄せて想定し備える！備えあれば憂いなし
Your safety is your own responsibility
I must admit that the more I want to be prepared, the more I feel I need to take with me.
Ready for any weather
Rain gear
Backpack cover
Prepared for injury
First aid kit
Prepared for the worst
Headlamp
Emergency blanket
など
Those are great. But do you think they're all necessary?
Have you ever used a headlamp or emergency blanket on a day hike?
No. But just in case something happens.
Arguing in a circle...
We're still trying to find a happy medium. Until then, we'll continue to look like we're hiking on different mountains.
Happy trails, everyone!
万が一の備え
軽さ
技術や体力、経験値の高さにもよるしね

Vol.160
Year-Round School Club Activities
(部活の楽しみ方)
New middle schooler Haru decided to join the badminton club at school. Between practice and tournaments, the club meets five or six days a week.
Many of my best memories from middle and high school are from club sports.
部活は青春の象徴みたいなもの
Club sports filled most of my free time.
You surely know Steve pretty well by now, and you can expect him to offer a different perspective.
What!? Six days a week?
?!
Nothing but badminton!
You'd think they were training to become pros.
When Steve was growing up, the sports he played changed with the seasons. He might play on the soccer team during fall, switch to basketball in winter, then play baseball in spring.
AUTUMN
Football
Soccer
Volleyball
WINTER
Basketball
Hockey
Fencing
SPRING
Baseball
Track
Tennis
など(学校による)
※夏休み中はナシ
えーと
Baseball was my favorite, but I played other sports in the off-season.
Hmm, that would be interesting. Maybe more fun.
バド部と陸上部で最後まで悩んでた人
With Japan's declining birthrate, schools are starting to have trouble recruiting enough players to field full teams. Adopting a seasonal sports system could be a way to fill out the teams.
様々なスポーツをすることで体の使い方が偏らないというメリットもあり

中学生になったハルは学校のバドミントン部に入部することにしました。週に5～6日は練習があると聞いて、スティーヴは……

**fill** いっぱいに満たす，埋める

**pretty well** ほとんど

**by now** 今はもう，そろそろ

**nothing but** ～だけ，～のみ

**pro** プロ（の選手）

**declining birthrate** 出生率の低下，少子化

**have trouble ~ing** ～するのに苦労する

**adopt** 導入する，採用する

**fill out** 膨らませる，大きくする

日本の学校とアメリカの学校では、スポーツ活動に対する考え方やその目的が異なるようです。

**objective** 目的，目標

**have a different approach to** ～に対して異なる取り組みをする

**loyalty** 忠実，忠誠

**multiple** 多数の，複合の

**wide-ranging experience** 幅広い経験

**half-hearted** ゆるい

**placement** クラス分け，配置

**varsity** 代表チーム

**former professional** 元プロ選手

**come first** 何よりも優先である

**eligible** 資格のある，望ましい

Vol.161
The Objectives of School Sports
（部活に求めるもの）
Japanese and American schools have different approaches to sports activities. They also seem to have different objectives for their sports programs.
JAPAN
Loyalty to one sport promotes personal development.
ひとつの道を
長く深く
U.S.A.
Participating in multiple activities builds wide-ranging experience.
A B C D E F G
広くバランスよく
Japanese sports teams have games and tournaments on weekends. In the U.S., school competitions are usually on weekday nights. This lets the kids use the weekends to meet friends or work at a part-time job.
ふーん
Kids in Japan should be better at the sports then, right?
The American way seems half-hearted.
It seems so. But there are three aspects that are stricter than Japan.
1 Placement based on skill
Kids often have to go through tryouts to make the team.
TRYOUT
アメフトや野球など
無事にパスしても…
Varsity
選抜選手による学校代表チーム
Junior Varsity
いわゆる二軍
誰でも気軽に入れる日本とは違うね
（ちなみに、もっと極めたい子は、地域のクラブチームに入るのが一般的）
2 High-level training
Coaches are often former professionals from outside the school or teachers with special skills.
しっかり指導
素人の顧問はあり得ない
3 Academics come first
Players must maintain a certain grade-point average to be eligible.
疲れた～ 勉強ムリ～
A single club formed and led by students that anyone can join, or multiple teams offering a wide variety of experiences and strong leadership. Which do you think is best for kids?

# Vol.162 The Flat Stanley Project
## （ぺちゃんこ人形プロジェクト）

カナダの教師が立ち上げ、アメリカ全土に広まった“あるプロジェクト”に、ミドリも参加することになりました。

About a decade ago, an innovative teacher in Canada created The Flat Stanley Project to inspire students to read and write. School-kids embraced the project, and it quickly became popular across North America. Last year, it crossed the sea to Japan.

### What is the Flat Stanley Project?

まずこの本を授業で読みました
FLAT STANLEY
by Jeff Brown
ドアの隙間から忍び込んだり
封筒に入って旅に出たり

The Flat Stanley books tell the adventures of Stanley, a boy who accidentally gets flattened, which leads to some unexpected benefits. In one episode, Stanley is sent across the country in a letter envelope.

Joining the official Flat Stanley Project is easy.

A) Register on the website
http://www.flatstanleyproject.com

B) Select a person from the mailing list

C) Begin correspondence

Midori's class conducted their own Flat Stanley project.

**STEP 1**

The students each mail a cutout picture of themselves to a relative or friend.

in
公式テンプレートもあるけど
自分で作ったよ

**STEP 2**

The recipient takes photos of the cutout and sends it back with a description.

アメリカに住む祖母

**STEP 3**

The students learn about the location from the photos and descriptions.

地理や文化なども

Kids love the anticipation of receiving a report of their own Flat Stanley. The official website says some Flat Stanleys have even been sent to NASA and the White House.

I'm secretly hoping someone will send one to us.

---

**decade ago** 10年前に
**innovative** 創造力に富む
**inspire** 動機づける，鼓舞する
**embrace** 受け入れる，採用する
**cross the sea** 海を渡る，外国へ行く
**get flattened** ぺちゃんこにつぶされる
**unexpected benefit** 思いもよらない恩恵
**register** 登録する，手続きをする
**correspondence** 手紙のやり取り
**cutout** 切り抜き
**description** 記述，説明
**anticipation** 期待

ハロウィンに欠かせないもの。それはゾンビや魔女、そしてかぼちゃのジャック・オー・ランタンです。

**in a previous life** 前世で

**barred from** 〜を禁じられる，阻まれる

**doomed to** 〜する悪い運命にある

**roam** 歩き回る，うろつく

**just once** 一度だけ

**less than a dollar** 1ドルしない

**patch** 〔畑の〕1区画

**ramble** ぶらつく，探求する

**maze** 迷路

**hayride** ヘイライド《干し草を積んだトラック・荷車での遠乗り》

# Vol.163 Halloween Pumpkins
（ハロウィンのかぼちゃ）

Everybody knows about all the decorations put up for Christmas. But even in October, we are busy decorating the house. Instead of Santas and Christmas trees, we are putting up zombies and witches and setting out a jack-o'-lantern.

The jack-o'-lantern is a spirit who did bad things in a previous life. He was barred from heaven and is doomed to roam the earth forever.
（※発祥の地であるアイルランドやスコットランドではカブ。アメリカに伝わってからカボチャになった）

Don't we all want to try carving a pumpkin just once? I sure do. But the stores here don't usually sell pumpkins that are big enough. You can find them online, but they are really expensive.

ハロウィーンかぼちゃ
う〜ん…
3,000 to 5,000 yen for a pumpkin
…and it's only good for a few days.
費用対効果としてどうよ
カービングするとすぐ傷み始めます

You can find pumpkins in stores in America for less than a dollar. But if you want to have more fun, you can go to a pumpkin patch and hunt for your own pumpkin. That's what our relatives in Northern California do every year.

Pumpkin Patch
You ramble through a huge field of pumpkins until you find one just the right size.
入場料 2ドル/人
カボチャ代 2ドル/個くらい

（↑クリスマスも毎年、ツリーファームでツリーを切り出している家族）

The pumpkin patch farms make it even more fun with mazes, hayrides, and other attractions for kids.

HAYRIDE
いいなー

# Vol.164 Making the Most of Dressing Up
（本気で楽しむハロウィンの仮装）

One of my favorite parts of Halloween is seeing Facebook pictures of the costumes my friends and relatives in the U.S. make.
Many schools allow students to wear costumes to school and even have costume contests.
What can I dream up this year?
My friend H makes a costume for her son every year.
He's even won a prize for best costume.
This year, she's using more crafts in the costume she's making.
中華系スクールのコンテストで
中国のアニメキャラ
空き箱
ワインのコルク
割り箸
発泡スチロール
ミシン用ゴム糸
包装紙の芯
If you think it would be odd to see kids wearing costumes going to school, just think how weird it would be to see adults wearing costumes going to work! Many store and restaurant workers dress up, and a lot of company workers wear costumes to work too.
車で通勤中
In my friend's office, everyone joins the fun.
ひー
血のりや特殊メイクもした友人C
They're really making the most of the opportunity.
What a great way to stimulate the imagination!


ハロウィンの楽しみのひとつは、アメリカの友人や親戚が作った仮装の写真をFacebookで見ること。彼らが思いっきり楽しんでいる様子に、こちらまでわくわくします。

**make the most of** 〜を存分に楽しむ

**dream up** 頭に描く，考え出す

**win a prize** 賞を取る，受賞する

**weird** 奇妙な，風変わりな

**join the fun** 楽しむ

**stimulate the imagination** 想像力をかき立てる

中学生になったのを機にスマホを持つようになったハル。家族LINEにたくさんの略語が出てきて、びっくり！

**decide when the time is right for** ～に適した時期を判断する

**own** 自分の,〔～を〕所有する

**must not** ～してはいけない

**maximum** 最大限の

**parental control** ペアレンタル・コントロール《未成年者に悪影響を与えるウェブページへのアクセスを親が規制できる機能》

**what the heck** いったい何が

**shorthand** 省略表現

**homonym** 同音異義語

**acronym** 頭字語《頭文字を並べたものが1つの単語として発音可能なもの》

Vol.165
The Language of the Internet I
（ネット用語①：略語）
When our son, Haru, started middle school, we decided the time was right for him to have his own smartphone. Other parents seem to agree. Data shows over 60 percent of middle-school students own smartphones.
Games
Videos
Other
LINE 80%
ハルの使用状況
CHECK
RULE 1
The smartphone must not be brought into Haru's room.
RULE 2
Maximum one hour of chat messaging per day.
Parental Control
アクセス制限なども かけてます
The smartphone is even convenient for us parents to communicate with him. One recent chat session went like this:
Steve
See you at the station.
HARU
ICU
Steve
I don't CU. Where RU?
What the heck is that?
Oh, of course! It's shorthand.
Words shortened to homonyms and acronyms to reduce typing.
4 for
U you
2 to, too
R are
C see
小文字でもOK
使用例
OIC (Oh, I see)
RU? (Are you?)
Me2 (Me too)
OMG Oh, My God
LOL もしくは lol Laugh Out Loud (爆笑)
KISS
HUG
PLZ Please
THX Thanks
JK Just Kidding
XOXO Kisses and Hugs
など
※女子高生ではない
Cool! I'm going to use them too. CUL8R なんてね (See you later)
にひひ
Be careful! You could end up sounding like a young schoolgirl.
数字を使うのは20代くらいまでが多い
BTW By The Way
FYI For Your Information
W/O Without
ASAP As Soon As Possible
など。
BYO Bring Your Own
←パーティーやBBQのときなどに
Many acronyms have been around much longer than the Internet and are still common.
通っぽく

# Vol.166 The Language of the Internet II
## （ネット用語②：絵文字と顔文字）

Emoji are everywhere in e-mail and messaging apps. People use them to add emphasis to typed messages.

July 17 World Emoji Day

世界でいちばん使われている絵文字の一つ

寿司や天ぷらも同様


Emoji carry meaning across language borders.

（Emotionから派生した単語だと思っている人が多いらしい）

使用例

Thank you.
（含.申し訳ないという気持ち）

That's great!
（含.ちょっとあきれる気持ち）

But just like words, emoji can have different meanings.

| JAPAN | Emoji | U.S.A. |
|---|---|---|
| OK，マル |  | Exercise, jumping rope |

Emoji faces can be very nuanced. Take the Apple and Google smiley face emoji for example.

ネガティブ
苦笑に見えなくもない
Apple
Google
ポジティブ
Impression

あー。
日本はテストで合ってると「○」をつけるけど、米国は違うしね
✓（チェック）をつけるのが米国式


Emoticons are faces created using text symbols. They are very different in Japan and the U.S.

| JAPAN | Emotion | U.S.A. |
|---|---|---|
| (^_^)(^o^)(^^) | Laughing, fun | :-) :-D X-D |
| (*_*)(>_<) | Sad | :-( :-< X-( |
| (T_T)(;_;) | Crying | :_( |
| (^_-)-☆ | Wink, joking | ;-) :-P |
| (’Д’) | Surprised | :-o |

Why are emoticons sideways in English?

慣れないから首が傾いちゃう


An American named Scott Fahlman created the first emoticon.

Americans express emoticons more with the mouth than the eyes. Sideways faces allow more flexibility to represent the features of the mouth.

:-)
楽しさがUPすると…
:-)))
口が増える!!


If we are careful not to overuse them, emoji and emoticons are very handy. Plus, they're fun!

入力したメッセージを強調したりニュアンスを加えたりする絵文字や顔文字。英語ではどのように使うのでしょうか。

**add emphasis to** ～を強調する

**World Emoji Day** 世界絵文字デー《7月17日を絵文字の使用促進を目的とした記念日としている》

**jumping rope** なわとび

**nuanced** 微妙に異なる

**emoticon** 顔文字

**sideways** 横向きの

**represent** 表す，象徴する

**careful not to** ～しないように気をつける

**overuse** 使いすぎる

私の子ども時代に比べ、たくさんのクリスマスプレゼントを受け取っているハルとミドリ。ちょっと過剰ではないのかと、気がかりで……

Vol.167
The Joy of Christmas
(クリスマスの喜び)
When I was little, my brother and I each received one present at Christmas.
当時、大流行していた
ローラースケート
待ってました!!
サンタさんからのプレゼント
携帯型液晶ゲーム機ゲームウォッチ
私
弟
Our kids receive presents from us parents as well as from numerous relatives overseas. I'd say they receive at least seven presents each!
Santa
Parents
Grand-parents①
Grand-parents②
Grand-parents③
Uncle
Aunt
しかもそれぞれ一つとは限らない
※スティーヴの両親は離婚後、各々再婚している
Hmm, I hope they don't get spoiled.
気持ちはありがたいけど
Will they really appreciate the generosity?
Did you get that many presents?
Well. Um. Yeah.
昔の写真
In America, Christmas Day is not only about receiving gifts, it's also about spreading the Christmas spirit of giving.
Merry Xmas!
クッキーやアメなど
宅配の人などにも
徳を積むのに似た行為なのかも
贈りものをするのは
徳
After some thought, my parents decided to give shared experiences with the kids. They say experiences are more valuable than possessions.
観戦チケットや観劇チケットなど
Ballet Concert
SPORTS
一緒に見に行けば思い出も作れてNice!


A as well as B　AもBも
numerous　非常に多くの
spoiled　甘やかされて育った，駄々をこねる
appreciate　〔～を〕よく理解する，ありがたく思う
generosity　気前の良さ，豊富さ
shared experience　共有経験
valuable　有益な，貴重な
possession　所有，財産

# Vol.168 Returning Presents
（プレゼントの返品）

Spreading the Christmas spirit by giving presents is not just for children. Adults exchange presents too. Among close friends and family, it's not uncommon to provide the receipt along with the present.

お～
NICE☆SHOP
A Gift for You
GIFT RECEIPT
Jacket Price Code 1234567
Shirt Price Code 8910234
値段の表示はない
ひらり

Oops! I thought the giver had mistakenly left it in the box. Actually, she had purposely put it in.

If you don't like it, bring it back to the store and choose something you like.
アメリカの親せき
え～
いただきものを返品するとかすごい罪悪感が…

Although people are usually reluctant to return items in Japan, in the U.S., stores are often crowded even after Christmas with people returning gifts they don't want.

わ！
すごい人…
Next, please!
30分待ちも珍しくない

Many stores have a return policy of "no questions asked." Just bring the item and the receipt, and they will exchange it for a store gift card of the same value.

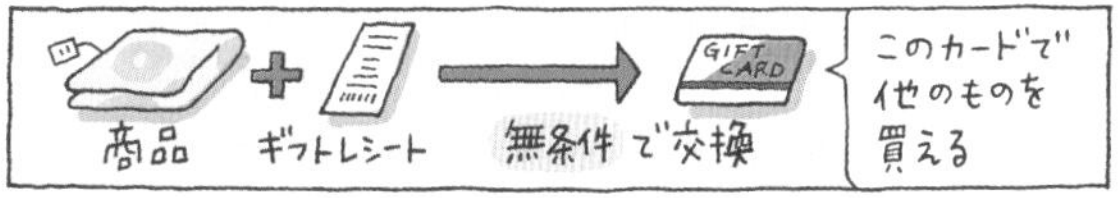
商品
ギフトレシート
無条件で交換
GIFT CARD
このカードで他のものを買える

驚くほど簡単
中にはレシートが不要な店も

An easy return policy makes it easier to buy a gift, but the stores must not like that about 10% of gifts are returned after Christmas. Wouldn't it feel strange to give a gift while thinking it may just be returned to the store?

もらったプレゼントにレシートが入っていました。うっかりかと思いきや、わざと一緒に入れられていて——

- **return** 戻す，返品する
- **exchange** 交換する
- **among** ～の間で
- **receipt** 領収書，レシート
- **Oops!** おっと！
- **mistakenly** 間違って〔～する〕
- **reluctant to** ～するのに気が進まない
- **crowded** 混雑した，いっぱいの
- **return policy** 返品条件
- **no questions asked** 理由を問わずに，無条件に
- **feel strange** 違和感を覚える

故郷の名産物を味わうのは楽しいもの。カリフォルニアのアーティチョークはご存じですか？

Vol.169
A New Dish for New Year!
(ふるさとの味)
あけましておめでとうございます
今年もよろしくお願いします
How are you spending the New Year's holiday? If you are like me, you are probably savoring some of the special foods from your hometown.
お雑煮好き〜
Steve is from California, where they have one dish that is quite unique.
ARTICHOKE
Artichokes are softball-sized vegetables belonging to the thistle family. In California, they sell for about a dollar each.
ゴツくてトゲトゲしい。
これほんとに食べられるの？
断面図
先がとがっている
※The "heart" is the most delicious part.
It's not the most attractive-looking vegetable, but the taste is very nice. Here's how to prepare an artichoke.
❶ Cut off the thorns
カボチャ並に固い
❷ Boil or steam for about 30 minutes
レモン汁が入った水
タケノコっぽい味
❸ Eat one leaf at a time
可食部(内側)
マヨネーズなどのディップ
歯でこそいで食べる
たくさんの残骸が…
Most of the artichoke is inedible. Only the meaty base of the leaves and the heart can be eaten. Even so, the taste is worth the effort. Californians love it.
If you ever see one in the grocery store, give it a try. I highly recommend it.

savor 〔飲食物を〕味わう，〔経験などを〕楽しむ

quite unique とても独特だ

artichoke アーティチョーク

thistle family キク科

attractive 感じの良い，魅力的な

thorn とげ

at a time 一度に，同時に

inedible 食用ではない

meaty 肉厚の，食べ応えのある

heart 中心，芯

worth 〜の甲斐がある

grocery store 食料(雑貨)品店

# Vol.170 Heaters I（我が家の暖房事情）

The middle of winter is the coldest time of the year. How do you keep away the cold? Air conditioners and electric carpets are probably the most commonly used types of heaters.
こたつにみかんは冬の風物詩
でも、こたつの魔力に勝つ自信がないから、絶対に買わないと決めてる
We have an older house near the mountains and need some more heavy-duty equipment to keep the rooms warm.
Kerosene Fan Heater
パワフル!
Kerosene Stove
加湿器も兼ねられて煮炊きもできるスグレモノ!
They certainly provide a lot of heat, but the fumes are a concern.
There are also some environmental issues.
限りある資源の消費やCO2の排出量とか
All this effort we put into heating our home — the carpets, the electric, gas, and kerosene heaters, the habit-forming kotatsu — could be avoided if we only had:
Central Heating!
Like at grandma's house!
The holy grail of home heating. We'll warm up to that topic in our next postcard.


1年で最も寒い時期がやって来ました。古い日本家屋に住む私たちの暖房器具は石油ファンヒーターがメインですが……

**middle of winter** 冬の半ば，真冬

**keep away** ～を近づけない，避ける

**heavy-duty** 極めて丈夫な，頑丈な

**equipment** 機器，装置

**kerosene** ケロシン，灯油

**fumes** 〔有害な〕煙，蒸気

**concern** 懸念，心配

**habit-forming** やみつきになる

**holy grail** 究極の理想

**warm up to** ～で活気づく

アメリカではセントラルヒーティングが主流です。我が家のように各部屋を個別に暖めるのではなく、家中の部屋を一緒に暖めます。

pretty much　ほとんど，大方

norm　基準，標準

individually　一つひとつ，個別に

via　～を通って，経由して

thermostat　温度自動調節器，サーモスタット

electric bill　電気代

keep in mind that　〔that以下〕ということを心に留めておく

viable　適用可能な，通用する

airtight　空気を通さない，密閉した

highly insulated　高度に断熱された

drafty　〔家・建物が〕すき間風の入る

# Vol.171 Heaters II: Reheated
## (セントラルヒーティング)

Central heating is pretty much the norm in the United States. Central heating usually covers all the rooms in a house rather than each room individually, like in our house.

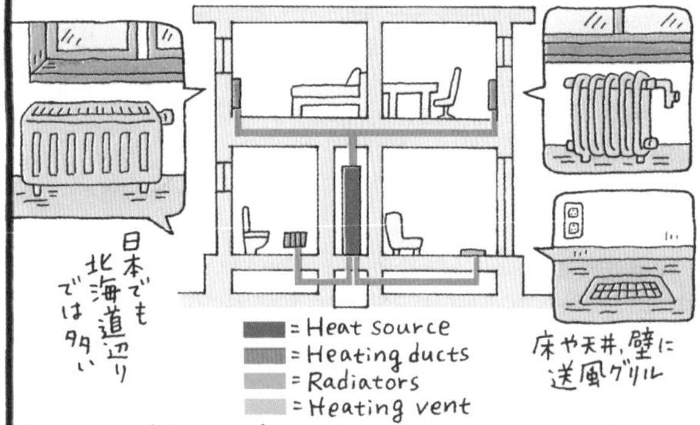

日本でも北海道辺りでは多い
床や天井、壁に送風グリル
= Heat source
= Heating ducts
= Radiators
= Heating vent


Heat is delivered to all of the rooms via ducts from a central heating unit. Each room has a thermostat, but they are usually set at the same temperature throughout the house. This makes it comfortable to move from room to room.

寒いのイヤだけど覚悟を決めてお風呂やトイレへ
しんどい
夜中の逡巡
こういうのとは無縁に


Yes, this uses a lot of electricity, but the average monthly electric bill is still less than $150 (about ¥16600). That doesn't seem too expensive. Keep in mind, however, that electricity rates are lower in the United States than most countries.

なんと!
U.S. electricity rates are about HALF the Japan rates!
自国でエネルギー資源をまかなえる強みだね


Central heating is viable because homes are built airtight and highly insulated. Our 40-year-old home in Japan is drafty and likely has little or no insulation.

We can only dream about living in a house with central heating some day. Hopefully that will help us feel a little bit warmer this winter.

夏の湿気に対応する通気性の良さが特長

# Vol.172 The Best Way to Dry Clothes
（衣類乾燥機の違い）

Steve and I have an agreement about using our clothes dryer. We use the dryer for towels and his clothes; we hang the kids' clothes, my clothes, and other items outside on a clothesline.
乾燥機が当たり前のアメリカ育ち
Our DEAL
外干しが基本の日本育ち
The weather can change this. When pollen is in the air, for example, everything goes into the dryer.
There's no denying that the American models are very attractive.
They're huge!
家庭用なのに業務用みたい
Washer
Dryer
アメリカの義母宅で
よく、双子みたいに並べて置かれている
They're power-ful!
It's all dry in less than an hour.
日本だと3時間以上かかるのが普通 ※ガス式は別
ホカホカ〜
熱いくらい
そのためこんなことも！
Beware! Some clothes will shrink.
いやーん
I first thought the difference was due to the technology, but it seems to be mainly because of the voltage levels.
Japan 100V
US 220V
Those are the common voltage levels for electric dryer.
Neither voltage level is better than the other — they're just different. I'm used to hanging clothes outside to dry. Steve's standard is to put all of the clothes in the dryer. Just like the voltage, neither approach to drying clothes is better, they're just different.

家で衣類乾燥機を使うと、アメリカの義母宅で使った乾燥機のパワフルさを思い出しますが……

**have an agreement about** 〜について合意に達する

**pollen** 花粉

**there is no denying that** 〜は否定できない，〜であるのは明らかだ

**in less than an hour** 1時間足らずで

**beware** 注意する，用心する

**due to** 〜が原因で

**voltage level** 電圧レベル

**neither** どちらの〜も…でない

ハルとミドリがDNA検査を受けると聞いたら驚かれるかもしれませんが、心配ご無用です。

- **bet**　～だと確信している
- **shock**　ひどく驚かせる，ショックを与える
- **identify**　確認［識別］する
- **biological parent**　実の親
- **scene of a crime**　犯行現場
- **ancestry**　先祖，祖先，家系
- **lineage**　血筋，血統
- **identity**　正体，独自性，アイデンティティー
- **verify**　確かめる，照合する
- **origin**　先祖，血統
- **saliva**　唾液
- **vial**　小瓶

Vol.173
DNA Test Step 1: Preparation
（DNAテスト①：準備）
We're having our DNA tested!
I bet this will shock many people.
ね
Aren't DNA tests used to identify someone's true biological parent? Or to find proof that someone was at the scene of a crime?
聞くに聞けない…
Don't worry. Our kids are having their DNA tested to learn their true ancestry.
Most Americans have lineages that go back to other countries, and knowing where their ancestors came from is an important part of their identity.
Mother: Irish descent
Father: Italian descent
Happy St. Patrick's Day
3月に祝う
ラビオリの味
しっかり受け継がれるイタリア系の鼻と
DNA tests are becoming popular in America as a way to verify one's origins. Steve's mother sent some DNA testing kits to our kids as Christmas gifts.
It's very easy to do. Simply put some saliva in a vial and mail it to the testing company.
ancestry DNA
$80～$100くらい
結構いっぱい
Put your saliva into the test vial.
What information will be found in our kids' DNA?
Will there be any surprises?
All we have to do now is mail it in and wait.
Mail it to the testing company. The results come back in two months.

# Vol.174 DNA Test Step 2: Shipping Saliva
(DNAテスト②：発送)

After the kids filled two vials with their spit, I sealed them in the small boxes and headed to the post office.
1 郵便
こちらに記入して下さい
はい
But when I went to fill in the international customs form, I ran into some problems.
内容品の詳細な記載
Detailed description of contents
内容品の価格
Value
えーと…
Contents? Should I write "saliva"?
Value? Does it have any value?
なんならプライスレス??
I ended up writing "Saliva for DNA test" and valued it at "$0."
"DNA test"…?
明らかに困惑
That might be a "specimen." I'd better check.
上司
東京国際郵便局に問い合わせよう
なんか大事になってる
DNA testing is really popular now in the U.S. This is just a commercially sold DNA test kit with some spit in it.
しどろもどろ
The postal clerks explained that they had to be cautious about "specimens" to protect against terrorism or viruses.
They finally let me send it after they had me write "Not an infectious substance" on the customs slip.
I hope the test kits make it to the testing center.


DNA検査のために子どもたちの唾液を入れた小さな箱を郵送しようとしたところ、予想外の問題が発生しました。

**shipping** 発送，出荷
**spit** 唾，唾液
**seal** 密封する
**customs form** 関税申告書
**run into a problem** 問題にぶつかる
**specimen** 検査サンプル，試料
**commercially** 商業的に
**postal clerk** 郵便局員
**cautious about** ～に警戒する
**infectious substance** 感染性物質
**make it to** ～までたどり着く，到達する

COLUMN
7

# The Spirit of Self-confidence

When I came back from the United States near the end of summer vacation, I realized that I feel more confident about my body and the way I dress in the United States than in Japan.

For example, I have a dress that looks like the drawing on the right. I was never able to wear it in Japan, even though I was obsessed with it, because I cared so much about what others would think, probably a little too much. When I wore it in the United States, my cousin complimented my outfit saying that it looked good on me. I felt really happy and proud of myself for building up the courage to actually wear it. My cousin also wore a one peace skirt. We walked a lot in the outfits, so we had a lot of chances to be seen by people. I felt confident in myself even though I would've felt quite insecure about my muscles (especially my thighs). I was also expecting some disapproving looks. But there was also no disapproving looks or any negative comments. A compliment from a total stranger came towards us unexpectedly. She said, "I love your outfits. It looks good on you guys!" It felt fresh and just amazing.

I came back to Japan hoping I could keep the spirit of self-confidence. Two days after coming back, my mom and I went to a ballet recital with my ballet teacher and her daughter (one of my best friends). I went in the same one peace skirt. I thought it'd be a good experience to get more confident about myself. I got on the train confidently, but soon became insecure because of the judgmental looks coming from some of the people on the train. I also felt like people were giving me disapproving looks when I was walking on the street. I still tried to stay as confident as I can but it was quite hard.

In japan I feel like the standards for beauty eliminates people like me from feeling beautiful. I hope I can become more confident in myself so that I can wear whatever I want to wear. I also hope that I can spread the joy I felt in the summer to others and make them smile and also feel confident in themselves.

■ **self-confidence** 自尊心 ■ **obsessed with** ～に魅了される ■ **compliment** 褒める，好意を示す ■ **thigh** 太もも ■ **unexpectedly** 不意に ■ **feel fresh** 爽快さを感じる ■ **judgmental** 批判的な ■ **eliminate** 排除する

STEVE
来日33年目の
江戸好きアメリカ人
KIKUE
ワタクシ
HARU
息子。
中学2年生
MIDORI
娘。
小学5年生

# 8th Year

2018

桜の下で日本酒を酌み交わしながらお花見——日本ではよく見る光景ですが、アメリカではそうもいかないようで……

**drinking alcohol** 酒を飲むこと
**finally** やっと，ついに
**lay out** 広げる，配置する
**sip** 少しずつ[ちびちび]飲む
**common scene** よく見られる光景
**illegal** 法で禁じられた
**public space** 公共の場
**private property** 私有地
**excessively drunk** 過度に酔っぱらった
**pleasure** 楽しみ，喜び

# Vol.175 Drinking Alcohol Outside
## （屋外で酒盛り）

Spring has finally arrived. It's the season to lay out a blanket under the cherry blossoms and sip some delicious sake.
まー飲んで
どうも
カンパーイ！
うぇーい
This is a common scene in Japan, but not in America. In many places in the United States, it's illegal to drink alcohol in a public space.
えー
Not even in a park or at the beach! What about a BBQ?
If it's private property, it's OK.
In fact, it's even illegal to be excessively drunk on the street, even when returning from a party.
これもアメリカ的にありえない図
You know how in American movies, you sometimes see someone hiding a bottle or can of alcohol in a brown paper bag? Now you know why.
こういうやつね
That also may be one reason why BBQ parties are often held at people's homes.
屋外飲みサイコー
Cheers!
We're looking forward to enjoying all the pleasures of a Japanese picnic in the park.

# Vol.176 A Room of One's Own I : The Door
(子ども部屋①：ドア)

It's well known that in America many kids have their own bedrooms from when they are babies with the idea that it fosters a sense of independence. We decided that Haru was ready for his own room when he became a middle school student. That may be a little later than usual in Japan.

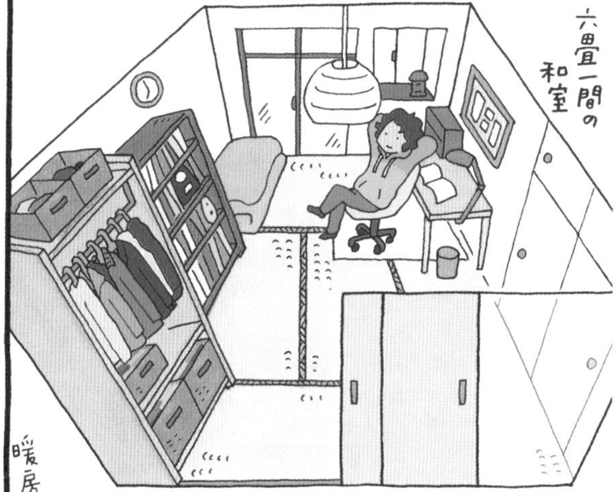
六畳一間の和室

暖房中は除いてだけど

In Japan, people generally consider their room to be their own private space and keep the door closed most of the time.

Haru, however, keeps his door open most of the time when he's there and even when he's not there. In this respect, we take the American approach.

Where Steve grew up, a closed door often meant the person wants privacy or doesn't want to be bothered. The rest of the time, doors remained open.

Someone getting dressed?
Sleeping?
A private conver-sation?
立ち入り厳禁!
閉じられたドアは
という看板を立てているようなもの

Haru is at the age when personal privacy becomes very important. We are well aware the day is coming when the door could be closed most of the time. We parents are keeping an eye on our maturing son's development.

中学生になって自分の部屋ができたハル。そのドアは基本的にいつも開けっ放しです。なぜなら——

**of one's own** 自分自身の
**sense of independence** 自立心
**private space** 私的空間
**most of the time** たいていの場合(は)
**in this respect** この点において
**privacy** プライバシー《私生活を他人に知られたり干渉されたりしない権利》
**bother** 煩わせる
**remain** ～のままである
**well aware** はっきりと意識している
**keep an eye on** ～から目を離さない，～を見守る
**mature** 大人になる，成熟する

ハルの部屋の掲示板に貼られた紙は、彼が自分の部屋を持つための大切な約束です。

bulletin board 掲示板
electronics 電子機器
neat 整頓された
pile 積み重なり，山
allowance 手当，小遣い
savings 貯金
come with ～がついてくる
plumbing 配管，水道設備
weeding 草とり
associate 関連付ける，連想する
make progress 進歩する
gradual 段階的な
steady 着実な

Vol.177
A Room of One's Own II: Room Rules
(子ども部屋②：ルール)
Haru has an important message pinned on the bulletin board above his desk.
ROOM RULES
Make bed every day in the morning
No food or electronics in the room
Room must be neat every Saturday by 6:30
No clothes piles
We respect that your room is your private space.
We will always knock before entering.
Prepare bath every night.
Help Dad for 1 hour each weekend.
Allowance ¥2,200/Month 10%+ to savings
This is part of the responsibility that comes with having his own room.
(同じタイミングでおこづかい制も始めたため，それも絡んだ内容になっている)
He helps with various household chores on the weekends.
下にバケツを置いてからね
こう？
Fixing the plumbing
Weeding the back yard
など
Most people probably associate one's own room with a quiet place to study. We do too, and we have also linked it with self-management and independence.
In the year he has had his own room, Haru has made gradual but steady progress meeting the conditions of the Room Rules.
服の山はまだちょくちょくできてるけどね

# Vol.178 Food for the Convalescent I: Ingredients（義母への療養食①：材料）

My mother-in-law recently had successful surgery on her stomach. We made an un-planned trip to visit her as she convalesced in her home. The surgery had left her very weak, and she had lost her appetite.
Even water tastes bad...
Because we live so far away and cannot be part of her daily life, we were very happy to be there to lend support in her time of need.
Assistance
孫はいるだけで喜びになる
My main job was to make the meals. After we arrived, one of my first stops was the supermarket to stock up on supplies.
What I found at the local supermarket
TOFU
SILKEN(絹)
FIRM(木綿)
EXTRA FIRM
Udon
Miso
Sesame Seed Oil
Mirin
Soy Sauce
KIKKOMAN
Rice Vinegar
Rice
NISHIKI
錦
米
Supermarkets in California usually have well-stocked Asian Food sections.
ポッキーやえびせんなんかも売ってるよ
Pocky
What I brought from Japan
ほんだし
そうめん，片栗粉
カットわかめ
白ゴマ，練りゴマ
高野豆腐
切干大根
車麩，板麩
She loves Japanese food, and I am hoping to help her regain her appetite.
Next time, I'll let you know what I made for her.


腸の手術を受け、自宅療養している義母のために急遽、渡米しました。療養食を作るために私が用意したのは——

**convalescent** 回復期

**surgery** 外科手術

**convalesce** 快方に向かう

**lose one's appetite** 食欲をなくす

**lend support** 力を貸す，助ける

**in one's time of need** 困ったときに

**first stop** 一つ目の目的地［計画］

**stock up on** 〔商品を〕買いだめする，買い込む

**regain appetite** 食欲を回復する

義母に何とか食欲を取り戻してほしい……！まずは消化にいいものをと思って、にゅうめんを作ったところ――

effect　効果

determined to　～することを固く決心している

easy to digest　消化しやすい

seaweed　海藻

have some more　もう少し食べる，おかわりする

stimulate one's appetite　食欲をそそる

not only A but (also) B　AだけでなくBも

regain one's health　健康を取り戻す

Vol.179
Food for the Convalescent II: The Effect（義母への療養食②：効果）
My mother-in-law had almost completely lost her appetite after her surgery. I was determined to help her get it back. When I thought about something that was tasty and easy to digest, the first idea I had was noodles in broth.
Wheat gluten（お麩）
Soy sauce broth
Seaweed
Some vegetables
Somen
にゅうめん Nyumen
She loved it!
...It's delicious! What is it? Can I have some more?
パァ…
Stimulates the Appetite
水すらまずいと言っていたのに
よっしゃ！
As her appetite returned, I gradually added to the menu.
お酢にみそ、とくにヒットがや！
きゅうりの入ったはりはり漬け
にんじんとピーマンのゴマみそ炒め
みそケチャップライス
豆腐田楽
It's now three weeks later. We have returned to Japan, and she is eating normally. She's making Japanese dishes too. She buys the ingredients on Amazon and watches how to prepare the dishes on YouTube.
She has not only regained her health, but has a new interest. I've found another reason to love my country's food.
今や煮干しとかつお節でだしをひく義母。おにぎりも好き

# Vol.180 Bridal Shower
## (ブライダルシャワー)

With spring in full swing, many women are preparing to become June Brides.

Steve and I were married 17 years ago, and among my many precious reminiscences is one very vivid memory of interesting gifts I received from my American relatives.

ギョ
スケスケ!
SEXY
こんなのばっかり
From, Steve's aunt
From Steve's sister

I was very surprised and not a little embarrassed, but these types of gifts are a custom at "bridal showers."

About one month before the wedding date, the bride's friends and family-to-be hold a bridal shower for her. Only women are invited, so they have a chance to talk frankly and laugh freely before the marriage. After having a bite to eat, they give the bride presents, like sexy panties, that might be out of place at other parties.

あのBachelor Partyの女性版のようなものですね
(注)あくまでもイメージです
(独身最後に、女人禁制でハジける新郎と友人たち)

One part of the custom is to collect the gift wrapping paper and ribbons and make a "rehearsal bouquet" for the bride to use during the wedding rehearsals.

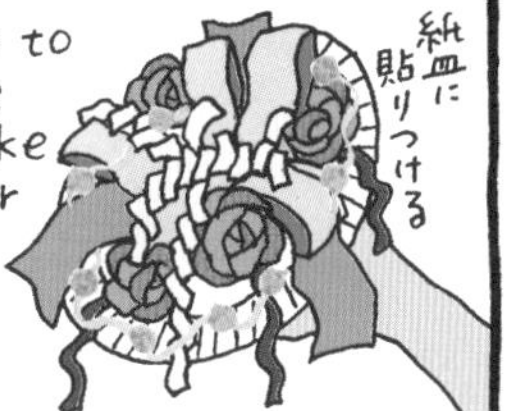
紙皿に貼りつける

My bridal shower was an eye-opening experience, and I will never forget how much we laughed and the warm welcome my family-to-be gave to me.

結婚した当時の思い出として忘れがたいのは、ブライダルシャワーとしてアメリカの親族から贈られた品々です。

**bridal shower** ブライダルシャワー《結婚する女性のお祝いパーティー》
**in full swing** 最高の状態で
**reminiscence** 思い出，思い出すもの［こと］
**vivid memory** 鮮やかな記憶
**not a little** 少なからず，かなり
**embarrassed** 恥ずかしい，どぎまぎして
**have a bite to eat** 軽い食事をする
**out of place** 場違いである
**rehearsal** リハーサル，練習
**eye-opening experience** 目を見張るような経験

アメリカに行くと必ず、スティーヴは洋服を買う日を設けます。彼がおしゃれにうるさいから、ではありません。

Vol.181
Clothing Sizes
（服のサイズと体型）
Every time we travel to the U.S., Steve sets aside one day to shop for clothes. That may sound like he's a fashionista, but he's not. There's a practical reason for it.
まとめ買いしておかないと
The clothes I've bought in Japan don't fit right.
丈が短い
股に食い込む
REI
We have the same shops in Japan. Why doesn't he just buy them there?
GAP
UNI QLO
Eddie Bauer
Well, the brands might be global, but the sizes and styles are usually designed to match the local preferences.
That's why clothes in Japan don't fit him the same as clothes bought in America.
That doesn't mean that the clothes in America all fit him perfectly.
Asian
European
体の厚みにも差が
Body Type
いつも袖を折り返してる
The sleeves are too long!
注 イタリア系は肌の色も黄色人種寄り
Maybe it's his Italian genes, but the sleeves and legs of American clothing are often too long for him.
帯に短し、たすきに長し？
Someday, I'd like to see how Italian clothing fits him, but he might not like to be so stylish.


**set aside a day to** 〜するために一日空けておく

**sound like** 〜のように聞こえる

**fashionista** ファッショニスタ，最新ファッションに敏感な人

**preference** 好み，優先傾向

**same as** 〜と同じである

**sleeve** 袖，たもと

**gene** 遺伝子

**stylish** 流行の，洗練された

# Vol.182 Summer School Visit in Japan
## (夏休みの体験入学)

Several of our Japanese friends living overseas return to Japan during the summer vacation. Schools let out early in America, and the kids have time to participate in Japanese schools before summer vacation starts in Japan.

ボクも小学生時代
毎夏してました
友人の息子Leoくん。中日ハーフ。在米12年
アメリカから来ました。
よろしくお願いします


Joining a Japanese school really helps Leo improve his Japanese and get to know his Japanese culture. Mother and son both look forward to it.

Cleaning up!
After-school activities!
Leoくんのお母さん
えっそんなこと?


Leo's mom likes that her son and his classmates are responsible for helping keep the school clean. Schoolkids in America don't get the same experience.

I think it's great that they learn a sense of responsibility.
アメリカでは業者が掃除する
日本


In America, many states require that children aged 12 or younger must be accompanied by a guardian or an older sibling at all times. Leo likes that he is free to go out by himself everywhere in Japan.

公園行ってサッカーやろうぜ
うん!!
ぐっ
Freedom!!


Some of the things we take for granted really deserve new appreciation.

海外に住む日本人家族の子どもたちが、夏休み前の日本の学校に体験入学するのは珍しいことではありません。

- **several of** ～のうちの数人[いくつか]
- **let out** 〔授業・会などが〕終わる
- **get to know** ～を知るようになる
- **responsible for** ～に対して責任がある
- **require** 要求する，義務付ける
- **accompanied by** ～が同行する
- **guardian** 保護者
- **sibling** きょうだい
- **take ~ for granted** ～を当たり前のことと考える
- **deserve** 価値がある
- **new appreciation** 新たな認識，改めて実感する価値

いつ来るかと恐れていたハルの反抗期は、思いのほか穏やかで、ちょっと拍子抜けしています。

teenage rebellion　10代の反抗，反抗期
in the throes of　～に苦しんでいる
angst　不安
dread　恐れる，ひどく心配する
onslaught　猛攻，襲来
adolescence　青年期《思春期から成人期までの過渡期》
to tell you the truth　実は，実を言うと
considerate　思いやりのある
surly　無愛想な
feel irritated　むしゃくしゃする
no big deal　大したことない
play a role　役割を果たす

# Vol.183 Teenage Rebellion
（ハルの反抗期）

Haru recently celebrated his 14th birthday. He should be in the throes of teenage angst. I've been dreading the onslaught of adolescence in my nice young boy.
うるせー！
くそババア
とか言われちゃったりしてー？
やだなー
でもそのうち
あー、かわいい…
But, to tell you the truth, it hasn't been as bad as I was expecting.
Sharing relationship
ボク、指揮者もやるよ
合唱コンクール見に来る？
ママ、それおかしくない？
ボクはおかしいと思う
Clearly stating opinions
Considerate
明日は自分でおにぎり作ってくから
朝、寝てていいよ
He was a little surly for while when he was a fifth grader, but that seems to have settled down. I asked him about it.
なんか拍子抜け
Haru, do you feel like you want to rebel against us? Or do you feel like that period is over?
えー
I think this is what my rebellious stage is like. Sometimes I feel irritated. But that's about it. It's no big deal.
His attitude is probably mostly due to his personality. But I think the way our family interacts may also have played a role.
1 Everyone shares their opinion
Why?
Because I think...
アメリカは「伝える」文化
日本は「察する」文化
2 Reverse relationship
これどういう意味？
あー それはね
ENGLISH
（小3くらいから。父子間でも）
Our dear, sweet 10-year-old Midori may be another story. That may be the difference between girls and boys.
フン
べつにっ
最近なんかムカムカするー
The first sign?

Vol.184
Sleepovers I
(お泊まり会①)
Social groups commonly become a high priority for girls in the fifth grade. Girls seem especially eager to fit in with their chosen group. Midori is no exception. She's become adamant about participating in group activities and having the same items as her friends.
帰国子女が多い学校なので友達もこんな感じ
We are BFF
Best Friends Forever
ミドリ
アメリカ育ちのHちゃん
メキシコ育ちのKちゃん
Rちゃん
The girls especially love having sleepovers.
Taylor Swiftが大人気。他、"We Are the World"をみんなで熱唱したり
帰国子女が多いとそうなるのかー
At Karaoke
Nearly all of the songs were in English.
At Home
They mainly used apps to make music videos of themselves
イマドキ〜
曲に合わせてコマ撮り動画を撮ったり編集したりするスマホのアプリで
B612やTikTok
The girls seemed to have had a good time, and the sleepover seemed to have been a success. I was so relieved...
...and exhausted.
ぐったり
布団の用意やら食事の支度やら
When shall we do it again?!
That's what we did at our sleepover. Next time, I'll show you some things that our family in America has done at its sleepovers.


小5になったミドリは、仲良しグループのメンバーとの関係が何よりも大切なようです。最近はお泊まり会も増えています。

**sleepover** 外泊，お泊まり会

**social group** 社会集団

**high priority** 高い優先度

**eager to** 〜に熱心である

**adamant about** 〜に関して譲らない

**have a good time** 楽しく過ごす

**relieved** ホッとした，解放された

**exhausted** 疲れ切った，消耗した

子どもたちは大喜びなお泊まり会ですが、受け入れる親としてはちょっと億劫、というのが正直なところで——

get excited about　～にワクワクする

less enthusiastic　いまいち気乗りしない

quite a bit of work　かなりの労力

remember　覚えている，心に留める

sleeping bag　寝袋

devise　考案する

# Vol.185 Sleepovers II

（お泊まり会②）

While Midori and her friends get excited about having sleepovers during summer vacation, as a parent, I'm decidedly less enthusiastic.
Preparing futons
Cleaning up
Planning meals
何にしよう
There seems to be quite a bit of work involved.
I asked Steve's brother in America how parents there usually prepare for sleepovers.
That's certainly a lot of work. Here, it usually doesn't take so much effort.
Steve弟。シングルファザー
First, the kids are reminded to remember they are guests in someone's house.
Hello! Thank you for having me over.
初回のみ。2回目からは Hello. How are you? くらいでOK
（日本語の「お邪魔します」みたいな定型句はない）
Point 1 Showered before visiting
Point 2 Bring your own sleeping bag and pillow
カーペットの家が多いから そのまま敷いて寝られる
Meals are very simple.
Dinner Pizza delivery
PIZZA
Breakfast Pancakes
+ ・Chocolate syrup ・Fruit ・Bacon or Sausage とか
Setting a basic standard makes hosting a sleepover so much easier.
Steve's brother also devised some interesting house rules for sleepovers, which I'll share next time.

# Vol.186 Sleepovers III（お泊まり会③）

Steve's brother in America has simplified sleepovers by having the girls bring sleeping bags and pillows and by ordering pizza to be delivered. He has even gone one step further by creating the SSR.

Sleepover
Survival
Rating


The SSR is based on your ability to have a successful sleepover.

Each category is rated on a score of 1 to 10.

Your overall SSR will be used for future decisions to have sleepovers.

He cleverly created the list so the kids would see it as a game. The checklist was a great success for both the kids and parents. The other kids' parents have even started using it.

| Fun Factor | Parent Relaxation | Departure |
|---|---|---|
| • Did you have fun?<br>• Were you kind to one another?<br>• Did you do something creative with your time? | • Did you do your best to allow the parent(s) to rest and relax?<br>• Did you follow the house rules?<br>• Did you help with cleanup?<br>• Did you go to sleep when asked? | • Did you leave the place cleaner than you found it?<br>• Was the departure done without a fuss? |

子どもは子どもで楽しみつつ、
親は親でリラックスして過ごせるように
Let's clean up!
OK!
PIZZA
Shhhh!


The checklist is designed not only to help the kids have fun, but it also provides instruction on how to behave when you're a guest in someone's home. With that in mind, parents may even start requesting their kids to have sleepovers.

姪のお泊まり会に慣れているアメリカの義弟に話を聞いてみると、すてきな工夫がたくさんありました。

**simplify** 簡単にする，単純化する

**go one step further** さらに一歩進む

**rate on a score of 1 to 10** 10点満点で評価する

**overall** 全部の，総合的な

**cleverly** 賢く，上手に

**factor** 要因，係数

**one another** お互い

**departure** 出発

**without a fuss** 騒がずに，ぐずぐず言わずに

**provide instruction on how to** ～する方法を指導する

**with that in mind** その点を考慮して

ハルには同い年のいとこがアメリカにいます。彼女の話を聞くと、日米の教育の違いが見えてきます。

passive learning　受身の学習
engage in　～に従事する，携わる
curriculum　カリキュラム，教育［履修］課程
required　〔科目が〕必修の
fine arts　美術
elective　選択科目
culinary arts　料理
divided into　～に分けられる
humanities and sciences　文系と理系
furthermore　さらに
fulfill　履行する，満たす
pursue　追求する，進む
inherently　本質的に

# Vol.187 School Life I : Methods
（学校生活①：学び方）

Haru and his cousin in the United States are the same age. She's already in high school, though, because the school year in America starts in September.

| U.S. (September Start) | | JAPAN (April Start) | |
|---|---|---|---|
| | 9th grade (Freshman) | 3年生 | 中学 |
| High school (4年間) | 10th 〃 (Sophomore) | 1年生 | 高校 |
| | 11th 〃 (Junior) | 2年生 | |
| | 12th 〃 (Senior) | 3年生 | |

同い年なのにかたや
High schooler
Middle school student

学習スピードはあまり変わらず
数学なんかはむしろ
日本の方が進んでるかも
Math
数学

Whenever we hear about her school activities, we're reminded of how different the American and Japanese education systems are.

## 1 Role of Teachers

Classes in Japan are typically "passive learning," where students receive information from the teacher. Students in the U.S. engage in "active learning," where they do presentations to the class and the instructor guides class discussions.

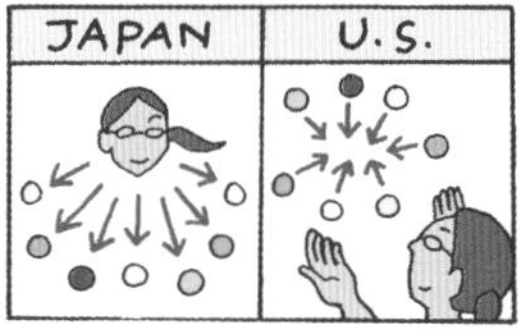
JAPAN
U.S.

## 2 Curriculum Options

Required
•English
•Math
•Science
•History
•Fine Arts
•Physical Education
•Foreign Language など
Electives
•Journalism •Design
•Culinary Arts •Business
•Engineering •Auto Shop
•Leadership •Wood Shop
•Communications
•Environmental Studies
•Home Economics など
コンピューターやボランティア、インターンシップなどが含まれることも
大学みたい！
実践的でおもしろそう！

Courses are not strictly divided into humanities and sciences, and furthermore, Haru's cousin doesn't even have a homeroom. Students create their own class schedules to fulfill the course requirements.

Information and learning are actively pursued, rather than just received. The school system inherently teaches students the American values of freedom and responsibility.

# Vol.188 School Life II: Report Cards
（学校生活②：評価方法）

Haru and Midori have classes for native English speakers at their school. The test scores and report cards for those classes are bewildering to me.

## Test Scores

正
誤
JAPAN
U.S.A.
ギョッ
Test Midori
間違いだらけ!?
ちゃんと合ってるよ
Good!
日米で正誤表記が異なる


## Report Cards

Teachers evaluate students on several items, including how actively they participate in class.

トップ項目
Report Card:
Class Participation 10/10
Quizzes 8/10
Assignments/Homework 29/30
Term Project 15/15
Midterm Exam 14/
Final Exam 17
Grade (in percent)
Grade

I think the reason that class participation is so important is because it is integral to the American style of teaching. The quality and success of student-led instruction depends on active student participation.

Homework research presentation
One student presents their research and conclusions, then the other students think about and discuss the topic
ナルホド。でもー


Students learn to listen to various ideas, analyze them, and then form their own opinions.

The categories on the report cards not only indicate that American-style education aims to cultivate knowledge, but that it also instills a democratic approach to the education of the country's children.

子どもたちが参加している英語ネイティブ向けの授業では、採点の仕方も成績のつけ方も欧米式です。

- **report card** 成績表，通信簿
- **bewildering** ひどく困惑させる
- **evaluate** 評価する
- **participate in** ～に参加［関与］する
- **assignment** 宿題，課題
- **integral to** ～に不可欠な
- **student-led** 生徒主導の
- **instruction** 教育，指示
- **analyze** 分析する
- **indicate** 指摘する，示す
- **instill** 染み込ませる，教え込む
- **democratic approach** 民主的アプローチ

１年半の間がんと闘ってきた義母が亡くなりました。数週間後、私たちは葬儀に出席するためアメリカへ渡りました。

say farewell　別れのあいさつをする

pass away　亡くなる，逝去する

funeral　葬式，葬儀

ashes　遺灰，遺骨

urn　骨つぼ

pantry　食品庫，食料貯蔵室

console　慰める，元気づける

caring and loving　思いやりがあって愛情深い

memorial service　告別式

cherish　〔～を〕大事にする

dear to　（人）にとって大切な

# Vol.189 Saying Farewell to Mom
（義母との別れ）

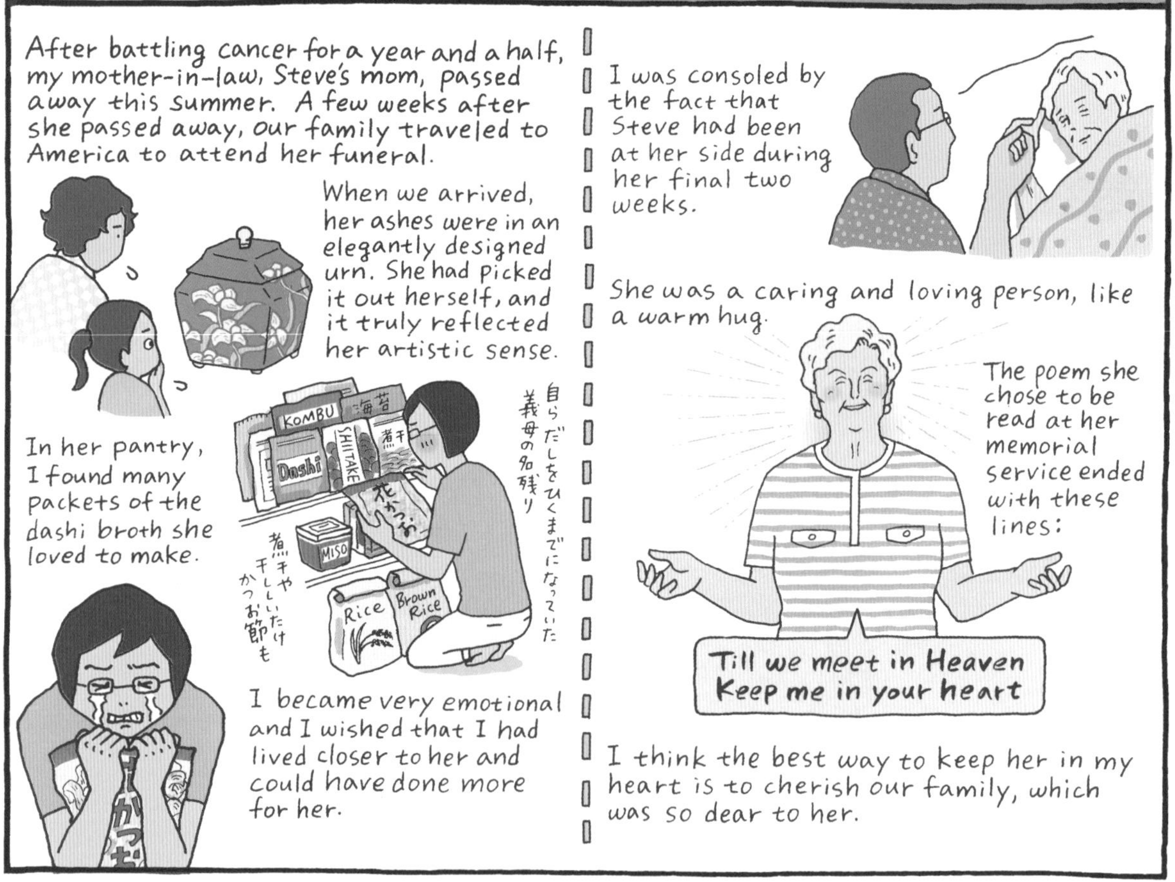
After battling cancer for a year and a half, my mother-in-law, Steve's mom, passed away this summer. A few weeks after she passed away, our family traveled to America to attend her funeral.
When we arrived, her ashes were in an elegantly designed urn. She had picked it out herself, and it truly reflected her artistic sense.
In her pantry, I found many packets of the dashi broth she loved to make.
KOMBU
海苔
Dashi
SHIITAKE
煮干
花かつお
MISO
Rice
Brown Rice
自らだしをひくまでになっていた義母の名残り
煮干や干ししいたけかつお節も
I became very emotional and I wished that I had lived closer to her and could have done more for her.
I was consoled by the fact that Steve had been at her side during her final two weeks.
She was a caring and loving person, like a warm hug.
The poem she chose to be read at her memorial service ended with these lines:
Till we meet in Heaven
Keep me in your heart
I think the best way to keep her in my heart is to cherish our family, which was so dear to her.

# Vol.190 The Memorial Service I
（告別式①）

My family published my mother-in-law's obituary in several publications. This is a common way to announce that a person has passed away and to let people know details about the funeral.
顔写真入り
日本のお悔やみ欄よりスペースが大きい
The obituary provides a brief personal history and some words about her.
抜粋
She is survived by her husband, four children, and four beloved grandchildren.
The ceremony was quite different from those I have experienced in Japan.
ハワイに10年暮らした義母にちなんで
Bouquet of tropical flowers
Typical dress-up outfits
In general, family members wore black clothing, but there aren't strict rules like in Japan.
シャツやネクタイは義母がいちばん好きだった紫色
露出が多くても真珠以外のアクセサリーをつけてもOK
姪めい
義父
男性もノーネクタイが多い
The guests wore clothes of various colors, like you would wear to visit someone's home. It was quite different than a memorial service in Japan, where everyone usually wears the same black clothing.
While it was a sad day for everyone, the bright colors created a strong feeling of warmth among family and friends.


訃報、供花、服装……アメリカの葬儀にまつわる様々なことが日本のそれとは異なっていました。

obituary 追悼記事, お悔やみ欄
let someone know （人）に知らせる
brief 大まかな, 簡潔な
personal history 経歴
survived by someone （人）を残して先に逝く
beloved 最愛の, いとしい
in general 一般に, 概して
strict rule 厳格な規則
bright color 鮮やかな色
strong feeling 〔引き起こされる〕強い感情
warmth 暖かさ, 優しさ

日本で言うところの精進落としや納骨もまた趣の異なるものでした。そこに温かみを感じつつ、私なりのお別れをしました。

remind A of B　AにBのことを思い出させる
reunion party　同窓会
lively　陽気な，明るい
dwell on　～をくよくよ考える
suffering　苦しみ，苦痛
eternal happiness　永遠の幸せ
joyous　喜びに満ちた
send-off　見送り
disorienting　方向感覚を失わせる，混乱させる
ingrained　染みついた，植えつけられた
altar　祭壇，供物台

# Vol.191 The Memorial Service II
## （告別式②）

After the memorial service for my mother-in-law, everyone drove to my sister-in-law's home. There was a buffet and a computer monitor displaying photos. Everyone was talking to old friends and relatives. It reminded me of a reunion party. I was surprised by how lively it was compared with similar events I have attended in Japan.

アメリカ
有志の人が思い出をスピーチしたり
日本
黒尽くしで言葉少な

Rather than dwelling on death and sadness, it seemed more like a celebration of moving on to a better place.

CELEBRATING THE LIFE OF
Suzanne
葬儀のプログラムも

Death can be the end of suffering and also the start of eternal happiness. In this spirit, a joyous send-off seems appropriate.

Although it was a little disorienting, I felt that I could express my feelings when we buried her ashes.

こっそり数珠も持参した
ちょっとお焼香に近い感じも。
骨壺を穴に納めた後、希望者はその上に一握りの土を入れていく

At an unconscious level, there was a moment at her graveside when I felt how deeply ingrained Buddhist customs were in me.

I realized that there are many types of funerals, but in the end it is a very personal matter.

After returning to Japan, we set up a small altar in our home for my mother-in-law.

寂しくないように義父と一緒の写真
形見の指輪
ミドリが置いた旅のお土産なども
お香
水
おりん

# Vol.192 The Challenges of the Japanese Language（日本語の難しさ）

Haru and I recently attended a talk given by the TV celebrity Daniel Kahl. Can you believe he's been in Japan for over 40 years?

オラも間もなく還暦だす
タレントで山形弁研究家
若い頃のダニエルさん
んだんだ
だいぶ恰幅（かっぷく）がよくなったけど
軽快トークは相変わらず。
90分間、しゃべり通しでした！


The entertaining talk included humorous anecdotes about the struggles foreigners have with the Japanese language. He shed light on many issues that I've often heard Steve talk about.

## Challenge #1 Missing subjects

We often omit the subjects of sentences. This can make it really hard for a listener to catch on to what we're talking about.

不安
今は誰の話…？


## Challenge #2 Indirectness

We tend to express our thoughts indirectly when we don't want to ruffle listeners' feathers.

いりません
（直接的）
これだと冷たくてキツイ感じで角が立つ
No, thank you
結構です
（婉曲的）
結構には「見事」とかの意味もあるし
結局いるの？いらないの？となりそう
英語では、YES・NOをシンプルにハッキリと直接的に言う


Japanese listeners infer a speaker's subject and the implied meanings behind the words. Sometimes it can take some pretty strong powers of conjecture to understand.

When talking in Japanese with non-native speakers, making an effort to speak plainly and leave out any guesswork might make it easier for them to understand what you are saying.

タレントのダニエル・カールさんの講演にハルと2人で参加しました。外国人が日本語で苦労する話をユーモアを交えて楽しく語っていました。

**struggle** 〔奮闘が必要な〕大変な課題
**shed light on** 明らかにする，浮き彫りにする
**subject** 主語，主題
**omit** 省略する，割愛する
**catch on** 理解する，わかる
**indirectness** 間接，婉曲
**ruffle someone's feathers** （人）の機嫌を損ねる
**infer** 推測する，察する
**implied** 暗黙の，言外の
**conjecture** 臆測，推測
**guesswork** 当て推量

大切なクリスマスツリーの飾りつけは、家長であるスティーヴの担当です。手順に沿って進めていきます。

**no small feat** 並大抵のことではない，なかなかの成果である

**skirt** 囲い，覆い

**head of a house** 家長，世帯主

**take care of** ～を引き受ける，担当する

**associated with** ～と関係がある，～を連想させる

**particular** 特定の，特別な

**abundance** 裕福さ，豊かさ

**mark a start of** ～の始まりを飾る

# Vol.193 Decorating the Christmas Tree

（クリスマスツリーの飾りつけ）

In our household, December means Christmas, and Christmas means a big Christmas tree. Decorating a tree is no small feat, and Steve guides us through the many steps.

| | |
|---|---|
| STEP ❶ | Put up the tree. |
| STEP ❷ | Wrap electric lights around the tree. |
| STEP ❸ | Hang the ornaments. |
| STEP ❹ | Lay the skirt under the tree. |
| STEP ❺ | Put the star on top. |

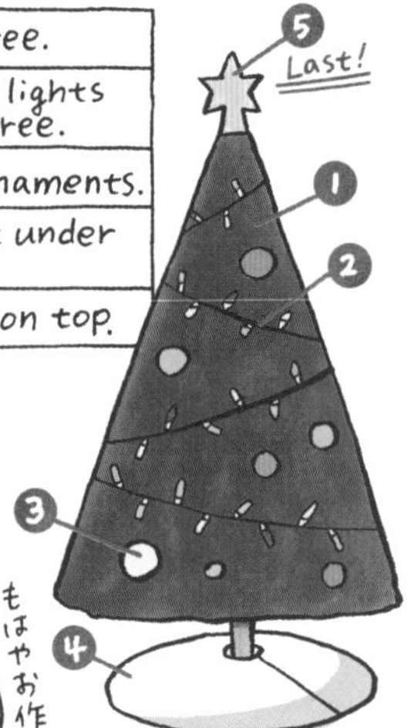

❺
Last!
❶
❷
❸
❹


（我が家のツリーは組立式で180cmくらい）

The head of the house usually takes care of Steps❶,❷and❺. My father-in-law guides the activities at his house in America.

ふう
❶❷は意外と神経を使う
もはやお作法？


The most fun part is hanging the ornaments on the tree. We usually hang the basic ornaments first and then add the special ornaments afterward.

The special ornaments are all associated with particular memories.

Basic ornaments
もともとはリンゴだった
Symbols of abundance and life
Special ornaments
ミドリの初めてのクリスマスにもらったもの
Midori's 1st Xmas 2008
Symbols of family travels and events

This one's my favorite!
Grammy gave this to me…
Xmas ornaments

The star represents the birth of Christ or hope.


The tree is complete when the star is placed on top.

Decorating the Christmas tree marks the start of the biggest family event of the year.

Vol.194
Housecleaning
(大掃除)
How is your year-end housecleaning coming along? One of our household chores this year was to repaper the shoji doors.
ボスッッ
次、ボクね
子どもたち的ハイライト
Best Chore Ever!
I admit, I really like it when the house is completely clean and everything is in order for a fresh start in the new year. But I have to say that cleaning and putting everything in order gets kind of hectic and stressful.
年賀状まだ書いてない
換気扇や水回りの掃除もやらないと
はい…
年末進行で締め切り早まります。ヨロシク
担
There's just too much to do.
Is this the way everyone in the world winds up their year? No, not at all.
My relatives across the Pacific do major housecleaning when the weather turns warmer.
さむっ
苦行に近いよね
たしかに寒い中での窓拭きとか
年末は、Xmasの来客に備えて、ちょっと片付けるくらいらしい
They call it Spring Cleaning.
Maybe it's just my Japanese nature that feels the need to clean up before the new year starts. I'd like to reset my approach. Maybe I could clean the ventilation fans and bathrooms now, and then space out cleaning the other rooms through the year. Can I overcome my compulsion to clean? Could you?
イラストを担当しました
おまけ
おすすめのお掃除本
プロが教える掃除術。洗剤3種でラクラク!
掃除の解剖図鑑
正しくできれば一生役立つ
(エクスナレッジ刊)
A Monk's Guide to a Clean House and Mind
Shoukei Matsumoto
(Penguin Books)
14言語で翻訳されている『お坊さんが教えるこころが整う掃除の本』の英語版

新年を迎えるにあたって家の中がきれいに整えられているのは気持ちがいいもの。でも、多忙を極める年末にすべてこなすのは困難で……

come along　進歩する

repaper　紙を張り替える

put ~ in order　～を整理する

get kind of　少し～になる

hectic　非常に忙しい，大忙しの

wind up　～を締めくくる

Japanese nature　日本人としての気質

ventilation fan　換気扇

space out ~　～とは別のことを考える

overcome　乗り越える，打ち勝つ

compulsion　衝動

感謝と招福のために飾られるしめ飾りには、地域によって様々な形があります。また、クリスマスリースとの共通点もあり……

straw　(麦)わら

harvest　収穫

talisman　お守り

ward off evil spirits　厄よけをする

prosperity　繁栄，幸運

region　地域，地方

distinct feature　目立った特徴

pastime　気晴らし，娯楽

admire　称賛する，見惚れる

hybrid of A and B　AとBの雑種，合同

wreath　花輪，リース

origin　起源

Vol.195
New Year's Decoration
(祈りのカタチ)
What type of shimekazari do you hang at your house? The Japanese custom of displaying straw decorations at the year-end originated as a show of appreciation for the past year's harvest and as a talisman to ward off evil spirits and invite prosperity in the New Year. Each region's shimekazari has distinct features, and there are said to be hundreds of variations.
全国的によく見られるごぼうじめ系
関東に多い輪飾り・玉飾り系
この部分はあったりなかったり
九州に多い鶴系とか
One of my favorite pastimes at New Year's is to admire the shimekazari I see while walking to our local shrine.
あっちのもいいね
実家の母
鶴
亀
眼鏡
動物やモノをかたどったものなども
しゃもじ
Sometimes I see versions that are a hybrid of shimekazari and a Christmas wreath. Despite being worlds apart in origin, it's interesting how similar their purposes are.
しめ縄
だいだい 橙
えび 海老
ゆずりは 譲葉
稲わら
裏白(潔白)
しで 紙垂(神)
Ward off evil spirits
Wish for a long and prosperous life
Gratitude for the harvest
リボン
ベル
ヒイラギ
常緑樹
りんご
松ぼっくり
ヒイラギの実(太陽)
As different as we may be, we all wish for the same things.
Best wishes for a happy and healthy New Year!

# Vol.196 Vocabulary Building Step I
## （語彙力を高める①）

How many times have you heard that simply reading is a good way to increase your vocabulary? I hear this at almost every parent-teacher meeting.

Reading books helps expand vocabulary and the ability to express oneself. Please encourage your child to read as much as possible.
ですよねー。日本語だってそうですもんね
英語クラスの先生


Our now-teenage son, Haru, has always read quite a bit since he was young and has a pretty diverse vocabulary.

英語も日本語も
Words
Phrases
Words
Idioms
Words
言葉の森を歩く


Our 10-year-old daughter, Midori, isn't as much of a bookworm.

I don't wanna read a book!
めんどくさーい
読むのはマンガばっかり
これはどう？
これもおもしろいよ


Considering their differences in reading habits, we were a bit worried that Midori might not be developing the vocabulary she should. However, Midori filled out her vocabulary quite a bit over the past year. She seems to be absorbing words from the videos she loves to watch.

iPadで海外のYouTuberを追ったり
NETFLIXでシリーズドラマを見たり


It dawned on me that books aren't the only way to pick up new words. Although watching videos is a step removed from reading and writing, we are very happy that Midori has found a way that works for her to increase her vocabulary.

語彙を増やすために読書がいかに有効か。分かってはいても読書嫌いのミドリに本を読ませるのは大変です。でも──

- **vocabulary building** 語彙の構築
- **parent-teacher meeting** 保護者面談
- **expand** 拡大させる，拡張させる
- **diverse** 多様な，それぞれ異なる
- **bookworm** 大の本好き
- **over the past year** ここ１年で
- **absorb** 吸収する
- **dawn on me that** 〔that以下〕と気がつく
- **step removed from** ～から一歩離れた

YouTubeや動画で英語の語彙を増やしているミドリの最近のお気に入りは――

**adolescent** 思春期[青年期]の若者

**ugh** 〔嫌悪・軽蔑などを表わして〕うえっ，げっ

**gather round** 周りに集まる

**fiercely** 激しく，猛烈に

**sensible** 分別[良識]のある

**studious** 勉強好きな

**boatload** 大量，多数

**patter** 早口のおしゃべり

**nemesis** 歯が立たない敵

**intriguing** 興味をそそる，魅力的な

**love interest** 恋愛対象

**squint** 目を凝らして見る

Vol.197
Vocabulary Building Step II
（語彙力を高める②）
Our 10-year-old, Midori, is building her English vocabulary by watching movies and YouTube videos. These are some of her favorite shows.
Haschak Sisters
Four adolescent American girls singing songs and making videos
YouTube
Brainchild
A science show aimed at kids
The Good Place
A comedy series about a woman mistakenly sent to what appears to be heaven
NETFLIX
Gilmore Girls
A family comedy-drama centered on a mother-daughter relationship
チャンネル登録者数526万！
「Boys Are So Ugh」とかすごく好き〜
再生数5599万回
On weekends, the whole family gathers round the TV to watch "Gilmore Girls."
シーズン⑦＋続編まであるうちの③まで見たところ
英語のシャワー
身近で自然な言い回しがいっぱい
オススメ♪
The variety of characters makes "Gilmore Girls" fun to watch!
I usually get what I want.
Lorelai
Single mother who fiercely guards her independence
Rory
Sensible and studious high schooler
Lane
Clever drummer with a strict mother
Lorelai and Rory talk a boatload — 50 percent more than most other shows. Their clever patter is full of jokes and pop-culture references.
お金持ち。保守的
ほかにもいろんな人が
Emily
Lorelai's mom and nemesis
Jess
Intriguing but troubled — one of Rory's love interests
If you squint, Jess kinda looks like Haru.
いよっ Jess!

# Vol.198 Valentine's Day
## (アメリカ式バレンタインデー)

Do you do something special for Valentine's Day? How about White Day?

The Valentine's Day custom in our family is a mix of Japanese and American styles. The four of us gather around the dining room table and exchange chocolates.

(ホワイトデーはなし)


One year, Midori came home on Valentine's Day feeling downhearted.

None of the boys gave me choco-lates.
女子から友チョコはもらったけど
Well, the Japanese custom is for the girls to give chocolates to the boys today.


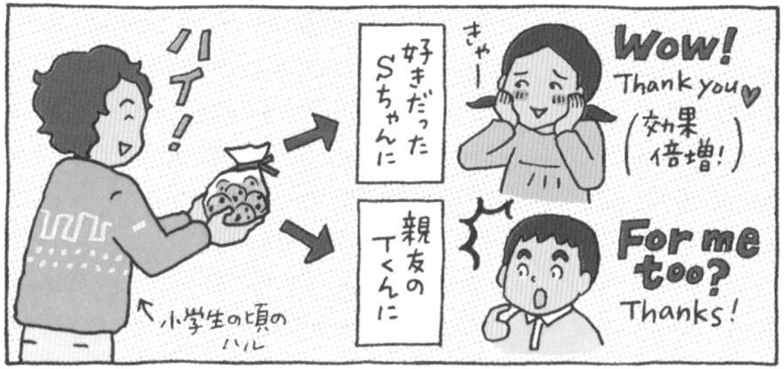

ハイ!
好きだったSちゃんに
きゃー
Wow! Thank you
(効果倍増!)
親友のTくんに
For me too? Thanks!
小学生の頃のハル


(└→ ※中学生になってからは日本式に切り替えた)

In times past, Valentine's Day in America was a special day to get your courage up to declare your love to someone, but in modern classrooms it has become a day to show friendship.

男性から贈るのが多いけどね

多いよ…
My son's teacher notified parents that if a student was going to give something out, they had to give them to all of their classmates.
アメリカ在住の日本人ママ
メッセージカードやちょっとしたお菓子、シールなど
I'll always be your friend!
From
手を加えてオリジナル性を出すことも
To From


Of course, supermarkets gladly lend a hand by setting up special areas with 32-piece candy packages, which is sure to cover all the students in a class.

That sounds like a lot more work than the obligatory chocolate custom we have in Japan. However, the kids can anticipate receiving notes or candies from every student in their class, and most kids diligently prepare one item for each of their classmates.

アメリカ式のバレンタインも取り入れている私たちですが、最近のアメリカ式は少しまた事情が異なるようで……

**do something special for** ～に何か特別なことをする

**downhearted** 落胆した

**get one's courage up** 勇気を奮い立たせる

**declare one's love to someone** （人）へ愛の告白をする

**notify** 〔正式に人に〕通知する

**lend a hand** 手を貸す，手伝う

**obligatory** 必須の，義務的な

**anticipate** 期待する，楽しみに待つ

**diligently** 熱心に，コツコツと

ミドリは「The Young Americans」というミュージカルを作り上げるワークショップに参加しました。

put on 〔ショー・劇を〕催す，上演する

theatrical 演劇の，劇風の

to no end 〔喜び・不満などが〕とても，果てしなく

rave べた褒めする，熱く語る

put briefly 端的に言えば

outreach 出張［支援］活動

improve 向上させる，磨きをかける

initial expectations 当初の期待

exhilarating 刺激的な，爽快な

have the time of one's life 楽しく過ごす

sense of self-worth 自尊心

Vol.199
The Young Americans I
（ヤングアメリカンズ①）
A few weeks ago, Midori joined a group called the Young Americans to put on a theatrical musical. She enjoyed it to no end and came home raving about how much fun it was.
The Young Americans
今までに4回参加したよ
What do the Young Americans do?
Put briefly...
They lead song and dance workshops aimed at helping participants discover their potential.
The instructors are students of the College of the Performing Arts in Southern California.
学校では教育学についても学んでいる
In just three days, they organize and inspire the kids to perform a full stage show.
（20曲以上の洋楽を歌ったり踊ったり）
International Music outreach Program
The group runs workshops in North America, Europe, and Asia. They've been coming to Japan every year since 2006 and holding workshops in cities around the country.
ECCも協賛してるんだ
チラシ
It might help her English, and she can meet people from other countries.
She might improve her singing and dancing.
ミドリ向き♪
Those were my initial expectations when we signed Midori up for her first workshop. But throughout an exhilarating three days, she and the other participants received much more than that.
Midori had the time of her life and grew in ways we didn't expect.
English
Singing
Dancing
Sense of self-worth
Respect for others
Self-expression
Teamwork
Next time, I'll share some of the things they did.

Vol.200
The Young Americans II
（ヤングアメリカンズ②）
The Young Americans program runs for three days. The final rehearsal takes place behind closed doors, but parents can observe the workshops and final stage show.
Day 1
Day 2
Day 3
A.M.
P.M.
Work-shop
Work-shop
Work-shop
Rehearsal
SHOW
150～300人もの子どもたちが、グループに分けられて、各グループごとに振り付けを教わる。
The kids are quick learners, and you can really see each child pushing them-selves to perform.
It's also fascinating to watch the instructors encourage the kids and keep the pace going.
The kids learn dance moves and songs (mostly in English) in sessions that last 15 to 30 minutes.
Of course, some kids are apprehensive about joining in, but the instructors gently encour-age them to try.
The kids are coaxed to participate. They are not forced to do anything.
Instructors stay with shy kids to help build up their courage.
ミドリも他の人を見ながらワンテンポ遅れて踊っていることしばしば
In such a short time, no one expects perfection, because that's not the objective.
Good Job!!
ジブンニハクシュ～！
Yeah! We did it!!
The praise is not for ability; it's for having the courage to try.
More about this life lesson next time.

このプログラムは3日間にわたって行われます。見学していると、参加する子どもたちを勇気づける様々な工夫が見られます。

take place behind closed doors　非公開で行われる

observe　見学する，よく見る

quick learner　飲み込みが早い

push oneself to　～に向けて頑張る

fascinating　興味をそそる

apprehensive about　～について心配する

coax　〔～させるために人を〕うまく説得する

expect perfection　完璧さを期待する

objective　目標，目的

praise　称賛，褒めること

ソロパートや振りつけのアイデアなど、子どもたちから何かを引き出し、自信につなげようとする試みがたくさんありました。

relatively 比較的
amazingly talented 非常に才能がある
moved by ～に心を動かされる
absolute 絶対の，完全な
no matter how good ~ is ～がどんなに優れているとしても
from the sidelines 傍観者の立場から
go along with ～に沿う，同調する
self-esteem 自尊感情，自己肯定感
liberating 解放的な
motivate 〔人を〕動かす，やる気にさせる

Vol.201
The Young Americans III
(ヤングアメリカンズ③)
During the Young Americans' song and dance workshops, an instructor will occasionally call one of the kids over to talk about performing a solo in the show.
舞台袖や廊下の隅でマンツーマンで教わったりする
ミドリも何度かソロパートを割り振られたことあり
歌やダンス以外にパントマイムやせりふ・手話などもあり
Sometimes kids with special skills are chosen, but most of the time the selections appear to be relatively random.
ダンス経験者
中にはここで初めて才能が花開く子も
けなげさに涙
Some of the kids are amazingly talented, but the audience is really moved by kids who are trying their absolute best no matter how good they are.
The kids work out the routines themselves. The instructors guide them by volunteering ideas from the sidelines.
Now let's make a dance to go along with the song. Does anyone have an idea?
これからみんなで振りつけを考えるよ
アイデアがある人〜?
インストラクターは2人組で英語と日本語をうまく織り交ぜて説明
Build the courage to speak up
Consider other people's opinions
ジブンニハクシュ!!
Seeing how the Young Americans workshops encourage self-expression and help kids build self-esteem, it's easy to understand why so many kids return again and again.
It's so fun and liberating!
I like how they motivate kids by praising them.
大好き!
アメリカ的!
次回はボクも参加しようかな

STEVE
来日34年目の
江戸好きアメリカ人
KIKUE
ワタクシ
HARU
息子。
中学3年生
MIDORI
娘。
小学6年生

# 9th Year

2019

イースターは、欧米では主要な祝日ですが、日本ではあまり馴染みがありません。アメリカの親戚の家で初めて参加しました。

**caught on** 人気がある, 盛んである

**mysterious** 不可解な, 謎めいた

**resurrection of Jesus** イエスの復活

**pre-Christian** 西暦紀元前の

**spring equinox** 春分

**fertility** 多産, 繁殖力

**feast** ごちそう

**fan out** 四方八方に散る

**prize** 賞品, 景品

**dud** 失敗, 役立たず, はずれ

Vol.202
Easter
(イースター)
Easter is a major holiday in the United States and Europe that hasn't caught on in Japan. Until last year, it was kind of mysterious to me.
What is Easter?
What's an Easter egg hunt and who's the Easter Bunny?
毎年日にちが違うのも謎
答え
Easter is a Christian holiday celebrating the resurrection of Jesus. Importantly, it is based on a pre-Christian celebration of spring and takes place on the first Sunday after the full moon after the spring equinox.
子だくさん
Life
Fertility
Symbols
When I was young, we went to a relative's house for a big dinner every year.
この日は店も休みになるところが多い
Easterのごちそう
ローストハムやキャロットケーキなど
Last year, the kids and I experienced our first Easter with Steve's relatives.
While the parents talked and prepared a feast, the kids went on an Easter egg hunt. They fanned out in the backyard searching for colorful plastic eggs with prizes inside.
大人があらかじめ隠しておく。
昔は本物の卵がメインだった
たっぷり
やった!
The prizes
Normal
Candy
Special
Money
Duds
A rock
A leaf
Easter this year is on Sunday, April 21. It might be fun to add a little Easter tradition to a spring picnic.

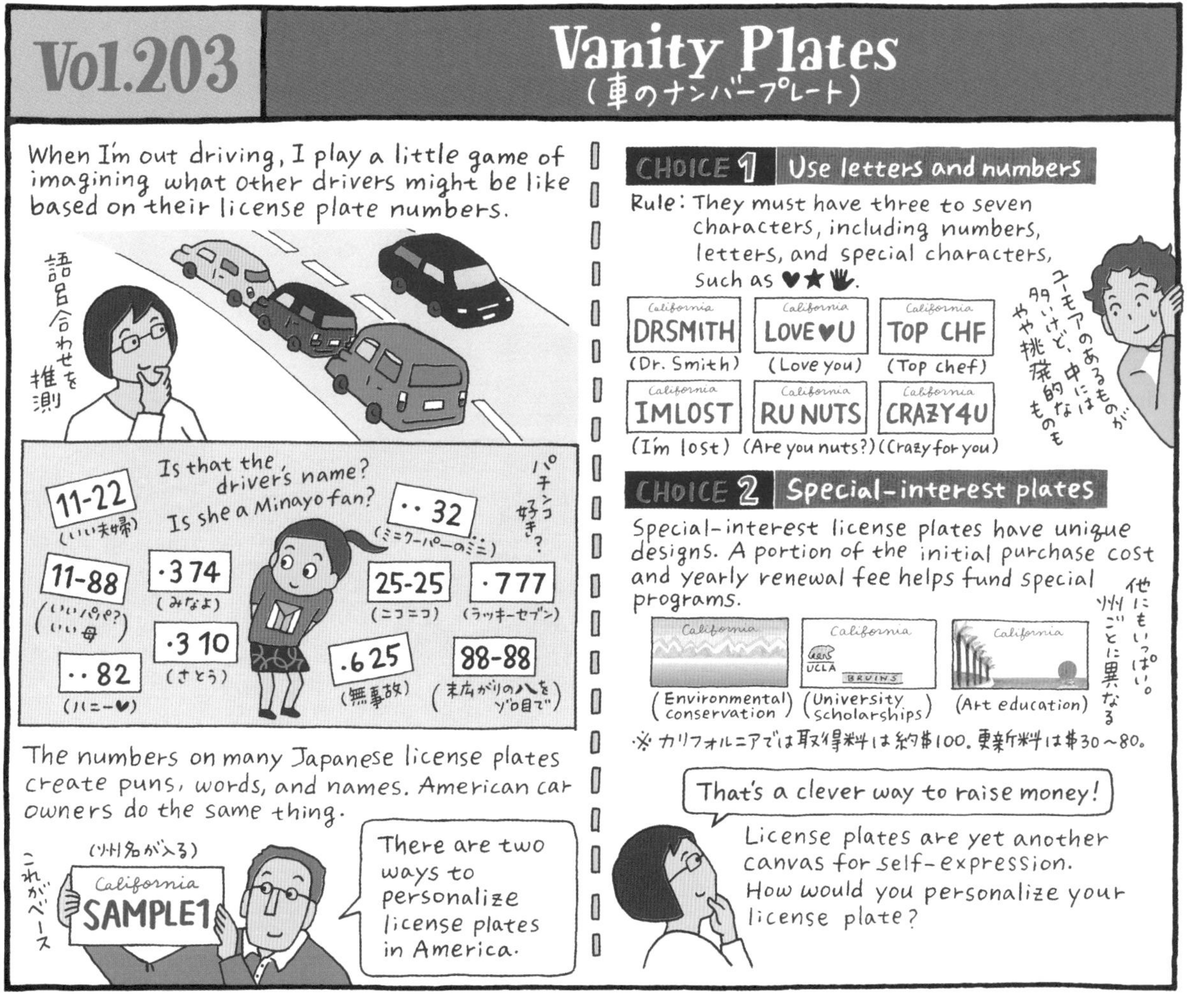
Vol.203
Vanity Plates
(車のナンバープレート)
When I'm out driving, I play a little game of imagining what other drivers might be like based on their license plate numbers.
語呂合わせを推測
Is that the driver's name?
Is she a Minayo fan?
パチンコ好き?
11-22
(いい夫婦)
11-88
(いいパパ? いい母)
··82
(ハニー♥)
·374
(みなよ)
·310
(さとう)
··32
(ミニクーパーのミニ)
25-25
(ニコニコ)
·777
(ラッキーセブン)
·625
(無事故)
88-88
(末広がりの八をゾロ目で)
The numbers on many Japanese license plates create puns, words, and names. American car owners do the same thing.
これがベース
(州名が入る)
California
SAMPLE1
There are two ways to personalize license plates in America.
CHOICE 1 Use letters and numbers
Rule: They must have three to seven characters, including numbers, letters, and special characters, such as ♥★✋.
California DRSMITH
(Dr. Smith)
California LOVE♥U
(Love you)
California TOP CHF
(Top chef)
California IMLOST
(I'm lost)
California RU NUTS
(Are you nuts?)
California CRAZY4U
(Crazy for you)
ユーモアのあるものが多いけど、中にはやや挑発的なものも
CHOICE 2 Special-interest plates
Special-interest license plates have unique designs. A portion of the initial purchase cost and yearly renewal fee helps fund special programs.
California
(Environmental conservation)
California UCLA BRUINS
(University Scholarships)
California
(Art education)
他にもいっぱい。州ごとに異なる
※カリフォルニアでは取得料は約$100。更新料は$30~80。
That's a clever way to raise money!
License plates are yet another canvas for self-expression. How would you personalize your license plate?

ドライブ中、他の車のナンバープレートからあれこれ推測しています。ナンバーに込められた意味を探るのは楽しいです。

**pun** ダジャレ，語呂合わせ
**personalize one's license plate** 車のナンバープレートに好きな番号を選ぶ
**choice** 選択，選択肢
**character** 文字《数字・符号も含む》
**Are you nuts?** 正気？ 気は確か？
**crazy for** ～が欲しくてたまらない
**special-interest** 特定の関心事，特定利益団体
**initial** 初期の
**fund** 資金を供給する
**conservation** 保護，保存

今年は、私たち夫婦が地域の「子ども会」の会長を務める番です。子ども会には、毎年決まった行事があります。

community involvement　地域社会［コミュニティ］への参加
have a set schedule of events　定期的な行事がある
recyclable　リサイクル可能なもの
organize　計画する，企画する
complicated　複雑な，困難な
huge stack　山積み
somehow　何とかして，ともかくも
dream up new ideas　新たなアイデアを練る
fundraiser　〔資金集めの〕イベント
excursion　小旅行，遠足
self-sufficiency　自給自足

# Vol.204 Community Involvement I
（コミュニティへの参加①：子ども会）

This year, it's Kikue's and my turn to lead our neighborhood kids' group, the Kodomokai.
とうとうこの日が…
子供会
子供会会長
子供会会長
The Kodomokai has a set schedule of events every year.
Neighborhood festival
子供みこしや山車
初詣も
Bon Festival
Family BBQ
Welcome meeting
Collecting recyclables
Seven-years' worth of information and instructions
Organizing the events is quite complicated, and past Kodomokai leaders have left helpful materials. It's a huge stack!
秘伝の奥義の書に思えてきた
Somehow, I need to make sure we don't miss or forget anything.
While I was worrying about keeping up with the program, Steve was dreaming up new ideas.
アメリカでよくあるやつ
Hey, we could do a fundraiser—a car wash!
1台だいたい500～1000円くらいで
School groups often use car washes to raise funds for activities or a charity.
We could use the money for the annual excursion. It's fun, and the kids could learn about self-sufficiency.
We would love to do it, but that would mean more work on top of the regular events.
Which raises the question: What's the real purpose of the Kodomokai?

Vol.205
Community Involvement II
（コミュニティへの参加②：自治会）
When we joined the neighborhood kodomokai kids' group, we also enlisted in the local jichikai community association. After a few years, however, we started to ask ourselves:
What's the actual purpose of jichikai?
はて
自治会とは？
Jichikai organize activities to maintain and improve the quality of life in the community.
広報
防犯・防災
親睦
環境整備
回覧板
横断
Also, jichikai are quasi-governmental entities.
Jichikai have long been a backbone of local communities, but they are facing a crisis. Membership is dwindling as society ages and younger people are reluctant to join.
体力的にムリ
仕事と育児で手いっぱい
加入するメリットも感じないし
役員とか大変だし
高齢者世代
若い世代や非加入世帯
Informal neighborhood groups are also common in the United States. But their objectives are a little different from those of jichikai.
Neighborhood Association
Citizens' groups discuss local topics and ways to make their neighborhoods safer and better
They meet when a problem in the neighborhood arises.
（運営委員はいる）
If they need to, they even propose solutions to the local government.
土地利用の在り方について など
行政とのつながり方も
They are kind of like an activist group.
能動的！
うーん
Jichikai are definitely more structured, but they seem to have a hard time changing things.
日本はトップダウン。アメリカはボトムアップ
Maybe jichikai need updating. Do you have any ideas?

子ども会に参加したのをきっかけに、「自治会」にも入りました。しかし数年後、私たちは自問自答するようになりました――

**enlist** 参加する，協力する

**community association** 地域自治会

**improve** 向上させる

**quasi-governmental entity** 準政府組織

**backbone** 支え柱

**dwindle** 縮小する，落ちる

**reluctant to** ～するのに気が進まない

**informal** 非公式の，私的な

**propose a solution** 解決策を提案する

**activist group** 活動家団体

**structured** 組織化された

**updating** 更新

自治会や子ども会に疑問を感じながらも、私たちが会員であり続ける大きな理由のひとつは、スティーヴの「ある意識」にあります。

**doubt about** ～に対する疑問

**acutely aware of** ～を非常に強く感じる，痛感する

**real challenge** 真の難題

**wonder if** ～ではないかと思う

**build a bond with** ～との絆を築く

**block party** ブロックパーティー《町内の（一部の）交通を遮断して行う野外パーティー》

**mingle** 入り交じる，人と話をする

**burden of responsibility** 責任の重圧

**lifesaving** 命を救うことができる

**brighten** 輝かせる，明るくする

Vol.206
Community Involvement Ⅲ
（コミュニティへの参加③：内と外）
Despite all our doubts about the jichikai and kodomokai, one of the main reasons we remain members is:
I want to be accepted in the "uchi 内" of our community.
日本人でなくても地元出身者でなくても
Steve is acutely aware of the "uchi and soto" aspect of Japanese society.
…
日本人の内と外を意識するとき
ガイジンはそういうとこアレだよねー
口口口 口口口
もちろん悪気なし
We do our best to participate and fit in, but sometimes it's a real challenge.
時間が長い
飲まされる
床座りしんどい
食事もイマイチ
強要はされないけど
まーまー
いわゆる飲ミニケーション
終日イベントを終えた後の打ち上げ@自治会館
We wonder if there is a less trying way to build bonds with our neighbors. The neighborhood groups in the United States gave us an idea —— a block party.
エアー遊具を借りたりすることも
手作りでもテイクアウトでもOK
BLOCK PARTY
Tables and chairs are set up on a street that has been closed to traffic. People bring food and drinks to share. The adults mingle and talk while the kids play together.
Many people feel joining jichikai brings a burden of responsibilities. Highlighting the benefits of jichikai could attract members. Knowing your neighbors can be lifesaving in times of emergency, and jichikai events brighten the community. That could be a really good first step.
イベントごとにスタッフを立候補制にしたり
必要なら有償制にするのもアリだよね

Vol.207
New Teeth, New Responsibility
(新しい歯と親の責任)
Eleven-year-old Midori is losing the last of her baby teeth as her adult teeth come in. Unfortunately, the dentist has been finding small cavities.
ガーン
虫歯4か所ですね。うち3本は永久歯。
生え変わるときは要注意なんですよ
4本も?! しかも永久歯も…
半年前の健診では虫歯ゼロだったのに〜
We're lucky in Japan that our national insurance includes dental treatment. U.S. insurance plans usually don't. That may be one reason why there's so much emphasis on prevention there.
Parents are responsible for their childrens' teeth, including teeth alignment.
We tend to agree. So Midori's continuing cavity problem makes us feel like we're failing her.
アメリカの水道水はフッ素入り
However, the latest discovery of cavities has spurred Midori to action. She's been brushing very carefully lately.
歯は一生ものの財産
ミドリ書
おまけ Tales of the Tooth Fairy
Oh no!
I swallowed my tooth!
The Tooth Fairy won't come…!!
What if you put your pillow on your belly.
Tooth Fairyとは?
It's an American custom that if you put a tooth under your pillow at night, the Tooth Fairy will come and exchange it for a coin.
That night
一応、歯は枕の下
Pillow
The next morning
The Tooth Fairy never fails!
やった!
Pillow


永久歯が生えてきて、最後の乳歯が抜けつつある11歳のミドリ。残念なことに、歯医者さんで小さな虫歯が見つかってしまいました。

**baby teeth** 乳歯
**adult teeth** 永久歯
**dentist** 歯医者
**national insurance** 国民保険
**dental treatment** 歯の治療
**emphasis on** ～に重点を置くこと
**teeth alignment** 歯並び
**fail** 〔～を〕失望させる
**spur someone to action** 行動を起こすように(人)を駆り立てる
**swallow** 飲み込む
**belly** 腹，腹部
**never fail** 決して裏切らない

反抗期らしからぬハルの態度に、「内にため込んでいるのでは?」と私の父（ハルの祖父）は不安に思っているようです。

rebel with a cause　理由ある反抗
turbulent period　混乱期
unreservedly　遠慮なく，素直に
resentment　腹立たしさ
harbor　〔悪意・考えなどを〕心に抱く
flame　炎
flare up in anger　カンカンに怒る
put out　〔明かり・火を〕消す
self-reliant　自立的な
insight　洞察力
defiant behavior　反抗的態度
mature adult　成熟した大人

Vol.208
Rebel with a Cause
（反抗は必要?）
It's commonly thought that the teen years are a turbulent period. Yet 15-year-old Haru is very pleasant and well-mannered. That, however, worries my father.
大丈夫か?
I wonder if he's holding something inside?
反抗期のイメージ
無愛想，暴言，部屋へ引き込もるなど
別に…
うるせー
ハルの日常
He gladly helps Midori practice.
もっと粘って!
騎馬戦の大将馬に決まったミドリ
He spends most of his time in the living room.
自室に勉強机もあるけど
米津玄師の「Flamingo」やWiz Khalifaの「See You Again」など
He sings unreservedly in the bath.
I'm not doing anything I don't want to do.
えー
Haru told us that he remembers a time when he felt anger and resentment.
When he was angry, it seemed like he was harboring a silently burning flame.
昔
There was a time when he would let the flame flare up in anger.
今
But now, he feels he can just put out the fire himself.
Nice
Mastering self-control is a key step toward being self-reliant.
反抗 自立
ベキ
Haru's insight is a reminder that a teenager's defiant behavior is not just about independence; it's also about becoming a mature adult.
「反抗期」じゃなくて「自立準備期」とかにしたらいいのでは

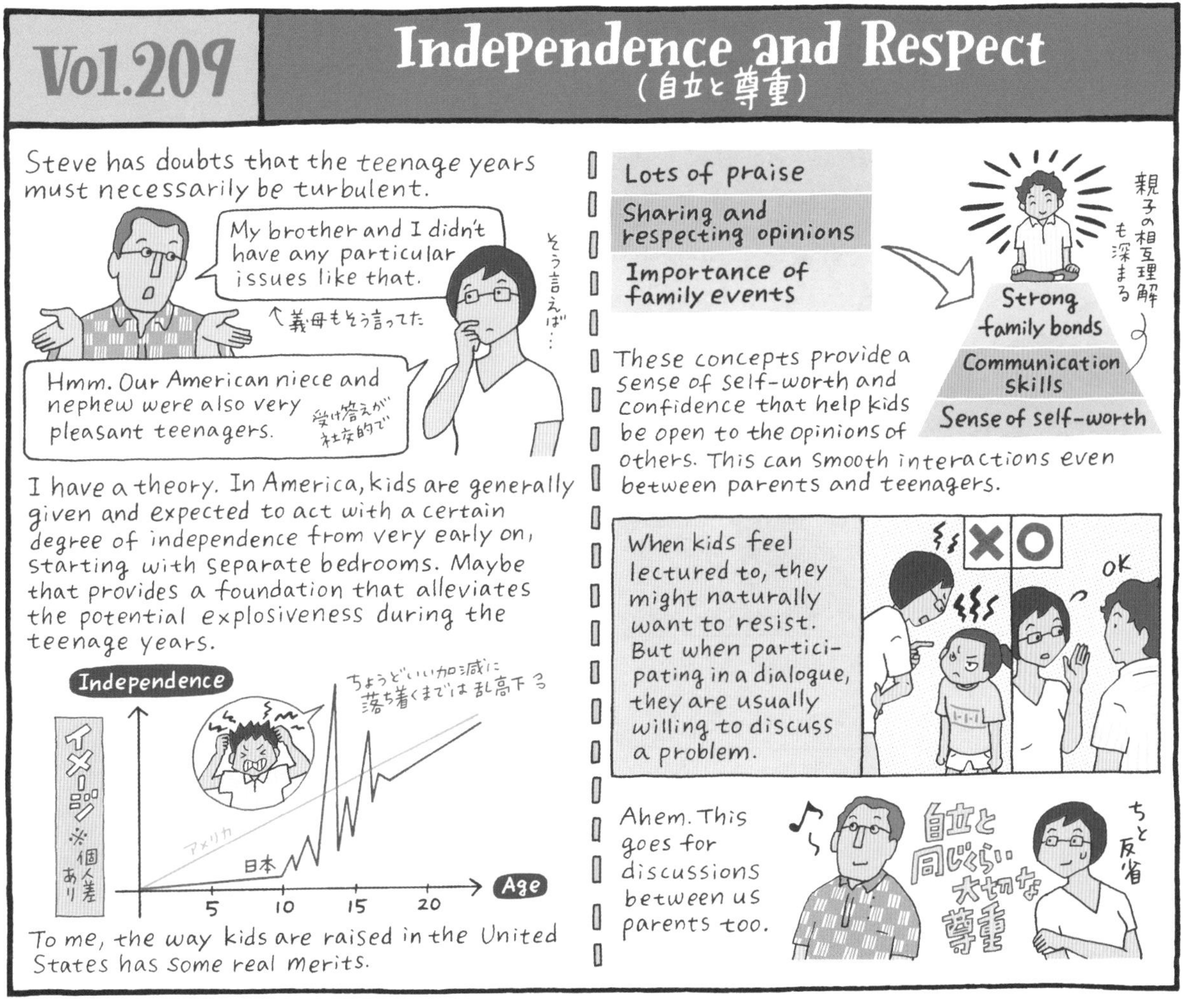
Vol.209
Independence and Respect
(自立と尊重)
Steve has doubts that the teenage years must necessarily be turbulent.
My brother and I didn't have any particular issues like that.
↑義母もそう言ってた
そう言えば…
Hmm. Our American niece and nephew were also very pleasant teenagers.
受け答えが社交的で
I have a theory. In America, kids are generally given and expected to act with a certain degree of independence from very early on, starting with separate bedrooms. Maybe that provides a foundation that alleviates the potential explosiveness during the teenage years.
Independence
ちょうどいい加減に落ち着くまでは乱高下す
アメリカ
日本
イメージ ※個人差あり
Age
5
10
15
20
To me, the way kids are raised in the United States has some real merits.
Lots of praise
Sharing and respecting opinions
Importance of family events
親子の相互理解も深まる
Strong family bonds
Communication skills
Sense of self-worth
These concepts provide a sense of self-worth and confidence that help kids be open to the opinions of others. This can smooth interactions even between parents and teenagers.
When kids feel lectured to, they might naturally want to resist. But when participating in a dialogue, they are usually willing to discuss a problem.
OK
Ahem. This goes for discussions between us parents too.
自立と同じくらい大切な尊重
ちと反省

必ずしも激しい反抗期があるとは思えないというスティーヴ。私の知るアメリカの10代を参考に考察してみました。

respect　尊重
have doubts　疑う
necessarily　必ず，必然的に
pleasant　感じの良い
theory　持論，見解
alleviate　軽減する，和らげる
explosiveness　爆発性，強烈さ
merit　利点，価値
interaction　意思の疎通
dialogue　対話
willing to　～する意思がある
ahem　えへん《咳払いの声》
go for　～に当てはまる

常々ペットを飼いたいと思っていた私たち。ようやくそのときが訪れて、２匹の猫を家族として迎えることになりました。

**pet-adoption agency** ペットの里親あっせん機関

**shelter** 保護施設

**get ready to** ～する準備をする

**vow** 誓約

**on the advice of** （人）の助言で

**silver mackerel tabby** 〔猫の〕サバトラ

**purr** 〔猫がゴロゴロと〕のどを鳴らす

**like attention** 注目されるのが好きだ

**for only a short time** 短期間だけ

**satiny** つやつやした，滑らかな

**meow** ニャー《猫の鳴き声》

Vol.210
What's New Pussycat? Meow, Meow, Meow（子ネコがやってきた！）
We had always wanted a pet and the timing was right, so now we are the proud owners of two cats. We were introduced to the cats by a pet-adoption agency.
まずはお見合い
チチチ…
かわいい〜
うは〜
ちっさーい
「Manaネコハウス」のスタッフさんたち
About 6 weeks old
The kittens came from a shelter in Gunma Prefecture.
環境省2017年データより
（関東でいちばん殺処分率が高いのが群馬で、86％）
よろしくお願いします
じゃあ、お引き渡しは1週間後で！
We had a lot to do to get ready to become pet owners, starting with a vow.
譲受誓約書
1. 責任をもって生涯飼育します
2. 完全室内飼いで飼育します
Clean the house
不要品を処分
電気コードを整理
猫砂だけでこんなに?!
Shop
On the advice of the adoption agency and friends, we got our house in order and stocked up on cat supplies. Finally, we were ready to bring home our new family members.
ゴロゴロゴロ…
（爪切りのときも）
Gen Silver Mackerel Tabby Male ♂
Gen is very friendly and starts purring whenever he is near us.
兄弟ではない。けど、仲良し
……Meow
ごはんのときだけ
Moco Silver Mackerel Tabby Male ♂
Moco likes attention, but he likes to be held for only a short time. He has a satiny meow.
Welcome to the family, Gen and Moco!

Vol.211
Naming the Cats
(ネコの名付け)
It was a lot of work for us to prepare to take in two kittens. But perhaps the most difficult part was deciding on names.
We put some photos of the cats up on a pillar by the dining room table to help us brainstorm.
お見合いの日にミドリが撮った写真
Some of the proposed names
このフェイスは隈取りポイントでしょ
KABUKI (歌舞伎)
MON (紋)
Peanuts
Oliver
TASUKI (たすき)
IZUMO (出雲)
Jam
Coco
首の周りが白くてたすきがけしてるみたいだし
かわいい名前がいい～
歌舞伎!? ぜったいやだ～
Cool
Two Tendencies
Cute
Steve did a Google search and printed out a long list of names. We each marked the ones we liked, but very few overlapped.
どうよ
Simba, Axel, Milo, Leo, Tiger, Roxy, Oreo, Jinx など
Over 300 names!
そもそもどれも日本人の私にはなじみが薄くピンと来ない
And then there were also...
Bilbo and Frodo? 『The Lord of the Rings』より
そーだ!
すごく良くない?!
源氏と平家とか?
老師と阿闍梨!
くらっ
How can we ever decide?!
When did we make the final choices? In the car on the way to pick them up, of course.
Gen (玄)
Moco (雲虎)
Cute-sounding names and cool kanji
Phew... What a relief to finally have names! I learned that people's tastes clearly arise from their preferences and their backgrounds.


2匹の子猫を引き取るために大わらわでしたが、最も大変だったのは、名前を決めることだったかもしれません。

**kitten** 子猫
**decide on** ～を決定する
**pillar** 支柱，柱状のもの
**brainstorm** 意見を出し合う
**proposed** 提案されている
**tendency** 傾向，性質
**overlap** 重なる，重複する
**on the way to** ～に行く途中で
**phew** ふぅ，はぁ《息を吐く音》
**relief to** ～して安心する
**arise from** ～に起因する
**preference** 好み

結婚してカタカナ姓を名乗り始めたら、思わぬ困難が日常的に発生するようになりました。それは――

primarily　主に
associate ~ with...　～と…を結びつける
married name　結婚後の姓
trial and error　試行錯誤
method to　～する方法
ensure　確実にする
correctly spelled　正しくつづられている
phonetic code　欧文通話表，フォネティックコード
Lima　リマ《ペルーの首都》
surname　姓，名字
failed attempt　失敗した試み

Vol.212
The Katakana Life
（カタカナ姓であること）
Japanese names are primarily written in kanji characters. So when we hear someone's name, we naturally try to associate the name with kanji. But what if your name does not have kanji?
記録の記に久しぶりの久に恵む～で「記久恵」です
とか
When I took the married name Ballati, written in katakana, I faced a new challenge.
バ・ラ・ティです
バラキさん…？
すでに違う
…
あっ
茨城のバラに木！ですね？！
どんな漢字
それ
After many trials and errors, before saying my name, I now clearly tell people that it is not based on kanji.
えっと
My name is written in katakana…
（漢字じゃないですよ～っ）
English has a method to help ensure a name is correctly spelled. It's called a phonetic code.
Phonetic Code
A phonetic code pairs a letter with a common word to ensure the listener gets the correct letter.
B as in baseball.
A as in apple.
L as in Lima.
BALLATI
みたいな感じで
B? P? D? V?
M? N?
とかわかりにくいもんね
This method gave me another idea for explaining how to write my surname.
バラバラの「バラ」に，テストの「テ」，小さい「ィ」です
伝われ～
おまけ　Failed attempts
バラエティの「エ」を抜いて「バラティ」です
翌日
コメディさんだっけ？
いやいや
バレッタさんだよね

Vol.213
The Benefits of Staying Behind
(留守番の役得)
This past summer, my husband and kids visited his family in California for two weeks while I stayed at home with our two cats. It was the first time in 18 years of marriage that I've had such a long time to myself.
After seeing them off at our nearby train station, I felt quite sad and lonely.
行っちゃった…
子供会会長
参加必須の会議や資源回収のため、渡米を断念(涙)
It's going to be a lonely two weeks…
帰りの車中
One night, I visited a friend whose husband is from Ireland.
Now's your chance to do those things you've always wanted to do but couldn't.
It's really refreshing!
父子のみの里帰りによる留守番の経験アリ
私は窓の桟を掃除しまくったよ←エライ!
The best things I did during the two weeks:
Met friends for dinner and drinks
今夜は終電コースで!
Watched all the Japanese movies I've been wanting to see.
BEER
We always seem to choose Western movies.
Ate all the goya chanpuru I wanted. (It's not a family favorite.)
DVD
鑑賞中 たいてい太ももには愛猫が♪
「万引き家族」「日日是好日」「湯を沸かすほどの熱い愛」「お葬式」「モリのいる場所」など
I still had to work, but the two weeks were a nice vacation from my duties as a mother and wife. I wouldn't mind doing it again sometime.
Refreshed
まあ次回は私も一緒に渡米したいですが


スティーヴと子どもたちだけで渡米し、私は一人でお留守番。2週間、自分ひとりの時間を過ごしました。

**benefit** 利益, 恩恵

**stay behind** あとに残る

**time to oneself** 自分のための時間

**see someone off at the train station** 駅で(人)を見送る

**lonely** 孤独な, 寂しい

**chance to do** ～をする機会[チャンス]

**one's duty as** ～としての務め

**mind** 〔～を〕嫌だと思う, 気にする

**sometime** あるとき, いつか

長い間、アメリカ的なハロウィンパーティーを楽しんできましたが、このところメキシコの要素も増えてきています。

**Day of the Dead** 死者の日《死者を偲んで感謝し生きる喜びを分かち合うメキシコの伝統的な風習》

**host a party** パーティーを開く

**spooky** 不気味な

**honor** 〔～に〕尊敬の念を持つ

**tomb** 墓所, 墓石

**Papel Picado** （スペイン語で）切り絵

**Calavera** （スペイン語で）ガイコツ

**be in someone's thoughts** （人）の頭に浮かぶ

**with a touch of** ～のような

Vol.214
Halloween and the Day of the Dead（ハロウィンと死者の日）
For the last 10 years or so, we've been hosting Halloween parties with friends.
Costumes
シャンプーハット→
総勢20人くらい
UNi CORN
757
Pot-luck
Spookyなものも少々
←ポテトサラダ
←ソーセージ
口だけで取る
Trick-or-treating
ご近所さんに協力してもらって
Bobbing for apples
Every year, we do the traditional American Halloween things. Over the last few years, though, a Mexican element has started to grow.
In Mexico, people celebrate "Dia de Muertos" (the Day of the Dead) during the first days of November. Like "O-bon," the holiday honors relatives who have passed away. However, they do it by dressing up, holding parades, and decorating tombs with festival colors.
Papel picado
Decoratively cut tissue paper
Calavera
Brightly colored skulls to create the image of a happy rebirth
ガイコツメイクで仮装したり
My mother-in-law once painted her face like a fantastic calavera.
くるっ
How do I look?
She'll be in our thoughts when we celebrate Halloween with a touch of the Day of the Dead.
「死者の日」を知るならこの映画がおすすめ！
リメンバー・ミー

# Vol.215 Emergency Evacuation
## (台風で緊急避難)

We hope that our readers came through last month's super typhoon Hagibis safe and sound.

Our city issued evacuation advisories all through the day. When the storm grew stronger in the evening, we moved to a temporary evacuation center, which is a nearby elementary school.

The house should be fine, but "should" isn't good enough in this situation.
我が家はハザードマップでイエローゾーンに隣接
Sleeping Bag x4
Moco & Gen in a Cat Carrier
Emergency Bag x3


About 10 other families had also sought refuge in the school's gymnasium. Each group used the school's folding chairs and gym mats to set up their own territory.

ビュウウウウ・・・
(風の音)
トランプや折り紙を持ち出し袋の中に入れておくの、おすすめ!
Getting some actual sleep was tough.
照明まぶしい。
床、カタイ
コーフンしてて一睡もできず →


In the end, we stayed only a few hours until the storm blew over. It was a good learning experience and we'll be better prepared if we need to do it again. That said, evacuating with pets poses special challenges. I'll talk about them next time.

Note to self: Put sleep masks and earplugs in the emergency kit.

超大型台風「ハギビス」が来たとき、私たちの住む市では終日、避難勧告が発令され、私たちも避難することにしました。

- **emergency evacuation** 緊急避難
- **come through** 耐え抜く，生き延びる
- **sound** 健康な，健全な
- **issue an evacuation advisory** 避難勧告を出す
- **temporary** 一時的な
- **seek refuge in** ～に避難する，逃げ込む
- **territory** 領域，陣地
- **tough** きつい，厳しい
- **blow over** 〔嵐・危機などが〕過ぎ去る，静まる
- **pose a challenge** 難題をもたらす

避難所を利用したことはよい経験となりましたが、ペットとの避難は課題もあることに気づかされました。

take refuge　避難する

front entrance　正面玄関

facility　施設

good argument　説得力ある議論

Environment Ministry　環境省

leave ~ behind　～を置き去りにする

allergy　アレルギー（反応）

hygiene　衛生状態

odor　におい

make a noise　物音を立てる，騒ぐ

designate　指定する

Vol.216
Evacuating with Pets
（ペットと避難）
During the recent typhoon, we took refuge in an evacuation center. Fortunately, the danger passed quickly, but visiting the center was a good experience to prepare for a real event.
何事もなく済めばラッキー。実地訓練したと思えばいい
One lesson we learned was that evacuating with pets is not so simple.
You may bring them in with you, but if there are any problems, then we would ask you to leave them by the front entrance.
あ、ハイ
受付
Our evacuation center allowed us not only to bring in the pets, but also to keep them with us inside the facility.
同行 … ペットを避難所に連れてくことまではOK
同伴 … ペットと避難所内で一緒に過ごすのもOK
みんな好意的でホッ
猫ちゃんだ～かわいい～♥♥
Inside the evacuation center
However, there are good arguments for and against allowing pets in evacuation centers.
This would make for an interesting debate.
Should pets be allowed in evacuation centers?
Pro
Con
The Environment Ministry recommends bringing pets to centers.
でもNGの避難所も多いらしい
Moco and Gen are part of our family. We can't leave them behind!
人の心を和ませる力もあるよ
Allergy issues
Hygiene issues
Odors
Pets making noise
These could cause real problems for some people.
What should we do?
うーん
Centers could designate areas where pets are allowed and not allowed. Pet owners should also be sure their pets don't bother other people.
Does that sound like a good solution? What do non-pet owners, think about it?

# Vol.217 Year-End Festivities and Fun
（年末の家族イベント）

The season of family events is here, starting with Thanksgiving, which is followed by Christmas and New Year's. Our family has one more big event. Every year in December, my parents host a rice-pounding party.

ヨイショ!
返しが抜群にうまい父方の叔母

きなこに納豆、大根おろし。おいしー

About 30 of our relatives from both sides of my family gather to pound rice and enjoy fresh rice cakes. We make enough for people to take home and enjoy on New Year's Day.

One of the best parts of the day is the Family Concert, in which our talented and not-so-talented relatives perform.

いとこ夫婦のデュオ
いとこのフラダンス
二胡やクラリネット、津軽三味線や和太鼓なんてことも

This year, we will play the handbells.

達者組（1人5〜6本担当）
四苦八苦組（1人3〜4本担当）
母（指導役）
弟
父

（※月1回集まって練習してきた、サン・サーンスの「白鳥」など）

It's great to get the family together for events other than marriages and funerals. We're hoping to keep this family tradition going for years to come.

感謝祭に始まりクリスマスにお正月と、イベント盛りだくさんの季節がやって来ました。我が家にはもう一つ、大きなイベントがあります。

- **year-end** 年末の
- **festivity** 行事，にぎわい
- **pound rice** 餅をつく
- **rice cake** 餅
- **take home** 家に持ち帰る
- **not-so-talented** あまり優れていない
- **family tradition** 家風，家族のしきたり
- **keep ~ going** ～を存続させる
- **for years to come** この先何年も

猫のいたずら防止のためにツリーなしになった今回のクリスマス。でも、クリスマス・スピリットは健在です。

**descend on**
〔場所に〕訪れる

**make plans for**
～の計画を立てる

**family get-together**
家族の団らん［集まり］

**custom to don**
着る習慣

**show gratitude**
感謝の意を表す

Vol.218
The Christmas Spirit
（クリスマスツリーはなくても）
The Christmas season is descending on towns and neighborhoods across Japan. Has everyone made plans for Christmas Day? We are looking forward to our annual family get together, but something will be missing this year.
What's Christmas without a Christmas tree?!
オモチャ天国とキャットタワーになる予感しかない
まだ子猫でいたずら盛り
Christmas Eve (the 24th)
Family dinner, open presents from each other.
わーコレ欲しかったやつ
Christmas Day
(morning)
やったー!
Open presents from Santa.
(lunch)
My parents join us for a relaxed lunch.
Merry Christmas!
CAKE
いらっしゃい
Christmas Day is a busy day. Steve and Midori have made it a custom to don Santa suits and make surprise visits to nearby friends.
Ho Ho Ho Merry Christmas!
Here's some candy for you♪
ちょっとしたお菓子
ドン・キホーテで購入
長靴
OMG! Look at you! How are you?
What's this? Thank you.
For us, Christmas is about showing gratitude and spreading joy. That's the spirit of Christmas.
楽しいしね
When you give and receive gifts, can you feel the Christmas spirit?
「プチお歳暮」と思えばしっくりくるかも

Vol.219

# Root Vegetables
## (おせちと根菜)

Every region and every family has their own version of "o-sechi" dishes for New Year's. But they all have one thing in common — lots of steamed root vegetables.

野菜がしっかり摂れて
壱
弐
参
参の重は
お煮しめ


Many of the vegetables represent good fortune, so even though they're not the most sumptuous-looking ingredients, there are usually a lot of them.

| | |
|---|---|
| れんこん (Lotus root) | たくさん穴が開いている ⇒ A bright future |
| 里芋 (Taro) | 子芋・孫芋がたくさんできる ⇒ A flourishing family |
| にんじん (Carrot) | 「ん(運)」がつく ⇒ Good fortune |
| ごぼう (Burdock root) | 長く根を張る ⇒ A long-lasting family or family business |
| こんにゃく (Konnyaku) | 結んである ⇒ Good relations, harmonious marital relations |

We love burdock and lotus roots, but in Europe and the United States, they're mostly considered to be just roots and are not so popular as food.

えぐみもあるし
たしかに根っこ感すごいよね


Konnyaku, on the other hand, is gaining popularity as a health food.

The English called it "devil's tongue" for how it looks. The texture and smell kept it from wider usage.

花
スライムっぽい
加工されてこんにゃくになる部分


It's becoming popular as a health food marketed in various shapes, including as noodles and rice.

GLUTEN-FREE
LOW-CALORIE
Miracle Noodle
SHIRATAKI
Miracle Rice
SHIRATAKI


During the upcoming Summer Olympics, it will be interesting to see what Japanese things attract the attention of foreign visitors.

Have a Happy New Year!!
年女でーす♪


おせち料理に欠かせない根菜ですが、欧米ではマイナーな食材です。でも、近年あるものが注目されています。

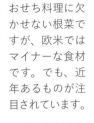

**have ~ in common** ～を共通に持つ
**steamed** 蒸し加熱した
**good fortune** 幸運
**sumptuous** 豪華な, ぜいたくな
**long-lasting** 長続きする
**family business** 家業
**harmonious** 仲のよい, 円満な
**marital relation** 婚姻関係
**gain popularity** 好評を博する, 人気を得る
**texture** 質感, 食感
**keep ~ from...** ～を…させない
**usage** 使用(法)
**attract attention** 注目を集める

日本でもアメリカでも、くしゃみをするときは口をふさぐのが正しいエチケットですが、いくつか違いがあります。

**sneezing** くしゃみ
**nothing to sneeze at** ばかにできない
**proper etiquette** 正しい礼儀作法
**ew** おえっ，げっ
**spittle** つば
**snot** 鼻水
**germ** 細菌
**call for** ～を必要とする，要求する
**followed by silence** 〔主語に〕続いて沈黙が訪れる
**stay warm** 暖かくして過ごす
**catch a cold** 風邪をひく

# Vol.220 Sneezing is Nothing to Sneeze At

(くしゃみをするとき)

Sneezing is universal. In Japan and the United States, the proper etiquette is to cover your mouth when you sneeze. There are some differences, though.
Japan
America
Use your hand or a handkerchief
ハクション!
Use your sleeve
Achoo!
Ew. Spittle and snot get on your hand. Then when that hand touches something else, it can spread germs.
ひじや服なら
そういう心配は不要
たしかに…
Well, that makes sense. So in our house, we use our sleeves.
American custom also calls for even more action when someone sneezes.
Achoo!
「お、大丈夫?」「お大事に」くらいの感じで
Bless you!
Thank you.
When someone sneezes, another person nearby, even a stranger, will say, "Bless you!"
In America, people feel awkward if a sneeze is followed by silence.
Doesn't that sound like something people in Kansai might do?
例
人が転んだとき
Tokyo
見て見ぬふりをする「やさしさ」
…
あっ
Kansai
笑い飛ばす「やさしさ」
冷たいわー
アンタ大丈夫か
ハデにコケたねー
地面が揺れたで
I hope everyone is staying warm this winter. Please be careful not to catch a cold.

# Vol.221 Valentine's Day Preparations
（バレンタインの準備）

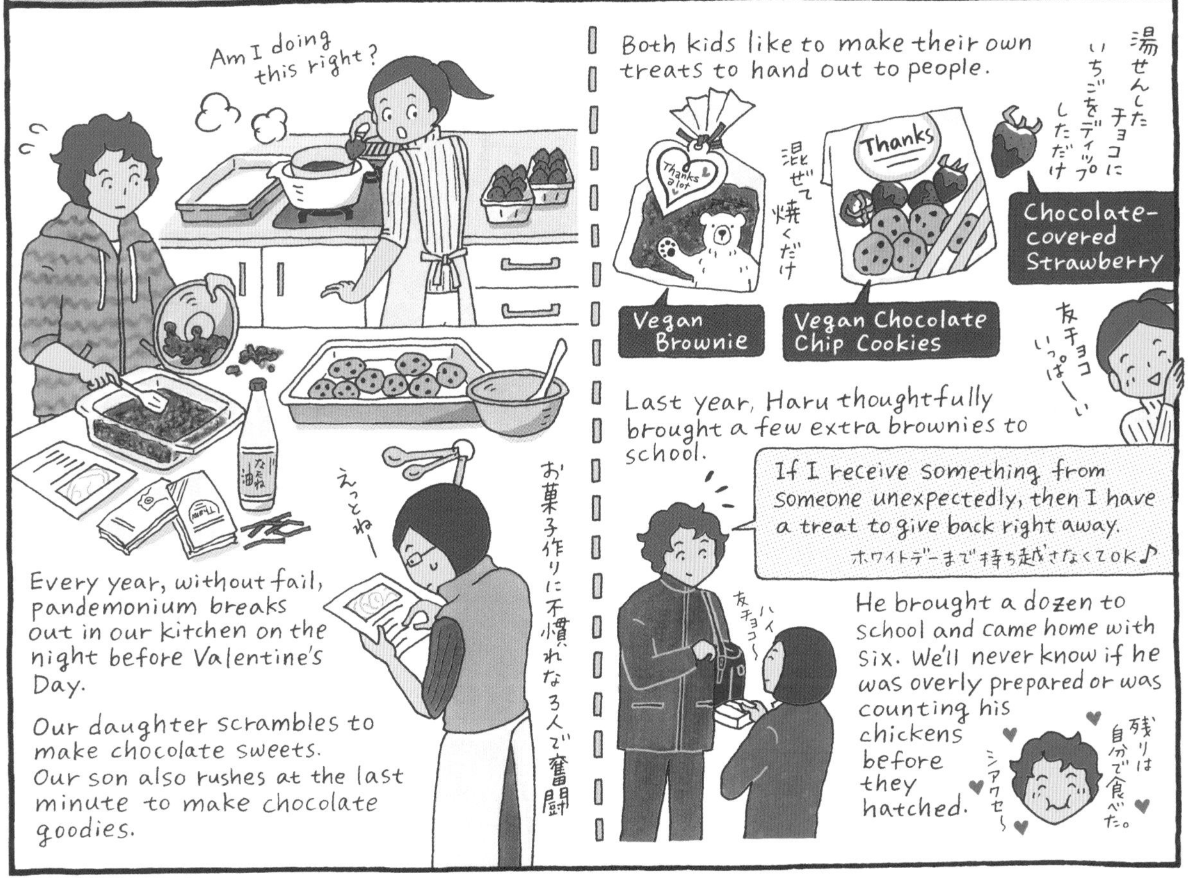
Am I doing this right?
Every year, without fail, pandemonium breaks out in our kitchen on the night before Valentine's Day.
Our daughter scrambles to make chocolate sweets. Our son also rushes at the last minute to make chocolate goodies.
えっとね〜
お菓子作りに不慣れな2人で奮闘
Both kids like to make their own treats to hand out to people.
Thanks a lot
Vegan Brownie
混ぜて焼くだけ
Thanks
Vegan Chocolate Chip Cookies
湯せんしたチョコにいちごをディップしただけ
Chocolate-covered Strawberry
友チョコいっぱ〜い
Last year, Haru thoughtfully brought a few extra brownies to school.
If I receive something from someone unexpectedly, then I have a treat to give back right away.
ホワイトデーまで持ち越さなくてOK♪
ハイ友チョコ〜
He brought a dozen to school and came home with six. We'll never know if he was overly prepared or was counting his chickens before they hatched.
シアワセ〜
残りは自分で食べた。

毎年バレンタインデーの前夜は大混乱に陥る我が家のキッチン。娘も息子も慌ててチョコレートのお菓子を作るからです。

**without fail** 必ず，確実に
**pandemonium** 大混乱，修羅場
**break out** 起こる，勃発する
**scramble to** 慌てて〜する
**at the last minute** 直前に，ギリギリになってから
**goody** 菓子，おいしいもの
**treat** おやつ
**hand out** 配る，手渡す
**thoughtfully** よく考えて，熟慮して
**unexpectedly** 思いがけなく
**count one's chickens before they are hatched** 捕らぬ狸の皮算用をする

私は決して料理上手ではありませんが、スティーヴやアメリカの家族にほめられるのは、和食の特徴のおかげかもしれません。

presentation 見栄え，体裁
heated up 加熱する
preparation method 調理法
visually appealing 見た目に魅力的な
put a lot of work into ～に多大な労力を注ぐ
by comparison 比較すると
garner 獲得する
compliment 賛辞，称賛
assemble 集める，組み立てる
put quite a bit of effort into ～にかなりの努力を払う
have some room to ～する余地がある

# Vol.222 Home Cooking
## （家庭料理とお弁当）

I'm not a chef. However, Steve and his family are always saying how good my cooking is. Sometimes it's a little embarrassing.

Delicious!
You're a great chef!!
Café Kikue is the best!
イイヤヤヤ

I suspect that they are impressed by the presentation and preparation of Japanese food.

**American style**

- ★ One plate
- ★ Heated up
- ★ Eating out or take-out is common

肉（レトルト） 野菜（冷凍）

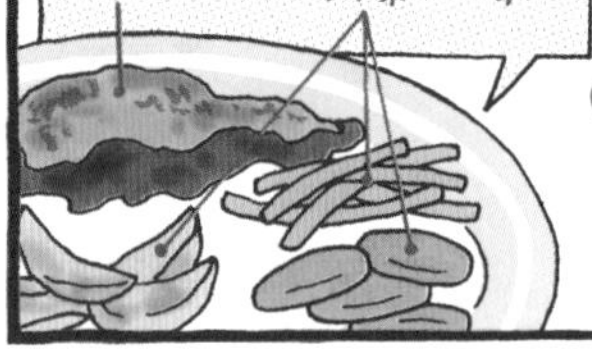

**Japanese style**

- ★ Lots of small dishes
- ★ Various preparation methods
（切る・炊く・煮る・焼く・あえる など）

1
2
3
4
5

Japanese food is visually appealing. And this makes it seem like we put a lot of work into it. By comparison, we do. Even what we think is an ordinary bento box lunch garners compliments.

OMG!
It's so colorful.
And healthy!!
まるですごく豪華な幕の内弁当のような高評価…
冷凍
前日の夕飯のおかず

**A typical American brown-bag lunch**

It's super simple to assemble.
（子供…ピーナツバター＆ジャム / 大人…ミート）サンドイッチ

フルーツも少々
紙袋に入れたり

This made me realize that Japanese put quite a bit of effort into food preparation. We probably have some room to relax our standards a little.

Vol.223
Sumo
（デコポン）
Right around this time each year, one of our family's favorite fruits steps into the ring.
おデコポーン！なんて
名前もいいよね。
デコポン
（不知火）
It's easy to eat!
・皮がむきやすい
・種なし
It's got a nice balance of sourness and sweetness.
They're big and filling.
This popular Japanese fruit is now being sold in some supermarkets in the United States. But it's being sold under a new name. What do they call it?
SUMO Citrus
Nice name!
It's a large citrus fruit with a chonmage on top!
1Lb $3〜4くらい
One Sumo costs about ¥150 to ¥200. Although about the same as in Japan, the price is a little high for one piece of fruit, but that gives it a little prestige.
Fruit there is generally cheaper than here.
とくにカリフォルニア
温暖な気候。フルーツの産地
ORANGES 2Lb $1
CANTALOUPES 2コ $5
PEACHES 1Lb $2
SEEDLESS GRAPES 1Lb $3
とか
（1Lb≒450g）
The dekopon Sumo is still a newbie on U.S. fruit aisles, but we think it's a Yokozuna for flavor and are rooting for it to quickly rise in the ranks.
ガンバレ
不知火
SUMO
デコポン

毎年この時期になると大好きな果物——デコポンの出番がやってきます。最近ではアメリカのスーパーでも販売されているそうです。

right around this time　今頃
ring　〔試合が行われる〕リング
sourness　酸味
under a new name　新しい名前で
prestige　名声，高い評判
newbie　初心者，新入り
aisle　通路
root for　〜を応援する
rise in rank　ランクが上がる，昇進する毎年３月17日は聖パトリックデーを祝うために、緑色の服を準備します。アイルランド系アメリカ人の家族と一緒に祝ったときは――

**break out** 〜を準備する，取り出す

**revered** 崇敬されている

**patron saint** 守護聖人

**maternal side** 母方

**heritage** 血統，血筋

**ancestor** 先祖，祖先

**Holy Trinity** 《キリスト教》三位一体

**fermentation** 発酵

**bay leaf** ベイリーフ，ローリエ《月桂樹の葉を乾燥させたもの》

Vol.224
St.Patrick's Day
(聖パトリックデーのお祝い)
Every year on March 17, we break out our green clothing to celebrate St. Patrick's Day. St. Patrick is revered in Ireland for spreading Christianity and is the patron saint of Ireland.
Two years ago, we celebrated St. Patrick's Day with the maternal side of Steve's family, who have Irish heritage.
Steve's mother's ancestor emigrated from Ireland in the 19th century.
通った鼻筋とブルーの瞳
義母
義母の弟
くつ下だけ、とかでもOK!
The Shamrock
(three-leafed clover)
★National flower of Ireland
★Symbolizes the Holy Trinity
·Father(神)
·Son(キリスト)
·Holy Spirit (聖霊)
緑のものをつけてないとつねられるよ
Ya gotta wear something green!
この時期は、スーパーなどにも緑グッズがたくさん売られる
At the gathering, we ate some traditional Irish foods.
白ワインに着色料
Soda Bread
·No yeast
·Baking soda
·No fermentation
シンプルで素朴な味
Corned Beef
Brisket and boiled vegetables
(塩漬け肉)
·Beer
·Beef stock
·Bay leaves
·Pepper
Slow-cooked for several hours
Onions
Potatoes
Carrots
Cabbage
The St. Patrick's gathering celebrated the family's roots and identity as Irish-Americans. In a way, it's like a green Christmas.
Happy St. Patrick's Day!

Vol.225
An Unfinished Spring
(尻切れトンボの春)
March has been a month of chaos and confusion.
えっ…!?
I'm asking that all schools be closed temporarily beginning on March 2 as a safety measure to prevent the spread of the COVID-19 virus.
速報 首相表明
※2/27(木)夜
Our kids, who were set to graduate from elementary school and middle school, had different reactions.
There's just 12 days left until my commencement ceremony. Now I can't even see my classmates anymore.
Will the ceremony be canceled altogether?
歌も呼びかけも練習してるのに…
小6
Woohoo!
No final exams.
中3
中高一貫なので「卒業」に思い入れなし
My arms are killing me!
一日で全部持ち帰り
All of a sudden, they have a long vacation from school. Although they do have homework, they've quickly settled into a rather lazy lifestyle.
Yeah, let's get the hammer.
友達とオンラインゲーム中
Commencement was drastically shortened, and they didn't even sing at the event. Unfortunately, the slimmed down ceremonies may not provide a good sense of closure to the school year.
We really hope the virus situation settles down in April and that the kids —all kids— can at least have opening ceremonies for the new school year.
故郷のカリフォルニア州でも非常事態宣言が出たりして気がかりです

３月は混乱と困惑の月でした。新型コロナウイルスの感染拡大を防ぐため、すべての学校が臨時休校となりました。

**chaos** 混沌，カオス

**safety measure** 安全対策

**prevent the spread of ～** ～のまん延を防ぐ

**be set to** ～することになっている

**commencement ceremony** 卒業［学位授与］式

**altogether** 完全に，すっかり

**killing me** 耐えられない

**all of a sudden** 前触れもなしに

**settle into** 慣れる，なじむ

**lazy lifestyle** だらけた生活

**drastically** 大幅に

**settle down** 落ち着く

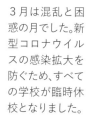

COLUMN
8

## Combining cultures

When I was in elementary school, I fell in love. Minecraft was a game that gave me a sense of freedom, creativity, and dreams. The three-dimensional world composed only of large blocks ignited my creativity. I started planning and sketching my ideas in a notebook, block by block. I carried that notebook everywhere and jotted down ideas in my spare moments. I filled three notebooks that way. I enjoyed planning out buildings more than constructing them.

Being a virtual architect was stimulating, but my interests started shifting towards real world possibilities. I discovered architecture and delved into it. I found the evolution of human home designs fascinating and was intrigued by all the different styles of architecture. I set my path to become a real-world architect.

As I read books and further deepened my knowledge, I began to develop my own taste. Designs with multiple distinct styles emphasizing each other's unique characteristics fascinated me. It was a delight to discover unexpected combinations of styles working together to create a complementary design.

Our house has a mix of Japanese and European styles. There are both western hinged doors and Japanese sliding doors. Our bay windows are equipped with shoji screens. Some of our western rooms with hardwood floors have lamp shades made of Japanese paper. You could say that I grew up in a literally multi-cultural house.

I believe my taste in architecture arose out of this rather unusual environment and the comfort I feel in it. One of my visions as an architect is to design buildings that combine cultures and styles seamlessly to create a unified concept.

Just like our house and family, cultures can fit together, inspire, and enrich, not only architecture, but anything you can imagine.

■ **combine** 結びつける，混ぜ合わせる ■ **three-dimensional** 3次元の ■ **ignite** 火をつける，燃え立たせる ■ **jot down** ～を手早くメモする ■ **delve into** 掘り下げて研究する ■ **intrigued by** ～に興味をそそられる ■ **complementary** 補う，補完する ■ **hinged door** 開き戸 ■ **unified concept** 統一された概念

MOCO
GEN
STEVE
来日35年目の
江戸好きアメリカ人
KIKUE
ワタクシ
HARU
息子。
高校1年生
MIDORI
娘。
中学1年生

# 10th Year

2020

年度始めの４月は、多くの人にとって新生活の始まりです。新生活には家電もあれこれ必要になりますが──

appliance　家電
mark the start of　～のスタートを切る
recent graduate　新卒（者）
vitality　活力
inflow of　～の流入
accompanied by　～が付き物である
pre-equipped　備え付けの
fridge　冷蔵庫《refrigeratorの短縮語》
brand-new　新品の，真新しい
make do with　～で間に合わせる
get started on the right foot　幸先のよいスタートを切る

Vol.226
Appliances for a New Beginning
（新生活と家電）
April marks the start of a fresh new year in many ways. Children are beginning a new school year, and many recent graduates are starting new lives on their own. Everyone seems to have renewed vitality and hopes for the year ahead.
I'm a high schooler now, and Midori started middle school.
久しぶりに前髪作ったよ♪
Basic Appliances for a New Lifestyle
Vacuum cleaner
Microwave oven
Refrigerator
Washing machine
Rice cooker
など
However, the inflow of new things into your life is often accompanied by an outflow of money.
In America, rental apartments usually come pre-equipped with appliances.
Imagine moving to a new place and not having to buy a fridge or oven. What a help that would be!
イイネ!
True. It's one less thing that you have to spend money on, but there are positives and negatives.
悲喜こもごも
Yes!
Oh my gosh! It's brand-new!
前のとこよりグレードアップ!
It works just fine.
Owner
うるさい
ブーン…
Hmm. My grand-parents had one like this.
Is it better to spend some money to buy a new one? Or to make do with the old appliance?
Which would you choose to get a new beginning started on the right foot?

# Vol.227 Connections
## (緊急事態宣言下のつながり)

We've been staying inside as much as possible ever since school let out. In our family, it's been more challenging for the kids than the adults.

We work at home anyway
食事作りが増えたけど習い事の送迎はなくなったし
School's been out since March 2nd. With school club activities and other lessons canceled, they have almost nothing to do.
ヤル気出なーい
最近筋トレにハマりだしたハル
Homework


Haru has always been fine doing stuff on his own, so he's not so put out. Midori, however, has a tight group of friends. To keep in touch, she's been heavily relying on Line, which the kids have been using very creatively.

Homework help
(LINE電話で)
How do you do this one?
Haru, can you help us?
困ったら兄に聞くことも
Drawing contests
(LINEビデオ通話で)
OK, now let's do summer, blue and… miniskirt!


The kids have found novel ways to stay busy and entertain themselves. I have a new appreciation for modern technology, as well as for our kids' adaptability and ingenuity.

In fact, we're all using Line to keep in touch with family and relatives in Japan and overseas.

Information
Sharing
Fun Stuff
アメリカの姪
My classes are all online until summer vacation. Ugh!
きれいな写真やおもしろ動画など
実母


We're maintaining social distancing without being socially distant. We're talking much more often than before. It'd be nice to keep it up when this scourge passes.

一斉休校となってから、私たちはなるべく家の中で過ごしています。我が家では大人より子どもたちの方が大変なようですが——

**as much as possible** できるだけ
**anyway** どっちみち，とにかく
**put out** （人）の心を乱す
**tight** 密接な，親密な
**keep in touch** 連絡を取り合う
**rely heavily on** ～に大きく依存する
**novel way** 目新しいやり方
**adaptability** 適応力
**ingenuity** 創造力
**keep it up** そのまま続ける
**scourge** 苦難の原因

家にいる時間が増える中、小さな楽しみを見つけたり、後回しにしていた雑事をこなしたり、工夫して過ごしています。

stay inside　家にいる
just for fun　遊び感覚で
enhance　高める
glimpse　ちらっと見る
lighten someone's mood　(人)の気分を明るくする
for one reason or another　どういうわけか
put off　先送りする, 後回しにする
clutter　散乱しているもの
non-perishable foods　保存食
sew　縫う
complaint　不満
help out　〔人を〕助ける, 援助する
over time　時間とともに

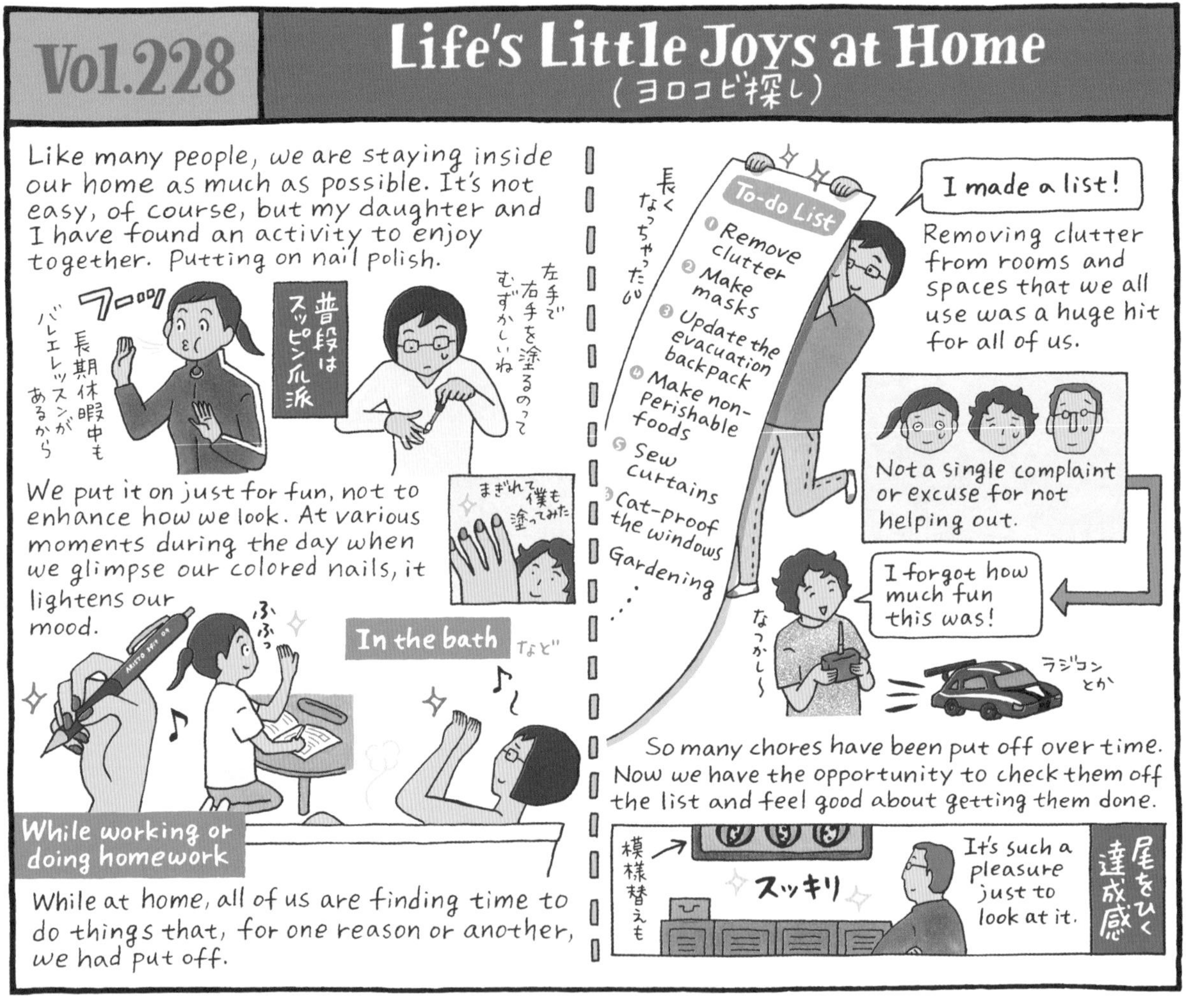

Vol.228
Life's Little Joys at Home
(ヨロコビ探し)
Like many people, we are staying inside our home as much as possible. It's not easy, of course, but my daughter and I have found an activity to enjoy together. Putting on nail polish.
フーッ
長期休暇中もバレエレッスンがあるから
普段はスッピン爪派
左手で右手を塗るのってむずかしいね
We put it on just for fun, not to enhance how we look. At various moments during the day when we glimpse our colored nails, it lightens our mood.
まぎれて僕も塗ってみた
ふふっ
In the bath など
While working or doing homework
While at home, all of us are finding time to do things that, for one reason or another, we had put off.
長くなっちゃった
To-do List
1 Remove clutter
2 Make masks
3 Update the evacuation backpack
4 Make non-perishable foods
5 Sew curtains
6 Cat-proof the windows
Gardening
...
I made a list!
Removing clutter from rooms and spaces that we all use was a huge hit for all of us.
Not a single complaint or excuse for not helping out.
I forgot how much fun this was!
なつかし〜
ラジコンとか
So many chores have been put off over time. Now we have the opportunity to check them off the list and feel good about getting them done.
模様替えも
スッキリ
It's such a pleasure just to look at it.
達成感尾をひく

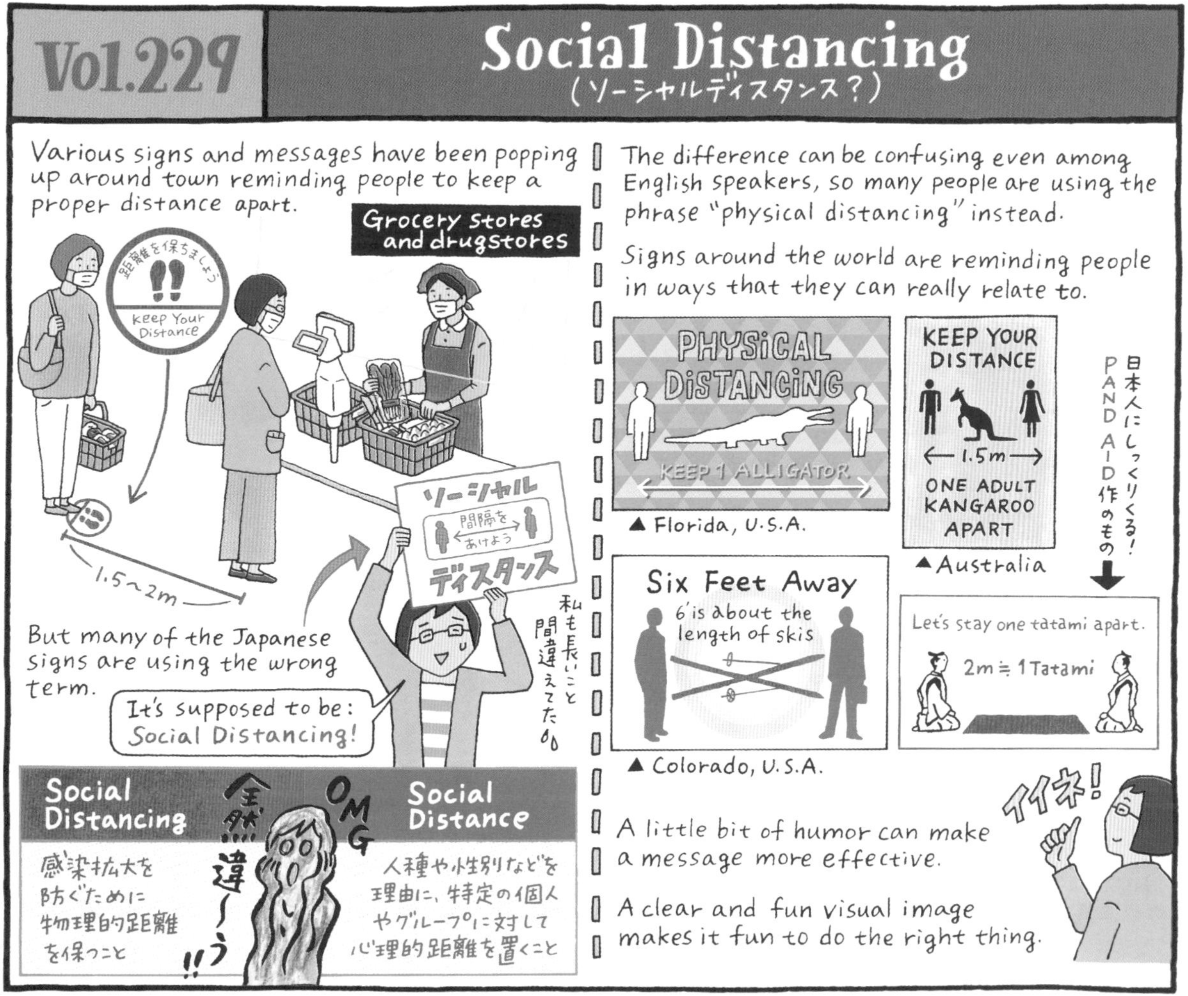
Vol.229
Social Distancing
(ソーシャルディスタンス？)
Various signs and messages have been popping up around town reminding people to keep a proper distance apart.
Grocery stores and drugstores
距離を保ちましょう
Keep Your Distance
1.5〜2m
ソーシャル
間隔をあけよう
ディスタンス
But many of the Japanese signs are using the wrong term.
It's supposed to be: Social Distancing!
私も長いこと間違えてた。
Social Distancing
感染拡大を防ぐために物理的距離を保つこと
全然違〜う!!
OMG
Social Distance
人種や性別などを理由に、特定の個人やグループに対して心理的距離を置くこと
The difference can be confusing even among English speakers, so many people are using the phrase "physical distancing" instead.
Signs around the world are reminding people in ways that they can really relate to.
PHYSICAL DISTANCING
KEEP 1 ALLIGATOR
▲ Florida, U.S.A.
KEEP YOUR DISTANCE
1.5m
ONE ADULT KANGAROO APART
▲ Australia
日本人にしっくりくる！ PANDA I-D作のもの
Six Feet Away
6' is about the length of skis
▲ Colorado, U.S.A.
Let's stay one tatami apart.
2m ≒ 1 Tatami
イイネ！
A little bit of humor can make a message more effective.
A clear and fun visual image makes it fun to do the right thing.

適切な距離を保つよう注意喚起する看板やメッセージが街中に登場しています。しかし、日本語の看板の多くは誤った用語を使っています。

**social distancing** 対人距離の確保
**pop up** 出現する
**remind someone to** （人）に〜することを気付かせる
**proper** 適切な
**wrong term** 間違った用語
**physical distancing** 物理的距離の確保
**alligator** アメリカワニ
**make ~ more effective** 〜の効果を高める
**do the right thing** 適切な行動をする

休校になって6週間後、ハルが一言、興味深いことを言いました。頭の中での日本語と英語の切り替えが遅くなったと感じているそうです。

- **language switching** 言語の切り替え
- **away from** ～から離れて
- **reflex** 反射神経
- **get rusty** 腕がなまる，さび付く
- **interact with** （人）と交流する，関わり合う
- **come to think of it** 考えてみると
- **conduct a ceremony** 式を執り行う

## Vol.230 Language Switching and Society

（脳内言語スイッチと社会）

After six weeks away from school, Haru made an interesting comment.
伸びた
だぶだぶ
I think I'm slower at switching between Japanese and English.
日本語で会話中なのに英語で考えちゃってたりして
Maybe it's 'cause I've been away from school for so long.
At school, he's constantly changing back and forth depending on whom he's speaking to. Now that Haru is home every day, his language reflexes are getting a little rusty.
E English
J Japanese
学校で
休校中
相手に合わせて返球するイメージ
帰国子女が多いので、英語も多め
返球相手は家族だけ
Our kids often interacted with their classmates, even during summer vacations from school. Come to think of it, school is our kids' "society."
部活や講習もあるしね
Haru and Midori reconnected with their society when their school conducted an online entrance ceremony.
In the Living Room
校歌も歌ってみた
制服も着てみた
新中1
新高1
知ってる先生の登場に盛り上がる
1年C組 ○○先生
おー ○○先生だ！
いえーい
※30分くらい
校長挨拶
先生の紹介
YouTube
ホームルーム
Zoom
I wonder how much online schooling will re-create society for our kids. I'm hoping for the best.

Vol.231
The Online Lifestyle
(オンライン生活)
I've been doing calisthenics with my kids while following along with the radio in the mornings.
Truth is, it's part of their homework.
Their school launched online schooling right after Golden Week.
運動不足の体に効く
Physical Education
Do calisthenics at least 3 times a week
YouTube 配信や schoolTakt など
スマホでもOK
教材の共有や課題のやりとり、質疑応答ができる授業支援システム
語学学習用には Edmodo
schoolTaktに似てるけどディスカッションも可能な教育系SNS
Remote School
Once a week via snail mail, the school sends textbooks and worksheets to kids.
The students send back the worksheets.
It's a hybrid of digital and analog schooling.
It's going pretty smoothly.
動画を見返したり
LINEで友達と一緒にやったり
わかりにくいところはハルに聞くことも
We like that we can study at our own pace!
問題を熟考できるし
通学がない分時間のゆとりがあってやりたいことができる
However, online lessons don't work so well for other types of classes.
画面に接近してみんなをチェックする先生
Ai-chan, straighten your leg more!
Zoom
C'mon girls, pull in those stomachs!
全身が映るように2〜3m離す必要あり
猫が〜
Online Lesson
It seems like the future is suddenly upon us.
Although this surge into the future is a little exciting, it still feels like something is lacking.
I'm kinda glad that the online life can't replace real personal contact.

子どもたちのオンライン授業が本格的にスタートしました。思いのほかスムースに順応しているように見える子どもたちです。

**calisthenics** 体操

**launch** 開始する

**physical education** 〔学科としての〕体育

**via snail mail** 郵便［郵送］で

**at one's own pace** 自分のペースで

**c'mon** さあ、がんばって《come onの省略形》

**be upon someone** （人）のところに来る

**surge into** 〜に押し寄せる

**lack** 欠いている、足りない

**replace** 〔〜に〕取って代わる

この半年で、怒涛のように新しい言葉が登場し、生活様式も大きく変わりました。

**sea change**　大転換，著しい変化
**boatload of**　大量の～
**declaration of emergency**　緊急事態宣言
**Three C's**　3つの密，3密
**self-quarantine**　自主隔離
**triage**　トリアージ，重症度判定検査
**write down**　書き留める
**accomplish**　成し遂げる，達成する
**take the initiative to**　率先して～する
**flip**　ひっくり返す
**positive affirmation**　肯定的な承認
**not-altogether-displeased**　まんざらでもない
**boost**　後押し

# Vol.232 New Lifestyle Habits
## （新しい生活習慣）

The last six months have brought a sea change in our lifestyles and a boatload of new words.

Cluster
Self-quarantine
COVID-19
Declaration of emergency
Pandemic
The Three C's
New lifestyles
Triage
Social distancing
濃密すぎて少し前のこととは思えない…
まあ現在進行形だけど


We're now washing our hands frequently and taking more care about general hygiene. We also created a Well-Done List where we write down things we've accomplished.

### Well-Done List

| Midori | Haru | Kikue | Steve |
|---|---|---|---|
| • 部屋の断捨離 | • 筋トレ | • マスク作り | • 草むしり |
| • 毎日，読書 | • マスク作り | • ぬか床再開 | • 掃除機のノズル掃除 |
| • ごはん作り トマトスパゲティ 納豆チャーハン | • ブラインドタッチ習得！ | • 冬物セーター洗い | • サイクリング |
| | • 掃き掃除 | • ラジオ体操 | • ヨガ |

Rather than a To-Do List of things we need to do, everyone writes down anything they've taken the initiative to get done.

Well-Done List
3月からスタート。どんどん長くなっていく
ダイニングに貼ってある
ミサンガ作ってみた
麦茶作っといたよー


Since the new COVID-19 lifestyle tends to create an atmosphere of not being able to do things, a Well-Done List flips the emphasis to being positive about what we can do.

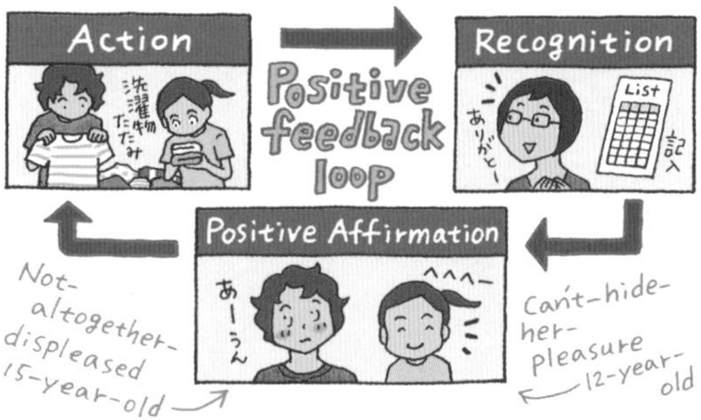

Action
洗濯物たたみ
Positive feedback loop
Recognition
List
ありがとー
記入
Positive Affirmation
あーうん
^^^ー
Not-altogether-displeased 15-year-old
Can't-hide-her-pleasure 12-year-old


The growing list also seems to be a nice boost to everyone's self-esteem. We may just keep the list up for a while.

Vol.233
Touch-Typing
(ブラインドタッチ)
I started using a computer after college. I didn't really learn to type. Instead, I got used to typing, so my typing style is unconventional.
当時のPC
今見ても近未来的デザインのMac
50cm近い奥行き
約20年後の今
Five-Finger Typing
なんちゃってブラインドタッチ
速い。けど、うるさい
カタカタタ！
タ！
タ!!
タタ！
今じゃこんなに薄型
Younger generations are starting to use computers much earlier than my generation did. They've made amazing progress during just a few months of online schooling.
I can type really fast now!
I can type without looking at the keyboard.
ブラインドタッチ、マスターしたよ！
自慢♪
Ah, you mean touch-typing! That's great.
トトト
げ
“ブラインドタッチ”って和製英語だったのか…！
知らなかった
完全なるtouch-typing。静か
Steve learned to type in high school nearly 40 years ago, and now typing classes are becoming standard even in second grade in the U.S. In our high-tech society, it makes sense that technology skills should be part of the early core curriculum.
はじめはゲームみたいなプログラムで
高学年になるとパワーポイントなども使いこなす
お
ま
け
▶
The quick brown fox jumps over the lazy dog.
This sentence uses all the letters of the alphabet. It's good practice for learning to type with every finger. How fast can you type it out?
オススメ！


オンライン授業のおかげでタイピングがレベルアップした子どもたち。ハルは、いわゆる「ブラインドタッチ」も身につけたようです。

**touch-typing** ブラインドタッチ《キーボードを見ないで正しく文字を打ち込むこと》

**unconventional** 一般的とはいえない

**make amazing progress** 目覚ましい進歩を遂げる

**high-tech society** ハイテク社会

**core curriculum** 必修科目

**type out** タイプで打つ

ハルが16歳になりました。アメリカでは運転免許を取得できる年齢です。そこで、私たちは特別なお祝いをすることにしました。

Vol.234
Sixteen Candles
(16歳のお祝い)
Our son recently turned 16 years old, which is a sort of coming-of-age point in American culture. In many states, 16 is when you can first acquire a driver's license. Many high schoolers even drive themselves to school.
助手席に免許保持者を乗せて、高速道路も。
アメリカの姪(16)も現在、公道で練習中。
It's common to throw a special party. For girls, it's celebrated as "sweet sixteen."
Sweet 16
A dance party, outdoor movie party, pool party...
We've got to think of something special to do for Haru.
We surprised Haru (and his lucky younger sister) with a day at the racetrack. Not watching, but driving go-karts! Racers speed around a 540-meter track for eight minutes. Top drivers reach a speed of 70kph.
(音、大きい)
30kph くらいで安全運転だったハル
16
うう こっちが緊張する～
Haru was uncharacteristically quiet as he waited his turn. After he crossed the finish line, though, he was a new person.
That was great! I wanna go again!!!
Before
…
パァァ
3年後は私の番♪


**coming-of-age** 成人の

**acquire a driver's license** 運転免許(証)を取得する

**surprise** 〔～を〕驚かす

**racetrack** 〔競争するための〕トラック

**kph** キロメートル毎時(= kilometers per hour)

**uncharacteristically quiet** いつになく静かな

**cross the finish line** ゴールする

**be a new person** まるで人が変わったようだ

Vol.235
The Coronavirus and Quality of Life
(コロナ禍のQOL)
Schoolkids are already nearing the end of their foreshortened summer holidays.
When schools reopen in fall, many classes in California will even be completely online.
リーダーシップ力が高く評価されている
ニューサム州知事
(男前)
Regions that have low transmission risk rates for two consecutive weeks will be allowed to hold in-person classes.
Teachers will be routinely tested.
Tokyo ought to take a page out of that playbook.
感染者、増えてるし
Somehow or other, I really hope they can experience as much regular school life as possible.
三密は避けるにしても
The School Life
行事
部活
友情
The new lifestyle makes it a challenge for students to maintain their usual quality of life.
At Haru and Midori's school, the students are in deep discussions to figure out how they can hold their annual school Culture Festival.
いつもみたいにできないならやらなくていいんじゃない?
展示ものだけにするとか?
三密を考えるとアトラクション系の出店はNGだよね
外部の人を入れなかったらどうかな?
屋外の模擬店ならOK?
でも高3は今回が最後だし
It's a tough problem, but by hook or by crook I hope they'll find a way to have a fulfilling school life.
Schoolkids are working harder than ever during this pandemic and truly deserve an A for effort!
ぎゅっ!
みんなすっごくよくがんばってる!!

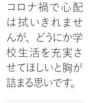

コロナ禍で心配は拭いきれませんが、どうにか学校生活を充実させてほしいと胸が詰まる思いです。

foreshorten 短縮する

transmission risk 感染リスク

for ~ consecutive weeks 〜週間続けて

in-person class 対面授業

ought to 〜すべきである

take a page out of 〜をお手本にする

somehow or other ぜひどうにかして

cultural festival 文化祭

tough problem 困難な問題

by hook or by crook どんな手を使ってでも

fulfilling school life 充実した学校生活

deserve an A A[優]に値する

ハルが生徒会役員に選ばれました。選挙演説では、多様性と自己表現を阻む校則について疑問を投げかけました。

elected to be　～に選ばれる

student council　生徒会

campaign speech　選挙演説

evolve　発展する

school regulations　校則

gender　ジェンダー,〔社会的・文化的〕性

perpetuate　〔～を〕長続きさせる

out of step　〔社会などと〕調和していない

sensibility　感受性, 感性

methodical approach　系統的アプローチ

status quo　現状, そのままの状態

Vol.236
School Dress Code I
（学校の服装規定①）
Haru was elected to be on the student council at his school. In his campaign speech, he talked about an issue that was on his mind.
Society is constantly evolving and becoming more diverse.
I will open discussion about school regulations related to diversity and self-expression and find a way to update the regulations.
一番の動機は役職への興味だけど
コロナ対策でモニター演説会に
The diversity and self-expression issues he was talking about were:
Hairstyles and school uniforms!
I don't believe gender should be the basis for having different rules for girls and boys.
Hairstyle
Why are there rules for boys and girls?
NG 男子の結び髪
NG 女子の坊主
勉強に支障が出るとも思えないし
Uniforms
Why must girls wear only skirts?
Why not long pants too?
選べたらいいかも
Haru says perpetuating fixed concepts based on gender is out of step with the sensibilities of modern society. He thinks that needs to change.
Impressed by Haru's logical and methodical approach to taking on the status quo about school uniforms, I took a look at how schools in America deal with the issue. I'll share with you what I found next time.
30年前の私
ウエストを折り返しスカート短くしてたなぁ

# Vol.237 School Dress Code II
## (学校の服装規定②)

アメリカの公立高校では、生徒の服装はほとんど自由ですが、私立の学校では服装規定がある場合も。詳しく見てみると――

Students at public high schools in the United States are mostly free to dress however they want. There are usually some rules, though.

BEER!
酒、タバコ、ドラッグ、政治的なものはNG
キャミソールなど、肌の露出が多いセクシーなものはNG
未成年への誘惑を避けるってことで納得!


Private schools, on the other hand, can have quite strict dress codes. My niece's school has some carefully defined rules.

1 Approved unaltered polo and outerwear.
(色やデザインは選べる)
など
両手を挙げてもおへそが出ないシャツ丈にする
意外と細かいね
2 Clean, intact jeans, dress slacks or khakis. Shorts to the knees.
ダメージやほつれは×
スウェットパンツやヨガパンツ、パジャマも×
3 Shoes with backs or back straps.
(ビーチサンダルやミュールは×)
理由 非常時に対応できるように
衝撃!
パジャマも想定範囲に入ってるとは


Private Catholic schools in the U.S. have an image of enforcing very strict dress codes.

Standard of Japan
They have so much more freedom of choice than at our school.
たしかに
…
男女差だってないし
靴下まで含めて一式、学校指定

Lots of choices within a set range
OR
One choice
どれにしようかな
これ以外は認めません
学校


It's a conflict between a school wanting to maintain a sense of decorum and students wanting to be able to express themselves. Haru has made it a personal objective to find a point of compromise between the two at his school.

**defined** 決められた
**approved** 承認された
**unaltered** 無地の
**intact** 傷がない
**khakis** カーキズボン
**have an image of** ～というイメージを持つ
**enforce** 〔～を〕強要する
**conflict** 不一致，対立
**sense of decorum** 礼儀の観念
**personal objective** 個人的目標
**point of compromise** 妥協点，落としどころ

次期アメリカ大統領選挙まであと約１か月。選挙当日になるとSNSには、投票済みステッカーを貼って投票所から出てくる人々の写真が溢れますが――

presidential election　大統領選挙
inundated with　〜でいっぱいだ
vote　投票する
display　見せる, 誇示する
civic duty　市民の義務
apparel　衣料, 装飾
Electoral College　選挙人団
candidate　候補者
popular vote　一般投票
riveting　心を奪われるような
fever　熱中

# Vol.238 The U.S. Presidential Election

（アメリカ大統領選挙）

The election of the next U.S. president is only about a month away.

On election day, online social networking sites become inundated with pictures of people exiting voting centers with stickers saying, "I voted."

I VOTED
nyc votes
THE BRONX
QUEENS
BROOKLYN
しゃれてる
New York Cityのもの
I Voted
I VOTED
I VOTED TODAY
デザインいろいろ。国旗を用いたものが多い
赤い羽共同募金みたい


This year, however, more states are allowing online voting, so fewer people may have a chance to proudly display their civic duty. Not to worry, a completely new type of election apparel has been appearing on the internet.

今回ならではのアイテム
I YOUR VOTE MATTERS
BIDEN HARRIS '20
VOTE
TRUMP 2020


The U.S. uses a system called the Electoral College for presidential elections. Even if a candidate wins the popular vote, it's the Electoral College that actually elects the president. Election day news can be riveting.

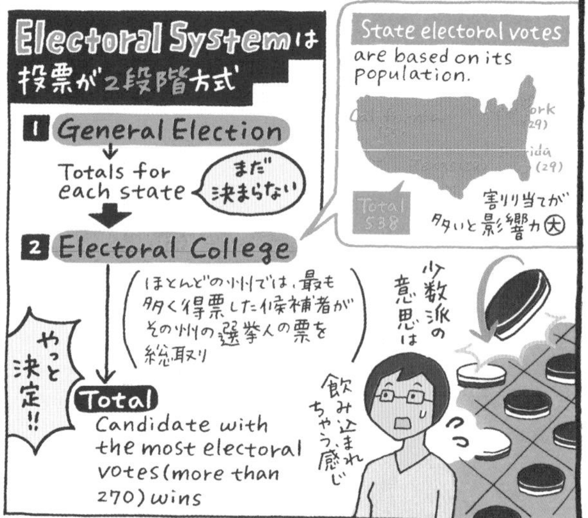

Electoral Systemは投票が2段階方式
1 General Election
Totals for each state
まだ決まらない
2 Electoral College
（ほとんどの州では、最も多く得票した候補者がその州の選挙人の票を総取り）
やっと決定!!
Total
Candidate with the most electoral votes (more than 270) wins
State electoral votes are based on its population.
Total 538
割り当てが多いと影響力大
少数派の意思は
飲み込まれちゃう感じ


Election fever is especially hot in the United States this year. Let's hope the outcome is very clear.

在外投票しました
I VOTED

Vol.239
Spirit Week
(楽しい学校行事)
High schools in the United States have a tradition of holding an annual Spirit Week.
Each day of the week, students come to school in clothes designed to match a specific theme.
愛校心と結束力を高める!
うちの学校でもできたらいいな!
MON
Pajama Day
TUE
Stripe Day
とにかくストライプ
WED
Old Person Day
THU
Twin Day
友達とお揃い
FRI
Decades Day
90年代とか
ネオンカラーな
The student council can choose any theme they can imagine.
Crazy Hair Day とかも
The students attend classes in their outfits.
Eh?! The teacher's in pajamas too!
お~
仮装する・しないは個人の自由
「日常」の中に「遊び」♪
In America, it's not unusual to see people going to work wearing Halloween costumes or decked out in green for St. Patrick's Day. It's easy to see where the idea gets its start.
Here in Tokyo, it would take a fair amount of courage to dress up and commute on the train.
But there's no doubt that a playful outfit would brighten up people's day.

アメリカの高校では毎年「スピリット・ウィーク」を開催します。その週は毎日、生徒たちは特定のテーマに沿った服を着て登校します。

**specific** 特定の，具体的な

**decade** 10年，ひと昔

**attend a class** 授業に出席する，受講する

**eh** えっ

**deck out** 美しく着飾る

**take a fair amount of ~ to** …するのにかなりの～を要する

**commute** 通勤［通学］する

**there is no doubt that** ～ということは疑いようがない

**brighten up someone's day** （人）の1日を明るくする

私たちが住む市はドイツに姉妹都市があります。１年前、親善使節団として来たドイツのティーンエイジャーを我が家で受け入れました。

**friendship and goodwill** 友好親善

**sister city** 姉妹都市

**delegation** 代表団，派遣団

**keep someone busy** （人）を忙しい状態に保つ

**stand out** 突出する，際立つ

**in person** 直に，直接

**come in handy for** ～に役立つ

Vol.240
Friendship and Goodwill I
（日独友好親善のホームステイ①）
The city we live in has a sister city in Germany. One year ago, we hosted in our home a German teenager who came over as part of a goodwill delegation.
Florian
Age 15.
Speaks German, English, French
サッカー大好き。憧れのマルコ・ルイス選手と同じ髪型
書類審査や面接の末選ばれたメンバーなんだね
3か国語もすごいねー
おイケメン
メンバーリスト
ボクと同い年♪
Our local community association kept him quite busy during his 10-day visit. He was out and about all day, almost every day, experiencing Japan.
Cultural Activities
Japanese Taiko Drums
Tea Ceremony
Making Udon
Wearing Kimono
うまい!
Japanese Calligraphy
It all looked so fun and interesting! One experience stood out for the strong impression it left on Florian.
Even Bus Tours!
スカイツリー
鎌倉
富士山
雷門
浅草
Shibuya Scramble!
There were probably three times more people than in my whole town!!
One point of interest for our kids was hearing the German language in person and just how much they could not understand of it.
わー
わからないってこういうことか
英語に苦労する母の気持ちがわかったか
ハハハ
他のメンバー
ドイツ語
Google Translate came in handy for learning interesting words.
ヤバイ
マジで
カワイイ
とかも教えた

# Vol.241 Friendship and Goodwill II

## (日独友好親善のホームステイ②)

About a year ago, we hosted a young man who was part of a goodwill delegation from our city's sister city in Germany. Just 15 years old, Florian was a cordial and gracious young gentleman.

He's so well mannered. He looks you straight in the eye when he talks to you.
誠実さが感じられる

He was also very conscientious.

Carefully arranged toiletries.
Futon made nicely every morning.

やば
It's time to go!
Yes, I'm ready.
Germans really are super punctual!!
Prepared to go.
5 minutes beforehand!

I was most impressed by his willingness to try new things. He unhesitatingly tasted unfamiliar foods without pondering if he might like them or not. His enthusiasm inspired us to introduce him to deeper and wider discoveries.

STEP①
お団子
ぬれせん
あんこ
STEP②
みそ汁
つけもの
刺身こんにゃく
いなり寿司
STEP③
At conveyor-belt sushi restaurant
納豆巻きも
赤貝も
とびっこも
制覇

To me, Florian is a fine example of a young man who was raised right, and he reminded me that the way children are brought up can have a deep and long-lasting effect on their lives. Haru and Midori both say they want to visit Germany, and I want them to be ready and willing to get the most out of their experiences.

大切にされている器は
他の人にも大切に扱われる
それはたぶん人も同じ

ドイツから来たフロリアンは実にいい青年で、かつ意欲的でした。私たちもつい、いろいろ体験させたくなって――

**cordial** 友好的な，誠心誠意の

**gracious** 親切な，腰の低い

**look someone straight in the eye** （人）の目を真っすぐに見る

**conscientious** 丁寧な

**toiletry** 洗面道具

**punctual** 〔人が〕時間を守る

**willingness to** ～する意欲

**unhesitatingly** ためらわずに

**ponder** じっくり考える

**inspire ~ to** ～に…する気を起こさせる

**get the most out of** ～を最大限に楽しむ

よく知らない人と電話で話すとき、自分が無意識に声の高さを上げていることに気づかされました。なぜそうするのでしょうか？

pitch　音の高さ
unconsciously　無意識に
social behavior　社会的マナー
amiable　親切な，感じのよい
ingrained in culture　文化に根差している
civilized　品のある
favorable　好ましい
intimidating　威嚇するような
self-reliant　自立した
vacuous　愚かな
silly　分別のない
intended effect　意図した効果
struggle to　～するのに苦労する

# Vol.242 Perfect Pitch
（声のピッチ効果）

I was reminded recently that when I'm speaking on the phone to someone I don't know, I unconsciously raise the pitch of my voice.
ハイ… ハイ…
よろしくお願いします
地声は低め →
What a high pitch!
That's not her usual voice.
ムッ
仕方ないじゃん 自然になっちゃうんだから
Although it annoyed me to hear that while I was on the phone…
?
Why was I doing it?
It seems to be a social behavior in Japan to raise the pitch of your voice to try to sound amiable to people you don't know very well. It's so ingrained in our culture, that we do it unconsciously.
High Pitch
Cute, friendly, civilized, gracious, beautiful
In Japan, a high-pitched voice creates a favorable impression.
Low Pitch
Strong, intimidating
（※ちなみに、日本女性の声のピッチの高さは世界一との説も）
The impressions generated by voice pitch are quite different in the United States.
Low Pitch
Intelligent, cool, sexy, self-reliant
High Pitch
Mechanical, vacuous, silly
注：あくまでもイメージ
The importance of self-reliance is emphasized to us from a young age.
かわいさより強さ!
サッチャー元英国首相も低い声を出すためのボイストレーニングをしたのは有名な話
After marrying into Steve's family, I noticed that my voice pitch became very high when I was nervous, and the high pitch had the opposite of the intended effect on my new relatives.
I still struggle to express myself in English, but I now consciously try to keep my voice pitch down.
緊張すると声が上ずっちゃう
Relax…
Take a deep breath.
Since voice pitch communicates so much, it's worth working on it to improve your language skills.

# Vol.243 College Admissions
## (大学進学準備)

College admissions requirements are already starting to loom over Haru, just midway through his first year of high school. He's trying to navigate two very different systems in Japan and the U.S.

選択科目
三者面談
模試

| JAPAN | | U.S.A. |
|---|---|---|
| Entrance Examination | ≠ | Admission |

推薦やAOはアメリカ式に近いけど
入試の出来不出来が大きく影響
体調管理も重要
高校時代を総合評価
学力以上に人物評価が肝

The Japanese system focuses more on entrance exam results, while the U.S. system tries to evaluate a student's overall high school experience and potential.

| | | | |
|---|---|---|---|
| 全部で6項目 | 学力系 | 1 | GPA（4年間の評定平均） |
| | | 2 | SATやACT（習熟度を測る全国テスト） |
| | 人物評価系 | 3 | Essay（自己アピールの作文） |
| | | 4 | Letters of Recommendation |
| | | 5 | Extracurricular Activities |
| | | 6 | Interview |

SAT and ACT tests are offered up to seven times each year, and a student can take the tests as many times as they like.

You can submit your highest test scores.
プレッシャーが軽減できていいね

重!
厚!
ただし、official問題集のボリュームはえげつない
1314p
1kg
7cm
SAT
大学進学する高校生の必需品

Extracurricular activities are used to gauge a student's character, such as leadership and a sense of responsibility, and to highlight their special skills and experiences.

Student council
Arts
Sports
Participation in projects
Volunteer activities
など
やるコトいっぱい
宿題も多いのに

American students don't have to go to cram schools, but they need to be plenty busy with other activities to make a good impression.

College admission systems play a large role in shaping how Japanese and American high schoolers spend their time.

高校1年の半ばを過ぎたばかりのハルですが、早くも大学進学に向けた動きが始まりました。日本とアメリカでは大学の入学審査も異なります。

**college admission** 大学入学選考

**loom over** ～にぼんやり現れる

**navigate** 〔～の〕かじ取りをする

**evaluate** 評価する

**letter of recommendation** 〔他人に書いてもらう〕推薦状

**extracurricular activity** 課外活動

**gauge** 〔人の能力や性格などを〕判断する

**cram school** 学習塾，予備校

**play a large role in** ～において大きな役割を果たす

12月になると、海外の友人や親戚からクリスマスカードが届くようになります。多くのカードには、家族全員の写真が載っています。

**holiday card** クリスマス[グリーティング]カード

**season's greetings** 季節のあいさつ

**centered on** ～を中心とする

**whole family** 家族全員

**brighten** 〔～を〕輝かせる，明るくする

**best wishes for** ～をお祈りする

Vol.244
Holiday Cards
（ホリデーシーズンカード）
Come December, we start receiving Christmas cards from friends and relatives overseas. Many of the cards feature cheerful family photographs.
Happy HOLIDAYS
様々な宗教に配慮して Merry Christmasではなく "Happy Holidays"や "Season's Greetings" とする場合も増えている
WISHING YOU A VERY MERRY CHRISTMAS
表面は写真と活字。裏にちょっとした個人メッセージを書く
うちではツリーに飾っちゃったりも
元気そう！いい写真だね
The New Year's cards we send in Japan are really very similar to the Xmas cards, although not so many seem to be centered on pictures of the whole family.
Families with small children like to send photos of their kids, and it's true parents tend to take a lot of photos of kids when they are small and fewer as the kids grow up.
あけましておめでとうございます
Most photos on New Year's cards seem to be of children.
親は入ってても小さくだったり
お宮参りとか七五三とか
This year, our Xmas cards will have a family photo. We don't usually do that, but since we haven't been able to meet people as often lately, we thought a picture would help brighten the holidays.
知人の写真家さんが撮ってくれた→
MERRY Christmas
The Ballati Family
（ビスタプリントというサイトを利用）
Best wishes for a happy season!

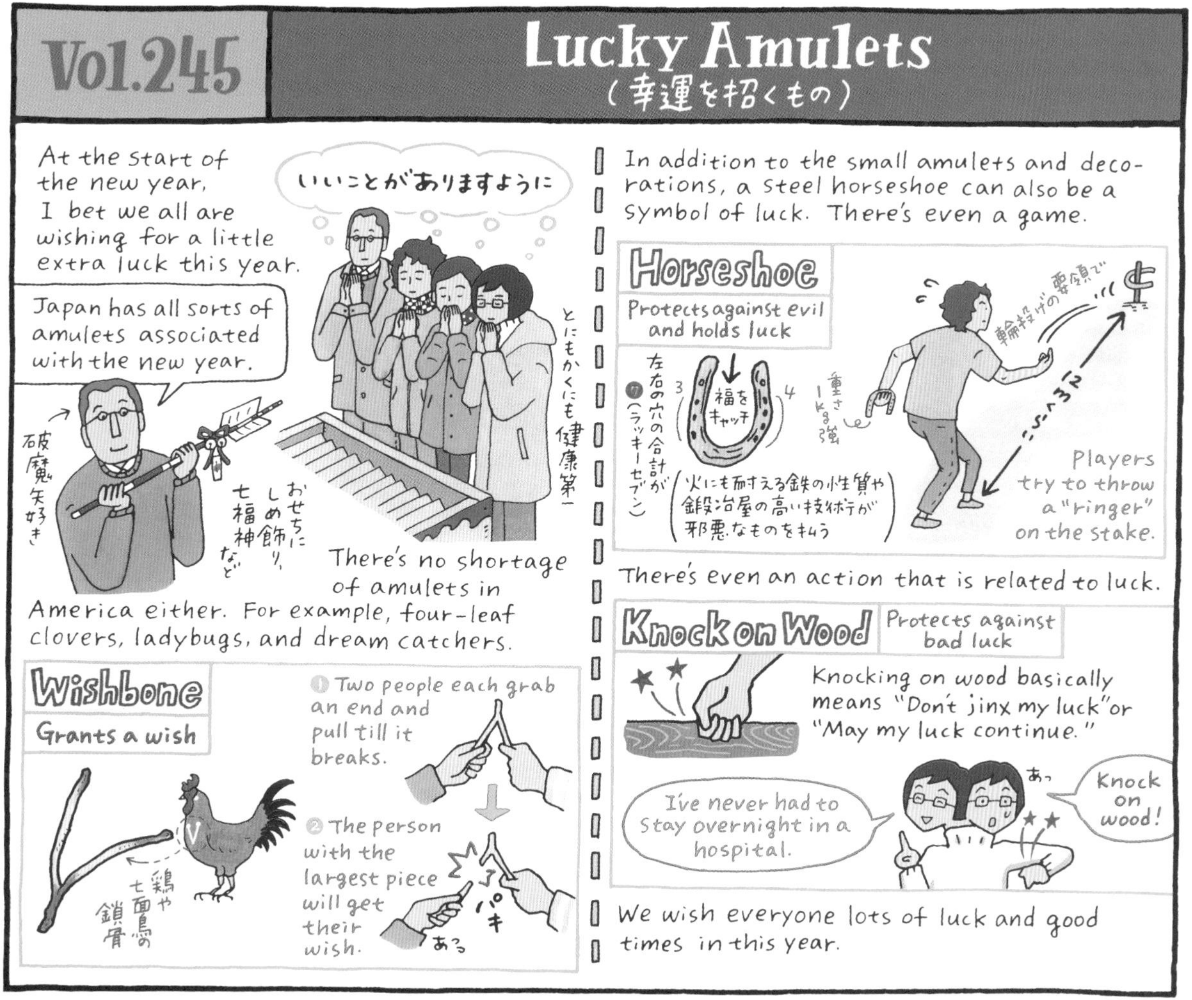

Vol.245
Lucky Amulets
(幸運を招くもの)
At the start of the new year, I bet we all are wishing for a little extra luck this year.
いいことがありますように
Japan has all sorts of amulets associated with the new year.
破魔矢好き
おせちにしめ飾り、七福神など
とにもかくにも健康第一
There's no shortage of amulets in America either. For example, four-leaf clovers, ladybugs, and dream catchers.
Wishbone
Grants a wish
鶏や七面鳥の鎖骨
① Two people each grab an end and pull till it breaks.
② The person with the largest piece will get their wish.
パキ
ある
In addition to the small amulets and decorations, a steel horseshoe can also be a symbol of luck. There's even a game.
Horseshoe
Protects against evil and holds luck
左右の穴の合計が7(ラッキーセブン)
3
4
福をキャッチ
重さ1kg強
火にも耐える鉄の性質や鍛冶屋の高い技術が邪悪なものを払う
輪投げの要領で
Players try to throw a "ringer" on the stake.
There's even an action that is related to luck.
Knock on Wood
Protects against bad luck
Knocking on wood basically means "Don't jinx my luck" or "May my luck continue."
I've never had to stay overnight in a hospital.
あっ
Knock on wood!
We wish everyone lots of luck and good times in this year.


幸運を願う気持ちはいずこも同じ。日本と同様、アメリカにもお守りやアイテムがいろいろあります。

**lucky amulet** 幸運のお守り

**associated with** ～にちなんだ，～と関連した

**shortage** 不足，欠乏

**ladybug** てんとう虫

**dream catcher** ドリームキャッチャー《北米の先住民族の伝統的なお守り》

**grant a wish** 望みをかなえる

**horseshoe** 馬蹄，蹄鉄

**stake** 〔地面に打ち込む〕杭，支柱

**jinx** つきを悪くする，不運をもたらす

**stay overnight in** ～に一晩泊まる

ミドリは、もうすぐ13歳。彼女はティーンエイジャーになる一歩手前です。最近、おしゃれに目覚めてきたようです。

- **on the brink of** ～の一歩手前で
- **in front of** ～の前に
- **fashionable clothes** 流行の衣服
- **hand-me-down from** ～のお下がり
- **self-image** 自己像，自分のイメージ
- **big issue** 大きな問題

Vol.246
The Birth of a Teenager
（ティーンの始まり）
Our little girl Midori is nearing her thirteenth birthday.
前髪作った
腰の位置が…
Hey, mom, I'm 3 centimeters taller than you!
She's on the brink of becoming a teenager.
お先に失礼しまーす
The teenage years start at age thirteen.
ちなみに「ハイティーン」は和製英語
10～12歳は違う
Ten
Eleven
Twelve
teenagerに含まれない
Thirteen
Fourteen
Fifteen
Nineteen
末尾にteenがある
She's been spending more time in front of the mirror lately.
小学生のとき
ただいまー
乱れ髪もへのかっぱ
最近
今日の前髪変～い
Of course, she's also becoming more interested in fashionable clothes. She loves to receive clothes that her older cousin in America has grown out of. She likes clothes handed down from Haru too.
GAP
Haru hand-me-downs
フィット感のあるものが多い
色柄は明るめ
Cousin hand-me-downs
However, she's also becoming interested in trying different styles.
I've been wanting this style.
今、流行りの
ふわっと感
ゆるっとしたオーバーサイズのセーター
ストレッチジーンズ（ここは従来通り）
Midori is entering a new stage of her life where self-expression and self-image will likely be big issues. We're looking forward to watching her grow.

# Vol.247 Teen Style
## （ティーンの服装）

Midori wears clothes bought in Japan and hand-me-downs from her American cousin. She prefers the American brands, and that got me wondering — How are they different? I compared the U.S. and Japan versions of Seventeen magazine.

日本版
Seventeen
1944年、アメリカで創刊。
1968年、日本版が発行された。
友達と〇〇〇へおでかけの日コーデとか
制服に似合うメイクとか
ゆるっとふわっと
Clothing, makeup, and hairstyle fashion tips for every occasion.
初デート
彼とビデオ通話
仲間とワイワイ
髪型いろいろ


The magazine layout has collages of photos and information that act like a how-to fashion guide. The models are mostly smiling and the clothing styles seem geared toward cute and charming.

アメリカ版
のサイトトップ
※1/14時点
seventeen
TRUMP 2020
2018年、紙媒体からオンラインに
(seventeen.com)


The U.S. online magazine has beauty tips and celebrity gossip, but also news and health articles, like about the pandemic and relationships. The styles are cool and even sexy, and the models have different ethnicities and physiques.

The styles are so free, like you just wear whatever you want.
色柄も明るめ多いし
へそ出し
スウェット
プラスサイズ
やっぱりへそ出し
足出し
ただし露出も多め
男子的に目のやり場に困らないのは日本の方かも～


日本で買った服やアメリカの従姉のお下がりを着ているミドリ。彼女はアメリカのブランドの方が好きですが——どう違うのでしょうか？

**teen style** 10代のスタイル
**prefer** ～を好む
**get A wondering** ～かもしれないとAが思うようになる
**fashion tip** ファッションに関するヒント
**layout** 割り付け，レイアウト
**collage** コラージュ
**gear toward** ～に合うようにする
**celebrity gossip** 有名人のうわさ話
**ethnicity** 民族性
**physique** 〔人の〕体格

生まれてくる赤ちゃんの名前を考えるのはとても楽しいことです。でも、スティーヴが挙げた名前の候補には驚かされました。

bicultural 二つの文化の
on the way 〔子どもなどが〕もうすぐ生まれる予定で
when it came to ～のこととなると
propose 〔～を〕提案する
How about ～ はどうですか？
joke 冗談を言う，からかう
as usual いつものように
half serious 半分本気で
have the good sense not to ～しない分別がある
get a chuckle くすくす笑う
close call 危機一髪

# Vol.248 Bicultural Naming Sense I
（名付けの感覚①：音の好み）

When a baby is on the way, one of the funnest parts of the process is thinking of names.
For our son, we wanted a name that would work in both Japan and the United States. When it came to proposing names, Steve and I started with very different ideas.
漢字 or Alphabet
「悠」の字とか使いたいなー
I like names with the letter Z in them.
字画はまあいいか。名字カタカナだし
Z?
Zoeとか Zachとかかな
How about Shozo(庄造)? Or Tarzan?
イメージ
Aaaaaaa
I thought he was joking (as usual), but he seemed to be half serious.
Then when our daughter was on the way...
Lots of girls have flower names...
How about Tulip? It's familiar but unique and has a good sound.
やっぱり大まじめ
漢字なら 富層とか？
ブッ
Well, we had the good sense not to keep those names, but we still get a chuckle when we talk about what might have been.
Whew, that was a close call.
正直今でも悪くないって思うけどなー

# Vol.249 Bicultural Naming Sense II
（名付けの感覚②：流行）

Every year, rankings of the most popular baby names are published for both Japan and the United States. A comparison of the two countries' top five names in 2020 reveals some interesting similarities.

| 生まれ年別の名前調査（明治安田生命） | | | Most popular baby names of 2020 (Baby Center) | |
|---|---|---|---|---|
| 男の子 | 女の子 | | GIRLS | BOYS |
| 蒼 | 陽葵 | 1 | Sophia | Liam |
| 樹・蓮 | 凜 | 2 | Olivia | Noah |
| | 詩 | 3 | Riley | Jackson |
| 陽翔 | 結菜 | 4 | Emma | Aiden |
| 律 | 結愛 | 5 | Ava | Elijah |

漢字一文字の名前が多いね
It looks like people prefer shorter names now.
国外でも通じやすい
Look at all the girls' names that end in "a." (日本も)
日本で「結」の字が多いのはコロナ禍で"結びつき"の大切さを実感した人が多かったかららしい
ぎゅ
結


One of the biggest differences between the countries is how long some names have remained at the top of the list.

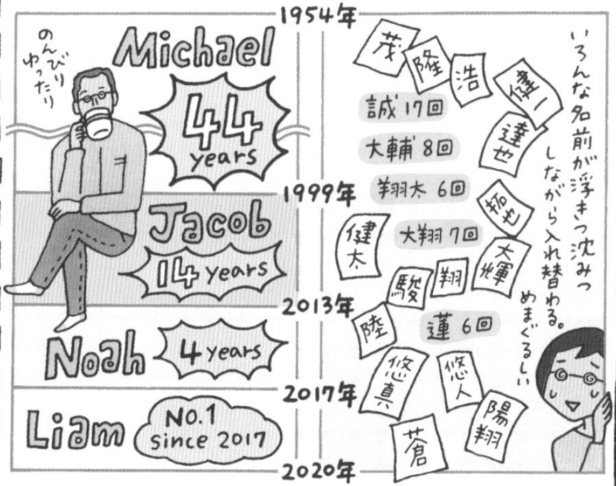

1954年
のんびりゆったり
Michael
44 years
1999年
Jacob
14 years
2013年
Noah
4 years
2017年
Liam
No.1 since 2017
2020年
茂
隆
浩
健一
達也
誠 17回
大輔 8回
翔太 6回
拓也
健太
大翔 7回
大輝
駿
翔
陸
蓮 6回
悠真
悠人
陽翔
蒼
いろんな名前が浮き沈みしながら入れ替わる。
めまぐるしい


It seems like names that were popular in the past can quickly come back into style. That might account for some names remaining on the American charts for years and even decades.

トメ（大正）
松江（昭和）
萌（平成）
「トメ」や「松江」にはならない令和っ子


毎年、日本とアメリカで赤ちゃんの名前の人気ランキングが発表されます。2020年のトップ5を比較すると、興味深い類似点がありました。

**publish** 〔正式に〕発表する
**comparison of** ～の比較
**reveal** 明らかにする
**similarity** 似ている点，類似点
**remain** とどまる，残る
**at the top of the list** リストの一番上に
**come back into style** 再流行する，また人気が出る
**account for** ～の主な要因となる

流行り廃りがあっても人気の名前が長く定着する傾向があるアメリカでは、同姓同名を防ぐのにミドルネームが役立ちます。

rise and fall in popularity　人気の浮き沈みがある

stick around　固執する

due to　～のために

instance　例，場合

multiple people　複数の人

come in useful　役立つようになる

gravity　重大さ，重要性

Vol.250
Bicultural Naming Sense Ⅲ
（名付けの感覚③：ミドルネーム）
A name may rise and fall in popularity, but they tend to stick around for a long time in the United States. Due to its large population, however, there are many instances of multiple people having the same first and last name.
In those cases, the middle name comes in useful.
Family Name
Surname
とも言う
First Name
Liam
Most popular boys' name in 2020
+
Middle Name
James
John
Robert
Michael
William
David
+
Last Name
Smith
Most common last name in the U.S.
The possibilities are endless.
音は同じでも、漢字表記などで区別化できるのが日本名
田中
など 紘子 宏子 寛子 裕子 浩子 広子 博子 弘子
Parents tend to choose a name they like for the first name, and select the name of a family member or relative for the middle name.
It shows respect and heritage.
有名人の名前、聖書や神話の登場人物の名前も結構あるけど
スティーヴの弟
姪
David (Uncle's name)
Julio (Grandfather's name)
Rose (Great-grand-mother's name)
It's a lot like using a character from a parent's name.
命名
記久恵
私の名前は祖父「久雄」から一文字もらった
However, people rarely use their full names other than for official reasons, such as on passports.
When someone does hear their full name, it usually carries a sense of gravity.
Stephen David Ballati, get over here right now...
イヤな予感しかしないんですけど

MOCO
GEN
STEVE
来日36年目の
江戸好きアメリカ人
KIKUE
ワタクシ
HARU
息子。
高校2年生
MIDORI
娘。
中学2年生

# 11th Year

2021

日本では結婚すると夫婦同姓にするよう定められていますが、国際結婚の場合は原則、別姓となっています。

---

**separate surnames** 別姓

**patriarchal system** 家父長制

**give a second thought to** ～について注意深く考える

**official family registry** 戸籍

**body** 主部，本文

**heading** 表題，見出し

**maiden name** 〔既婚女性の〕旧姓

**line through** ～に引いてある直線

**peculiar** 奇妙な，変な

**whatsoever** 何があっても，全く

**cultural norm** 文化規範

Vol.251
Separate Surnames
(夫婦別姓)
Japan has a patriarchal system where a woman usually adopts the husband's surname. Among international couples, however, it's not uncommon to use separate surnames.
When we married, I didn't give a second thought to adopting Steve's family name. But something strange happened to our official family registry.
ペンネームが旧姓だし～
「氏の変更届」を追加で提出する必要あり
Steve is only recognized in the body of the registry, not in the heading.
戸籍筆頭は日本人の私
本籍
東京都
〇年〇月〇日アメリカ合衆国 バラティ スティーヴと婚姻届出
氏名
バラティ 田村 記久恵
妻
記久恵
Our new family name is there, but my maiden name is too, with a line through it.
バラティ 田村
なんか感じ悪い
Some people argue that having the same name is important to create family bonds, even if it's just in the registry. Well, I'd like to show them how peculiar our registry looks.
An international couple we know has been using different names for more than 20 years.
Have we had any problems because of our different names?
Nope, none whatsoever!
きっぱり
ダンナさんはニュージーランド人
子どもたちの名前はお父さんの姓をミドルネームに
It's only complicated when trying to follow the cultural norm. I wonder, though, how difficult is it to just let couples decide for themselves which name they want to use?
What if you could have as many names as you want?
ブラジルみたいに
Or let people be free to choose any name they want for their family.
野村と田中が結婚して五十嵐にしたい，とか
わりとレアだし♪
結婚しても「バラティ」はキープしたいなー
田村家之墓
Even if the names are different, family is always family.

Vol.252
Breadwinners
(食パンの魅力)
The most common type of bread in Japan is white bread. People love the soft texture. Steve, however, is less than satisfied with that.
もっちり
ふわふわ
トーストしてカリッとしてても
Where are the nutrients?
白すぎるし、甘すぎる!
It has no density!
本格ベーカリーのパンでも、まだ物足りない
Wide Variety of Breads in U.S. Supermarkets
There're all sorts of brown breads, like whole grain, wheat, and rye.
100% WHOLE WHEAT
壮観!
日本のものに比べるとかなりドライ
Great mouth feel, distinct flavors!
They're both yummy in their own way♪
If Japanese bread is white rice...
...then American bread is like brown rice.
The end slices are also flavorful!
The standard school lunch in America is a sandwich with fruit and a snack, like potato chips. American kids love PB&J sandwiches. (And because they're easy to make, so do their parents.)
PB&J Peanut Butter and Jelly Sandwich
まさかの掛け合わせ
砂糖や甘味料が入ってないもの
(※ピーナッツクリームではない)
PEANUT BUTTER
ジャム(定番はいちご)
いちご
Put them together.
Spread on each slice of bread.
Give it a try!

日本の食パンの多くは、その柔らかさともちもち感を売りにしていますが、スティーヴには納得がいかないようです。

white bread 精白パン

less than satisfied with ～に満足[納得]していない

nutrient 栄養素

density 密度，濃さ

brown bread 黒パン

whole grain 全粒の，未精白の

wheat 小麦

rye ライ麦

mouth feel 口当たり

distinct flavor はっきりとした[独特の]風味

in one's own way それなりに，～らしさがあって

flavorful 風味豊かな

日本で物件を探すときは南向きであることが重要視されますが、カリフォルニアでは窓からの眺めが大切なポイントです。

**place in the sun** 太陽の当たる場所

**southern exposure** 南向きであること

**essential** 絶対必要な，不可欠な

**mold** カビ，菌

**hang out laundry** 洗濯物を干す

**direct sunlight** 直射日光

**damage** 損傷を与える

**frosted** 〔窓ガラスなどが〕艶消しの

Vol.253
A Place in the Sun
(住まい選びの基準)
When selecting a place to live in Japan, many people think a southern exposure is not only best, but essential.
南
夏
冬
Protects against mold.
Place to hang out laundry to dry.
Checklist Point #1
Lots of Sunlight
In Steve's home State of California, however, too much sun can be a problem. Many people try to avoid houses with too much southern exposure.
Too much direct sunlight can damage furniture and floors.
So what do people in California look for when choosing a place to live?
North-facing living room (義母の家)
シェード カーテン や ブラインド
Checklist Point #1
The View
Curtains are almost always open (if there are curtains at all).
Our home here in Japan faces south. Although the windows on the north side are frosted, we have windows on all sides. Very few have curtains.
Like our family, our home is a mix of east and west.
障子はあるけど開けてるよ
眺めっていっても ウチの場合，庭木や隣の畑くらいだけどね

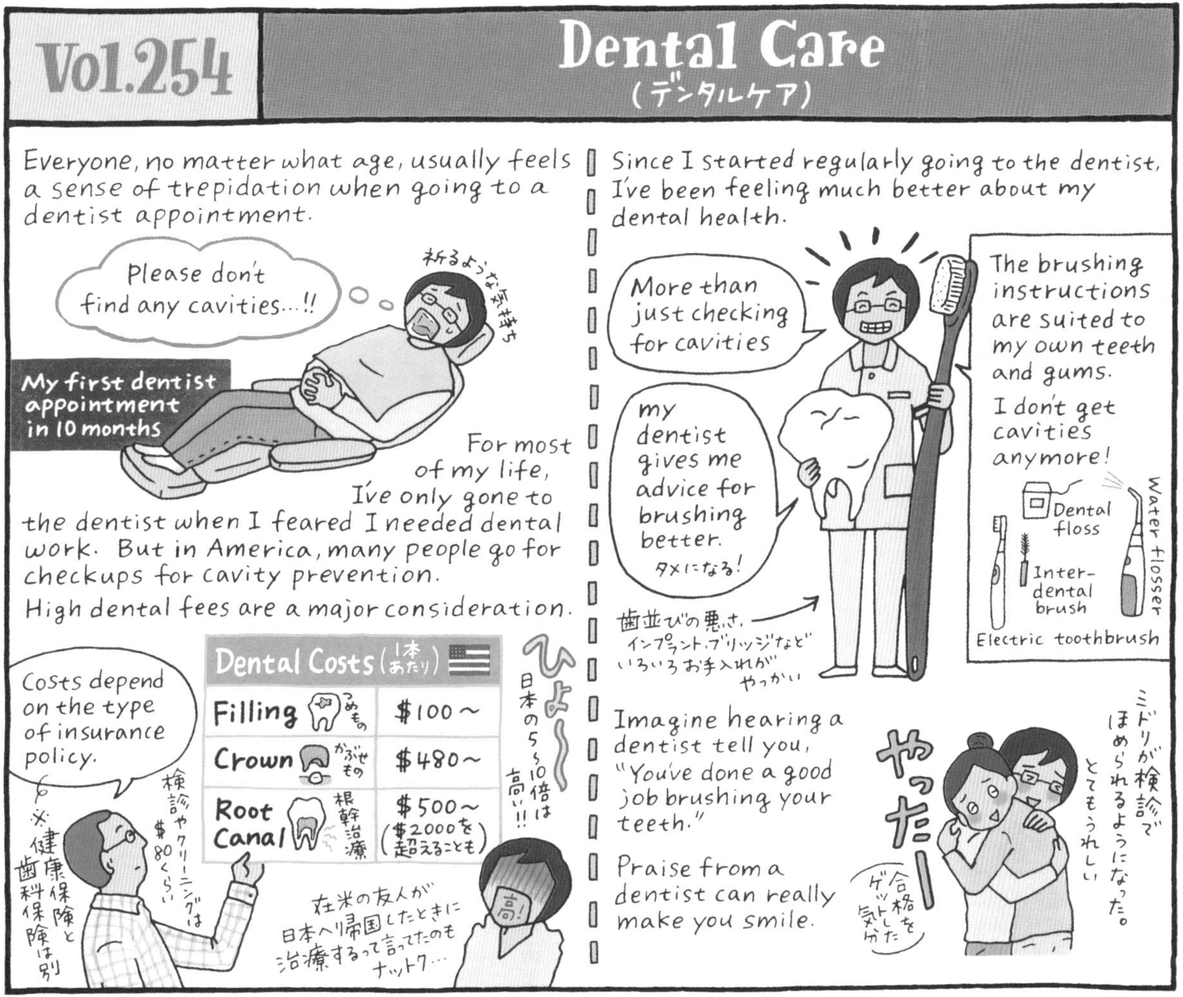
Vol.254
Dental Care
(デンタルケア)
Everyone, no matter what age, usually feels a sense of trepidation when going to a dentist appointment.
Please don't find any cavities...!!
祈るような気持ち
My first dentist appointment in 10 months
For most of my life, I've only gone to the dentist when I feared I needed dental work. But in America, many people go for checkups for cavity prevention.
High dental fees are a major consideration.
Dental Costs (1本あたり)
Filling つめもの $100〜
Crown かぶせもの $480〜
Root Canal 根幹治療 $500〜 ($2000を超えることも)
ひょ〜
日本の5〜10倍は高い!!
Costs depend on the type of insurance policy.
※健康保険と歯科保険は別
検診やクリーニングは$80くらい
高!
在米の友人が日本へ帰国したときに治療するって言ってたのもナットク…
Since I started regularly going to the dentist, I've been feeling much better about my dental health.
More than just checking for cavities
my dentist gives me advice for brushing better.
タメになる!
歯並びの悪さ、インプラント、ブリッジなどいろいろお手入れがやっかい
The brushing instructions are suited to my own teeth and gums.
I don't get cavities anymore!
Dental floss
Water flosser
Inter-dental brush
Electric toothbrush
Imagine hearing a dentist tell you, "You've done a good job brushing your teeth."
Praise from a dentist can really make you smile.
やったー
合格をゲットした気分
ミドリが検診でほめられるようになった。
とてもうれしい

歯医者に行くときは、年齢に関係なく誰でも不安な気持ちになります。私はずっと歯の治療が必要そうなときだけ行っていましたが――

**trepidation** 恐怖, 不安

**dentist appointment** 歯医者の予約

**go for a checkup** 健診を受ける

**cavity prevention** 虫歯予防

**major consideration** 大きな要因

**regularly** 定期的に

**suited to** 〜に向いている

**gum** 歯ぐき, 歯肉

我が家の猫、モコとゲンは家の外に興味津々です。油断すると玄関から脱出しそうになるのでヒヤヒヤします。

**microchip** マイクロチップ（を埋め込む）

**Fido** ファイドー《任意の飼い犬を指す愛称》

**fluffy** フワフワした

**become curious about** ～に好奇心がわく

**slip out** そっと抜け出す

**collar** 〔ペットなどの〕首輪

**mandate** 命じる，命令する

**implant** しっかり埋め込む

**subcutaneous** 皮下の

**stray** 道に迷った，はぐれた

**squeamish** 神経質な

**reunite with** ～に再会する

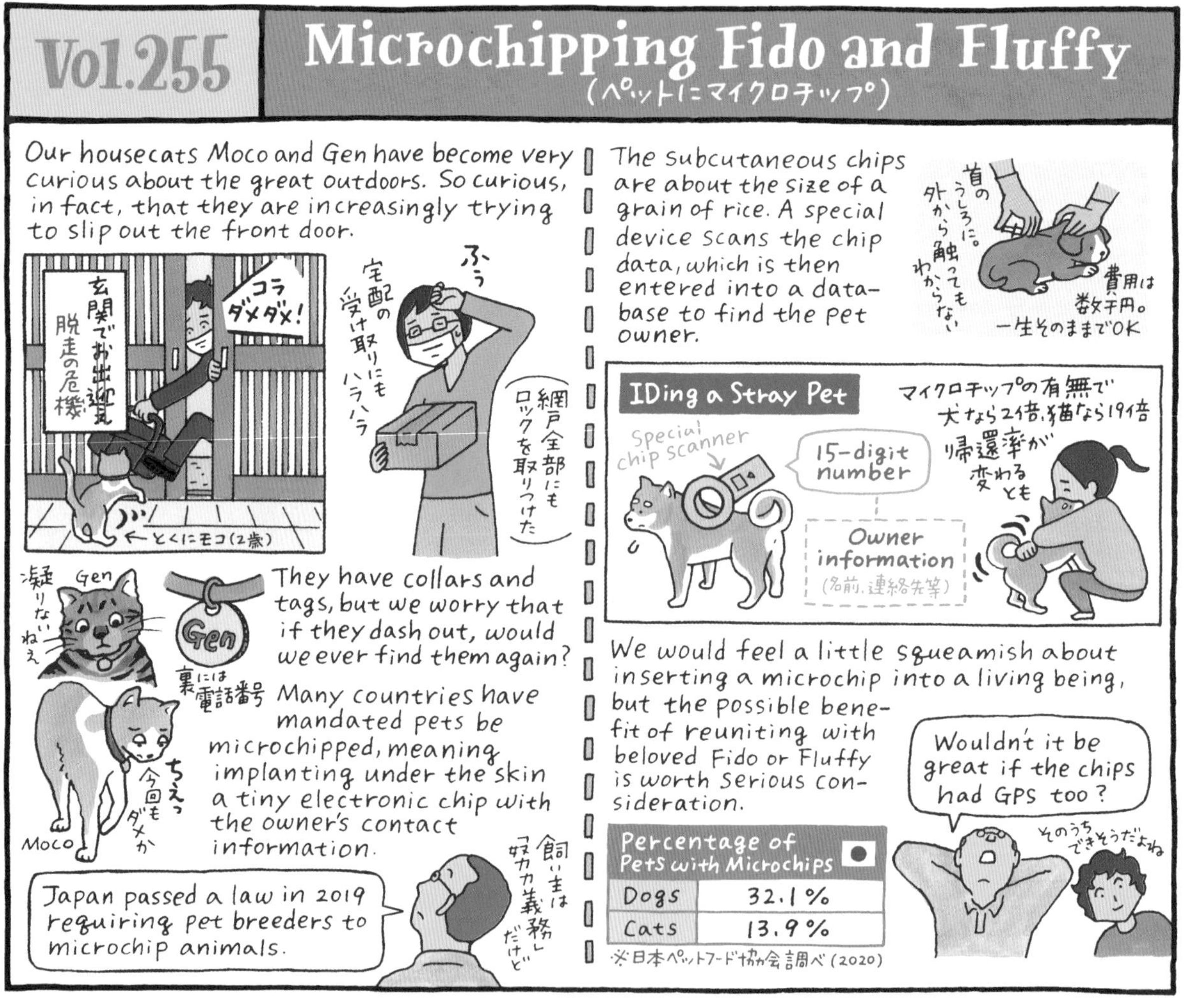

Vol.255
Microchipping Fido and Fluffy
（ペットにマイクロチップ）
Our housecats Moco and Gen have become very curious about the great outdoors. So curious, in fact, that they are increasingly trying to slip out the front door.
玄関でお出迎え
脱走の危機
コラ ダメダメ！
とくにモコ（2歳）
ふう
宅配の受け取りにもハラハラ
網戸全部にもロックを取りつけた
They have collars and tags, but we worry that if they dash out, would we ever find them again?
Gen
凝りないねえ
Gen
裏には電話番号
Moco
ちえっ 今回もダメか
Many countries have mandated pets be microchipped, meaning implanting under the skin a tiny electronic chip with the owner's contact information.
Japan passed a law in 2019 requiring pet breeders to microchip animals.
飼い主は「努力義務」だけど
The subcutaneous chips are about the size of a grain of rice. A special device scans the chip data, which is then entered into a database to find the pet owner.
首のうしろに。
外から触ってもわからない
費用は数千円。
一生そのままでOK
IDing a Stray Pet
Special chip scanner
15-digit number
Owner information
（名前，連絡先等）
マイクロチップの有無で犬なら2倍，猫なら19倍帰還率が変わるとも
We would feel a little squeamish about inserting a microchip into a living being, but the possible benefit of reuniting with beloved Fido or Fluffy is worth serious consideration.
Percentage of Pets with Microchips
Dogs 32.1%
Cats 13.9%
※日本ペットフード協会調べ（2020）
Wouldn't it be great if the chips had GPS too?
そのうちできそうだよね

Vol.256
Vaccination Expectation
（ワクチン接種への期待）
I recently booked a reservation to receive COVID-19 vaccination shots. It wasn't for me; it was for my parents.
当日
手分けして二重態勢に
Internet Team
父を担当
15分前からスタンバイ
母を担当
弟
やっぱりつながらない
Flip-phone Team
…あ! 取れた!
数時間かかるかと思ってたのに
開始2分で完了
こっちも取れたよ
ネットであっさり取れて拍子抜け
（※自治体によるらしい）
Right now, those of us in our 40s and 50s in Japan are still waiting for our turns to come.
Meanwhile, the vaccinations are moving quickly in the United States.
Friends our age were vaccinated in early May, and teenagers were eligible to get shots a few weeks later.
Anyone aged 12 or older can receive a vaccination.
In the U.S., vaccination centers have been set up in hospitals, drugstores, baseball stadiums, and even large parking facilities. Vaccine recipients often receive gifts for coming in.
NY
Stickers
Cloth mask
Vaccination card holders
VACCINATE NEW YORK
I got vaccinated!
CA
Surgical MASK
HAND SANITIZER
Oxy Watch
UNO
なぜかUNOも
同じ州でも会場によって異なるそう
Baseball Ticket
Some places are even giving out food and sports tickets.
Our family usually doesn't get the annual flu shots. But, although we have some reservations about the COVID vaccines, we plan to get the shots when our turn comes around.
ボクの分はまだちょっと悩み中
様子を見つつ考えます
I hope I can see my cousins soon…!!
もう2年も会えてない😢
アジアンヘイトも収まってほしいよ〜

先日、両親の新型コロナワクチンの接種予約を手伝いました。自分の分は一体いつになるのかわかりません。

**expectation** 予想，期待，待望

**book a reservation** 予約を取る

**flip phone** 折りたたみ式携帯電話

**meanwhile** その一方で

**eligible to** ～する資格がある

**parking facility** 駐車施設

**recipient** 〔ワクチンの〕接種者

**flu shot** インフルエンザの予防接種

**come around** 巡ってくる

私の両親はすでにお墓を用意しています。厚意から「スティーヴもそこに入ればいい」と言ってくれているのですが——

memorialize 〔～を〕記念する
cemetery （共同）墓地
plot 区画
ancestral 先祖から伝わる
tomb 墓所，墓標
grave 墓，墓所
scatter one's ashes 遺灰をまく，散骨する
meaningful 意味を持つ
columbarium 納骨堂
have second thoughts 考え直す
end the practice 慣行をやめる
make someone wonder （人）の疑問を誘う

Vol.257
Memorializing Loved Ones I
（故人を偲ぶ方法①）
About 10 years ago, my parents bought a cemetery plot for themselves.
墓石はまだない
We would like you to come visit us when we're gone.
終活の一環として用意したの
えっ
Steve, you can rest in it too.
あ…ありがとうございます
In Japan, which maintains ancestral tombs for generations, being invited to share one means you've become part of the family. But, in California where Steve is from, single-person graves and scattering ashes are common.
My grandparents' ashes were scattered in places that were meaningful to them.
生前好きだった山に
実家の庭の木の根元に…
目印の石
ぶごごく
Steve may have felt a little uncomfortable about being put in a grave with someone else.
I think I'd like my ashes to be scattered somewhere.
お義父さんたちの気持ちはありがたいし大切にしたいけど
祖国に骨を…とかはないらしい
Me too.
Plus, we have no idea where the kids will end up living.
※散骨に関しては自治体等にご確認ください
Attitudes in Japan are changing. More people are choosing apartment-like columbariums and some would rather end the practice altogether. Even my parents seem to be having second thoughts.
It makes me wonder, what's the purpose of leaving behind tombs?
おまけ
本家のお墓に行く楽しみ
田村家代々之墓
記久恵の久！
久右衛門だって
先祖代々の石碑
嘉永?!

Vol.258
Memorializing Loved Ones II
(故人を偲ぶ方法②)
When my mother-in-law passed away a few years ago, we respected her wish and placed her ashes in a gravesite. My father-in-law pays daily visits.
Expansive park-like cemetery with lots of greenery
Various types of tombstones
愛犬と一緒に。車で10分
Parking is available conveniently close to the gravesite
In Japan, people commonly attend memorial ceremonies at Buddhist temples for many anniversaries after someone's passing. Our family in America doesn't have such a custom.
盆暮れ、お彼岸のお墓参り
数年ごとの法要
一昨年、祖父母の33回忌に参加
In Christianity, which is the prevalent religion in the United States, there are no further ceremonies after the funeral. People visit gravesites privately. Christians in American culture believe the spirit goes to heaven after death, and the person's memory lives on in people's hearts.
義母のお墓にも同様の言葉が刻まれている
SMITH
(義父もここに入る予定)
When you think of me, I'll be there in your heart.
Because of the pandemic and living in a different country, we haven't had a chance to visit my mother-in-law's gravesite for quite a while. So that way of thinking gives us some comfort.
行事など家族の折り目には必ず
形見の指輪を身につける
The memories you carry in your heart are the most precious.
「星の王子さま」にあるみたいに星を見て思いをはせるっていうのもいいよね
樹林葬か宇宙葬希望

数年前に義母が亡くなったとき、彼女の意思を尊重して、遺灰を墓地に納めました。義父は毎日お墓参りをしています。

gravesite　墓地

pay a visit　訪問する

Christianity　キリスト教

expansive　広大な，開放的な

prevalent　広く行き渡っている

further　さらなる，追加的な

for quite a while　かなり長い間

give someone comfort　（人）に慰めを与える

夏休みが３か月近くにもなるアメリカでは、子どもたちが参加するためのサマーキャンプや教育プログラムが大人気です。

**on top of that**　それに加えて

**as rare as**　～と同じくらい珍しい

**supervised by**　～に見守られる

**STEM**　科学・技術・工学・数学，理系科目《Science, Technology, Engineering, and Mathematicsの頭文字》

**in advance**　先立って，前に

**sleepaway**　寝泊まり

**enroll in a program**　プログラムに登録する

# Vol.259 Summer Vacation for the Parents and Kids（親と子の夏休み）

Students in Japan and America are enjoying the best part of the school year — summer vacation.

American schoolkids look forward to nearly three months off from school during the hot summer. On top of that, school homework is as rare as summer snow.

新学年にあがる前だしね
あっても読書くらい
こちとらプリントやドリルの山に自由研究とか
Nearly 3 months (June to August)
Summer Vacation
About a month and a half (July to August)


Many kids look forward to attending a summer camp for part of the summer. And since elementary school-aged kids are required to be supervised by an adult, many working parents are eager to send them.

Sports
Arts&Crafts
Performing Arts
STEM
Outdoor など
（online ものも増加中）


Some summer camps and educational programs are extremely popular. Reservations can fill up six months in advance.

たとえば
There're all sorts of programs, and price tags too.
Day only （1日数時間×5日間）
$100~500 (Price for 5 days)
Sleepaway （1～3週間）
$1500 (per week)
自治体や教会主催だと安め
JAN
Summer Camp


Yes, it can be expensive.

But parents see summer as a chance for their kids to have unique experiences.

Haru is also trying something new this summer. He's enrolled in an online program for high schoolers offered by a college in the United States.

時差のため夜中の受講
コロナ禍で旅行も部活もムリそうだしね…
College-run online program
いたしかたなし！

# Vol.260 A Life of Lessons
## (習いごと)

Like Haru and Midori, their American cousins participate in extracurricular activities. One big difference, though, is the number and variety of lessons they've taken.

1 or 2 for longer than one year
バレエのみ8年
十部活でバドミントン5年
サッカーは2年、野球は4年
Ballet
Baseball
Soccer
Karate
Trombone
Soccer
Baseball
Drums
Lacrosse
Soccer
Baseball
Guitar
Rhythmic Gymnastics
Indian Dance
Contemporary Dance
Painting


The idea is that lessons provide experience and trying different things can help a person find what they are good at and enjoy doing. The places offering the lessons also make it easy to join in.

Zero enrollment fee
You'll never know unless you try
Short-term commitment
Affordable
Designed to be fun
(指導はゆるめ)
低年齢のうちはとくに


In Japan, once you sign up, you are basically committing to continuing. Lesson plans in the U.S. are often shorter. This has two advantages — little pressure to continue, and a sense of accomplishment from finishing a segment.

Finish!
1クールごとに
↑10回とか数か月とか
More!
No more!
I'm signing up again!
What shall I do next?


"I want to get better!" Kids with desire and motivation can move up to the next level. At the higher, more serious levels, many are looking ahead to college.

姪も選抜チームに。遠征多数で本格的
(費用もUP!)
Scholarship
College
Favorable evaluation for college entrance


Midori has been doing ballet for many years now for no higher reason than she enjoys dancing. In its own way, that's enriching too.

「好き」だけで続けて8年目


ハルとミドリのように、アメリカのいとこたちも課外活動に参加しています。しかし、ひとつ大きく違うのは、習い事の数と種類の豊富さです。

- **trombone** トロンボーン
- **lacrosse** ラクロス《ホッケーに似た球技》
- **rhythmic gymnastics** 新体操
- **enrollment fee** 入学［入会］金
- **affordable** お手頃な価格の
- **short-term commitment** 短期間の参加
- **sense of accomplishment** 達成感
- **segment** 一区切り
- **look ahead to** 〔将来のことを〕見据える
- **enrich** 高める

かつてないほど多くの自転車が走っているのを目にします。コロナ禍で、世界的な自転車ブームが巻き起こっているのです。

than ever　かつてないほど（に）
absolutely right　100％正しい
trigger　引き起こす，もたらす
companion　〔付き添う〕仲間，友
meet up for　～に集まる
check out　～をよく調べる
athlete　運動選手，スポーツ愛好家

# Vol.261 Global Cycling Boom
（サイクリングブーム）

If you think there are more bicycles than ever out on the road these days, you're absolutely right. The COVID-19 pandemic has triggered a worldwide cycling boom.
Steve's been doing solo bike rides since his twenties, but he's recently found some cycling companions.
タイヤが細くてスピードが出るロードバイク
A good 2-hour ride in the cool of the morning feels great.
減量もできてスッキリ♪
One morning last year, he met an American guy who lives nearby and is also a cyclist. Now, he and a group of guys meet up for long rides on the weekends.
アメリカ人やアイルランド人など4人
うれしい発見！
近所にまさかこんなにいたとは
Steve's brother in California has also started cycling. They use Strava to check out and comment on each other's rides.
Strava is a free website and app that records activities and provides performance data. It's a sort of social network for cyclists, runners, swimmers, hikers — athletes of all kinds.
STRAVA
★ GPS tracking and data (Route, time, speed, etc.)
★ Follow other athletes
へ〜 こんないいルートが！
おっ。この人のタイムに挑戦してみようかな。フフフ…
オリンピックコースの一部を試走した二人
その後のTV観戦も楽しそうでした
In spring, Steve and Haru started going out for weekend rides together. Steve really enjoys the father-son time.

Vol.262
The Joy of Reading
（異なる言語で読書をすること）
As bookworms, both Steve and I spend a lot of time reading. We both read at night before going to sleep. However, the books we like to read are quite different.
Relaxing Time
Japanese
文芸書がほとんど
English
Literature, Essays, Historical Fiction, etc.
The books are also in different languages, which makes it tough for us to talk about what we're reading.
Books we read in other languages are usually for special study rather than enjoyment
えーっとこの単語の意味は…
余白にあれこれ書き込みながら
趣味の日本民俗学の研究書
Our kids read in both languages. So we get lots of chances to talk about books with them.
READY PLAYER ONE
by Ernest Cline
ファンタジー好き
This was a real page turner!
実際、授業中にも読んじゃったし
忘れられない1冊！
衝撃の構成!!
こころ
夏目漱石
THE HOBBIT
J.R.R. TOLKIEN
It's a fantasy, but it seems so real.
泣ける話が大好物→
（※漢字がない分、洋書の方が読みやすいらしい）
They're so lucky! Their language skills give them access to a whole other world of books…!
単純にうらやましい
We all have growing stacks of books we want to read by our beds. The Japanese word for this phenomenon is becoming known in English.
家族からのオススメ洋書
Wonder
Matilda
The Book Thief
1945
Tsundoku（積ん読）
Acquiring reading materials that pile up without being read yet.


スティーヴも私も本好きで、就寝前の読書が欠かせません。最近、子どもたちと本の情報を共有できるようになりました。

**bookworm** 大の本好き，本の虫

**special study** 特別な学習

**give someone access to** ～を利用する手だてを（人）に与える

**stack of books** 本の山

**phenomenon** 事実，現象

**acquire** 入手する，購入する

**reading material** 読み物，読書の素材

**pile up** 積み重なる，たまる

最近、世界のゴミ焼却炉の半分以上が日本にある、という驚くべき事実を知りました。そして、やはりゴミの焼却量も日本が一番多いのです。

organic waste
　食品廃棄物

garbage incinerator
　ゴミ焼却炉

content　含有量

high temperature
　高温の

garbage disposal
　生ゴミ処理機

food scraps　生ゴミ

municipality　地方自治体

sewage system
　下水設備

efficient　効率的な

burden　負担，重荷

give ~ another try
　～をやり直す

compost〔～を〕堆肥にする

Vol.263
Organic Waste
（生ゴミとのつき合い方）
I recently learned a surprising fact: More than half of all of the garbage incinerators in the world are in Japan. As you would expect, Japan also burns the most waste too.
焼却量は約3300万トンにも
およそ1000基
（他国は、多いところでも100基台）
国土が狭く、人口が多い日本で焼却に頼らざるを得ないのは理解できる話ではあるよね…
About 40% of the garbage in Japan is organic waste, which has a lot of moisture in it. Burning garbage with high water content requires high-temperature incinerators.
生ゴミの80%が水分
But why does Japan have more waste incinerators than even the U.S.? The reason is that most kitchen sinks in the U.S. have a garbage disposal to process food scraps.
Garbage Disposal
ガガガガ
水を流しながらON
ON
Food Waste
この中で砕く
臭わない。害虫の発生を防ぐ
Some municipalities even require homes to have garbage disposals.
排水処理槽を経由して下水へ
The disposals send waste through the sewage system to wastewater treatment facilities. Maybe that's more efficient than burning it, but it seems like it just shifts the burden. The ideal solution would be to reuse organic waste.
With that in mind, we've started giving composting another try.
分解しやすいように細かく刻んでから入れたりしてると
ごはんの取り分けをして育てている気分に♪
Composting to make rich soil

# Vol.264 Japanese Pitfalls
## （日本語の落とし穴）

Steve is an old Japan hand and makes his livelihood as a professional translator, but he still gets tripped up sometimes by loanwords and onomatopoeia in Japanese.

### Pitfall #1 Loanwords

The Japanese syllabary has a tough time matching some sounds.
こっちの方が元の発音に近いと思うんだけど
Train→トレイン
Almond→アルモンド
Bazaar→バザール
English clearly pronounces the n, r and l sounds.
人名もかなり厄介


### Pitfall #2 Onomatopoeia

※日本語はとてもオノマトペが多い

いやー暑かった!
止まった途端汗がブシュワッブシュワッって噴き出したよ
He's coining his own word again...
感じはとても出てるけど


There are no set grammar rules or ways to create onomatopoeia. Explanations often end up being very fuzzy or with the inscrutable reason that "it feels like what it means."

そういうときはドッと、とかブワッと、とかかなー
え、じゃあボッと、とかジュッとなら?
うーん…


Steve has translated the whole gamut of materials, from business reports to signboards, but one of his toughest jobs was when he tried his hand at a manga.

シーーン…
キュイーン
バキッ
ゴゴゴゴゴ
Hush… (Silence…と訳されることも)
Zoom?
Zing?
Screech
???
CRACK
RUMBLE
ウーン
Oof


Japanese is said to be one of the most difficult languages to learn. Certainly, kanji is challenging, but those simple-looking words written in katakana might be even harder.

翻訳者として日本語に相当慣れ親しんでいるスティーヴですが、外来語やオノマトペにつまずくことがまだまだあります。

- **pitfall** 隠れた危険，落とし穴
- **Japan hand** 日本通
- **make one's livelihood as** 〜で生計を立てる
- **get tripped up by** 〜に惑わされる
- **loanword** 外来語，借用語
- **onomatopoeia** オノマトペ，擬音語
- **syllabary** 音節
- **coin** 〔新しい言葉を〕作る
- **set rule** 既定のルール
- **fuzzy** 不明瞭な
- **inscrutable** 不可解な，謎めいた
- **whole gamut of** ありとあらゆる〜

長年、我が家の年中行事として楽しんできたハロウィンは、もともとアイルランドで始まったものです。

**Celtic** ケルト文化の

**have fun with** ～と楽しい時間を過ごす

**turnip** カブ

**folklore** 民間伝承，言い伝え

**boundary** 境界（線）

**blur** ぼやけ，不鮮明

**earthly** 地上の，この世の

**Samhain** サウィン《ケルト暦で1年の始まり，夏の収穫を祝う行事》

**ward off** 避ける，追い払う

**poverty** 貧困，不毛

Vol.265
Celtic Halloween
（アイルランド式ハロウィン）
Our annual Halloween parties since the kids were small have become a family tradition. We couldn't gather with friends last year, so we had fun with just the four of us.
（家の中の飾りつけもした）
Wig
HAPPY Halloween!
写真をいつものみんなに送信！
What are we going to do this year?
家族の中でいちばん楽しみにしている人
Maybe we can find some ideas if we look at how they do it in Ireland, where Halloween began.
How about Jack-O'-lanterns made from turnips?
カボチャより細工がしやすそう
In Celtic folklore, the boundaries blur between the earthly and spiritual worlds after the harvest, and the spirits of the dead desire to return to their homes. These spirits don't belong in our world, and some are evil.
Samhain
ちょっとお盆っぽいよね
↑母方がアイルランド系
A special dish for ghostly visitors
Scary costumes ward off evil spirits
Colcannon
Mashed potatoes and cabbage.
Barmbrack
Bread with dried fruits.
Symbolic items are baked in.
油紙に包んで
Ring → marriage
Coin → wealth
Cloth → poverty
など
誤飲注意

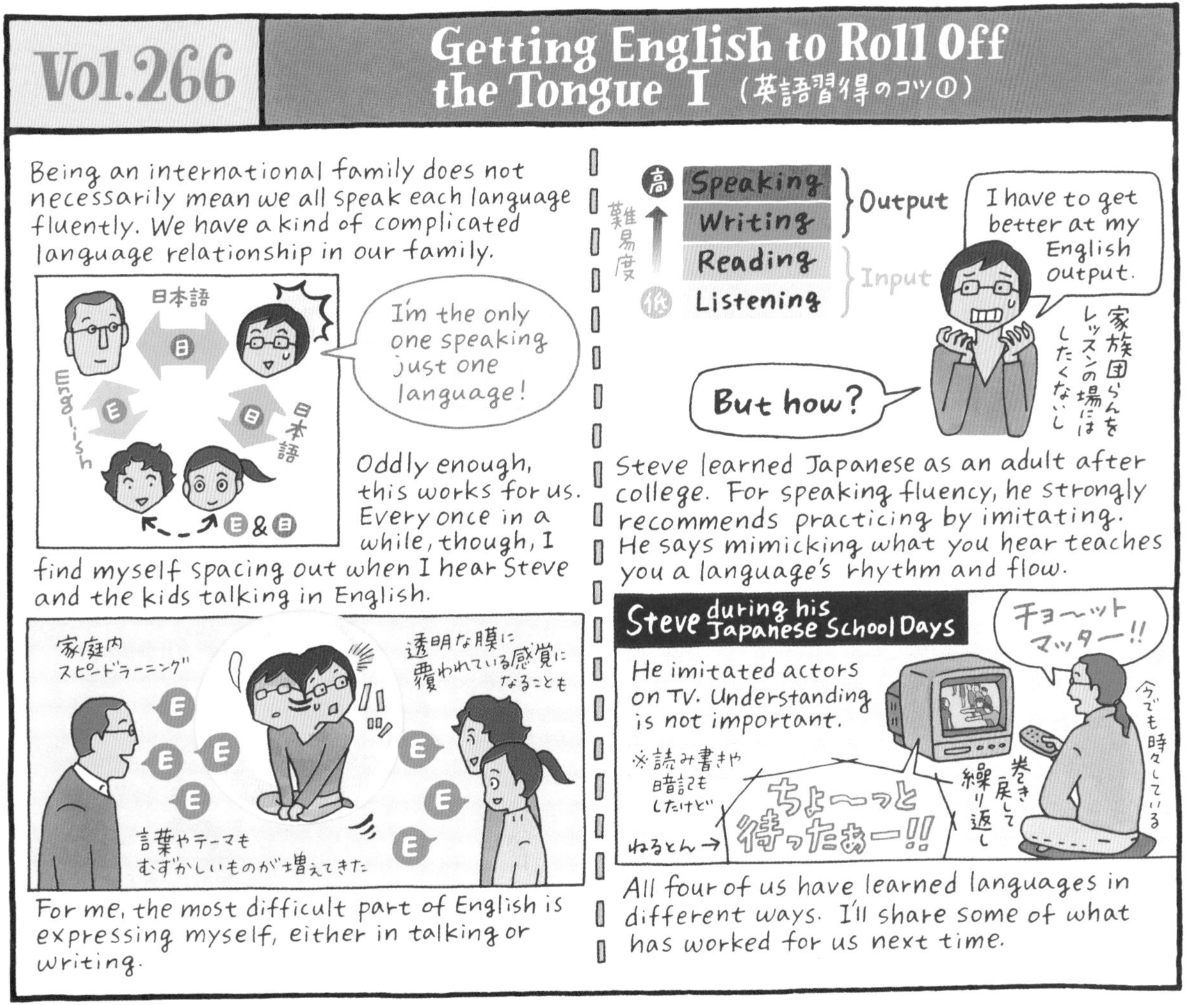

Vol.266
Getting English to Roll Off the Tongue I (英語習得のコツ①)
Being an international family does not necessarily mean we all speak each language fluently. We have a kind of complicated language relationship in our family.
日本語
日
English
E
日
日本語
E & 日
I'm the only one speaking just one language!
Oddly enough, this works for us. Every once in a while, though, I find myself spacing out when I hear Steve and the kids talking in English.
家庭内スピードラーニング
透明な膜に覆われている感覚になることも
言葉やテーマもむずかしいものが増えてきた
For me, the most difficult part of English is expressing myself, either in talking or writing.
高
難易度
低
Speaking
Writing
Reading
Listening
Output
Input
I have to get better at my English output.
家族団らんをレッスンの場にはしたくないし
But how?
Steve learned Japanese as an adult after college. For speaking fluency, he strongly recommends practicing by imitating. He says mimicking what you hear teaches you a language's rhythm and flow.
Steve during his Japanese School Days
He imitated actors on TV. Understanding is not important.
※読み書きや暗記もしたけど
ねるとん→
ちょ〜っと待ったぁー!!
巻き戻して繰り返し
チョーットマッター!!
今でも時々している
All four of us have learned languages in different ways. I'll share some of what has worked for us next time.


国際結婚家庭だからといって、必ずしも全員が多言語を流ちょうに話せるわけではありません。我が家で言えば、そう、私がいい例です。

**roll off the tongue** 発音しやすい，言いやすい

**fluently** 流ちょうに

**every once in a while** たまに，ときどき

**find oneself** 気がつくと〜している

**space out** うわの空である

**express oneself** 自分の考えを表す

**imitate** まねをする，模範とする

**mimic** まねる，口まねする

英語を上達させたいなら——とスティーヴやハル、ミドリが私にしてくれた具体的な助言を紹介します。

**pointer** 助言, アドバイス, ヒント

**throw in** 投げ入れる, 手を貸す, 〔言葉・話題を〕持ち込む

**bit** 部分, 具体例

**keep a diary** 〔継続的に〕日記をつける

**keep one's chin up** 〔困難な状況で〕元気を失わない

**put in an effort** 努力する, 力を費やす

**shortcut** 近道, 手っ取り早い方法

**put one's nose to the grindstone** コツコツ取り組む, 一生懸命に勉強する

# Vol.267 Getting English to Roll Off the Tongue II（英語習得のコツ②）

When I asked for some pointers for getting better at English, the kids were quick to throw in their two bits.
You should try writing your own sentences.
Even writing short sentences is satisfying—and encouraging.
你吃饭吗？（ごはん、食べる？）
不吃（食べないなんて）
←第2外国語で中国語を勉強中
You could keep a diary.
私、見てあげるよ
So following their advice, I've been practicing English when I'm by myself.
えーっと… Today we'll have a parents' meeting at school.
車外の様子を実況中継してみたり
I'm looking forward to meeting Hannah's mom.
But, I'm sure my sentences have mistakes. Is it really good to practice that way?
Mom, it's fine to make mistakes!
Just keep trying. Keep your chin up!
ハイハイ 脱いだ 脱いだ
相手はそんなのすぐ忘れちゃうんだから
間違いを恐れる気持ち
恥
In the end, one thing that Steve has often said always comes back to me.
When I was an English instructor, students were always asking me, "What's the secret to learning English?"
The secret is that you need to put in the effort.
努力
There are no shortcuts to learning a language.
After 20 years in a dual-language household, I'm probably at my limit for "absorbing" English. If I'm going to improve, I'll need to put my nose to the grindstone.
千里の道も一歩から

Vol.268
Japanesey Gifts
(日本らしい贈りもの)
When sending gifts to family and friends overseas, we generally feel like we should send something Japanesey. However, we've sent so many Christmas and birthday gifts over the years that we're running out of ideas.
初期の頃のチョイス
Fan
Personalized paper lantern
スー&ダン
Hanko Seal
安加寿
(アンガス)
Plum liqueur
ぷらり
日本酒仕込み
It's like wine, and smooth.
Coin purse
大きく開いて使いやすい
Table runner Placemats
帯を再利用したものなど
It's gorgeous!
Papier-mâché dog
クリスマスオーナメントとして
T-shirts with Family crest
自分用にも買っちゃった
We are also exchanging Christmas gifts with the German family of the boy who stayed with us a couple of years ago.
Their gifts have a German sense to them♪
Made in Germany
Wooden tree ornament
❶ Incense
❷ Smoke comes out his mouth
かぶせる
Smoking man
Rauchernn
Made in Japan
Straw New Year's Decoration
説明を添えて
KABUKI FACE PACK
Japanese treats
想い出の味として
羊かん巻
ぬれせん
ゆずはちみつ
This year, maybe we'll send some quirky technology, which Japan is famous for.
Combination rechargeable heater and backup battery

海外の家族や友人に贈り物をするとき、日本風のものを送りたくなりますが、私たちはそろそろネタが尽きそうで、工夫が必要です。

**Japanesey** 日本式の，日本風の

**feel like** 〜したい気がする

**run out of ideas** アイデアが尽きる，ネタ切れになる

**plum liqueur** 梅酒

**table runner** テーブルランナー《テーブルの中央に置く帯状で長尺の布》

**place mat** ランチョンマット

**papier-mâché** 張り子の

**family crest** 家紋

**incense** 香，香料

**quirky** 突飛な，奇抜な

クリスマスで一番大切なクリスマス・スピリットをどう体現するか――スティーヴや子どもたちの試みを紹介します。

core element　中心的な要素，根幹
show goodwill to　～に友好を示す
charity　慈善，思いやり
colleague　同僚
postal　郵便（局）の，郵送の
adapt ~ to　～を…に適応させる
evolve　発展する
don　着用する
hand out ~ to　…に～を手渡す
put a smile on someone's face　（人）を笑顔にさせる

Vol.269
The Christmas Spirit
（私たちのクリスマス・スピリット）
For many people in America, Christmas is the biggest event of the year, when families gather for large feasts and to exchange gifts.
A core element of the season is spreading joy, or what is called the Christmas Spirit.
The Christmas Spirit is showing goodwill and charity to others.
Merry Christmas!!
Thank you!
People give gifts to show their appreciation to people around them, such as friends, colleagues, and postal and delivery workers.
CHOCOLATE
お菓子などのプチギフト
Love
Sharing
Caring
Steve adapted the Christmas Spirit to our local situation. We originally visited nearby friends and gave them homemade cookies, but the family custom has evolved over the years.
ハイどうぞ
わあ！
下校中の子どもたち
ちょっとくいだおれ人形っぽい。笑
Now, every year, Steve and the kids don Santa suits and walk around the neighborhood handing out candy to children. One year, Haru decided to wear a Santa hat to school, saying "I thought it would put a smile on some people's faces."
And that's how the Christmas Spirit spreads.
アラ
ちょっとしたサプライズとして
Christmas Spiritとはつまり，"お福分け"なのかも
Wishing you a Happy Holiday Season!

Vol.270
Thank You Cards
（お礼状）
しめかざりチェックが楽しいお正月の散歩
We hope everyone is looking forward to a fresh new start in the new year.
We are still enjoying the Christmas afterglow. We do some chores, however, like putting away the Christmas tree and…
Have you finished writing your thank you cards?
うんあとで
今ムリー
The children are obligated to send thank you notes for Christmas presents they received.
このときのために、もらったプレゼントはメモしておく
Grandma & Grandpa
Sweat-shirt
Uncle Randy
LEGO
Sending cards is common in the United States. Supermarkets and drugstores often have whole aisles dedicated to cards for every occasion.
For our relatives overseas, we combine the thank you cards and Japanese New Year's cards. The kids write their thank you messages on the nengajo.
HAPPY NEW YEAR!
2022
ミドリのイラストや発表会写真
Midori
Haru
裏面に
Dear Uncle Randy,
Thank you so much for the sweatshirt. It's really cool. I love it! That brand is one of my favorite brands. How did you know that? You're amazing! Thank you. Hope to see you soon.
Love, Midori
ハルが自分で作ったしめかざり
At the start of the year, the kids are also scrambling to finish their school homework. The last day of relaxing winter vacation is often (always!) quite hectic.
だから早く始めろって言ってるのに


クリスマスプレゼントをもらった人たちに、子どもたちはなるべく早くお礼状を書かなくてはなりません。

**thank you card** お礼状

**afterglow** 余韻，名残り

**put away** 片づける，しまう

**obligated to** ～する義務がある

**send a thank you note** お礼状を送る

**combine A and B** AとBを組み合わせる［兼ねる］

**sweatshirt** スウェットシャツ，トレーナー

**scramble to** 慌てて［大急ぎで］～する

**hectic** 非常に忙しい，大忙しの

今月はミドリの誕生日にケーキを焼く予定です。ベジタリアン対応のものを探すより、作った方が手っ取り早かったりします。

**veggie** 野菜(の)，菜食(の)

**come in many shades** 多くの色がある

**replaceable** 交換[代替]可能な

**commercial** 業務用の

**alternative** 代替手段，選択肢

**have on hand** 手近に持っている

**surprisingly** 驚いたことに，意外にも

**scrumptious** とてもおいしい

Vol.271
Veggie Sweets
(ベジタリアンスイーツ)
I'm going to bake a cake for Midori's birthday this month. I usually don't make desserts, but buying a cake can be a challenge.
Finding a cake with vegetarian ingredients is near impossible. It's easier to bake one myself.
欧米ではわりと手軽にヴィーガン製品が手に入るみたいだけど
Vegetarians come in many shades of green, but vegans like Steve try to avoid eggs and dairy products.
Vegan用
代替卵
大豆ベースの粉
水
卵液のようになる
Milk is easily replaceable with soy or nut milks. But what can replace eggs? Butter? Or cream?
Commercial alternatives are increasingly available, but can be expensive. I try to use common items we have on hand.
Shortcake
Cream made of
Tofu
Maple Syrup
Lemon Juice
Peanut Butter
アレルギー対応レシピなど、重宝してます
Gateau au Chocolat
Alternative Ingredients
Vegetable Oil
Maple Syrup
Apple Juice
Soy Milk
おから入り
DAIRY FREE
EGG FREE
(※ものによっては、バナナや練りゴマを代替に使うことも)
Of course, these ingredients aren't going to taste the same as traditional ones. But they can be surprisingly scrumptious in their own way.
しつこくない甘み
Tofu-based cakes aren't as heavy, so I eat more! (Usually too much…)
おいしい
I think I like this one even more than the other.
14歳になりました
14

Vol.272
Girlfriend Visit
(ガールフレンド来訪)
We had a wonderful and interesting start to the new year. Our son brought his girlfriend over to visit.
Hi. Thank you for having me.
連れてきたよー
ビョーク風味の強い小松菜奈といった感じのクール美人
Welcome.
Make yourself at home.
しっかりしろ私
I was so nervous. I couldn't even keep a conversation going.
Back in my day, meeting the parents was a big deal. It basically meant that you were planning to marry.
アメリカだと「クリスマスに招待≒婚約」かな
いろいろびっくり。でもすてき
My brother-in-law and 18-year-old niece in America recently went on a short vacation. With them were his girlfriend and her boyfriend. I was floored.
義弟の恋人の息子も!!
義弟の恋人
姪の恋人
めい 姪
義弟
They seemed so relaxed around each other that I was surprised to learn they had only been going together for a few weeks.
It's a little too soon to be meeting the parents, isn't it?
展開早いな。いや、うれしいけど
This is my pet lizard.
いつも通りの人
Is it just a coincidence that these two incidents happened at the same time? Or are people much more open about their relationships now? Either way, I think it's a good thing. In fact, that was a very nice day.
Come again anytime.
ハルの部屋が片付くし
ハイまた！

新年早々、ドキドキすることが起きました。正月三が日、ハルが我が家にガールフレンドを連れてきたのです。

**bring someone over** （人）を連れてくる

**make oneself at home** 楽にする，くつろぐ

**keep a conversation going** 会話を続ける

**relax around someone** （人）と一緒にいる状態でくつろぐ

**go together** 交際する，恋人同士である

**lizard** トカゲ

**big deal** 大事なこと，一大事

**floor** 圧倒する，打ちのめす

**coincidence** 〔偶然の〕一致

**either way** どちらにしても

成人年齢の引き下げに伴って、国籍選択の期限も早まることになりました。難しい問題がどんどん差し迫ってきます。

dual citizenship　二重国籍
statistics　統計（データ）
make a choice　（取捨）選択する
legal age of adulthood　法定成人年齢
cruel　ひどい，過酷な
response　対応，反応
worrisome　心配させる，悩ませる
split up　分断する，引き裂く
come to one's senses　正気に戻る，目を覚ます

# Vol.273 The Dual Citizenship Issue
## (多重国籍問題)

Statistics show that 1 in 50 babies born in Japan have one Japanese and one foreign parent. These children are often called "half" in Japanese. But what nationality is the child? We get this question all the time.

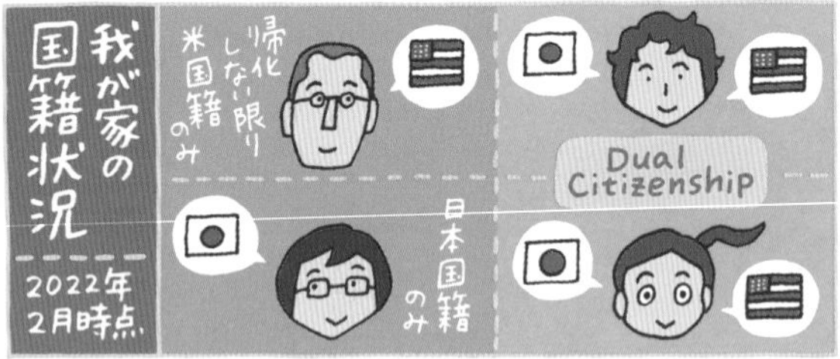

我が家の国籍状況
2022年2月時点
帰化しない限り米国籍のみ
Dual Citizenship
日本国籍のみ


The U.S. allows people to have multiple citizenships, but Japan wants you to choose just one. Because of that, Haru and Midori must make a choice between their two countries.

成人して2年後までにってことで"
Japan is lowering the legal age of adulthood to 18! (2022年4月〜)
They'll have to choose when they turn 20!!
すぐじゃん!!!
(ハル17歳 ミドリ14歳)


Our kids have roots in both countries, and they love them both.
How can they make the best choice for their future when they've had no experience living as an adult in society? It seems cruel to make them choose.

Choosing one...
means leaving the other.

選択義務は
履行（日本国籍を取得）。
外国籍に関しては
「離脱の努力」と
されていることから
重国籍のままでいる
人が少なからずいる
のが現状ですが、
あくまでもグレー。
PASSPORT
JAPAN PASSPORT


Japan's pandemic response of blocking foreigners from entering the country makes our situation even more worrisome. The single-nationality requirement could literally split up our family.

Over 64 countries allow dual citizenship. For our family's sake, we hope Japan will come to its senses and join the list soon.

国籍のカベ

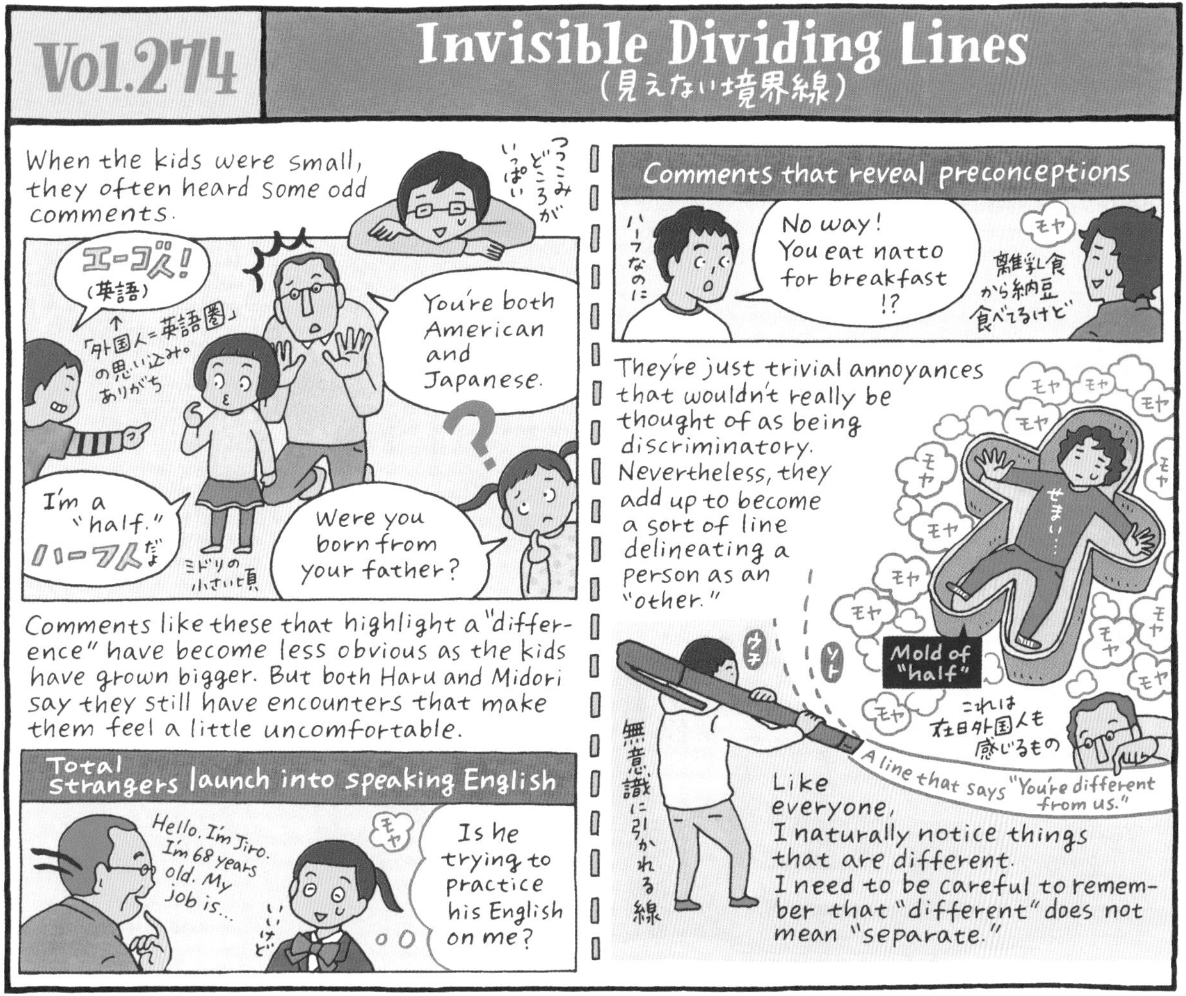

Vol.274
Invisible Dividing Lines
(見えない境界線)
When the kids were small, they often heard some odd comments.
つっこみどころがいっぱい
エーゴ人!
(英語)
「外国人=英語圏」の思い込み。ありがち
You're both American and Japanese.
I'm a "half."
ハーフ人だよ
ミドリの小さい頃
Were you born from your father?
Comments like these that highlight a "difference" have become less obvious as the kids have grown bigger. But both Haru and Midori say they still have encounters that make them feel a little uncomfortable.
Total strangers launch into speaking English
Hello. I'm Jiro. I'm 68 years old. My job is...
モヤ
いいけど
Is he trying to practice his English on me?
Comments that reveal preconceptions
ハーフなのに
No way! You eat natto for breakfast!?
モヤ
離乳食から納豆食べてるけど
They're just trivial annoyances that wouldn't really be thought of as being discriminatory. Nevertheless, they add up to become a sort of line delineating a person as an "other."
せまい…
Mold of "half"
ウチ
ソト
これは在日外国人も感じるもの
無意識に引かれる線
A line that says "You're different from us."
Like everyone, I naturally notice things that are different. I need to be careful to remember that "different" does not mean "separate."


内心「モヤッ」とすることがあるのは、子どもたちもスティーヴも同じようです。何がそうさせるのでしょうか？

**invisible** 目に見えない

**dividing line** 境界線

**have an encounter** 遭遇する, 出くわす

**launch into** ～を始める

**preconception** 先入観, 思い込み

**trivial annoyance** ささいな悩み

**discriminatory** 差別的な

**add up to** 結局～ということになる

**delineate** 輪郭を描く

**mold** 型

**separate** 接していない, 関連がない

ハルとミドリは学校のスピーチコンテストに参加しました。偶然にも、二人とも亡くなったアメリカの祖母のことを話したそうです。

sow a seed　種をまく［植える］

by coincidence　偶然に

late　今は亡き

precious moment　貴重な時間

regret　後悔する

set aside　〔～を〕傍らに置く

memento mori　汝の死を覚えよ《死、あるいは死すべき存在であることを思い起こさせるもの》

live life to the fullest　精一杯生きる

sage advice　賢明な助言

germinate　発芽する，成長する

sprout　発芽する，芽を出す

# Vol.275 Sowing Seeds

（種が芽を出すとき）

Haru and Midori recently participated in their school's annual speech contest. Students can speak on any topic they like, but by coincidence, both of them talked about their late grandmother in the U.S.

油絵をたしなみ
家族愛あふれていたグランマ
七五三も毎回来日

They talked about precious moments they had with her and how they regret taking that time for granted.

**Look Back from the Future**

I think you can avoid having regrets like that by setting aside your emotions and imagining how you will look back on yourself in the future.

A memento mori, an object serving as a reminder that death will come, can inspire you to live your life to the fullest.

僕にとってのメメントモリは祖母の油絵や祖母から贈られたセーターなど

**Book**

My grandmother often told me, "Always have a book by your side." I didn't think much about it at the time, but now that I've started reading more, I appreciate her sage advice.

Book

温度
光
酸素
3要素が揃って発芽する種

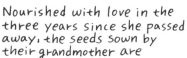

Seeds of wisdom and love germinate when the time is right.

Nourished with love in the three years since she passed away, the seeds sown by their grandmother are starting to sprout in the hearts and minds of her grandchildren.

It would bring us great joy if these Postcards have provided our readers with some seeds that will one day grow and blossom.

## とある日の私たち

家族写真を撮ろうと思い立ち、カメラをタイマー設定にして一斉に跳んだ。
全員がカッコよく宙に浮いた瞬間を狙ったものの、タイミングが合わない。
大笑いしながらみんなで20回近く跳んだ。
なんてことない、だからこそ大切な、とてもいい一日だった。

Special Thanks to
Sue & Don, Russ & Emily, the Tamuras, and our loving families in the U.S.A. and Japan.
Our international family and friends, and our kids' school.
The editorial team and the readers of Asahi Weekly, and H. Hasebe.

## あとがき

うちには家中、あちこちにメモ帳があります。居間はもちろん、寝室や車のダッシュボードにも。家族と過ごす時間の中でふとしたタイミングで転がり出てくるものを「あ、これは！」と思ったら大急ぎでメモを取る。リスが木の実を頬張るようにせっせとストックし続けたものを、隔週で小出しにして気がつけば11年の歳月が経っていました。

あと数年もすると、子どもたちは我が家から巣立っていくかもしれません。4人一緒に暮らすのもあと少し、子育てもカウントダウンに入ってきた感があります。家族としてひとまとまりに暮らしてきた濃厚な時期を、こうして描きとめられたことをうれしく思います。

ずっと快く描かせてくれた家族に心から感謝します。書籍化にあたり、家族のコラムを挟み込むことになりましたが、3人ともが二つ返事で引き受けてくれました。苦戦してもいましたが、それ以上に楽しんで書いてくれました。本当にありがとう。

また、私たち家族に関わってくれた、たくさんの人たちにも感謝を。皆さんとの関わりがなければ生まれなかった話がたくさんあります。とくに亡き義母Sueには特別な感謝を捧げます。

今後私たち家族がどんな道を辿るのか、まだ先は見えません。子どもたちがどこに根を張るのか、スティーヴや私はどこに骨を埋めるのか(歳を重ねると母国への帰巣本能が頭をもたげてくる、といった話をよく聞きます)、高齢となったそれぞれの親のことも気になります。パンデミックを経験したことで、家族が国をまたいで暮らすことの難点がより具体的な形で見えてきました。

それでも。今まで同様「いいとこ取り」を続けて、できる限り楽しんでいきたいと思うし、巣立っていく子どもたちも同様であってほしいと願っています。

「Have fun!」

これは私が家族を玄関で見送る際にする声かけです。日本語なら「行ってらっしゃい」、英語なら「Have a good day!」が定番ですが、それらを自分なりにかけ合わせた結果、こうなりました。

私たちにとっても、皆さんにとっても、今日が明日がこれからが、発見とおかしみに彩られた、すてきな一日でありますように。Have fun!

田村記久恵

## The Gift of Cultural Diversity

Looking through these postcards about our family is like a trip back in time. I can see how our family has evolved and how our kids have gone through experiences they will carry with them for the rest of their lives. They have learned practical skills like how to cook dinner and change shoji. They've had common life experiences like losing teeth, riding the train alone, and introducing a girlfriend to their parents that will shape the person they become. Unforgettable experiences like those happen in the course of everyone's daily lives.

The experience of culture, however, doesn't just happen on its own. Since we live in Japan, the kids have had many opportunities to join in cultural activities, from dancing at Obon to eating Osechi ryori. Passing on my American culture, however, took a conscious effort. Remembering holidays like Christmas and Halloween was easy because they are kid-oriented. But there were many years when Independence Day was passed over or when Thanksgiving consisted of just taking a moment to say thanks without a special meal.

How will bicultural kids like Haru and Midori carry forward their dual cultures into the future? Because they have two cultures, will the bonds to their Japanese and American cultures be weak? How do cultures survive in countries that have a diverse mix of people? If the United States is an example, individual cultures are personal, passionate, and resilient. Think of Cinco de Mayo, Mardi Gras, and Juneteenth as they are celebrated in America. At the same time, that cultural diversity enriches everyone.

As the next generation of bicultural kids move into society and Japan welcomes more people from overseas, culture in Japan will continue to thrive with abundant opportunities to experience joyous new celebrations and heartfelt ceremonies in addition to the great traditions of Japanese holiday festivities.

Steve Ballati

## テーマ別索引


【言語】 1, 2, 3, 8, 13, 23, 29, 30, 31, 39, 43, 51, 52, 53, 54, 55, 58, 83, 87, 96, 100, 103, 118, 121, 124, 136, 155, 157, 158, 165, 166, 192, 196, 197, 212, 230, 262, 264, 266, 267

【慣習】 6, 9, 14, 24, 26, 27, 28, 34, 47, 50, 69, 71, 76, 78, 79, 82, 95, 100, 101, 104, 126, 135, 143, 147, 150, 158, 159, 172, 173, 174, 203, 207, 212, 220, 233, 234, 242, 245, 248, 249, 250, 251, 254, 257, 258, 261, 272

【行事・イベント】 10, 11, 12, 15, 16, 17, 22, 36, 40, 63, 64, 65, 77, 85, 88, 89, 90, 91, 93, 111, 117, 137, 138, 140, 141, 142, 163, 164, 167, 168, 175, 180, 190, 191, 193, 194, 195, 198, 202, 214, 217, 218, 219, 221, 224, 244, 265, 269, 270

【子育て】 3, 5, 6, 18, 23, 27, 29, 30, 39, 43, 51, 56, 57, 67, 68, 72, 73, 74, 77, 79, 80, 81, 83, 84, 86, 96, 98, 99, 100, 101, 102, 103, 105, 106, 107, 118, 120, 134, 146, 151, 152, 153, 156, 176, 177, 183, 184, 185, 186, 196, 199, 200, 201, 207, 208, 209, 227, 232, 234, 243, 246, 247, 248, 249, 250, 259, 260, 272, 275

【学校生活】 4, 10, 58, 72, 81, 121, 124, 144, 149, 160, 161, 162, 182, 187, 188, 225, 230, 231, 233, 235, 236, 237, 239, 243, 275

【衣】 21, 25, 42, 44, 71, 108, 122, 125, 154, 172, 181, 246, 247

【食】 19, 32, 33, 41, 46, 61, 62, 94, 130, 131, 132, 133, 169, 175, 178, 79, 219, 222, 223, 252, 271

【住】 7, 8, 20, 38, 60, 74, 75, 92, 139, 170, 171, 172, 226, 253, 263

【読書】 48, 51, 84, 89, 99, 123, 144, 162, 194, 262

【社会】 5, 34, 35, 45, 49, 66, 67, 68, 70, 73, 119, 127, 128, 129, 145, 204, 205, 206, 229, 238, 251, 256, 273, 274

【おもてなし】 37, 112, 113, 114, 115, 240, 241, 268

【できごと】 59, 66, 97, 109, 110, 116, 127, 128, 129, 148, 173, 174, 178, 179, 189, 199, 200, 201, 210, 211, 213, 215, 216, 225, 227, 228, 231, 232, 235, 261

【ペット】 210, 211, 215, 216, 255


＊数字は該当するVol.を表しています。

# おまけ

あひる口コンテスト
@ダイニング
1位
2位
@個室
やってるつもり
ニッ?

# Steve #どこで覚えた #あひる口
#口元だけでなく目元も #ダントツ
#コロナ #自室隔離中のミドリと #ビデオ通話で家族団欒
#笑いすぎて涙が出た

刃先の角度をcheck
趣味:包丁研ぎ

# Kikue #老眼を初めて認識したのは包丁研ぎで
#メガネを取らないとよく見えない #もともと近眼

足指自由自在♪

# Midori #足指で #拾える
#華麗とズボラが背中合わせ #バレエ女子あるある？
#気がつけばガニ股になりがちなのも

# Haru #オンライン授業４日目
#変顔してたら #友達に #スクショを撮られ #送られてきた
#なぜ変顔 #遊びゴコロ

ピンクの
サングラスを
装着して
参加した日も

#オンライン授業5日目 #ヒゲを描いて参加 #なぜヒゲ
#チャレンジは続く #楽しそうで何より

**Postcards from a Bilingual Family**
**日×米家族の11年**

2022年12月6日　第1刷発行

著　者　田村 記久恵

訳　者　Steve Ballati

発行者　浦　晋亮

発行所　IBCパブリッシング株式会社
〒162-0804 東京都新宿区中里町29番3号 菱秀神楽坂ビル
Tel. 03-3513-4511　Fax. 03-3513-4512
www.ibcpub.co.jp

印刷所　株式会社シナノパブリッシングプレス



ISBN978-4-7946-0740-9

装　　丁＝山口桂子（atelier yamaguchi）
英文校正＝Ed Jacob

## 本書の続編「Field Notes of a Bilingual Family」は『Asahi Weekly』で読めます！

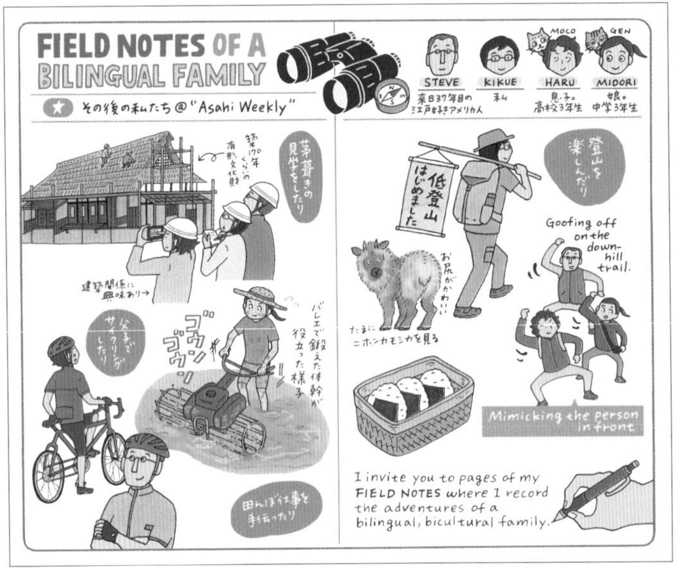
FIELD NOTES OF A BILINGUAL FAMILY
その後の私たち＠"Asahi Weekly"
MOCO
GEN
STEVE
来日37年目の江戸好きアメリカ人
KIKUE
私
HARU
息子。高校3年生
MIDORI
娘。中学3年生
茅葺きの見学をしたり
築170年くらいの有形文化財
建築関係に興味あり→
低登山はじめました
登山を楽しんだり
お尻がかわいい
たまにニホンカモシカを見る
Goofing off on the down-hill trail.
父子でサイクリングしたり
ゴウン ゴウン
バレエで鍛えた体幹が役立った様子
Mimicking the person in front
田んぼ仕事を手伝ったり
I invite you to pages of my FIELD NOTES where I record the adventures of a bilingual, bicultural family.

"Field Note"とは、野外活動で用いられる「観察記録ノート」のこと。
異文化比較を軸に描き続けた「Postcards from a Bilingual Family」を少し踏襲しつつ、
より自由に、我が家の活動を「観察ルポ」しています。